INTERN
GRAPHICS
GALLERY

PLUG YOURSELF INTO...

THE MACMILLAN INFORMATION SUPERLIBRARY™

Free information and vast computer resources from the world's leading computer book publisher—online!

FIND THE BOOKS THAT ARE RIGHT FOR YOU!

A complete online catalog, plus sample chapters and tables of contents give you an in-depth look at *all* of our books, including hard-to-find titles. It's the best way to find the books you need!

- **STAY INFORMED** with the latest computer industry news through our online newsletter, press releases, and customized Information SuperLibrary Reports.

- **GET FAST ANSWERS** to your questions about MCP books and software.

- **VISIT** our online bookstore for the latest information and editions!

- **COMMUNICATE** with our expert authors through e-mail and conferences.

- **DOWNLOAD SOFTWARE** from the immense MCP library:
    - Source code and files from MCP books
    - The best shareware, freeware, and demos

- **DISCOVER HOT SPOTS** on other parts of the Internet.

- **WIN BOOKS** in ongoing contests and giveaways!

TO PLUG INTO MCP: ➤

GOPHER: gopher.mcp.com
FTP: ftp.mcp.com

WORLD WIDE WEB: **http://www.mcp.com**

INTERNET GRAPHICS GALLERY

PAUL DE GROOT and DICK OLIVER

with Lane Boyd

Internet Graphics Gallery

Copyright© 1995 by Que® Corporation.

Library of Congress Catalog No.: 95-71445

ISBN: 0-7897-0137-5

97 96 95   6 5 4 3 2 1

Interpretation of the printing code: the rightmost double-digit number is the year of the book's printing; the rightmost single-digit number, the number of the book's printing. For example, a printing code of 95-1 shows that the first printing of the book occurred in 1995.

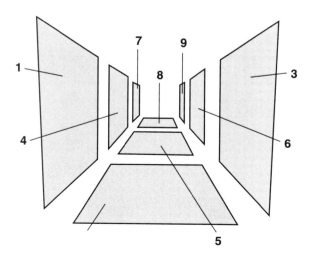

1 *Beethoven*, Dan Farmer

2 *Ideal Cities*, Daniela Bertol

3 *Poolball*, Dan Farmer

4 *Song #4 (icterus)*, Brian Evans

5 *untitled landscape*, Michael Gerstein

6 *Feather*, Dick Oliver

7 *unknown*, Unknown artist

8 *The Anti-Warhol*, Ron English

9 *unknown*, unknown artist

Credits

President and Publisher
Roland Elgey

Associate Publisher
Stacy Hiquet

Publishing Director
Brad R. Koch

Editorial Services Director
Elizabeth Keaffaber

Managing Editor
Sandy Doell

Director of Marketing
Lynn E. Zingraf

Publishing Manager
Thomas H. Bennett

Acquisitions Editor
Beverly M. Eppink

Product Director
Benjamin Milstead

Production Editor
Mitzi Foster Gianakos

Assistant Product Marketing Manager
Kim Margolius

Technical Editors
Anthony Schafer
Doug Welch

Acquisitions Coordinator
Ruth Slates

Operations Coordinator
Patty Brooks

Editorial Assistant
Andrea Duvall

Book Designers
Ruth Harvey
Kim Scott

Cover Designer
Dan Armstrong

Production Team
Stephen Adams
Bryan Flores
DiMonique Ford
Trey Frank
Amy Gornik
Damon Jordan
Julie Quinn
Kaylene Rieman
Jody York

Indexer
Mary Jane Frisby

Composed in *Cheltenham Light* and *Bodega Sans* by Que
Corporation.

To Jean, and to Emily, Geneva, Burton, and Heidi, whose love and commitment through several long episodes of bookwriting blues let a dream come true.

Paul De Groot

Paul De Groot is assistant managing editor of the Southam New Media Centre, formed by Southam, Inc. to move Canada's largest-circulation newspaper chain into the world of interactive and online media.

Born and raised in Seattle, he was a reporter and photographer for various Canadian newspapers for 17 years, covering a variety of beats, including civic affairs, politics, education, science, health, and religion. His computer hobby turned into a full-time job when he became newsroom network administrator and then coordinator of electronic publishing at the Edmonton Journal. He lives in Edmonton with his wife Jean, four children, a hyperactive dog, a hypoactive snake, and about 37 computers, most of which are in almost-working condition. ▲

Dick Oliver has authored and coauthored several graphics programs, articles, and books, including *Tricks of the Graphics Gurus*, *PC Graphics Unleashed*, *FractalVision: Put Fractals to Work for You*, and *Fractal Grafics 3D*. Dick is president of Cedar Software of Morrisville, Vermont, which specializes in new approaches to advanced graphics and 3-D modeling. He also publishes the *Nonlinear Nonsense* netletter, an online web site and paper newsletter covering creative computer graphics. You can contact him at **dicko@netletter.com**. ▲

Lane Boyd lives and writes in Austin, Texas, where he works as a Publishing Specialist for SEMATECH, a semiconductor R&D consortium. He is a former reporter and editor for computer magazines *MicroCAD News*, *Unisys World*, *The Sun Observer*, *HP Workstation*, and *Digital Desktop*, some of which still exist. He spends most of his free time avoiding the hot Texas sun by sitting in the hot Texas shade writing fiction and poetry; storytelling through a cast of action figures and green plastic soldiers; and webbing through the Internet, thankful for its recent release from its text-based prison. ▲

Acknowledgments

Paul De Groot's Acknowledgments

Several people have played important roles in the development of this book.

Graham Fletcher, of Corporate Computers, Inc. of Edmonton, gave me that first "wow" experience with Mosaic, and provided the Internet access which encouraged my own exploration of the net.

Doug Poff and other staff at Information Technology Services of the Cameron Library at the University of Alberta provided me with space to work in and that most precious gift, a very fast Internet connection. Without it, this book simply could not have been done in such a short time.

Florence Kuby at the Cameron Library came through with daily encouragement, and unlocked some important doors.

Ace Chatur and the staff at CompCanada put together hardware that worked flawlessly throughout the project.

Beverly Eppink, acquisitions editor at Que, somehow managed to be a tough critic, a demanding taskmaster, and a great collaborator all at the same time.

Linda Hughes, publisher of the Edmonton Journal, and Rick Laiken, managing editor of the Southam New Media Centre, showed tremendous understanding while I attempted to juggle authorship with other responsibilities.

Lane Boyd's Acknowledgments

Denise Potter, for Internet research, on-the-spot editing, and moral support.

Derek Pearcy, for unlimited use of his Macintosh and the T-1 connection it sits on.

Loyd Blankenship, for use of his Pentium-based computer.

Mom & Dad, Dana Blankenship, Nancy Lopez, and Lisa Wannemacher, for their wisdom and friendship.

We'd Like to Hear from You!

As part of our continuing effort to produce books of the highest possible quality, Que would like to hear your comments. To stay competitive, we *really* want you, as a computer book reader and user, to let us know what you like or dislike most about this book or other Que products.

You can mail comments, ideas, or suggestions for improving future editions to the address below, or send us a fax at (317) 581-4663. For the online inclined, Macmillan Computer Publishing has a forum on CompuServe (type **GO QUEBOOKS** at any prompt) through which our staff and authors are available for questions and comments. The address of our Internet site is **http://www.mcp.com** (World Wide Web).

In addition to exploring our forum, please feel free to contact me personally to discuss your opinions of this book: I'm **102121,1324** on CompuServe, and **bmilstead@que.mcp.com** on the Internet.

Thanks in advance—your comments will help us to continue publishing the best books available on computer topics in today's market.

Benjamin Milstead
Product Developer
Que Corporation
201 W. 103rd Street
Indianapolis, Indiana 46290
USA

Contents at a Glance

PART I ▼ BEST GRAPHICS SITES ON THE NET

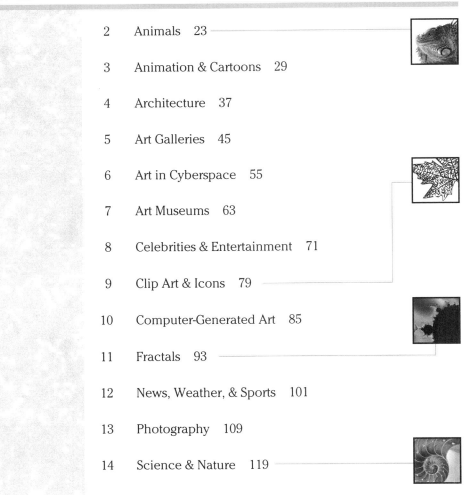

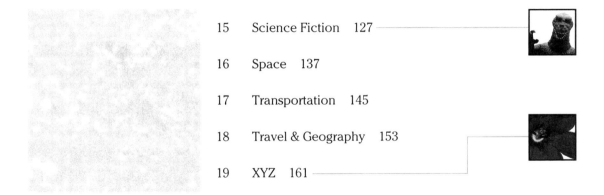

PART II ▼ FINDING MORE GRAPHICS

PART III ▼ WORKING WITH GRAPHICS ON THE NET

PART IV ▼ NET.GRAPHICS CD

Table of Contents

7 Art Museums 63

8 Celebrities & Entertainment 71

9 Clip Art & Icons 79

10 Computer-Generated Art 85

PART II ▼ FINDING MORE GRAPHICS

20 Graphics Sites from A to Z   171

21 Search Strategies & Techniques   427

PART III ▼ WORKING WITH GRAPHICS ON THE NET

25 Putting Graphics on the Net   535

Introduction

For MOST OF ITS quarter-century of existence, the Internet has been a visually drab place. Scientific principles were hotly debated, personal quarrels fought, and e-mail exchanged in a text-only environment, which was ruled by those who could master cryptic UNIX commands.

In recent years, graphical browsers such as Mosaic and Netscape have brought point-and-click simplicity to the Internet, and introduced a new visual language of buttons, icons, and inline images.

The new graphical Internet is bursting with activity as companies, individuals, and institutions "go online." With pictures online, educational institutions can illustrate their texts; artists can showcase their work; scientists can share their findings; and individuals can point with pride to their work, their lives, and their families.

Full-color publishing—which is still expensive in the world of traditional print—is child's play on the Internet. New ways of communicating are emerging as people exploit the power of visual images to explain, stimulate, and simulate the real world.

What This Book Is About

This book celebrates the promise of the transformation of the Internet into a rich visual environment. The images of our time and our world, from abstract art to painfully exact images of microscopic creatures, from cave paintings to futuristic science-fiction worlds, are now at your fingertips.

We're going to show you what's out there on the Internet by guiding you to places that make effective use of its graphical power. We'll go to art galleries where the world's most innovative artists display their work, to travel guides only available online, to images fresh from deep-space telescopes, and even to video cameras attached to the Net.

You'll see creative ways to use images, you'll find loads of sites where you will be entertained and informed, and you'll learn how to put your own images online. The CD-ROM included with this book will supply most of the software you need to create, capture, and modify your own images so you can put them on the Internet or send them to others via e-mail.

Who Should Read This Book

We've written this book for several audiences. First, even if you don't have Internet access, you'll want to read this book to find out what's out there. Most of this book is not very technical, and you can begin to catch the excitement of the online world when you realize that its way of conveying information—words and pictures—is something you're already familiar with.

Second, people who have computers and perhaps even Internet access often find it confusing and overwhelming. Where should you go and what can you do? You'll find answers here because we've picked out sites that represent the state of the art in using the Internet to convey information about and with graphics. The authors of this book visited about 3,000 of the better-known graphics sites on the Internet to come up with the hotlists of graphics sites. You'll find approximately 400 sites mentioned in this book.

And, because the Internet is changing rapidly, we're giving you the tools you'll need to find more of the great places to go on the Internet. Sadly but inevitably, some of the information in this book will be out-of-date by the time the first copy hits the bookstore. We're giving you the tools and the knowledge to use those tools, to help you discover for yourself new sites for graphics and pictures.

Third, even if you're familiar with the Internet, we'll save you a lot of time (and if you're paying for Internet access by the minute, a lot of money) by pointing you to the best sites.

Fourth, if you really want to put graphics to work, perhaps by using the Internet as a source of images for personal or business projects, or by using the Net to distribute or display your own graphics, we'll show you how to do it.

Types of Graphics on the Internet

Graphics on the Internet fall into a few major categories. The easiest for the newcomer to the Net to imagine are photographs online: pictures of people, animals and places, scientific images, and artistic works.

You'll also find movies and video online, such as clips from Hollywood films, television shows, or your favorite cartoons and animation.

As you can imagine, the Net is heavily populated with people who know and love computers and software, so you'll find many intriguing examples of images that are actually created by computers. Some are fantastic and abstract designs, while others are very realistic. Yet others are pictures of the normally invisible, such as the energy fields around a molecule, the flow of air around an airplane, or relationships between financial indicators over a period of time.

Other artists on the Net use computers to manipulate photographs in new and startling ways, taking conventional images and transforming them through digital wizardry into contorted shapes, dazzling new colors, or seamless blends of reality and fantasy.

In the world of art, you'll find classical paintings, the most famous images and sculptures from centuries of art, along with the work of today's artists. Many of those artists work in traditional media, such as watercolor, acrylic, or bronze, while others create their art through digital wizardry.

How This Book Is Organized

To guide you through the images on the Net, we've divided this book into several sections.

The introductory chapters, which you're reading now, outline what we're trying to do, and how you can make use of the graphics on the Net.

The next section covers images by subject or type, such as animals, travel, animation, or computer-generated art. We devote three of the chapters here to visual arts, exploring the ways that artists and art lovers are using the graphical power of the Net. These chapters cover:

▼ Art Galleries—art that is usually for sale, and is displayed on the Internet by galleries or by individual artists who may also display or show the art in a physical gallery.

▼ Art in Cyberspace—art that (in general) can only be viewed on the Internet, and is not displayed in a physical gallery. It may or may not be for sale.

▼ Art Museums—historical or classical works of art that are found in art museums or private collections, and usually are not for sale.

In the center of the book, you'll find a 16-page gallery where we show off the work of some of the Net's finest artists. Some may be names you recognize, but most are newcomers whose work has never before been published offline. In this gallery, anyone, computer literate or not, will see the energy, the ferment, the opportunities, and the challenges that technology brings to the arts through the Internet.

Our alphabetical listing of sites is a detailed look at some of the most important graphics sites on the Net. In choosing sites, we considered the following:

▼ Does the site have enough graphic images to warrant a visit from someone interested in seeing graphics? Are the graphics well chosen, unique, or particularly striking?

▼ Is graphic quality high, with clean, well-cropped, and properly sized images, good color, and sharpness?

▼ Is this site well designed? Can you identify the contents easily, and quickly jump to the section you want? Is it easy to move around in the site? Are the links up-to-date? Do sections or items have understandable names? Are sections divided into manageable chunks and organized well?

▼ Are images well sized, neither so small that detail is lost, nor so large that you can't fit them on your screen?

▼ Is the site modem-aware? Does it use logos, thumbnails, and other graphic devices efficiently for those on slower connections to the Net? Does it tell visitors the size of larger images so they can tell in advance how long it might take to download the images?

NOTE We normally set our displays for 800 by 600 pixel resolution when working on this book. We often turned off the Netscape directory buttons to provide more screen space. In our case, an image deeper than about 425 pixels or wider than about 780 pixels would run off the screen.

Because the Net is changing so quickly, you'll need to know how to find sites on the Internet yourself. Our chapters on search strategies, and on online graphics directories, point you to the most powerful search tools to help you find what you want.

Once you find it, what do you do with it? The following chapters will make you an expert in retrieving, modifying, and using graphical images. We'll explain how you can retrieve those nifty graphics and put them on your own computer. As you explore the Net, you might want to work with some of your own graphics, perhaps to send images to friends via e-mail, or to put your own images on a Web page. We not only tell you step-by-easy-step how to do this, but in our chapter on putting graphics on the Net, we'll give you the tools—in the form of image viewers and other software—that you can use on your own computer.

By the time you've worked your way through our examples and step-by-step instructions, using the software on the CD-ROM or that you download from our Internet site, you'll have a lot more expertise, and get far better results with graphics than you may have thought possible. This is hot stuff, but you don't need to be a computer science graduate to do it.

We have seen many images displayed on the Net that could have benefited from the simple techniques this book explains. Even some experts who leaped into cyberspace some time ago don't know as much about graphics as you will after reading this book and using the software we provide.

The CD-ROM

The CD-ROM included with this book has several components. In our color gallery, we've only shown one picture from selected artists on the Net, but you'll find many more pictures from these artists on the CD-ROM. We've also supplied you with viewing software, so you can see and enjoy the images on the CD-ROM.

The CD-ROM also contains an HTML file listing all of the sites mentioned in this book. By opening this file in your Web browser, you can use it to go directly to the sites we've mentioned.

Finally, we've included a treasury of image decoders and encoders, programs for creating your own fractals, and programs for modifying and improving digital images, so you can put your new knowledge to work right away, without having to locate or purchase additional software.

What This Book Is Not About

A term like graphics, or even Internet, doesn't always mean the same thing to people, so we want you to know that this book doesn't cover certain areas.

It's not a book about programming or graphical programming techniques. You'll see the results of those techniques here, but to find out how they're done you should look for books specifically about graphics programming.

It's not a book about how to get on the Internet. We do cover the basics about connecting to the Net and setting yourself up to view graphics, but if you need more information, consider a book that specializes in those topics or talk to access providers who can help you get on the Net.

If, after seeing some of the snazziest pages on the Internet, you want to create your own, you should consider a book on HTML, the language most widely used on the World Wide Web. We'll show you how to prepare images to put on Web pages, but the actual construction of those pages is beyond the scope of this book.

Finally, this book is not an art review, or comment on the artistic merit of the graphics at various sites. Okay, so you may be able to figure out what we like and what we don't like, which is inevitable when there's so much to choose from. However, we don't consider ourselves art experts, and if sometimes we sound like that, it's just pretend.

CHAPTER 1

A Link Is Worth a Thousand Words

In This Chapter

> * Why graphics are behind the explosion of interest in the Internet

> * How graphical browsers like Mosaic and Netscape have made the Net a friendlier place

> * How you can use the Internet's graphical power for personal pleasure, business, educational purposes, and for keeping in touch with other people

In Other Chapters

> * For more information about downloading graphics from the Internet, see Chapter 23.

> * To use the software tools on the CD-ROM to view and modify graphics, see Chapter 24.

The Internet is one of the most amazing phenomena in human history.

This isn't just hype. You've probably heard this before and at one time you thought "that's just those propeller-heads again, off in their own little world."

Admittedly, if you're not connected to the Internet yet, you do represent about 90 percent of the population right now. Whoops, the meter ticked and it's now 89 percent. That's how fast this phenomenon is moving.

But the Internet is much more than a toy or digital playground. Many people already make their living from providing Internet services. Many scientists and computer professionals rely on the Internet to communicate with each other daily. And increasingly, businesses and government are finding the Internet a powerful and inexpensive way to communicate with their customers and citizens.

Then there's the rest of us.

The fact that "access to the Net" is not part of the Universal Declaration of Human Rights suggests that you can muddle along without it. (On the other hand, you probably don't know what's in the Universal Declaration of Human Rights anyway. But we do, because we were on the Internet and went to gopher://gopher.undp.org:70/00/unearth/rights. And it actually does say that "Everyone has the right of equal access to public service in his country," which not many years hence may require that you have access to online services. See what you're missing?)

But we're not going to try to prove the Net's worth to you. We'll just say that it enables more people to get in touch with other people and their worlds of work, play, family, and community faster than anything else.

The numbers bear that out. Statistically, interest in the Internet is skyrocketing. The rate of increase of new users is still increasing. Did you get that? Not the number of new users. But the rate that they are getting on and using the Net is still increasing. This is big, and it's growing faster than ever.

A Picture Is Worth a Thousand Links

Graphics is a significant part of that growth. In fact, it explains much of the Internet's explosive popularity in the last few years. After all, the Internet has been around for more than 25 years, but it's only since 1994 that it has worked its way into our everyday vocabulary.

What happened in 1994? In one word: Mosaic.

In July of 1993, some graduate students at the National Center for Supercomputer Applications at the University of Illinois released the first version of a program that enabled people to find their way around the Internet by simply clicking on a word or picture. The words and pictures would show up automatically on their screens.

The difference between getting around the Internet this way, and getting around the old way, where users had to type obscure commands and addresses on a screen full of text, was dramatic. The old way was for hackers and for people who needed to use this technology so badly they would wrestle their way up the learning curve, sweating and swearing. The new way was so simple that, in theory, you didn't even have to know how to read, let alone type, to get around.

Mosaic, as this software was called, was an elegantly simple solution to a problem that had eluded traditional online services: how could they show graphics and smart-looking fonts, without dramatically slowing the whole system? Mosaic leveraged some capabilities that already existed on the Internet with some capabilities of newer personal computers, such as their ability to display graphics and fonts. Its developers produced something about which every programmer dreams: a "Killer App," an application so innovative, powerful, and useful that people buy computers just to use it.

So the Net was easier and it also became far more graphical. By graphical, we mean that information is conveyed by pictures, video, images, and diagrams, as well as by text. Most human beings rely on their eyes to process more than 70 percent of the information they receive. So being able to convey information through pictures has added immensely to users' enjoyment and appreciation of the Internet and has fueled a huge public interest. It is reaching the point, say many observers, where it will take its place as a "fourth medium," next to television, radio, and print.

To give you an idea of how pervasive graphics have become, the authors of this book visited about 3,000 of the better-known graphics sites on the Internet to come up with our hotlists of graphics sites. You'll find approximately 400 sites mentioned or listed in this book. We're certain that we only skimmed the surface, and by the time you read this book several hundred new graphical sites will have been launched.

Graphics is what this book is about: how you can find pictures and images on the Internet that can increase your enjoyment, understanding, and who knows, maybe even your income. This isn't a book about everything on the Internet. We've ignored many worthy and important places on the Internet that don't have pictures, not because they're not worth visiting, but because we want to focus on images and graphics, showing you how they are used to provide information and pleasure.

Browsers

Programs like Mosaic are called "graphical browsers," because they let you click your way around the Internet, "browsing" the information and pictures that other people, companies, and universities make available. Mosaic is not the only browser, but it's a good one, and it's free. Variations on Mosaic may or may not be free.

Many commercial online services such as Prodigy, CompuServe, America Online, and the Microsoft Network, have built graphical browsers into their services. If you're a member of one of those services, you needn't worry about special software as long as you have the latest version of the access software these companies provide their users. The most popular browser on the Net as we write this book is Netscape, which is free to educational and non-profit organizations, but which others are supposed to pay for. Anyone can download the program from the Internet without paying for it, although the license says you should pay if you are a private or corporate user. All of the screen shots in this book show the Netscape browser (and yes, we paid for our copy).

The key to browsers is the "link." A link can be either text or a picture. Text that is a link is often identified by being a different color or having an underline. Images that are links have a colored border. Clicking on a link will take you to another document or another image. That document or image might be on the same computer as the link, but it can just as easily be on another computer thousands of miles away. It sounds simple, and it is.

Bookmarks

Another popular and important feature of most browsers is the "bookmark." Microsoft's Internet Explorer, part of the Windows 95 Plus Pack, calls this "favorite pages." Many FTP and Gopher programs, and especially graphical browsers like Mosaic and Netscape, incorporate bookmarks.

Bookmarks are very important, because they make it easy to mark places you want to visit again. Technically, most Internet addresses look like this: 155.187.10.12. Hardly makes you want to go there, right? Fortunately, the wizards of the Internet have ways to replace the numbers with more readable addresses and names, such as "Virtual Art Gallery." They hide most of the other stuff from you, unless, of course, you want to look at it. That means that instead of entering 155.187.10.12 in your software, you can click on "Virtual Art Gallery" to access an Internet site. You can save these references, and their associated technical information, as bookmarks. Bookmarks make it easy for you to find your way back to a site you really like.

You can collect your favorite bookmarks in "hotlists." Every time your computer starts your Internet software, it can also load your hotlist of favorite bookmarks. To get to your favorite site you can then simply pull down your hotlist from a menu and click on the site's name, and your browser will immediate start connecting to that site.

Graphical Internet browsers are available for most popular computers, but which you can use may depend on how powerful your computer is. Netscape, for example, requires at least a 386 Intel processor running Microsoft Windows, or a Macintosh with a 68020 processor.

A *hotlist* is a list of your favorite or most frequently visited bookmarks. Typically, it is stored in a file on your computer, and when you start your Internet software, the program reads your hotlist and makes it available from your program menus, where it's easy to access.

To access your bookmarks you can just open the hotlist and click on the bookmark for the site you want to visit.

We use the term "hotlist" to describe our own collection of favorite graphics sites. To make it easier for you to locate them, we've taken the hotlist we built while working on this book and included it on the net.graphics CD in the back of this book.

You can replace your own hotlist with ours by selecting the file QUELIST.HTM as your browser's default bookmark file, or you can look at a file we have set up to be viewed from your browser, called QUEPAGE.HTM. Select Open file from the menus of your browser, and work your way to the hotlist file on the CD. You'll see our list with the names of the sites mentioned in this book, with brief descriptions of each site, corresponding to the chapters of this book. Click on a highlighted link, and off you'll go.

For more information about connecting to the Internet and configuring a browser for graphics, see Chapter 24, "Viewing & Using Graphics from the Net."

For an even more thorough treatment of browsers, you can pick up books like *Using Netscape*, *Using the Internet*, or *Using Microsoft Internet Explorer*, all from Que.

Commercial Online Services and the Internet

This book focuses on the Internet, and on sites reachable through Internet software, rather than on commercial online services such as CompuServe, America Online, Prodigy, the Microsoft Network, Genie, or eWorld. That's not because these services have nothing to offer. All the authors of this book continue to use several of these services, in spite of the availability of the Internet, because they offer services or features that aren't available on the Internet.

In some cases, they have thousands of images, excellent search tools to find them, and are far better organized than the Internet. They tend to have easy-to-use navigational tools that are consistent throughout their services. They have reliable manuals, and they have help-lines where you can get assistance from real human beings when you can't find or use something. Most of this is not true of the Internet.

Another advantage of commercial online services is that they are still accessible with older computers that can't handle Mosaic and Netscape. And because all the major online services have gateways to the Internet, with graphical browsers, you can use this book to access graphical sites using those services. Finally, they are sometimes cheaper, especially for occasional use, than what some dedicated Internet access companies charge.

This book focuses on the Internet because it is new, and changing, and the number of people who use it is larger than that of all the commercial online services put together. In addition, there are few reliable guides on where and how to view and use graphics in particular.

The most compelling reason to focus on the Internet in a book about graphics and images online is that Mosaic and its variations and descendants, such as Netscape, handle graphics more smoothly and naturally than any of the software (other than their Internet browsers) currently available on commercial online services.

Ways to Use Images on the Internet

So there are "purty pichers" on the Internet. What good does that do you? Glad you asked. And we're glad you're using this book for your answer, because with a good guide to graphics they can be very useful in many parts of your life and work. Without a good guide, however, it would be easy to get lost or to spend a lot of time, and possibly money, in fruitless pursuit of that picture you want to see.

Wow!

First, what's wrong with pretty pictures? The Net is loaded with hundreds of images from the world's finest painters, photographers, and other artists. It's the largest showcase of art, both contemporary and classic, that you're ever likely to have in your home or office.

Some artists whose work is visible on the Internet (and in the color gallery in this book) are leading a new era of art. Freed from some of the constraints of physical tools, they can incorporate color, movement, cultural symbols, and even interactivity into their work, vastly expanding the language of art.

Because artists' work is easily accessible to anyone on the Internet, the barriers between artists and audience are disappearing. You don't need to go to New York to see what New York's newest young artists are up to. In fact, you're likely to see their work online before someone in New York sees it in a SoHo gallery.

The Internet also provides exposure for artists who work outside the traditional art centers. We'll point you to people in Holland, Haiti, and Australia, for example, whose work may never appear in a North American gallery, but whose work has as much artistic merit as anything that North Americans can find in their galleries. Now, it's only a mouse click away for anyone with Internet access (see Figure 1.1).

Some of the art online simply isn't available anywhere else. We'll point you to some superb travel photography that isn't available in any coffee-table book. It's only on the Net.

Figure 1.1
*"Couple on Horseback" by
Haitian artist Micius Stephane.*

http://www.egallery.com/egallery/disk8/img0005.jpg

And some kinds of art, you probably wouldn't normally be interested in if it weren't so easy to find on the Internet. Hearing someone's describe a fractal as multiple iterations of a formula to define a particular set of numbers is nothing like seeing a picture of a fractal, we can assure you (see Figure 1.2).

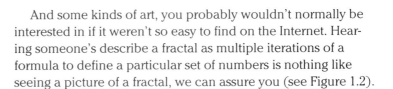

Figure 1.2

A fractal image entitled "Hot Peek" from Don Lebow.

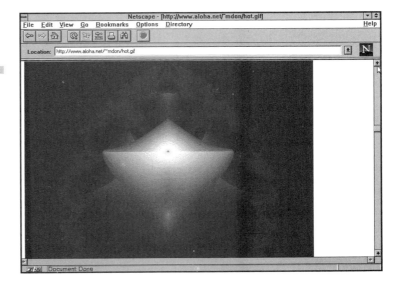

http://www.aloha.net/~mdon/hot.gif

And finally, where else, we ask, could you go to find out whether there's coffee in the coffee pot at Cambridge University's Trojan room? Case closed.

Education

Every new communications medium has promised a more informed public as its chief goal. Some have succeeded— books and education are practically synonymous—while others, like television, have brought mixed blessings.

We'll admit there's a lot of zany, crazy, and stupid stuff on the Internet. Some sites even specialize in lists of the stupid things people do on the Internet.

Fortunately, the Internet lets the stupid and sublime co-exist quite happily. And we're beginning to see ample evidence that this powerful medium has exceptional capabilities for education.

Take an obvious theme related to graphics on the Internet: art education.

You'll find images carved in French caves by Paleolithic artists, along with sensational work from the most innovative of today's artists (we'll leave you to speculate on the progress of art over the last 25,000 years or so).

You'll find many sites where most or all of the output of a particular artist is featured. Looking for something from, say René Magritte or Jan Ver Meer? Each has special galleries devoted to his particular work. Sites like the WebMuseum and the Vatican feature dozens of works from dozens of artists, and have hundreds of classic images online.

Many art museums are coming on to the Net, and many have special sections for educators. Teachers can download special educator kits of ready-made classroom units on art of a particular period or culture, including digital images they can print out or display on their computers.

Science is another area of particular interest to educators. The Internet offers an online, interactive frog dissection; stunning images and movies of the sun, planets, distant galaxies; live television coverage of NASA space missions; and comprehensive images of earth itself (see Figure 1.3).

Students can play with geometry, manipulating shapes and designs interactively, with no additional software required. They can find maps of any place on earth, explore the CIA World Factbook and view fragile medieval manuscripts that are no longer accessible to the public.

Figure 1.3

When galaxies collide: this stunning image from the Hubble Space Telescope shows a glowing ring of gas, already beginning to form new stars, emerging from the shock wave created when one of the two galaxies to the right collided with the center of the larger galaxy on the left. The insets on the left show details of the shock wave (top) and the main galaxy (bottom).

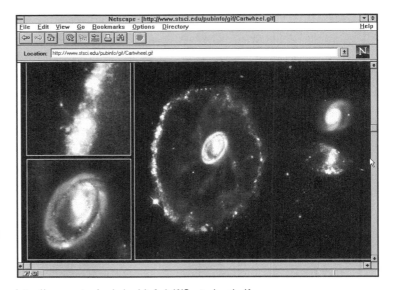

http://www.stsci.edu/pubinfo/gif/Cartwheel.gif

Business

We can think of a few good ways to use Internet graphics for business purposes. With not much incentive we're sure you can come up with some business needs of your own where graphics play a role.

An obvious way to use the Internet's graphics is in business presentations and newsletters (see Figure 1.4). Jazzing these up with graphics is critical in making a good impression, but it isn't easy to find the graphics you need. Furthermore, finding a picture for your presentation is only the first step; next you need to scan it into your computer so you can combine it with your presentation or with the text of your newsletter.

On the Internet, all images are already digital. Putting one into your presentation is as simple as saving it on your disk from the Internet, then popping it into your presentation from the disk. And if it's not completely suitable, our CD-ROM will supply you with the tools you need to modify, re-size, and crop the image to fit your requirements.

A map is a common feature of many slide shows, but it's often tough to find just the area of the world you want, and to get the right lighting. If your slide show is digital, you can simply capture the screen with the software we supply, or save the map image to disk for later viewing and cropping. If you want a slide for a projected show, a computer screen is just about the

Figure 1.4

This dramatic but simple balloon image from the Internet could find its way into a business report or presentation.

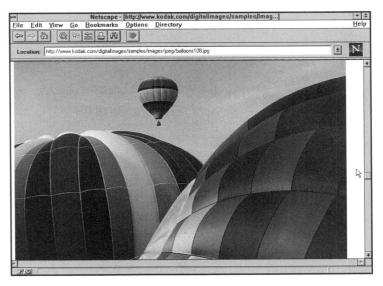

http://www.kodak.com/digitalImages/samples/images/jpeg/balloons108.jpg

right size for focusing with a camera at its nearest focus point. Get your map on screen and shoot away, trying a few different exposures to get something that will look good on your projection screen (slower shutter speeds will give better results).

An increasingly important business requirement, of course, is to present your business on the Internet itself. If you're thinking about using the Internet for business, we'll point you to some of the tools you need to present your business in the right light, including clip art and software. We'll also show you some sites that use graphics effectively. Those models will be useful in making your own site look good.

You may also find artists and photographers on the Net who can provide you with original art or photography to complement your company's image. Doing business over the Internet can be a fast, efficient way to view samples and preview the work of potential business partners.

Personal Pleasure

The graphics on the Internet can be used for many personal purposes. You can download screensavers directly from some sites on the Internet or convert the images you find into screensavers or decorative wallpaper for your computer screen.

Internet images can make great decorative art such as greeting cards, invitations, specialty cards, calendars, and gift wrapping. Many will look fine even with a black and white printer, while you may want to use a color printer to get the full effect of others. Whether you can do this legally or not depends on the artists. A few don't want their images downloaded at all. Most permit their use for personal purposes, and some encourage people to download their work and use it any way they like (see Figure 1.5).

Artists, especially those who work digitally, may find the raw material for some of their images on the Internet. Downloaded, the images can provide inspiration, or form part of the structure for a new image.

School reports will look better with the maps available on the Internet, and community newsletters can benefit as well.

Figure 1.5

Seasonal clip art from Sandra's Clip Art Server.

http://seidel.ncsa.uiuc.edu/ClipArt/graphics-sampler/christmas-and-winter.gif

Or, you can simply download pictures and put together a personal art gallery of your favorite images. Using the viewers we supply on the CD-ROM, you can view your personal collection anytime without logging on to the Internet.

Staying in Touch

You needn't always be a viewer of art. The Internet is also a tool you can use to display your own work, send images to other people, or collaborate with other artists if you have an artistic bent.

If you're an artist, or anyone who makes a product that would benefit from wide exposure through photos, diagrams, movies, or other graphics, run, don't walk, to the Internet and find a way to put your images on the Web. The software we provide can help you create and modify your images to make them look good. By visiting the galleries we identify here you'll find many examples of artists and artisans who are using the Internet effectively to reach huge audiences.

Several sites on the Internet specialize in collaborative art. (See Figure 1.6.) Variations on this theme include collages made up of the work of multiple artists; mail art in which artists e-mail work to each other, modifying the image each time it is

Figure 1.6

A collaborative art project from OTIS.

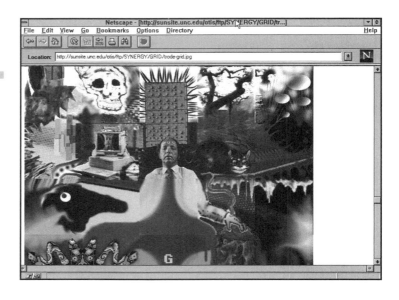

http://sunsite.unc.edu/otis/ftp/SYNERGY/GRID/trode-grid.jpg

passed along to the next artist; or exercises in image modification, where everyone begins with a basic image and modifies it to create new images.

Even things as simple as portraits, family pictures, or your latest vacation photos can be sent by electronic mail to people in distant places. As digital cameras, video capture technology, and Kodak's Photo CD technology take hold you'll find it easier than ever to create digital images that lend themselves to electronic transfer.

Many Web sites, especially those with an animal or hobby interest, are always looking for users to contribute pictures.

If your reaction when you visit a site is "I can do better than that," or "They should see my pictures of that scene," contact the Webmaster and offer your images. Many Webmasters of graphical sites don't have any images of their own. All their pictures have come from volunteers, friends, and other people on the Internet. They'd love to have a look at your pictures, and if your pictures offer something new for visitors, chances are good the Webmaster will put your pictures on the Internet.

Animals

SEARCHING FOR ANIMAL pictures on the Internet is not unlike searching for them in the wild.

You can't always find what you want when you want it. You just don't know what you'll find when you look. But if you look long and hard enough, you're sure to see something surprising.

In our investigations, for example, we ran across everything from a 350-pound Burmese python that lives in someone's home (actually it may be the snake's home that a human lives in—the snake would win in any contest over ownership!) to a site that specializes in fly parts (as in house flies).

Oh, and there are lots of dog, cat, horse, rabbit, fish, and wild animals sites around as well. Some sites specialize in a particular type or even breed of animal, while others are more general. In short, it's a zoo out there.

American Association of Zoo Keepers

 http://aazk.ind.net

Figure 2.1

A cougar, in the wild cats section of the American Association of Zoo Keepers site.

http://aazk.ind.net/animal_gifs/Cats/WildCats_CarolineBrett/WC.cougar.jpg

IN THAT CASE, who better to make sense of a zoo than the American Association of Zoo Keepers?

Their site truly covers its territory from Apes to Zebras.

There are whole sub-directories here devoted just to wolves or apes or birds, so there is a very good chance of finding something you like from the animal kingdom at this site. The images are often excellent quality as well, with many exceeding 400K in size.

By the way, the pictures are mostly of animals in their natural environments, which makes for better pictures.

The images are stored as files rather than as the usual World Wide Web thumbnail pictures, so you have to go by the text descriptions to figure out what's what.

However, the zookeepers are building a special directory that contains small previews of the full-sized images. When you get to the images section at this site, go to the preview directory first.

To save needless downloading time on large images you don't want, you can go to the preview section first, find the image you want, and download it quickly. If you like it, you can go back and download the full image from the main picture gallery. The preview page also has brief descriptions of the images, unlike many of the images in the main directory, which have only file names.

This site could use some housekeeping. A few file names were misspelled (for example, foggy instead of froggy) when we were there, and some obvious targets are in not-so-obvious places.

If you're looking for lion pictures, for example, there are no lions and no lion sub-directories listed in the main directory for animal pictures. You have to look in the safari directory to find them.

Fortunately, it's a fun place to browse, so a few bad hits aren't all that bad. Who wants to look at fog anyway?

The zookeepers also invite folks to e-mail them animal pictures, which adds to the disorganization. An animal name you don't recognize could turn out to be the name of someone's cat or parakeet uploaded here to gain Net immortality. ▲

Figure 2.2

This wolf can be seen up close at the American Association of Zookeepers site, in the wolves subdirectory.

http://aazk.ind.net/animal_gifs/wolves/wolves-08.gif

The Electronic Zoo

 http://netvet.wustl.edu/e-zoo.htm

Figure 2.3

Two deer in a photo on a Swedish graphics archive, accessed through the Electronic Zoo.

THE ELECTRONIC ZOO falls into the category of sites with indexes of other sites. Although it stores few images at its own site, it maintains a very authoritative list of animal sites on the Internet. So, if you don't find what you need at the American Association of Zookeepers, chances are good you'll find a link to it here.

ftp://ftp.sunet.se/pub/pictures/animals/2deer.gif

Figure 2.4

The Bulldog Picture Archive, dedicated to the most beautiful of dogs.

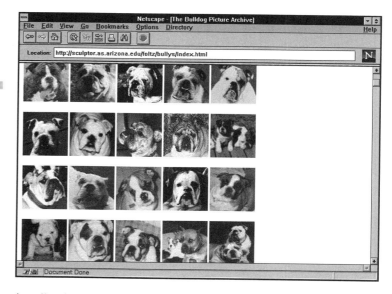

http://sculptor.as.arizona.edu/foltz/bullys/index.html

Click down a page from the opening menu until you see the icon named animals (it has an animal footprint on it). From there, click on the images icon, and voilà, you're looking at a lengthy list of images of every animal you can think of, and probably a few you hadn't.

As you would expect, there are plenty of cat, dog, and horse sites on the Internet. Interestingly, Netizens also seem to have an affinity for iguanas, snakes, and other reptiles. You may not have expected to find the Lemur Page or the Bulldog Picture Archive, which is devoted to the proposition that the Bulldog is the most beautiful of dogs. Then there's FlyView, a rather strange, but very scientific database containing hundreds of images of fly parts (the insect) used in genetic research. ▲

alt.binaries.pictures.animals

AS IS USUAL with newsgroups, you have to be in the right place at the right time. This is the right place to pick up animal pictures that haven't appeared before, though there is no archive site for the images that appear here. However, many of these images are picked up by those who collect animal pictures, so you'll find them in other sites on the Internet, usually without credit.

The nice thing about a newsgroup, however, is that if you're looking for something in particular, you can leave a message to that effect. The chances are good that someone out there has what you want, and can either steer you to it or upload the image to the newsgroup for you to use. ▲

Figure 2.5
Images of all kinds can be found in the alt.binaries. pictures.animals group.

alt.binaries.pictures.animals

Graphics Sites Reviewed in Ch 20

In addition to this chapter's best of the best, read about these sites in Ch 20.

Biological Sciences Database

http://www.calpoly.edu/delta.html

Images, scientific names, and QuickTime movies of animals, particularly of marine creatures, seabirds, ocean-going mammals, and marine reptiles.

Fish Information Service (FINS) Index

http://www.actwin.com/fish/

Good galleries of freshwater and marine aquarium fish.

Herpetocultural Home Page

http://gto.ncsa.uiuc.edu/pingleto/herp.html

Mike Pingleton's herpetology page, with numerous galleries of snake and reptile photos.

Interactive Frog Dissection

http://curry.edschool.virginia.edu/~insttech/frog/menu.html

Photos and movies illustrating how to dissect a frog.

Pet Pages

http://www.dynamo.net/dynamo/pets/pets.html

An Internet site where pet owners can put their dearly beloved furry and feathered friends on a Web page.

CHAPTER 3

Animation & Cartoons

THE MOST DIFFICULT step in finding downloadable cartoon and animation graphics using Netscape is not getting lost in deep .html directories. This should be no problem, however, if you're interested in losing large chunks of time to reading comix (read, comics) and staring at lush fields of subdirectory after subdirectory of high-quality anime (Japanese animation) scans. Lush is definitely the operative word.

We were glad we packed a virtual picnic basket to take with us while trekking through the field of cartoons and animation graphics. A healthy meal of Pentium chips and a fast modem (28.8) were barely enough to get us through downloading many of the larger cartoon and animated movie .mpgs.

Still, the club-like atmosphere between sites was well worth our stay in their part of the Internet. We followed as many links as possible, but still never reached any place appropriate to call an "end." That was fine with us, though. We brought lunch.

The St. John's Anime Film Society Gallery

 http://www.cs.mun.ca/~anime/afs/gallery.html

Figure 3.1

Robots are at the core of anime. The "Knight of Gold" is one of the larger graphics (96K) available through the Anime Gallery, in the subdirectory for "Mechs & Machinery."

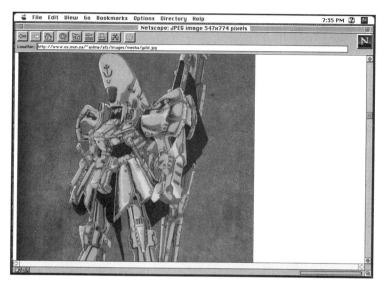

http://www.cs.mun.ca/~anime/afs/images/mecha/gold.jpg

THE ANIME GALLERY is relentless in its previewing of anime graphics. The gallery provides small thumbnails of each of the subdirectories, and the subdirectories are all preview-oriented. A good deal of the other anime pages we looked at on the Internet were long lists of references that accommodate the tremendous amount of available anime art, which means that you don't know what you're going to get until each image is downloaded.

Since there's so much anime (animation) and manga (comics), casual Web browsers are usually forced to click through every reference and suffer the lag time of long screen redraws. However, this site dumps a good portion of graphics onto its homepage before offering up a single link to an image index.

Scrolling down the page, you see a long list of anime and manga titles and a small preview graphic. Clicking on any one of those references takes you to another page of downloadable graphics and some background information on the story.

The Anime Gallery refers to the listings as "wings," roughly one for each film, series, or topic that has a serious number of images associated with it. There is also a "miscellaneous" wing for the images they liked but didn't know what to do with.

A majority of the images are slow-modem friendly—thumbnail images that are either one quarter or one eighth the size of the original. There are larger graphics available, too, but you really have to look for them.

NOTE Since the Japanese culture learned about animation from watching Disney movies, it shortened the word to "anime" to describe its cartoon-like movies. On the other hand, "manga" is the Japanese equivalent to "comic," the process of telling stories through pictures, an arche-typical art form older than Japanese culture itself.

Figure 3.2

The Knight Sabers serve as the heroines of the The Bubblegum Crisis.

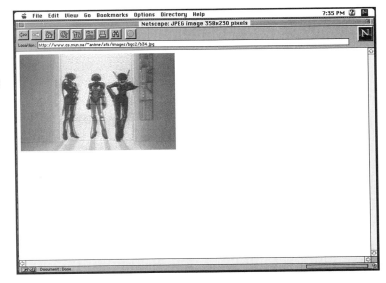

http://www.cs.mun.ca/~anime/afs/images/bgc2/b34.jpg

For example, the link to The Bubblegum Crisis ("Cyber punk... robots... hardsuits... killer babes!") leads to another long page of images from the animated movie. A sound library and an image index follow from there.

The image index on The Bubblegum Crisis link previews 24 images, but the .jpgs are only about 10K each, so they're small and might suffer on closer examination. Depending on how much of a connoisseur you are of Japanese manga (comics), this collection might be disappointing because the images, though intriguing, are too small to see clearly. Otherwise, it's a good collection of anime graphics scanned from animation.

Some larger graphics of Bubblegum Crisis Laserdisc covers can also be found at the base of this page (four images).

For a more extensive still-picture archive, The Anime Gallery links to the Venice FTP site, which provides a long list of filenames.

If you're interested in downloading chunks of animated QuickTime movies, follow the link to Rastlin's Anime Pages, and then select "QuickTime links and frame grabs." The resulting list is daunting. "The Kimagure Orange Road Movies—Part 1," for example, contains nine .gzipped movies, ranging from 7 to 24 megs each.

If you find that you're even more interested in anime after browsing through these pages, click on the subdirectory for Miyazaki Films and try out the Anime Pocket Guide. It'll tell you everything you need to know. ▲

Bone

 http://144.174.145.14/USERS/JAKE/Bone.html

Figure 3.3

Fone Bone dodges the water as his brother, Phoney Bone, climbs out of the barrel. Thorn grimaces while Grandma Ben smiles cheerfully.

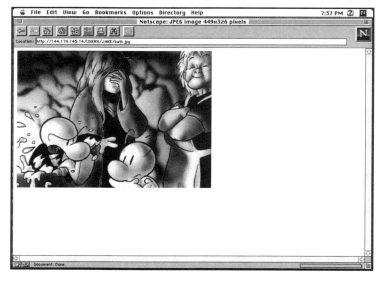

http://144.174.145.14/USERS/JAKE/bath.jpg

WE WERE APPREHENSIVE as the home page for the comic book *Bone* pulled up on the screen. Created by *Bebes Kids* & *Rover Dangerfield* artist Jeff Smith, we were sure that the Web site for such a widely popular cartoon would contain view-only graphics and tease us into running out and buying the latest edition.

Thankfully, we were wrong. Brightly colored excerpts from the comic are linked to each character description, as are scans of several covers from the comic book. The images should download when you click on them, or, in Netscape, you have the option to copy this image to your computer buffer.

There are B&W sketches of the characters spread throughout the site. The downloadable character pictures (.jpgs) are in full, rich, color, except for a few of the cover samples from other Jeff Smith projects.

The Bone site is easy to read and well organized. While some sites try to squeeze as much information on one page as possible, the Bone page quickly breaks down its graphics links to "Characters" and "Covers." Following the Characters links takes you to more sketches of the characters, plus additional pictures taken direction from the comic. The text here is large font and relaxing on the eyes.

There are only a few covers to download, but they're mixed into a complete index of the Bone comic. Readers are treated to a sneak peak of (as of this review) the upcoming "Bone #20," which is in B&W.

One of the prizes of this site is hidden beyond a few text pages. Click on the Introduction link, and then select the link to interviews with Jeff Smith, which is a page with yet another available character sketch of Bone. The first three interviews are rather short, but the link to "Jeff's interview with 'Him' from Lethargic Comics #9" reveals a treasure: seven large .gifs of an illustrated interview with Jeff Smith, written in the style of Space Ghost, Coast to Coast. Each of these B&W .gifs are about 500K in size and take some time to download or even view, but it's worth the time.

More art can be found following the link to Jeff Smith's home page and clicking on the "pictures" collection. There, you'll find a random assortment of other full color and B&W graphics by Jeff Smith. Some of them are devoted to Bone, others are photographs of the artist.

For cartoon collectors, there are several "jam" cartoons that shouldn't be missed. The jams are portraits of several different cartoon characters posing together. In this case, Bone is posing in three different sketches with several other popular characters, such as Cerebus, from *Cerebus*, by David Sim, and characters from Martin Wagner's *Hep Cat* comic book.

We did find a few links that were inaccessible at the time, but that might be from overflow traffic. Keep trying.

The Ordering Information link provides an index of Bone comics and addresses, but doesn't allow the Web browser to order online. Also the Mailing List link doesn't automatically subscribe you to **bone@erzo.berkley.edu**. We'll just have to survive with the excellent graphics for the time being. ▲

Figure 3.4

Jeff Smith drew this picture for the Wizards Creators Portfolio series of collectors cards. It features Bone and love-interest Thorn fleeing from the Rat Creatures.

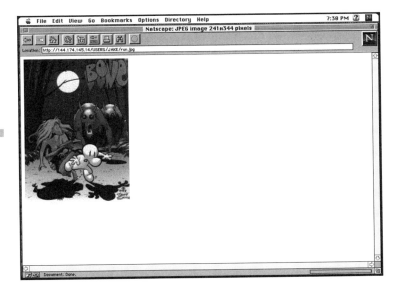

http://144.174.145.14/USERS/JAKE/run.jpg

The Uncanny X-Page

 http://ux4.cso.uiuc.edu/~m-blase/x-page.html

Figure 3.5

X-Men's Colossus, featured in the "Age Of Apocalypse Gallery" from SideWinder's Page For Gifted Youngsters. One of several links listed on the X-Page Image site.

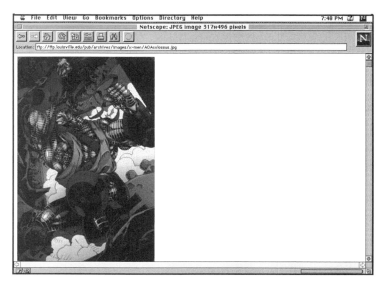

http://www.spd.louisville.edu/~mlviet01/pics/alter-x/AOAcolossus.jpg

THIS PAGE IS DEDICATED to lists of links for art from "The Uncanny X-Men," probably one of the most popular of American comic books. While there are no downloadable graphics on this page, the links send you to several large archives, specifically found under the heading "Sights And Sounds."

The link to the Index of Marvel Images (oddly also labeled "Robert Kohlbus' Non-Sports Card Collection") brings you to another short list of collections, all of which contain high-resolution scans of many of the featured trading card images. Some of the them are really large (319K for Dr. Doom 2099!); but if you're devoted, you can have the quality art all for your own keeping.

Still, their bulky file size allows you to have some very nice colored art that you might not be able to get anywhere else, unless you own all the cards and scan them in yourself.

Robert Kohlbus' Non-Sports Card Collection

http://empire.umd.edu/PICS/marvel

SideWinder's X-Men Page

http://www.spd.louisville.edu/~mlviet01/x.html

JSE's X-Men Graphics

http://www.ultranet.com/~jamie-se/xmengrph/xmengrph.html

Matthew Garrand's Marvel Image Archive

http://rpinfo.its.rpi.edu/~garram/Images.html

Figure 3.6

This image from JSE's X-Men Graphics page features the winsome Rogue of the X-Men casually holding up a car on her fingertip.

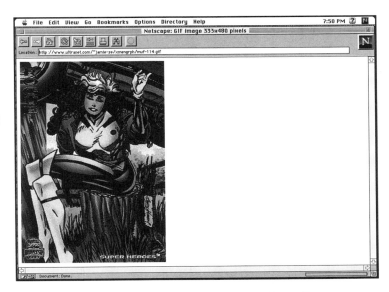

http://www.ultranet.com/~jamie-se/xmengrph/muf-114.gif

We thought it was a nice touch to see the presence of trading card companies, such as Fleer Flair Marvel Cards, on the Internet. If you're not a dedicated buyer/trader of collector cards, it's frustrating to walk through any bookstore and see the cards wrapped up in shiny mylar packaging—you don't get to see the art. This site contains images of 16 superheroines, each about 50K and easily downloadable.

JSE's X-Men Graphics page is a large collection (24, when we visited) of medium-sized .gif files of X-Men cover art and more trading cards (the page administrator says he tries to

not make duplicates of what other pages offer).

A tremendous amount of superhero art can be found in the link to Matthew Garrand's Marvel Image Archive. Here, you'll find a comprehensive, alphabetical listing of almost all Marvel superheroes. Each

subdirectory contains at least one graphic. The more popular heroes gave three or four images. Some of them are quite large, others aren't. Wolverine is the featured keeper of the archive, but the images are not constrained to X-Men pictures. ▲

GRAPHICS SITES REVIEWED IN CH 20

In addition to this chapter's best of the best, read about these sites in Ch 20.

Akira Picture Archive

http://www.informatik.tu-muenchen.de/cgi-bin/nph-gateway/
hphalle8/~rehrl/Akira.archive.html

Images from the Japanese animated movie *Akira*.

The Calvin and Hobbes Archive

http://www.eng.hawaii.edu/Contribs/justin/Archive/Index.html

A very full archive of the newspaper daily *Calvin and Hobbes*.

Comics 'n Stuff

http://www.phlab.missouri.edu/~c617145/comix.html

A resource site for finding all the comics you need on the Internet.

The Dilbert Zone

http://www.unitedmedia.com/comics/dilbert/

A home page for devotees of the *Dilbert* comic strip. Don't get caught reading these at work.

Venice

http://www.tcp.com/pub/anime-manga

An FTP site for Japanese animation and comics.

4

Architecture

To ARCHITECTS, the word cyberspace has special meaning. After all, they are experts in space and in the way humans interact with the spaces in which they live and work.

Development of the Internet and of cyberspaces in general are causing a revolution in architecture and architectural thinking. What does a "virtual factory" look like? How would you design the headquarters for a "virtual corporation"?

Architects are using the graphics capabilities of cyberspace in two primary ways at this point:

▼ to share ideas, and particularly ideas about using computers in architecture, and

▼ as a repository of images of historical and contemporary architecture.

At the time of this writing, we couldn't find some of the things we wanted to see, such as all the important buildings in New York, all the major Gothic churches of Europe, and all the buildings designed by Frank Lloyd Wright. Small sets of such images can be found, but no one has compiled those images in a complete form and put them on the Net.

In this chapter, we're going to look at two efforts, however, that make good use of cyberspace to show you architectural space, and we'll point you to additional resources.

Virtual Study Tour

 http://archpropplan.auckland.ac.nz/misc/virtual_tour.html

Figure 4.1

The Hadrianic Baths at Leptis Magna, built by Hadrian around 127 A.D.

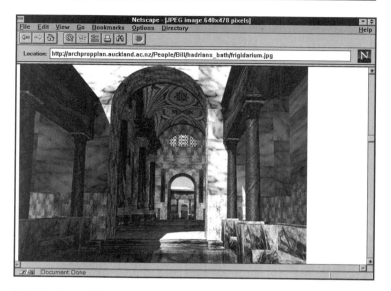

http://archpropplan.auckland.ac.nz/People/Bill/hadrians_bath/frigidarium.jpg

THE ARCHITECTURE Property and Planning Department at the University of Auckland, New Zealand has come up with the best organized collection of materials related to computer visualization of architectural spaces.

In one section, called In Memory of Architecture (see how quickly the virtual can overtake the concrete?) department members reconstruct historical architectural spaces on computer.

You'll find reconstructions of Hadrianic Baths, a temple of Ramses, a Japanese gallery, and a reconstruction of Mies van der Rohe's 1929 German Pavilion for an exposition in Barcelona.

The pavilion was a very modern, minimalist blend of horizontal and vertical planes and reflecting pools that turned the world of architec-ture on its ear. At the end of the exposition, the real pavil-ion was dismantled to be shipped back to Germany, but was never re-erected anywhere and is now lost.

If you've ever played the game Doom, with its whiz-bang scrolling and virtual real-ity play, you'll recognize the idea behind the Barcelona Pavilion. The Barcelona Pavil-ion is Doom for architects, and it is one of the cleverest sites on the Internet.

When you access this site and begin to take the "tour" with a graphical Web browser, just put your engine in park and hold on. The Web pages change automatically, frame by frame, to take you through the building. If you'd like to stop and look around at the end of the tour, you can do so because every image consists of three horizontally arranged frames. Clicking on the left frame turns your view to the left, clicking on the right frame turns your view to the right, and clicking on the middle frame moves you forward. In this way you can "walk" through the building in three-dimensional fashion, examin-ing its spaces at your leisure.

By the way, to see all of this and to find your way back to the beginning easily, go to the Preferences menu of your browser and turn off features like Location and Toolbar. You'll get more screen space that way. Also, to avoid extra downloading if you want to return to a location within the site, take advantage of your browser's bookmark feature: create a bookmark for the location of the opening screen so you can return to it whenever you like. Pressing Ctrl+A in Netscape, for example, creates a bookmark for the page you're currently looking at. (Or, you can also view the "history" of locations you've been to in the current session to go back to a specific page.)

If you click on the link to the University of Auckland at The Virtual Tour, you'll find a similar, but less interactive approach to the same concept. To help new students find their way around, the university built a virtual model of the campus. MPEG video, which you can download, provides fly-throughs, fly-overs, and fly-unders around campus.

Matiu Carr, a capable and innovative architectural modeler and a highly skilled Webmaster, completed much of the work at this site. Many people involved in architectural rendering and 3D graphics would be quite happy to have some of this New Zealander's experiments and works-in-progress as their finished work.

On the Virtual Study Tour's home page, you'll find a link simply titled Gallery. Follow it. It takes you to a section that covers more of Carr's work.

You'll find a takeoff on Corbusier's Garden City idea (also accessible from the main home page), and CAD models of a private home, including a short MPEG movie to show the client what he would see if he were standing in the central patio and turned in a full circle.

On the home page you'll also find a link to a student's gallery, which is worth pursuing to see how computer drafting, visualization, and rendering is influencing architecture. ▲

Figure 4.2

Clicking on the center frame moves through a computer recreation of a famous pavilion designed by Mies van der Rohe.

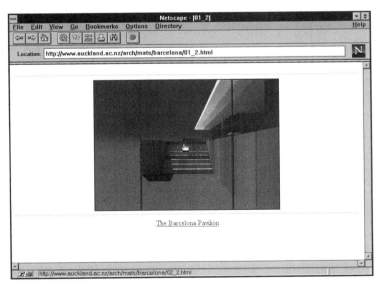

http://www.auckland.ac.nz/arch/mats/barcelona/01_2.html

Figure 4.3

Created as an exercise to help new students, computer-generated models of the University of Auckland campus and MPEG fly-overs, fly-throughs, and fly-unders.

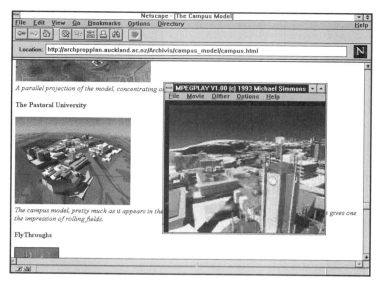

http://archpropplan.auckland.ac.nz/Archivis/campus_model/
campus.html

Figure 4.4

A movie to show a client how a home would look and other work from Matiu Carr.

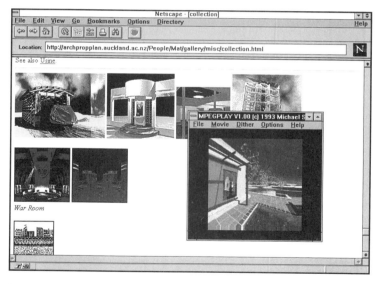

http://archpropplan.auckland.ac.nz/People/Mat/gallery/misc/
collection.html

LAVA

 http://www.bwk.tue.nl/lava

Figure 4.5

Museon/Omniversum, in The Haague, Netherlands, designed by Wim Quist

http://www.bwk.tue.nl/lava/galleries/museums/quist1.jpg

LAVA, A DUTCH acronym for The Lab for Architecture, was initiated in 1993 by students at The University of Technology in Eindhoven, Netherlands. Developed specifically to take advantage of the Internet, it is a place to trade ideas about architecture and provide pointers to other architecture sites on the Internet.

Two areas of this site are of particular interest. If you have an application that can read AutoCAD-style DXF files, several building models are available under the Modelshop link.

The rest of us will want to go to the Galleries section, and specifically to the Museums link in this section.

A museum is a common civic showpiece designed not only to hold its collection, but also to display the talents or artistic sense of its locale.

This exhibit offers pictures of the interiors and exteriors of many of the world's great museums.

The gallery covers 27 major museums from Germany, London, the Netherlands, the United States, and France. Many are by famous architects such as Mies van der Rohe, a key figure in the Bauhaus movement, Frank Lloyd Wright, and I.M. Pei, whose extension to the Louvre in Paris is featured at LAVA.

The museums database lets you look for a project by the name of the museum, the year it was built, the country it is in, or the architect who designed it. Once you find a museum and follow that link, you'll often find several photographs of the institution, such as interior and external views and special display areas. The section on New York's Guggenheim Museum, designed by Frank Lloyd Wright, has exterior views during and after construction, several shots of the interior, and a view of the skylight. ▲

Figure 4.6

Interior of the Guggenheim Museum of Modern Art.

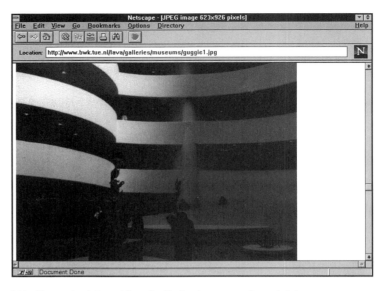

http://www.bwk.tue.nl/lava/galleries/museums/guggie1.jpg

GRAPHICS SITES REVIEWED IN CH 20

In addition to this chapter's best of the best, read about these sites in Ch 20.

Acanthus Virtual Gallery

http://cad9.cadlab.umanitoba.ca/Virtual_Gallery.html

Portfolios of three Canadian architects from the Prairies.

Archigopher

gopher://libra.arch.umich.edu:70/11

A small collection of images from Greece, plus some 3D and CAD drawings, archives on Kaminsky and Palladio, and a section on architecture on the moon.

ArchiWeb

http://www.archiweb.com/index.html

A collection of architectural information. Under construction when we visited, but it looks very promising.

Bill's Lighthouse Getaway

http://gopher.lib.utk.edu:70/lights.htm

A gallery of lighthouses on the east and west coasts of the United States.

Covered Bridges

http://william-king.www.drexel.edu/top/bridge/CB1.html

Photos and descriptions of more than 40 covered bridges in southeastern Pennsylvania and neighboring states.

Durham Cathedral

http://www.dur.ac.uk/~dla0www/c_tour/tour1.html

A thorough tour of an ancient, but still used, castle site that has figured prominently in English history.

Frank Lloyd Wright

http://flw.badgernet.com:2080

Images of some Frank Lloyd Wright architecture in Wisconsin.

Glensheen

http://www.d.umn.edu:80/glensheen

A well-illustrated visual tour of the elaborate Glensheen Estate near Duluth, Minnesota.

Los Angeles: Revisiting the Four Ecologies

http://www.cf.ac.uk/uwcc/archi/jonesmd/la

A Welsh architecture student takes a fresh look at Los Angeles.

Pompeii Forum Project

http://jefferson.village.virginia.edu/pompeii/page-1.html

A look at the architecture of ancient Pompeii, and its implications for city planning.

Renaissance and Baroque Architecture

http://www.lib.virginia.edu:80/dic/colls/arh102/index.html

A rich archive of photos of Renaissance and Baroque architecture.

C H A P T E R

5

Art Galleries

Two TRENDS IN recent years have made the Internet a great playground for commercial art galleries.

The surge in popularity of graphical browsers has made it possible to easily display art work on the Internet to a large number of the newcomers to the Net. Many of these people are ordinary consumers who were not inclined to fight their way to graphic images with command-line interfaces and Kermit, but who, with Mosaic and Netscape, are merrily finding their way around.

Second, restrictions on commercial use have evaporated or been pushed aside in recent years, so that galleries could openly advertise works for sale and even conduct transactions across the Internet.

We're going to look at commercial art galleries in this section. These are galleries whose primary purpose is the sale of art either from other artists or by the artist who operates the Internet site. We have another section, Chapter 7 "Art in Cyberspace," for galleries whose focus seems to be less commercial, and which concentrate on opportunities to simply display art.

We're finding an increasing number of traditional art galleries coming aboard the Internet; however, their commitment varies widely. Some show museum-like caution, putting up only one or two images from one or two artists. At the other end of the spectrum are galleries that exist primarily online and aggressively use cyberspace as the prime showplace for their art.

The Electric Gallery

 http://www.egallery.com/egallery

Figure 5.1

*"Preparation pour le Marché"
(Preparing for Market) by
Claude Dambreville.*

http://www.egallery.com/egallery/disk9/img0038.jpg

WE FOUND NO other gallery on the Internet that used online technology as thoroughly and as well as The Electric Gallery.

It is large, with hundreds of pictures. It is well organized, with several different ways to find the pictures that you want. It has large and small images, for those with slow Internet connections and those with fast connections. And it does an excellent job of displaying the art on its site.

This is a gallery that doesn't cheat the online community with minuscule images or crippled color palettes. The Electric Gallery recommends using a 1024 by 768 resolution screen with at least 65,000 color display for viewing the images, which are JPEGs up to 200K in 24-bit color. They're big, colorful, and beautiful. Even the thumbnails run 16K to 18K so you can get a good look at images without having to download everything. (You don't need SuperVGA and a high-color video card to access the site; you'll just find that the images look better and fit more easily into your viewing window if you

have better hardware.)

The Electric Gallery divides its collection into "wings." Each wing is further subdivided into rooms, each with about three pictures in it, from various artists in that wing. The wings (and the number of rooms when we looked) cover Haitian art (38 rooms), Southwest art (22 rooms), pictures from an art school in the Peruvian Amazon basin (14 rooms), a jazz and blues wing (6 rooms), a folk art wing (9 rooms), and a contemporary art wing (8 rooms).

In addition, there are 14 rooms in a special Journeys section, and three in a Northwest Myths section. That's 114

rooms—usually with three images per room.

You can navigate through this gallery by taking a shortcut to the rooms and clicking on a room. Once in a room, you can click to move to the next room or back to previous rooms.

An alternative is a "walking tour," which brings up three images at a time from the whole collection. Also, you can elect to view images by the artists within a wing. We'd recommend taking the walking tour first, and if you see an artist whose work appeals to you, view the collection by artist so you can see more of that artist's work.

http://www.egallery.com/egallery/disk2/img0227.jpg

Figure 5.3

Lozano Mita's "The Stream."

http://www.egallery.com/egallery/disk5/img0019.jpg

The Electric Gallery's specialty is ethnic and primitive art and one of its first, and still largest sections, is the Haitian wing.

Look beyond the images of Haitians as only boat-people or impoverished sugar cane workers to recognize that Haiti, with its African, French, and Spanish cultures and a historical tradition of independence, has a turbulent and artistically rich history.

The depth of the Haitian gallery here is awesome, with some 47 painters represented. Clicking on a painter's name brings up one to four representative images from that artist, plus a brief biography.

The artists here are the best that Haiti has to offer. Born in the 1920s and 1930s in many cases, their work has both the maturity of their experience and the vitality of their culture and island.

Many have sold or displayed their work in prominent galleries in New York and Paris. Some work with primitive themes, such as animals, plants, and village life. Others work with more traditional artistic subjects, such as portraits, landscapes, and seascapes. Most fall into realist or Impressionist styles, and have a joyful sense of color and the ability to compose disparate objects into intriguing wholes.

If you have a decent connection and the time to browse, you can easily spend a whole day in this gallery.

The newer Southwestern art section was not nearly as deep when we visited, with only two painters, Lawrence W. Lee and Mary E. Wyant, represented there.

The Amazon project shows the Amazon jungle with a clarity and beauty that might have eluded you in watching all those Hollywood movies about water snakes, alligators, and muscular women. These paintings are by young Peruvian artists who are dedicated to preserving the beauty of this unique watershed. They attend an institute called Usko-Ayar (which means "Spiritual Prince"), and their art is a way of preserving knowledge about the spirits, animals, and plants of the upper Amazon basin.

The Jazz wing has the spirit of great jazz: asymmetrical, yet balanced; casual, yet structured. You can not only look at the paintings here, but download a short B.B. King audio clip. These are mostly portraits of jazz and blues greats such as Miles Davis, Dizzy Gillespie, Charlie Parker, Billie Holiday, John Coltraine, Ray Charles, and John Lee Hooker.

The Folk Art Wing features mainly self-taught artists from around the world, including the Americas, Eastern Europe, and the Caribbean. Many have established reputations and have been shown in galleries.

The Contemporary Art wing showcases new young artists from various countries, and had eight names represented when we were there.

A special exhibit, Journeys, featured paintings by Adrian Wong Shue, whose Asian heritage and Jamaican upbringing provide material for a unique artistic path.

Shue explores themes from Greek mythology and everyday relationships, with an unusual palette of colors and strong, formal compositions.

Figure 5.4

"Rocky" fastens his chaps in this painting by Mary Wyant in the Electric Gallery's Southwestern art section.

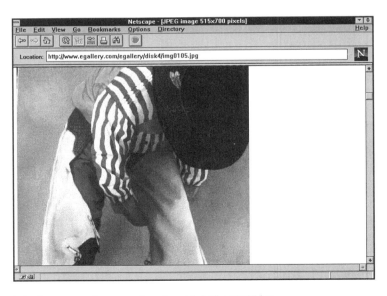

http://www.egallery.com/egallery/disk4/img0105.jpg

Figure 5.5
Zagaceta Alfredo's "The Little Birds," part of the Amazon Project.

http://www.egallery.com/egallery/disk5/img0016.jpg

Figure 5.6
"One Chance" (Miles Davis) by Gary Patterson and Marion Barnes.

http://www.egallery.com/egallery/disk6/img0003.jpg

Figure 5.7

"Cantina Watergate" by Manuel Garcia Moia of Nicaragua.

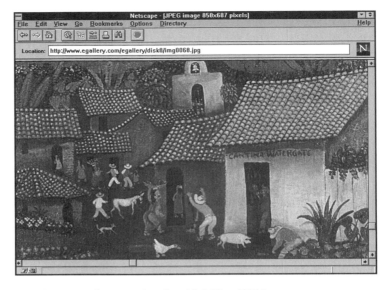

http://www.egallery.com/egallery/disk8/img0068.jpg

Figure 5.8

"Sundrift IV" by Sergey Cherep (Russia) in the Contemporary Art wing.

http://www.egallery.com/egallery/disk11/img1013.jpg

In the Northwest gallery, you'll find paintings with Northwest native themes by anthropologist and artist Frank Woll.

Woll's section offers the classic Northwest native totems as well as more narrative types of paintings that are more painterly than traditional Northwest art, but have the strong lines and drawing of that art.

Another section features the Abstract Realism of Rolland Golden, a much-exhibited American artist who covers the byways of the American landscape with confidence and boldness.

If you really like this gallery, you can download a special digital catalog (currently for Windows only) that has a searchable index of all the pictures and even a screen saver routine featuring the pictures in the gallery. It's seven megabytes, and if that's too much to download, you can order it on diskette. ▲

Figure 5.9

"Wolf and Owl Go Hunting," by Frank Woll in the Northwest Art section.

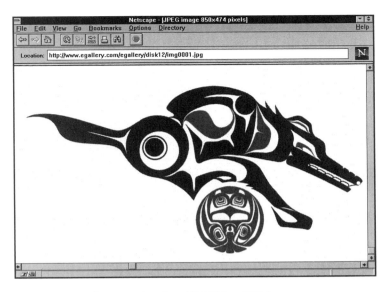

http://www.egallery.com/egallery/disk12/img0001.jpg

Graphics Sites Reviewed in Ch 20

In addition to this chapter's best of the best, read about these sites in Ch 20.

911 Gallery

http://www.iquest.net/911/iq_911.html

A gallery in Indianapolis that specializes in electronic media and computer-generated art.

Art.Online

http://bighorn.terra.net/artonline

An Internet display space for commercial artists.

Artix

http://www.artix.com/biz/artix

A Web site for many of the top Manhattan art galleries.

Art Metal

http://wuarchive.wustl.edu/edu/arts/metal/ArtMetal.html

A gallery displaying the art of several artists who work exclusively with metal.

ArtScene

http://artscenecal.com/index.html

A site based on a monthly magazine that covers the art museums and art galleries of Southern California.

Astarte Gallery

http://www.icl.co.uk/Astarte/Images/a11.gif

Astarte Gallery specializes in classical antiquities from all parts of the world.

Elliott Brown Gallery

http://www.ftgi.com/iar/1.html

A commercial gallery that also has an Internet site. The gallery specializes in artistic glass.

Impala Gallery

http://www.thegroup.net/impala/imphome.htm

The Impala gallery specializes in the arts and crafts of Asia, Egypt, and West Africa.

Isaacs/Inuit Gallery

http://www.novator.com/UC-Catalog/Isaacs-Catalog/Isaacs-Internet.html

A gallery specializing in the work of Inuit (Eskimo) carvers and artists.

JAAM

http://www.iNTERspace.com/art/jaam/jaam.html

JAAM specializes in the work of the Natives of the Pacific Northwest and the coast of British Columbia.

The Masters' Collection
http://www.portal.com:80/~jdoll/joes/masters/

Reproductions of masterpieces, available on the Net.

Merike Lugas
http://www.eagle.ca/~roda/RodMerArts/ArtGalIntro.html

A particularly well-done gallery from an individual artist who uses the Web effectively to market her work.

Virtual Portfolio
http://www.dircon.co.uk/maushaus/folio.html

An Internet showcase for the work of some of London's top photographers.

Wentworth Gallery
http://wentworth-art.com/wwg/index.htm

A selection of images from the Wentworth Galleries, a chain in the Eastern United States, with a good variety of art styles.

CHAPTER 6

Art in Cyberspace

THE STRUGGLING ARTIST of the past was always fighting for recognition. Snooty gallery owners, snooty museum curators, maybe even snooty black-velvet painting makers prevented the artist from the public recognition and acclaim he or she deserved, at least in the artist's eyes.

Things have changed. Now anyone can have a gallery, and show anything they want, any time they want, on the Internet. We're calling such galleries "cyber galleries." They generally don't have a real-life counterpart. That is, you can't walk into the gallery on a street somewhere and see the same paintings or work, in most cases. In addition, the art is on the Net not so much for commercial purposes as for the satisfaction of knowing that the statement one makes through art can be heard and seen by others.

The great thing about cyber galleries is that anyone can put up whatever they want, often at much lower cost than they could mount, frame, and hang their work in a regular gallery. The not-so-great thing is that low-quality or novice work that would never make the walls of a conventional gallery often finds its way onto the Internet.

In this chapter, you'll take a tour of some of these galleries. However, this is not a comprehensive or perfect list. We found so many cyber galleries out on the Net that we simply couldn't keep up with them. This chapter will expose you to some of the variety on the Net, as well as acquaint you with some of the better galleries we ran across.

Art on the Net

 http://www.art.net/Welcome.html

Figure 6.1

"Crowds in January" by Samia A. Halaby, at Art on the Net.

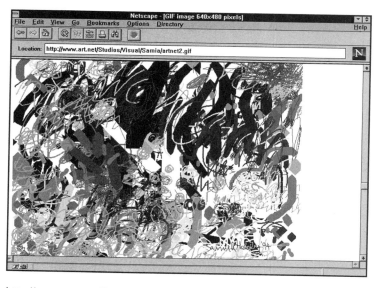

http://www.art.net/Studios/Visual/Samia/artnet2.gif

ART ON THE Net is a great place to begin when looking at this category of sites. It's very large, and growing fast. It's well organized, and gives you good tools for moving around and for locating the kind of art you want to see. Perhaps most important in a site of this type, it isn't rigid.

Art on the Net does not enforce standards on how artists use their individual gallery spaces, which makes this like a real artists' collective. Some artists show you their studio and talk about their travels; others write short essays on art. Some develop Web pages that meander through various artistic styles while others get right to the point with screens of thumbnails.

Some artists insist that their work is for viewing on the screen only. Others invite you to download and print images for your own enjoyment.

Many of the artists work in digital media, some work in traditional (now called "analog") media, and many have a foot in both camps, producing both kinds of work, or scanning their paper sketches and studies into the computer for finishing.

Using Art on the Net's menus you can easily get to the artists' galleries. Once there, however, you will follow the plan that each artist has for viewing work. The disadvantage is that some artists are better at organizing their material than others. On the other hand, art and artists are different, and the way you view it should perhaps change as well.

Art on the Net is non-commercial, that is, it asks that artists not post prices on their work. But artists are encouraged to publicize e-mail or snail mail addresses or phone numbers so Internet visitors can get in touch with the artist.

When we looked, it had about 65 artists from all around the world. From the home page you can click on artists' studios, to get to a list of artists by categories. This site has much more than visual artists on it—it includes musicians and bands, performance artists, poets, video artists, animators, and others. When we looked there were 44 artists under visual artists, with brief descriptions of their media and styles.

Figure 6.2
"Nuclear energy is our friend"
from Steve Standeford.

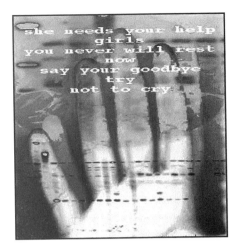

http://www.art.net/Studios/Visual/Pixel/handgene.gif

Figure 6.3
In "3:42pm Dec. 5, 1990"
photographer Troy Bennett
plays with texture and light in a
personal exhibition called
"Silence of Light."

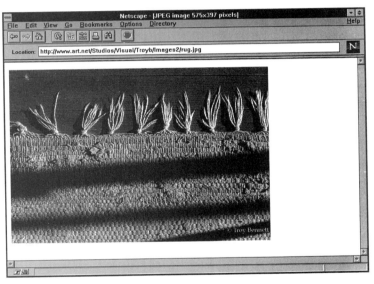

http://www.art.net/Studios/Visual/Troyb/Images2/rug.jpg

Some of the newer areas are very thin: sculpture and performance art each had one contributor when we looked, for example. However, these arts don't lend themselves to viewing on the Internet nearly as well as other arts do, so it's not surprising that painters and watercolorists form the vast majority of artists here.

When you get to the home page you'll have several options.

The link titled The Gallery takes you to a hodgepodge of offerings on Art on the Net: an introduction to new art shows, video clips of some featured musicians, a view of a particu-

lar artist who may or may not be elsewhere on Art on the Net, or a feature on a newcomer to Art on the Net.

This section is "curated" by someone, so it will be whatever that person decides to come up with. When we were there, dipping into the various

rooms brought us to a gallery of New Guinea wood carvers, a special section on Israeli artists, several galleries of paintings from individual artists, video clips of some musicians, and information and links to a new exhibit on art and technology, among other things.

Figure 6.4
Diane Fenster blends graphics and text into powerful, evocative images.

http://www.art.net/Studios/Visual/Fenster/ritofab_Home/cantofive.html

The meat of this site is listed under the home page's link to Artists' Studios. Click on that and you get to choose the general type of art you'd like to view—visual artists, musicians, performance artists, sculptors, animators, and others.

There's no way to sum up the experiences at this site. We loved Mary Vollero's little books (click on the images to "page" through the books), Tom Coffin's dazzling graphics, Tory Bennett's classy and thoughtful photos,

Henry Chiu's Snapdragon Chronicles. In fact, we went into almost every gallery in the visual artists section and found something we liked.

Art on the Net is also where digital artist Diane Fenster has her Web page. Fenster is an artist of such skill and depth

that she deserves recognition beyond the digital ghetto. Her series "Ritual of Abandonment," parts of which were displayed at her Web site when we visited, is a tour de force of images, associations, and symbols. ▲

Strange Interactions

 http://amanda.physics.wisc.edu/show.html

Figure 6.5
"Landscape Event Number Two" by John Jacobsen.

JOHN JACOBSEN was one of the first artists to use the Internet as a showcase, and his Strange Interactions gallery shows up again and again in any list of Net-based art galleries. It earns this recognition not only because of its relatively long presence on the Net, but because of Jacobsen's accessible, yet mysterious art.

http://amanda.physics.wisc.edu/allimages/landscape_event.jpg

Jacobsen juxtaposes people, geometric spaces and figures, and cultural icons of various kinds in a shadowy artistic space.

Though not well known off the Internet, at least outside his home in Madison, Wisconsin, Jacobsen's pioneering experience with the Internet illustrates its power as a vehicle for artists.

Within minutes of announcing, in a few newsgroups and elsewhere, that his art was available (originally via FTP and Gopher), users were coming in to look at it. Within the first 24 hours, people from 19 different countries had looked at the art, and one image was accessed more than 1,000 times in the first week. Compared with the often-lonely experience of an artist mounting his first exhibition in a real art gallery, it was a revelation.

Jacobsen works primarily in pencil, and in oil on wood. Symbols of the cyber-age—wires, telephone poles, and people who pass each other on the street but do not really meet, are major motifs of his work. At times he begins with a photo or newspaper clipping, adding paint, texture, and his own symbols to produce the final image.

Like many of the cyber artists on the Internet, Jacobsen does not make his living from art, but the chance to display his art, and the obvious enjoyment that others get from accessing his gallery, is a good reason to maintain a cyber gallery. ▲

A CYBER GALLERY OF YOUR OWN

If you think a gallery space on the Internet, accessible to millions of people, will cost a lot of money, think again. In many cases, you'll find such a display space to be cheaper than framing a single picture.

Art on the Net, for example, charges $60 a year, plus one work of art, which will be auctioned off on the Internet.

Art on the Net discourages artists from overt selling within their galleries, but Kaleidospace begins with the notion that it's a place for artists to put their work before potential buyers. It even handles basic credit card purchases over the Net for artists. The price for a space on Kaleidospace is based on the number of works of art you put on, but it starts as low as $100 for the one-time setup fee.

These sites will provide some assistance in putting your art into digital form. Or you can do it yourself, using the software provided with this book and the advice in Chapter 25, "Putting Graphics on the Net," which tells you how to convert your art into digital images for display on the Net.

6

Figure 6.6

"The Lovers" by John Jacobsen.

http://amanda.physics.wisc.edu/jpeg/The_Lovers.jpg

GRAPHICS SITES REVIEWED IN CH 20

In addition to this chapter's best of the best, read about these sites in Ch 20.

@Art

http://gertrude.art.uiuc.edu/@art/gallery.html

An exhibit focusing on "second-generation," computer-generated art where the computer and associated technology has begun to disappear.

Alternative Virtual Biennial

http://www.interport.net/avb/

A site that blends the visual vocabulary of traditional painting and art with modern themes.

Anecdote

http://anecdote.com/

An underground club in Ann Arbor, Michigan, that provides space on its walls for local artists. That art is also posted on the club's Internet site.

ArtNetWeb

http://www.awa.com/artnet/artnetweb/home.html

A site with writing, news, and several online galleries of art.

Bas van Reek Art Building

http://www.xs4all.nl/~basvreek/

Using the metaphor of a real art gallery, this site displays the work of several Dutch artists.

Cyberia Art Galleries

http://www.easynet.co.uk/pages/cafe/gall.htm

Work by several excellent U.K. artists.

Digital Collage

http://www.csulb.edu/Collage/index.html

An online gallery of student and faculty work from California State University Long Beach.

Digital Art Endeavors and Other Artistic Experiences

http://ziris.syr.edu/home.html

A cyber gallery that specializes in interactive and collaborative work, where people on the Internet (including you) participate in the creation of art.

FineArt Forum Gallery

http://www.msstate.edu/Fineart_Online/gallery.html

A variety of art, from installations, to galleries of photographs, and artists statements of various kinds.

Kaleidospace

http://kspace.com:80/

An Internet gallery featuring the work of a wide variety of artists working in music, film, animation, graphics, and other arts.

6

Fluxus Online

http://anansi.panix.com:80/fluxus/FluxusMenu.html

In-your-face, challenging, crazy art and words from a gallery that defines itself as part of a "wry, post-Dada art movement that flourished in New York and Germany in the 1950s and '60s, and influences many contemporary artists."

Grotesque in Art

http://www.ugcs.caltech.edu/~werdna/grotesque/grotesque.html

A site that explores the "principle anxieties of modern man" through the images of traditional and modern artists.

Net@Works Exhibition

http://www.interlog.com/~steev/exhibition.html

A survey of Canadian art, with an emphasis on installations, robotics, and holograms.

OTIS (Operative Term is Stimulate)

http://sunsite.unc.edu/otis.html

A massive (more than 200 artists) visual arts gallery where anyone can contribute and anyone can look.

Pavilion Internet Gallery

http://www.pavilion.co.uk/PIG/

A versatile collection of work, including poetry, photography, painting, and wire sculpture.

Pixel Pushers

http://www.pixelpushers.wis.net/

A gallery with work from some of the world's top digital artists.

ProArts

http://www.lanminds.com/local/proarts.html

ProArts is the cyber version of an annual show in the Bay area in which artists open their studios to the public.

7

Art Museums

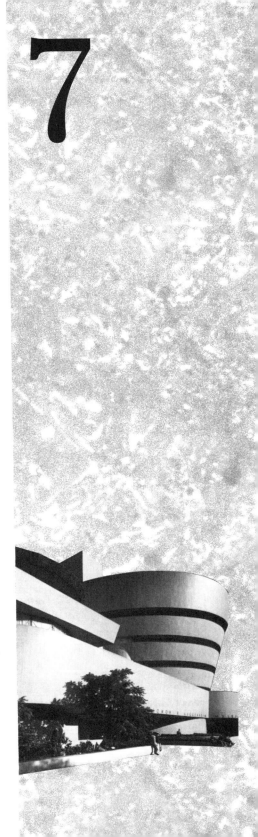

THE DEVELOPMENT OF graphical tools such as Mosaic and Netscape will probably revolutionize the way we view art. Great masterpieces are in most cases unique. If you want to see an original Picasso, Michelangelo, or da Vinci, you'll have to visit the museum that owns the original. A good alternative is to find a heavy coffee-table book that has the images you want to see.

Over the Internet, however, a growing number of galleries are putting images of their work online. You can visit the important photography collection at the Los Angeles County Museum of Art without having to travel to Los Angeles. You can use an Internet search engine, punch in the name of the artist you want, and go to a site that specializes in that artist, or that has some of his or her work online.

At least that's the way it should work.

In reality, most art museums are struggling with how much of their work to put online. While many of them have already established sites on the World Wide Web, the content reads like Everything-I-Could-Find-Out-With-a-Simple-Phone-Call: the hours that the building is open, who designed the building, and upcoming exhibitions. Many have online galleries containing selections from their collections or special exhibitions. But in most cases, you'll be lucky to find more than a couple of samples of art.

There are some exceptions, but most of the action appears to be taking place in online art museums, which collect great works of art, and organize them so that you can find what you want.

WebMuseum

 http://www.emf.net/wm

Figure 7.1

"The Marriage of Giovanni Arnolfini and Giovanna Cenami" by Jan van Eyck, is part of an exhibit on Gothic Art at Le WebMuseum.

PERHAPS MORE THAN any other, the WebMuseum demonstrated the power of the Internet to display and organize graphics when it opened in March 1994 as The Louvre (because it actually has no official connection, it had to change its name to WebMuseum).

http://star06.atklab.yorku.ca/wm/paint/auth/eyck/arnolfini/
eyck.arnolfini.jpg

MIRRORS

When a site becomes too popular, its host computer can't keep up with the demand for its services. Response slows to a crawl, weird things start to happen, and connections get dropped or data arrives incomplete. The solution is a *mirror*, which is a site somewhere else that has the same information on it. Everytime the host computer is updated, the mirror site is also updated. By splitting the traffic between the original host and the mirror, the load on each computer is reduced, and so is the network traffic. For example, if you're in San Francisco and elect to use the Paris site of Le WebMuseum rather than the Berkeley site across the Bay, all of the data you receive must be sent across the Atlantic and across the U.S. Other people who are using those links will experience slowdowns because of the traffic you create.

Many of us had that "Wow!" experience as we linked blithely to Paris and zipped through the famous paintings on display at one of the world's premier art galleries.

The site is so popular, in fact, that it is now mirrored in nearly two dozen locations around the world.

The WebMuseum is very much a collaborative effort. Experts or fans of particular painters from all around the world contribute images and explanatory text, and it seems likely that the WebMuseum will quickly become the largest repository of fine art on the Internet. In other words, if you're looking for a painting, look here first. If it's not there, keep looking because new paintings and new artists are constantly being added.

From the home page you'll see references to several special exhibits. These are comprehensive explorations of the work of particular artists or periods, and often include links to other sites on the Web, and to the Encyclopedia Brittanica, for background material.

When we were there, for example, the special exhibits covered Gothic Art, Cezanne, and a brilliantly illuminated Book of Hours from medieval France.

The Book of Hours is a good example of how the Internet can make art accessible: you can't see the originals even if you visit France, because the manuscript is too fragile for public display.

Navigating through the special exhibitions is much

like taking a personal guided tour of the artist's work. You look at a period or type of work, read about how it fits into the artist's overall work, then move on to the next section.

The Cezanne special exhibition is a happy blend of text and images. The images are arranged roughly according to the artist's various artistic periods. It's easy to browse and to see the work associated with a particular stage in the artist's life.

To gain access to the vast picture archives on the WebMuseum, click on the link to Famous Paintings, where you'll find individual galleries for each artist. The quantity of images in each gallery varies: some have only a few pictures, while others are comprehensive. However, virtually every

Figure 7.2

Wassily Kandinsky's "Autumn in Bavaria."

http://star06.atklab.yorku.ca/wm/paint/auth/kandinsky/
kandinsky.autumn-in-bavaria.jpg

painter of international significance is represented here. Most have some text providing a brief biography of the artist, and all the images are displayed with thumbnails, titles, and usually the year they were created.

One of the first special exhibitions put on by the WebMuseum was on Impressionism. Unlike a real gallery, where one exhibit disappears when a new one comes in (because there isn't room to hang both), this exhibition is still accessible at the WebMuseum. You'll find a link for it in the Famous Paintings section.

This is an extraordinary visual arts site, and a tremendous resource for anyone looking for an image, curious about a painter, or interested in learning more about art and art history. ▲

Figure 7.3

"Painting with Two Balls," from Jasper Johns, shows that the WebMuseum is not limited to old masters.

http://star06.atklab.yorku.ca/wm/paint/auth/johns/johns.two-balls.jpg

Christus Rex

 http://www.christusrex.org

THIS, MUSEUM CURATORS, is the art museum you want to imitate. By anyone's standards, its 1,300+ images from the Vatican's huge collection constitute an artistic treasure on the Internet, not to mention in real life. Compared with the paucity of small images most museums provide, the Vatican is several orders of magnitude ahead in exploiting the online environment. (Not bad for a 1900-year old institution.)

When it comes to its most famous images, the Vatican doesn't simply put a picture on its Web site. It puts four, five, even 10 pictures showing the same object or painting in overall view, detail, and, in the case of sculpture, from several different angles or in different lighting.

The site has some small 30-60Kb JPEGs which are easier for those with modem connections to download, but many images are also available in a 200-300Kb JPEG format for those who want to see the details.

All images are well marked, with a thumbnail, the name of

Figure 7.4

Sano Di Pietro's 1445 panel depicting the flight of the Holy Family to Egypt is among the Vatican's many classic paintings.

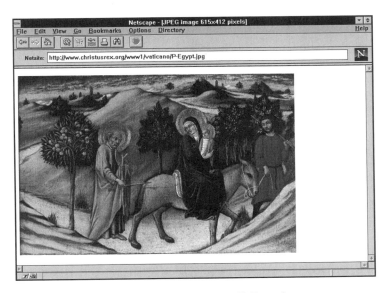

http://www.christusrex.org/www1/vaticano/P-Egypt.jpg

Figure 7.5

Michelangelo's "Creation of Adam," on the ceiling of the Sistine Chapel.

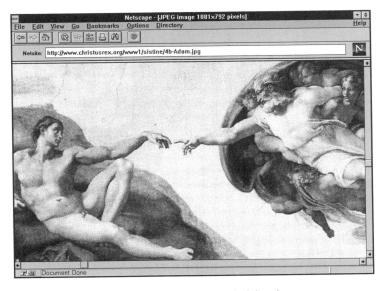

http://www.christusrex.org/www1/sistine/4b-Adam.jpg

the image, its type, and size in kilobytes.

The site is divided into four main areas: Vatican City, which covers the grounds and buildings, including the interior of St. Peter's Basilica; The Sistine Chapel, which covers just the paintings and sculpture in the chapel; the Raphael Stanze, which covers the paintings and decoration in the papal apartments; and the Vatican Museums, which covers the illuminated manuscripts, embroidered religious garments and cloths in the Vatican's library, tapestries, the paintings and sculptures in various galleries and other museums, and

archaeological treasures from Egypt and Italy.

In spite of the number of images, it's not difficult to find any particular one. Let's say we want to locate Michelangelo's glorious "Creation of Adam."

Since it's painted on the ceiling of the Sistine Chapel, we click on the link to the Sistine Chapel. More than 20 thumbnails will show up next, so after a wait, we scroll to the Scenes from Genesis section, where the thumbnail shows Adam reaching out toward the Creator.

Clicking on that thumbnail, we get 17 images from this painting, including close-ups of Adam, close-ups of the Creator, even close-ups of Eve, tucked tenderly in the crook of the Creator's arm, as well as additional images related to Eve.

Should you want to look at other images on the ceiling, there's a helpful map with all the images numbered that shows the perspective of lying on your back looking up at the ceiling. You'll also find—in a directory containing ceiling pictures in general—a photo showing the same view. This solves the critical dilemma of not being able to actually visit the chapel. Because you can't appreciate how they are arranged by seeing only the paintings, the lying-on-your-back view gives you that perspective.

Another famous piece of art, Michelangelo's "Pieta" (found in the Vatican City section, which includes St. Peter's Basilica), gets similar treatment. Because this is a sculpture, it's important to see it from different angles and in different lighting. The 10 images on this one sculpture accomplish this.

If you really want the grand tour, the next and previous buttons at the bottom of each directory let you take an online stroll through the whole collection.

Those on modem connections will find this a rather slow trip. If you're looking for something in particular, turn the thumbnail images off, because the descriptions for each image are quite complete.

Obviously we can't cover all of this site in detail, but it is a feast for the eyes and mind from what is probably the single most important repository of the art of Western civilization. ▲

Figure 7.6

The "lying-on-your-back" view of the Sistine Chapel ceiling.

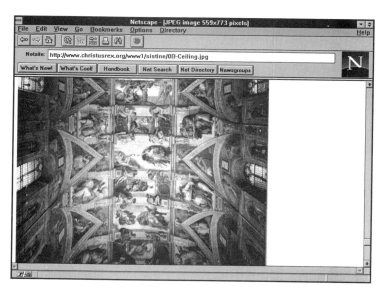

http://www.christusrex.org/www1/sistine/0B-Ceiling.jpg

GRAPHICS SITES REVIEWED IN CH 20

In addition to this chapter's best of the best, read about these sites in Ch 20.

African Art, National Museum of

http://www.si.edu/organiza/museums/africart/homepage/nmafa.htm

A museum showing Africa's artistic heritage through its ritual decorative, and household objects

Age of Enlightenment

http://dmf.culture.fr/files/imaginary_exhibition.html

A large exhibition, with paintings in a grand, heroic style from the period of the Enlightenment in France.

British Library

http://portico.bl.uk/

Various collections from one of the most important centers of Western intellectual history, with an eclectic assortment of online displays, with everything from images of maps, science, paintings of India, and others.

Essential Escher Gallery

http://www.umich.edu/~mransfrd/escher/

More than 200 Escher works, arranged by year, with commentary, etc.

Los Angeles County Museum of Art

http://www.lacma.org/

Images from the museum plus an extensive collection of photography by L.A.–area photographers.

Norton Gallery of Art

http://www.icsi.com/ics/norton/

Exhibits from the Norton Gallery, which offers previews of coming exhibits and images from its permanent collection.

Singapore Art & History Museum

http://www.ncb.gov.sg/nhb/museum.html

Good exhibits of Indian and Asian arts and crafts, photographs from Singapore's World War II years, postcards from 1900-1930, with excellent text and historical background.

Paintings of Vermeer

http://www.ccsf.caltech.edu/~roy/vermeer/

An exhibit on Vermeer with a clickable map showing the location of all his known paintings.

Photo Antiquities Home Page

http://deskshop.lm.com/photo.antiquities/index.html

Old photographs (Civil War, Daguerreotypes, etc.) and antique cameras and equipment.

Treasures of the Louvre

http://www.paris.org/Musees/Louvre/Treasures/

A small but high-quality collection of some of the world's most famous art treasures.

Wooden Toys

http://www.pd.astro.it/forms/mostra/mostra_i.html

An engaging and well-organized exhibit of wooden toys, most from the early 1900s.

World Art Treasures

http://sgwww.epf1.ch/BERGER/index.html

A carefully selected set of high quality photos on art from the Mediterranean and Asia, plus a devotee's journey through a sacred Egyptian temple.

Andy Warhol Museum Home Page

http://www.warhol.org/warhol/

A small collection of Andy Warhol's work.

8

Celebrities & Entertainment

▶ **W**HAT DOES IT take to be an international star?

Well, it used to take a great entertainment product, an agent or two, contracts with major record companies or studios, distributors, and so on. Now it also takes a Web site or a newsgroup.

Celebrities and their handlers are pouring into the Internet, partly because it's cool, and partly because it's a great way to keep in touch with fans all over the world.

Anyone who has browsed through a list of newsgroups on the Internet will recognize many of the names in the alt.fan groups. Brad Pitt, Conan O'Brien, Courtney Love, Barry Manilow, David Bowie, Elton John, Elvis, Frank Zappa, Harrison Ford, Jay Leno, Jimi Hendrix, John Denver, Mel Brooks, and other entertainment names all have alt.fan groups devoted to them. Outside the entertainment industry, you'll find groups for Dan Quayle, Stephen King, Bill Gates, Noam Chomsky, and many others.

If you're looking for pictures of these people, their projects, or their productions or performances, there's a good chance someone has put up an FTP or World Wide Web site devoted to them, and on that site you'll find the pictures you want.

In this chapter, we're going to look at some top sites that come at the celebrities issue from different angles.

Hollywood Online

 http://hollywood.com/

Figure 8.1

Sharon Stone in "The Quick and The Dead."

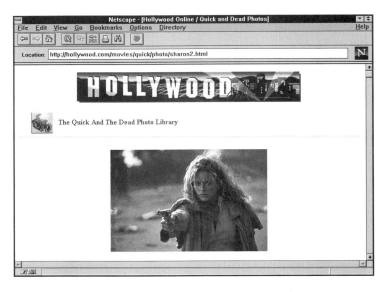

http://hollywood.com/movies/quick/photo/sharon2.html

THE ENTERTAINMENT INDUSTRY has been a key player in the drive for better graphics, and the idea is that someday down the road, you can load up a movie on your computer and play it.

We're getting there, and Hollywood Online proves it. This is a graphics-rich site built with all the pizzazz Hollywood can provide, which is to say, with loads of snazzy graphics and snappy menus.

Hollywood Online is mostly about the film industry, and at any given point it may be featuring a couple dozen current releases. Other than the film itself, there aren't many stones left unturned at this site.

You can get:

▼ A film's poster
▼ Action photos of all the stars
▼ A photo of the cast
▼ Video clips from the film

▼ The film's trailer (the short promotional previews that has all the good stuff in it)
▼ Screen savers with images from many films
▼ Interactive games and digital collectibles related to many films

The still images you'll find here aren't particularly large: most don't fill the screen, which means they download faster (and you won't be able to make 16×20 blowups to put on your wall).

Few pages are longer than two screen pages on your computer, and you don't get hit with a lot of graphics to download unless you specifically ask for them. That makes this site friendly for those with slower connections.

From the opening screen, click on Photos, to get to photo galleries for each of the films on the site. You'll see the film's advertising poster, pictures of all the major stars in action, and some action stills, all in color. Real film buffs will also find pictures of some less well-known players, such as directors, writers, or cinematographers.

Click on the Interactive button for accessories like screen savers, games, and so on. They will vary from film to film, depending on its theme.

Figure 8.2
The poster for the film "French Kiss."

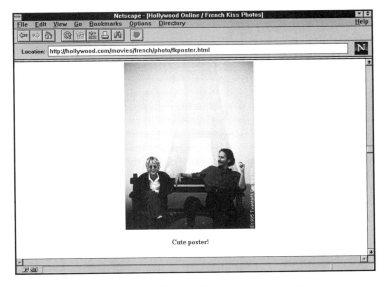

http://hollywood.com/movies/french/photo/fkposter.html

This being Hollywood, there's a lot of creative energy going into making interactive entertainment products, and some are quite clever.

If you click on the Videos button, you'll go to a similar screen of movie titles, except that this time you'll be able to download QuickTime or AVI clips from the film.

There's a bit of advertising on here too, and, this being Hollywood, this is not your standard fare. For a look at how the other half lives, you can browse through a few real estate ads showing the multi-million dollar Hollywood homes for sale in the real estate section. ▲

TIP Would you like to grab a still image of a favorite star's face or an action scene from a trailer you've downloaded? You actually don't need any special equipment to do so, if you're using Windows. Simply start running the movie using the appropriate viewer, and stop the movie at the appropriate point. Make sure the window with the movie is the active window (click on the title bar of the window to make it active). Then hold down the Alt key and tap the Print Screen key. This makes a snapshot of the active window and puts it on the Windows Clipboard.

Now open Paintbrush or the image editor of your choice—check out the CD-ROM included with this book for image-editing software such as Lview Pro. Go to the Edit menu of that software and select Paste. The current image on the Clipboard will be pasted into your image-editing software, ready for you to print or modify.

AVI and QuickTime files are better for this than MPEG files. MPEGs save space by eliminating information that doesn't change from frame to frame, so stopping them at a particular frame will often give strange results.

Be aware that the quality of these images will generally be quite poor, but if you want to use them for icons or thumbnails, they may be acceptable.

Rolling Stones

 http://www.stones.com/

Figure 8.3

If the Stones have been to your country, you'll find your national flag on a tongue.

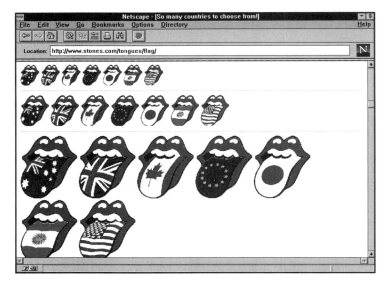

http://www.stones.com/tongues/flag/

THESE GUYS DON'T really need a Web site to make them famous, but they were one of the first groups to get onto the World Wide Web, and it's a great example of how you can make graphics available to your fans.

When we visited the sites, the Stones were well into the "Voodoo Lounge" stage of their career, and the theme of that tour was a stuck-out tongue, in many, many variations. You can even go to a spot on the site to download tongue graphics for use on your own home page. The tongues come painted with the flags of every country where the tour visited, plus numerous other variations in color and texture.

The Stones were not only one of the first groups on the Web, but their site has been at the leading edge of Internet technology, so be prepared for some surprises. When we visited, it was one of the first sites we'd seen to use Sun's Java technology to send small applications over the network.

It also has something called "Video Streamer Boxes" which show a "stream" of digital frames as though they were stacked on top of each other, pancake-style, to form a 3D object.

If you're not into playing with this really advanced stuff (so advanced that when we visited there was no user software available for some of it), there's always the traditional picture gallery, which has a link on the home page. You'll find pictures of all the band members individually, plus pictures of everyone together. You can also look at pictures from the covers of their CDs and albums.

The Stones also encourage their fans to send in photos they've taken of the band at a concert, so you'll find those listed in the Spoils of Our War section. ▲

Figure 8.4

A Video Streamer Box template.

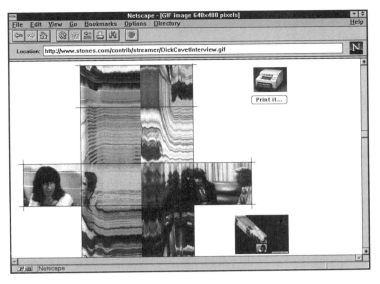

http://www.stones.com/contrib/streamer/DickCavetInterview.gif

alt.binaries.pictures.celebrities

THIS NEWSGROUP is the place to come for the latest and the unusual. Fans of various celebrities come by to gossip and to trade pictures of their idols.

You'll need to know how to retrieve encoded images from newsgroups to be able to look at these pictures. (See Chapter 23, "Getting Graphics from the Net," for more information on this process.)

This is not a moderated newsgroup, which means anyone can post anything here. You may find a certain amount of nudity here spilling over from other sections of the alt.binaries.pictures section.

This is where you'll often find some untouched or casual pictures of the stars as well, those that their fans or freelance photographers have taken. Unlike the pictures shown at studio-sponsored sites, these aren't always intended to show the stars in their best light. You may find pictures from early stages of a star's career, or pictures from the celebrity's personal life.

It's a bit like a supermarket tabloid: racy, unpredictable, and often pressing the boundaries of truth. That barely clad photo of a popular female star engaged in some risqué activity might actually portray some questionable moment early in her career—but it could also be a look-alike who, blessed with grainy film, bad scanning techniques, and marginal photography, can be made to look like the star. Where do rumors start? Right here, folks. ▲

Figure 8.5

A collection of celebrity photos pulled from the alt.binaries.pictures.celebrities list. From the left: Amy Jo Johnson, Jim Carrey, Trisha Yearwood, and Daisy Fuentes.

alt.binaries.pictures.celebrities

GRAPHICS SITES REVIEWED IN CH 20

In addition to this chapter's best of the best, read about these sites in Ch 20.

Robert Altman Communications

http://www.cea.edu/robert/x.index.html

Photos, by *Rolling Stone Magazine*'s long-time chief photographer, of major entertainment and music figures.

Cinemaven Online

http://useattle.uspan.com/maven/

A collection of press photos from many, many movies.

Desktop Cinema

http://www.iac.net:80/~flypba/movie.trailer.index.html

A comprehensive list of QuickTime movie trailers for film and television shows.

Entertainment Weekly

http://www.pathfinder.com/

Interviews, photos, and images from top entertainers.

Paramount Pictures

http://www.paramount.com/

A major studio puts its products on the Web.

People Magazine

http://www.pathfinder.com/

Stories, with photos, of top celebrities.

Supermodel Home Page

http://www.supermodel.com/

A page attempting to attract some supermodels.

Time-Life Photo Gallery

http://www.pathfinder.com/

The photo gallery, in the Photo Sight section, has images of famous people.

Walt Disney's Buena Vista Pictures

http://www.disney.com/BVPM/index.html

Movie previews, games, and mementos from Walt Disney's Buena Vista Pictures.

http://sashimi.wwa.com/hammers/index.htm

Celebrity photos from a photographer of the English entertainment scene.

Clip Art & Icons

THE RESOURCES OF this book will help you find the art you need, when you need it, using online sources.

This section is devoted to clip art, which is art designed to be grabbed and dropped into your documents or onto your Web pages. Much of it is black and white line art, which will reproduce almost exactly on your laser printer or photocopier as you see it here.

The most popular kind of document on the Internet is the World Wide Web home page, and it has created enormous demand for a new type of clip art: GIF and JPEG images that can be used to add backgrounds, horizontal rules and bars, icons, and other graphical devices to home pages. This chapter covers them also, with sites that specialize in these devices.

Be warned that clip art varies tremendously in quality. Some comes from poorly scanned originals and is barely printable, while other art is crisp and clear. Whether you can use the images you find will depend on you and the image quality your project demands.

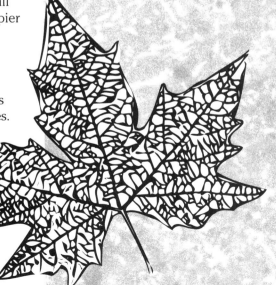

Your Automatic Icon File

If you're using a World Wide Web browser like Netscape, did you know that every icon or line you access on a Web page is temporarily stored on your computer even if you don't specifically download it?

If you check out your netscape.ini file under the [cache] section, you'll see a section that looks something like

```
cache dir=c:\tmpfiles\cache
```

If you have memory and disk cache sizes set higher than zero in Netscape's options/preferences/cache and network setting, when Netscape pulls down an HTML page, it puts the data in that page, including the text and icons, into the cache. This speeds up re-displaying the page if you go to it again within a short time. And rather than asking the host computer to send four copies of a button that appears four times on a home page, Netscape gets one copy, then pops it onto the screen three more times from its memory or disk cache.

If you hunt through the directory specified in the "cache dir" setting, you'll find many of these old buttons and text files sitting there. Unfortunately they all have an extension of .MOZ, which makes it difficult to figure out what's in each file. Windows Write is one program that can open any file (specify no conversion when opening the file, and don't save any changes when closing it). If you see, for example, the word GIF somewhere on the first line, try saving the file with a .GIF extension, which your browser or a file viewer on the CD can view. If the word JFIF appears near the front, it is a JPEG format file.

If you copy these files to another directory and rename them, you can re-use them on your own Web pages, subject to any copyright restrictions.

For more information about viewing and using graphics from the Net, check out Chapter 27 and some of the software included on the CD-ROM.

Sandra's Clip Art Server

 http://www.cs.yale.edu/homes/sjl/clipart.html

Figure 9.1
A contribution from Brad Stone at Sandra's Clip Art Server.

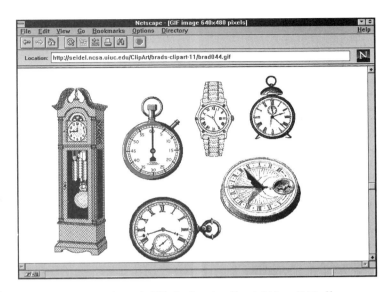

http://seidel.ncsa.uiuc.edu/ClipArt/brads-clipart-11/brad044.gif

YOU'VE PROBABLY HEARD expressions such as "almost like the original" or "just like new."

Sandra Loosemore's Clip Art Server is, in many cases, much better than the original. This is because clip art collections tend to be random collections of art without organization, without thumbnail images, and with at best, only descriptive file names to work with. At worst, DB098758.gif is a collection of airplane silhouettes, and DB098756.gif is a picture of a jack-o-lantern. And what was in DB098757.gif, anyway?

Take the well-stocked FUNET collection. It's an awesome collection of clip art, with several thousand images in it, but file names are your only clue, and you can't always tell from them the difference between the clip art in signs07.gif and signs09.gif. Also, it requires a special login on FTP.

Try Sandra's Clip Art Server before you go to FUNET, because this site has not only almost all of the FUNET art, but it has it in three modes: an HTML page listing the file names, keywords, and file descriptions; a UNIX tar (compression) file that includes all the images; and a link to FUNET if you want to see the original collection.

This site has around 3,000 files, many with multiple pieces of clip art, but more important, each file has a list of keywords and each individual collection has an index file that you could download and print out for future reference. Without much effort, you could use the fine organization here to create a searchable database of clip art images.

As well, all the images here are in the universally-recognized GIF format, while the original collections are in other, less-familiar formats. For example, the large Carnegie-Mellon English server clip art collection is in a Macintosh format not accessible for PC users.

FUNET does not exhaust Sandra's collection of clip art by any means. Under the Color Expressions link you'll find some original, well-done color clip art that would work well on stationary or Web pages. The images of animals, and plants could dress up a Web page and a number of background images here would make a good beginning for the main logo on an otherwise drab home page.

Figure 9.2

Clip art can be handy for adding seasonal or holiday themes to your work.

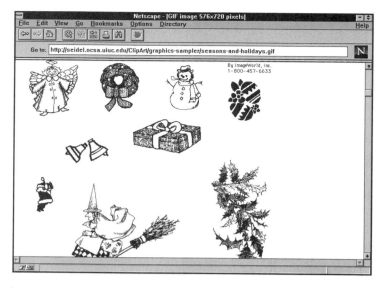

http://seidel.ncsa.uiuc.edu/ClipArt/graphics-sampler/seasons-and-holidays.gif

Figure 9.3

The small backgrounds in the Color Expressions area are designed to support text for use on Web pages and stationary or other purposes.

http://seidel.ncsa.uiuc.edu/ClipArt/color-expressions/backgrounds/pasture-bg.gif

The Carnegie-Mellon English server clip art collection, with nearly 600 files, is also here. The originals have those numbered names, which, thankfully, this site has improved with descriptions and keywords.

Another section contains Brad Stone's 1.5 megabyte "nice ware" collection ("If you use it, do something nice for someone."). The art here is excellent-quality line drawing that should reproduce well in other documents.

The site includes several smaller collections, some of which have a good selection of borders and corners for dressing up documents, plus more than 500 images garnered from the alt.binaries.clip-art newsgroup. ▲

GRAPHICS SITES REVIEWED IN CH 20

In addition to this chapter's best of the best, read about these sites in Ch 20.

Daniel's Icon Archive

http://www.jsc.nasa.gov/~mccoy/Icons/index.html

A very large, well-organized collection of balls, lines, and icons to add color and style to your Web pages.

EFF Graphics Archive

http://www.eff.org/pub/Graphics/

Icons with a "Freedom of the Net" theme, plus a good collection of miscellaneous icons, rules, and buttons.

Orthodox Christian Foundation Home Page

http://www.ocf.org/

A good collection of icons of icons, and some religious clip art.

Pattern Land!

http://www.netcreations.com/patternland/index.html

A great site for finding background patterns for Web pages.

SimTel

file://oak.oakland.edu/SimTel/msdos/deskpub/

Several zipped files of clip art, and a great archive of other graphics software.

TAEX Clip Art Collection

http://leviathan.tamu.edu:70/1s/clipart

An extensive clip art collection focusing on agriculture and food.

10

Computer-Generated Art

COMPUTERS ARE artistic tools in two ways.

One way artists can use computers is as electronic paint-brushes. The artist uses the computer as a digital canvas, duplicating what a paint brush or pen does, or perhaps laying down new colors and strokes that were not possible with conventional tools. The computer gives the artist some new tools, such as the Undo feature and the Save As function. These let an artist play with an effect, and produce variations on a theme without repeating the basic idea each time.

The other way artists can use computers is to create conditions for art or to use a programming language to describe an object or a pattern, and then stand back and watch as the computer does the actual drawing. Fractals are a common example. Plug some values into a formula and the computer calculates a result. The artist creates the original conditions and uses the mathematical values as tools for creative effort.

In this chapter were going to look at the other kind of art. We're giving it the name *computer-generated art* because it generally relies on the processing power of the computer to create new shapes and visual experiences.

Fractals are covered in another chapter, so we'll be looking at some other ways that computers create art in this chapter; we'll also look at art where the computer has been a major part of the design and creation stage.

(Art)ⁿ (or Art^n)

 http://www.artn.nwu.edu/

Figure 10.1

A kind of high-tech Stonehenge, these delicate shapes super-imposed on a landscape are computer projections of mathematical equations.

http://www.artn.nwu.edu/phsc/menageatrois.jpg

(ART)ᴺ (PRONOUNCED Art to the nth) is a fertile blend of science and art, where supercomputers, scientific data, and art collaborate to produce images that look at the real world in new ways. You'll find some ground-breaking technology here, both in the techniques used to produce the art, and in the images it depicts.

We've chosen (Art)ⁿ as our featured site because of the range of art represented here. Here, the artists work with not only abstract and mathematical beauty, but also apply their work to social issues and culture in the finest traditions of art.

The idea behind (Art)ⁿ is to generate powerful visual images based on scientific, mathematical, or natural phenomenon. Almost other-worldly in scope, complex mathematical theories, invisible viruses, and molecules are transformed into images that are not only useful to scientists

but compelling and beautiful as art.

(Art)ⁿ images are usually generated by high-powered Silicon Graphics workstations or even Cray supercomputers, and the artists often work in collaboration with scientific laboratories. (You'll often see the gallery's name displayed on the Internet as Art^n, by the way, because most browsers can't display superscript characters.)

A word of advice: This gallery has great depth and variety. It will take time to explore it all, but don't skip a section just because you aren't interested in something like fractals or viruses. You'll miss some of the coolest images on the Net, guaranteed.

The Romboy Homotopy

The heart of (Art)ⁿ is its galleries. Two of these internal galleries really stand out: the (Art)ⁿ/NCSA/EVL gallery, and the Virtual Photography gallery.

The (Art)ⁿ/NCSA/EVL gallery (NCSA stands for National Center for Supercomputing Applications, and EVL stands for Electronic Visualization Laboratory) is where you will find the rare and amazing Romboy Homotopy. This is not an obscure Liverpudlian rock band, but a 3D image that is generated by a certain type of mathematical formula and then enhanced by (Art)ⁿ. The resulting object is a voluptuous mass with smooth curves and projections, to which the (Art)ⁿ

Figure 10.2

This voluptuous image began as a four-dimensional mathematical equation called a Romboy Homotopy.

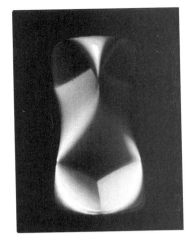

http://www.artn.nwu.edu/phsc/venus.jpg

Figure 10.3

An early form of biological warfare: Indians were given blankets infected with smallpox. In this image, an Indian boy's face is surrounded by an image of the deadly virus.

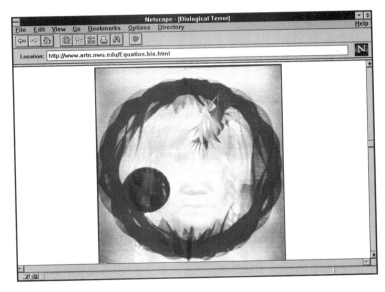

http://www.artn.nwu.edu/Equation.bio.html

artists add color and transparency. One so echoes a feminine shape that they have named it "Venus."

Prediction: It's coming soon to a poster shop near you.

Provocative Sculpture

On to the Virtual Photography gallery. This is further subdivided into galleries for Sculpture, Virtual Portraits, Scientific Visualization, Computer-Aided Design, and Architecture.

Until 3D glasses are part of the standard Net-surfing kit, you'll have to be satisfied with two-dimensional pictures in the sculpture section. But it's worth it. These images are not only visually intriguing, but politically and intellectually provocative.

Nude and biomedical images make a compelling and troubling statement about AIDS and sexuality. An exhibit on terrorism connects images from chemistry, biology, and economics with pictures of those who have been terrorized by their misuse.

Figure 10.4

Electron fields around a chromium chloride molecule are visualized as an interaction of rounded shapes.

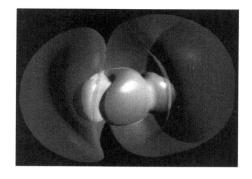

http://www.artn.nwu.edu/phsc/chromiumchlor.jpg

Figure 10.5

Supersonic shock wave around a hypersonic aircraft create an explosive image.

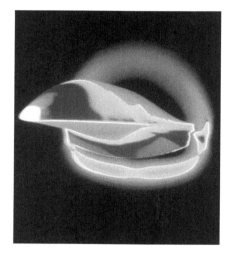

Scientific Visualization

In the Virtual Photography gallery, the Scientific Visualization gallery is further divided into sections for Viruses, Medical, Chemical, Aerospace, and Fractal Images.

You may be disoriented on entering the Viruses section: these beautiful images represent some of the deadliest bugs on the planet: HIV, polio, and flu- and cancer-causing viruses are on display here, in glorious color.

The Chemical section demonstrates the wonderful blend of science and art at $(Art)^n$. No one can see an atom, but mathematical descriptions of atoms can be transformed, by computers, into colorful and

http://www.artn.nwu.edu/phsc/hypersonic.jpg

descriptive images that can actually help scientists understand their fields better. They often make great art that wouldn't look bad on your living room wall, either.

The Aerospace section has as its focus some mundane scientific stuff, such as how air flows around an aircraft, but they make knockout graphics images. The entire spectrum of color is used effectively here to display differences in air pres-

sure or air speed, which normally wouldn't be visible at all.

Under Fractals, you'll find some playful stuff which indicates why computer folks are enthralled with fractal images. Exotic scientific disciplines such as chaos theory and four-dimensional mathematical formulas are used here as well as fractal mathematics, and are converted by the computer into colorful abstracts or realistic, but completely fictional, landscapes.

In the Computer-Aided Design area of the Virtual Photography gallery, you'll find images that really show off the computer as a tool for making artistic images. These aren't your average Paintbrush bitmaps. They show that in the hands of an artist who knows how to use a computer, the boundaries of art, science, and reality can be manipulated and explored in new ways. ▲

GRAPHICS SITES REVIEWED IN CH 20

In addition to this chapter's best of the best, read about these sites in Ch 20.

Alias/Wavefront

http://www.alias.com/

Fantastic images and short but punchy animations to show off some of the world's leading animation software.

Contours of the Mind

http://online.anu.edu.au/ITA/ACAT/contours/catalogue.html

A catalog from a show examining computers, thinking, and art. Not a lot of images, but quality is excellent.

Electronic Visualization Laboratory

http://www.ncsa.uiuc.edu/EVL/docs/html/gallery.html

Equipped with some of the world's most powerful supercomputers, artists and scientists work together to create images of both beauty and utility.

Geometry Center

http://www.geom.umn.edu/

Interactive games and exercises that illustrate principles of geometry.

Implicate Beauty

http://www.vanderbilt.edu/VUCC/Misc/Art1/Beauty.html

"Computational art," which focuses on mathematical processes that generate images, music, and animation. Includes some interactive features where you plug in some values and the host computer produces an image.

Interactive Genetic Art

http://robocop.modmath.cs.cmu.edu:8001/

Beautiful abstract images are created by visitors to this site who vote on the patterns they prefer. The computer later tallies the votes and plugs the values into a formula to generate a new image.

Interactive Media Technology Center

http://www.oip.gatech.edu/mmtltop.html

Graphics from multimedia presentations, QuickTime movies of simulated environments, and QuickTime VR presentations.

Land of the Squishy

http://www.btw.com/dce/

A gallery showcasing what can be done with special image manipulation tools such as Adobe Photoshop, KPT Bryce, and Ray Dream designer.

Marthart.com

http://www.wri.com/~mathart/

Experiments with geometry, virtual reality, and other forms of computer-generated art.

Persistence of Vision (POV)

http://www.povray.org/
Keywords: computer-generated art

An important site for ray tracing, with a Hall of Fame, loads of images from a monthly competition, and downloadable software if you want to try your own ray-tracing.

Sharky's Art Gallery & House of Graphic Delusions

http://www.aloha.com/~sharky/artwork.html

A ray-tracing gallery with some of the best ray-tracing online, including other Internet sites and important other sites such as CompuServe's Graphics Development forum.

Silicon Graphics Silicon Surf

http://www.sgi.com/

From the maker of some of the world's premier graphics machines come a set of galleries that show off what brute computing horsepower and good imaginations can accomplish. They call it "Serious Fun."

Stanford Computer Graphics Library

http://www-graphics.stanford.edu/

Demonstrations of how mathematics and computer rendering can color, change, and depict 3D objects and their reflections.

Vern's SIRDS Gallery

http://www.sirds.com/

A well organized collection of Single Image (Random Dot) Stereograms, or SIRDS.

10

Fractals

MANY OF US, while sitting through algebra or calculus classes in high school shared the same thought: Will I every need this stuff?

Fractals literally make you look at mathematics in a new way. Created on a computer by plotting the results of mathematical formulas, they generate some of the most provocative and imaginative images on the Net.

In the hands of a skilled computer artist, who may use other computer graphics tools such as ray-tracing and photographic image manipulation, these simple mathematical formulas become striking, powerful, and often perplexing images. Our eyes tell us these are real objects, but our minds say they can't exist. Others look as real as photographs, and yet are entirely mathematical.

We'll look at a few of the best sites on the Net to see and learn about fractals, then point you to a few more on our list of the top graphics sites on the Net.

What is a Fractal?

A fractal is a set of points that have been generated by a certain type of mathematical formula.

The formula feeds data back to itself, and then repeats its calculations, a process called *iteration*. Many fractal images are made up of thousands of iterations of a formula.

A fractal is generated by varying the numbers that are first plugged into the formula, or by tracking the values of different parts of the formula as they change in each iteration.

Fractals have a number of important characteristics. Because they are generated mathematically, you can enlarge a fractal infinitely. While other images will become blocky and lose resolution when you enlarge them, fractals can preserve their detail even when magnified thousands of times in their digital form.

In many fractals, each part is, in some way, an image of the whole, a characteristic sometimes called *self-similarity*. As you enlarge a fractal, you frequently encounter details identical to the original fractal.

The term fractal was coined by Benoit Mandelbrot, who derived it from the Latin word frangere, meaning "to create irregular fragments."

Fractals are often defined by the mathematical formula used to generate them. The original fractal type is called the Mandelbrot set, but many variations have been developed. And even with a given formula, by changing its variables and functions, tremendous variety is possible.

For more complete information about fractals you can get the document fractal.faq by FTP at ftp://rtfm.mit.edu/pub/usenet/news.answers/fractal-faq and on the World Wide Web at many sites, including The Spanky Fractal Database.

The Spanky Fractal Database

 http://spanky.triumf.ca/

THIS WHIMSICALLY NAMED site is a great place to begin with fractals. Spanky has a well-groomed selection of fractal libraries and links to many other places on the Internet.

It may not have the depth of some sites devoted to specific fractals, but it is a well-organized introduction. Its creator notes that much of the material in Spanky is available elsewhere on the Net, but he thought "it would be nice to have it all in one place." We agree.

Figure 11.1

I think that I shall never see a fractal as lovely as a tree, unless the fractal is a tree, as this one is.

http://www.geom.umn.edu/pix/archive/homepages/L-systems_all.html

Figure 11.2

This jewel-like image was generated using the Mandelbrot set. The dark, heart-shaped object at middle right is the basic Mandelbrot figure.

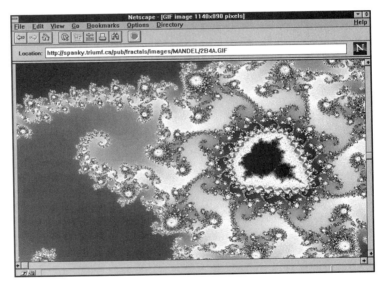

http://spanky.triumf.ca/pub/fractals/images/mandel/2b4a.gif

TIP You can make your own fractals with the program Fractint, available on the Internet via FTP for Amiga, DOS, Windows, and UNIX computers. A Macintosh version is in development. A Windows version is available at ftp://wuarchive.wustl.edu/systems/ibmpc/simtel/window3.

Figure 11.3

This image from The Spanky Fractal Database demonstrates the beauty and complexity of fractal images.

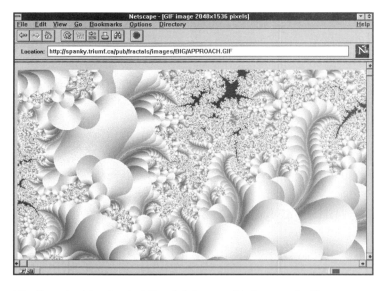

http://spanky.triumf.ca/pub/fractals/images/big/approach.gif

Figure 11.4

An example of a Lyapunov fractal.

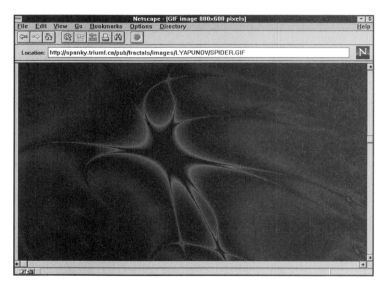

http://spanky.triumf.ca/pub/fractals/images/lyapunov/spider.gif

The database is divided into directories, each with a particular type of fractal or the work of a particular fractal designer.

The Noel directory contains dozens of fractals from Noel Giffin, the Webmaster of Spanky.

The IFS section shows fractals that produce highly regular patterns: fern leaves, pyramids, spirals.

The Lyapunov series generates ethereal traces of color in abstract patterns across the screen.

The Engstrom directory contains fractals from Henrik Engstrom who uses ray tracing to present strong contrasts between solid objects and almost liquid or gaseous regions, with vivid colors and composition.

Engstrom's own home page, at http://www.dtek. chalmers.se/Datorsys/Project/ qjulia/index.html, contains more of his powerful images.

Spanky also has "mini" and "big" galleries with small or large versions, respectively, of various fractal images that appear elsewhere on the site. If you see something you like in the mini gallery and would like a larger, more detailed version, search the other galleries: all of the mini pictures are available in larger sizes elsewhere.

The Zito directory contains fractals by Guiseppe Zito of Italy. We'd rate Zito's material as among the best and most original on the Net. Zito's formulas generate images with strong geometrical shapes and dazzling color gradations. He has his own site on the Internet, at http://www.ba.infn.it/www/wfractal.html. ▲

The Mandelbrot and Julia Set Explorer

 http://aleph0.clarku.edu/~djoyce/julia/explorer.html

Figure 11.5

The Mandelbrot and Julia Set Explorer lets you play with fractals to generate your own images. Notice the location of the mouse pointer in the image on the left. When the mouse was clicked, the image on the right was generated.

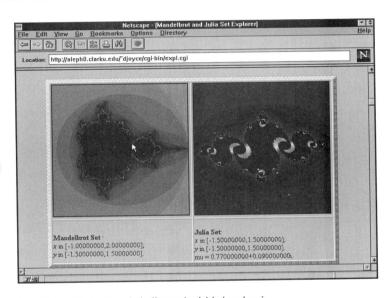

http://aleph0.clarku.edu/~djoyce/cgi-bin/expl.cgi

HAVE YOU EVER wanted to be an abstract artist, but didn't know where to begin?

Interactive fractal explorers are a great start. A simple click of the mouse and you generate dazzling images, in endless variety.

You simply click on part of a Mandelbrot image, and a new graphic is created. Depending on the site, it may be a simple magnification, or it may be a variation based on choices you have made.

You don't need any special software on your computer to do this. All the work is done by the host computer on the Internet, which creates a new image file based on your choices, then sends that new image file over the Net to you.

The Mandelbrot and Julia Set Explorer is an excellent site to begin basic fractal explorations.

When you access the site you see an image of the basic Mandelbrot set. Click your mouse anywhere in that image. The host computer will take the coordinates of your mouse click, and produce a new type of fractal, called the Julia set, from those coordinates.

The resulting fractal will be displayed next to the original Mandelbrot set.

The site offers many variations, which you can access from simple fill-in forms and checkboxes. In addition to generating a Julia set you can opt to enlarge the Mandelbrot set or modify values in the formula. You don't need to know what variables like *lamda* and *mu* mean. Just try a few and see what effect they have on the result. ▲

Sprott's Fractal Gallery

 http://sprott.physics.wisc.edu/fractals.htm

Figure 11.6

Each day John Sprott's site automatically generates a new fractal.

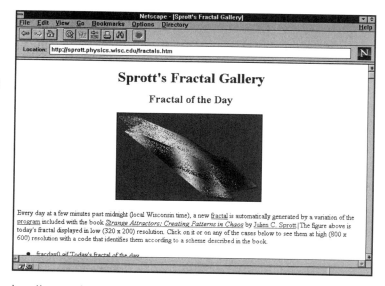

http://sprott.physics.wisc.edu/fractals.htm

JULIEN C. SPROTT, author of a major work on fractals and mathematical theories about chaos, has created one of the most comprehensive galleries of fractals.

The first thing you'll see on the home page is the Fractal of the Day, generated automatically by Sprott's computer.

Sprott covers many fractal types, with loads of well-designed images. While the site has a decidedly scientific bent, you needn't be a scientist to enjoy it.

Sprott doesn't give descriptive names to his fractals, so you'll have to guess a bit. Each section, which covers a different type of fractal, has a "catalog" image combining images of all the fractals in that section. However, you can't click on an image in the catalog image to enlarge it, so you'll still have to do some guessing about which filename—aGNGUVETSNWK or aGOHRHRNFLNO, for example— is the image you want. ▲

GRAPHICS SITES REVIEWED IN CH 20

In addition to this chapter's best of the best, read about these sites in Ch 20.

alt.binaries.pictures.fractals

The most active newsgroup for fractal designers, with new images constantly appearing.

3D Strange Attractors and Other Objects

http://ccrma-www.stanford.edu/~stilti/images/chaotic_attractors/nav.html

An artist applies powerful rendering tools to fractals.

Fractal Movie Archive

http://www.cnam.fr/fractals.html

Zoom through fractals, mountains, and even the Golden Gate in animations over, through, and under fractal landscapes.

Fractal Gallery

http://eulero.cineca.it/~strumia/FractalGallery.htm

A simple guide to understanding fractals and some outstanding images.

Hydra

http://reality.sgi.com/employees/rck/index.html

A fractal explorer that lets you move into three-dimensions, with a large gallery of fractal images.

Synthetic Images, Online Gallery of

http://www.seas.gwu.edu/faculty/musgrave/art_gallery.html

Landscapes and spacescapes out of fractals, plus a fractal animation.

CHAPTER

12

News, Weather, & Sports

NEWS, WEATHER, and sports are such a part of almost every person's daily life that its repetition on the Internet seems a bit superfluous when you can just pick up a newspaper, turn on the television, or talk to your neighbor.

But news, weather, and sports are more than information. They're about timeliness and participation. We want the most current information, the most credible information, we want a lot of it, and we want to express our own opinion about the issues; hence, the rise of live television broadcasts like CNN, ESPN, and their younger sibling "reality-based" television shows like *COPS* and *Court TV*.

Not only does the Internet bring you discussion groups, chatlines, and home pages devoted to just about any topic imaginable, but it also supports news, weather, and sports with images, photographs, and charts that would require an intensive investment in time and effort to collect in person.

Electric Examiner (The San Francisco Examiner)

 http://www.sfgate.com/examiner/index.html

Figure 12.1

A montage of photographs from The San Francisco Examiner's features series called, "The Caregivers."

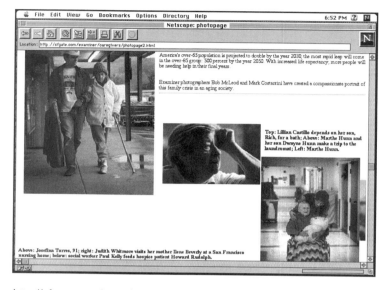

http://sfgate.com/examiner/caregivers/photopage2.html

THE SAN FRANCISCO EXAMINER is aggressively bringing itself onto the Web. The newspaper can be accessed through The Well, and, after finding only text at several other news links, we put the *Examiner's* URL into our bookmark upon seeing graphics for its daily features.

Further down on the home page are the feature articles. On this day, there was one about caring for the elderly in a series called, "The Caregivers." The link to the feature article was broken into categories, including the "Caregivers Photo Page," which contained a handful of images that accompany the long list of articles found under "Read the Stories."

The Examiner uses the advantage of Netscape (or any other WWW browser) to provide more information than a newspaper usually could. Visitors are able to access the background and photographs of the series reporters and photographers via the link to The Creators. Visitors can also access a Resource List for related information on the series, and pointers to other Internet links.

During our visit, we reviewed the files highlighting the United Nation's 50th Anniversary, centering on the "1945 photo page," where we found nine images from the early days of the U.N. *The Examiner* also had a .gif of the U.N.'s original charter. The article was supported by other sundry information, such as lists of U.N. participating organizations and press releases of local activities.

The Virtual Newsroom link was much cleaner than we expected. No scans of the cigarette butts or junk food containers that usually populate a reporter's life. Cleanliness didn't mean the Newsroom didn't need some housecleaning, however. There were several links in the newsroom that went awry and led to defunct URLs or to a notice of an URL change that sent us back to *The Examiner's* front page.

Figure 12.2

A scan of the original U.N. charter, retrieved from files supporting The Examiner's coverage of the U.N.'s 50th anniversary.

http://www.examiner.com/projects/UN_50/un50photos/resolution.gif

There are a number of interesting links in the Newsroom, such as the Digital Gallery, "pioneering work by American photographers." Clicking over to the gallery led to a page dedicated to Chris Gulker's photo book *Los Angeles: A Retrospective*. The following seven high-quality images are downloadable prizes. More housecleaning was needed here, too, though. A single click on any of the images sent us back to *The Examiner's* front page again.

The Examiner's Fat City Forum, where citizens are urged to "report waste and abuses of public money," was quite enjoyable. "You report the problems; we'll help build the solutions." However, only one of the two articles that followed, "Muni's repair crisis idles 20% of buses," contained any graphics—a chart of missed runs by San Francisco's bus system, tracked by weeks since Jan. 1994.

At the time of our visit, the home page was announcing that its online files would archive all the way back to 1988. Currently, *The Examiner's* archives allow you to revisit back issues through Wednesday, Jan. 4, 1995. Visitors are able to surf these archives by date or by keyword search, but none of them contain photographs. Perhaps that will be *The Examiner's* next mission. ▲

NOTE In our search for news, weather, and sports sites, we encountered the home pages of "information providers" who either charged for access or who required that you submit your name and a valid e-mail address before further exploring the site. We avoided reviewing these sites not because we didn't agree with their right to charge for a service (which they *do* provide), but because there are so many other sources of *free* information on the Internet. It is without a doubt that most visitors to the Internet will have many opportunities to pursue their own interests in for-profit pages, but we leave that to you to decide.

The GOES Weather Satellite

 http://climate.gsfc.nasa.gov/~chesters/goesproject.html

Figure 12.3

A color image of Peru's weather patterns taken by the GOES weather satellite, with credit to NASA-Goddard Space Flight Center.

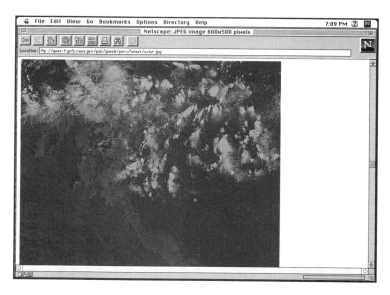

ftp://goes-f.gsfc.nasa.gov/pub/goes8/peru/latest/color.jpg

THE TECHNICAL STORY behind GOES (Geostationary Operational Environmental Satellites) is available through the GOES-I/M Project Brochure link. It depicts the mission of the National Oceanic and Atmospheric Administration (NOAA) to provide "continuous, dependable, timely, and high-quality observations of the Earth and its environment." Managing its responsibility by using interactive ground- and orbit-based systems, the GOES I-M satellites continuously send images back to Earth, most of which are available for the Internet audience.

But it's not as boring as it sounds. The images cached in this site bring the daily television weather forecast to its knees. (As an added bonus, the movie clips and high-resolution images are free of newscasters standing in front of the screen.)

A word of warning: The files on this site are as unpredict-

able as the weather. There are a great deal of useful weather maps and links to images, but the files on this site are not well labeled. Sometimes they are linked to another page, sometimes they download .tiff documents, and sometimes they download .mpgs. Many times, you may encounter image files well over 500Kb. You just never know what this valuable resource is going to bring you, which can result in several computer crashes while examining the site. Be careful and back up often.

In the GOES Hot Stuff link, for example, there is an FTP site containing an extremely long list of ambiguous file

names (for example, 9507151132G8I03.tiff). The difficulty with .tiff documents is that your normal .jpg viewer won't know what to do with it. You might have to use different imaging software, such as Adobe Photoshop, before viewing the B&W full-resolution GOES-8 images of Tropical Storm Chantal in the Sargasso Sea, including some one-minute interval imagery.

Still, there was the message, "WARNING: 10 MByte MacBinary file in Adobe Photoshop 3 format" for the "natural color" full-Earth image of Hurricane Andrew. *Whew.*

Figure 12.4

A false-color composite image of hurricane Hugo from GOES-7.

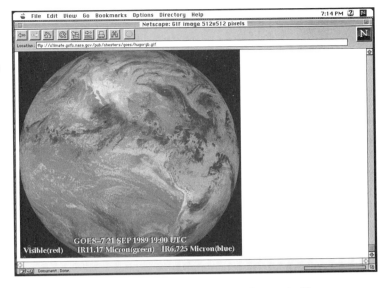

ftp://climate.gsfc.nasa.gov/pub/chesters/goes/hugorgb.gif

There were images and movie clips on just about every link on the GOES home page. A majority of the images are B&W, unless noted otherwise. The GOES-8 Results is primarily .mpgs, the GOES Data Servers on the Internet offer up more images and movie clips, and a link to the Space Environment Laboratory previews "Today's Space Weather."

Don't be fooled by the "GOES Chat" link, which visitors might expect to be one of the IRC-like chat forums that have become popular by users of Netscape. Instead, "GOES Chat" contains promotional images and movies, "novelties" such as "an accidental GOES-7 shot of the quarter moon on 14 June 1994" and a 96-frame, 672Kb movie of hurricane Andrew crossing Florida in 1992; imaging notes and some trivia.

A number of comparative images, charts, and explanations about the GOES I-M satellites can be found on the Introducing GOES-I link to an article written for the Bulletin of the American Meteorological Society in May 1994. The GOES-I satellite uses 10-bit images, versus the 6-bit images of GOES-7 shows the "expected improvement in detection of cloud-top features using higher bit depth visible imagery."

We tried for some time to access the Experimental Stuff that appeared to be an image map overlaid with hot-button boxes located over several large regions of the Western Hemisphere, but were continually turned away by URL errors. We encountered this problem quite often when clicking around this site, but shrugged it off to a "busy day on the Internet" since most of the links eventually let us in.

At the end of our look into satellite weather, we returned to the GOES Hot Stuff link, where the best images were stored. We downloaded the "crude multi-spectral QuickTime movie of full Earth for a day," sat back, and watched the clouds roll in. ▲

Figure 12.5

A series of images from the GOES-8 Sounder Channels, illustrating a storm and tornado outbreak over Georgia on May 15, 1995.

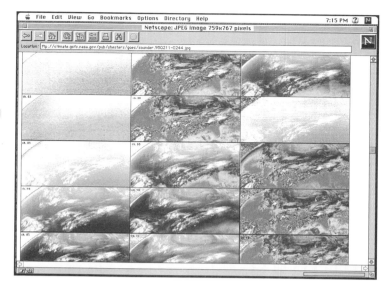

ftp://climate.gsfc.nasa.gov/pub/chesters/goes/sounder.950211-0244.jpg

The 19th Hole

 http://www.sport.net/golf/

Figure 12.6

A photograph of the Augusta National Golf Course, from the 19th Hole collection.

http://www.sport.net/golf/pics/ANGC.GIF

WE DIDN'T EXPECT golf to have a fundamental presence on the Internet, especially for graphics, but that's where we ended up and were glad for it. This is not just a site for images (which is good) but a sport supported by the Internet, which is somewhat unique. Like any sports-oriented site, The 19th Hole has its dedicated space for long lists of

Figure 12.7

The backside of the Camelback Golf Club scorecard.

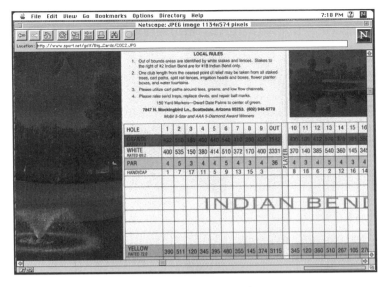

http://www.sport.net/golf/Big_Cards/CGC2.JPG

Figure 12.8

Only a true golf fan would upload a photograph of the bags of practice golf balls from the Masters tournament.

http://www.sport.net/golf/pics/master.gif

statistics and schedules, but it also uses the Internet to support the players of the game. We liked that.

Logging in to The 19th Hole, with its sandpit-colored background, we headed directly for the Art link. The art is divided into Scorecard Archive and Golf Art & Pictures. The latter leads to a lengthy list of random images. The file names are clear enough that most of the time you know what's in the file, and most of them contain a very short description. All of them are notated with file size.

While this gallery of images may not contain a fleet of photographs of every golf pro, we found it refreshingly eclectic in its selection of images. Among other available files, there are golf greens, a few archival photographs from golf's B&W days, the required photograph of Arnold Palmer, and a *Hagar the Horrible* cartoon where he carefully and fatherly tells his son the facts of life: "You'll be preoccupied and won't be able to think of

anything else. But don't worry, it's perfectly normal… it's called Golf."

For golf fans, the best section of The 19th Hole's art gallery is "Jimbo's Scorecard Collection." When we visited, the file contained front and back images of scorecards from 28 different golf courses, most of them located in the south and southwest, from the Lubbock (Texas) Elm Grove Golf Club to the Rolling Hills Golf Course in Tempe,

Arizona. The current exceptions include Jimbo's collected cards from five golf courses at the Disney World Resort in Orlando, Florida, and the Laukaan Peurunkagolf in Finland.

The images of the scorecards are readable, but it appears as though a few of the cards were carried around in somebody's back pocket, with the occasional large crease down the middle of the image. Regardless, golfers are able to examine the shapes and styles of the various fairways and predicted ranges and handicaps.

In the Headlines section, visitors will find the regular news stories (linked to ESPN's SportsZone server) and several subdirectories of schedules, current tournament results and rankings, and the syndicated *Sandy Bunker's Golf Tips*. The almanac will take you to even more results and rankings information.

The real help that The 19th Hole offers is its classified ad section. The For Sale, Wanted, Clubmakers, and Miscellaneous sections contained a large host of ads placed by Internet-savvy players and companies. While we didn't have any golf clubs to sell, we liked that you could place your own classified ad without shelling out any dues for using the site or the service. Visitors do have to give their name and e-mail address, but that's a part of the advertising game.

Visitors can also link to other golf sites, including the Golf FAQ and the Golf Home Page at Dartmouth, where you can find all you need to know about making good clubs. ▲

Graphics Sites Reviewed in Ch 20

In addition to this chapter's best of the best, read about these sites in Ch 20.

Dmitri's OJ Simpson Trial Center

http://www.cs.indiana.edu/hyplan/dmiguse/oj.html

Up-to-date images and current events from O.J. Simpson's televised trial.

OneWorld Online

http://www.oneworld.org/index.html

A global-news home page with illustrated news articles.

CHAPTER

13

Photography

PHOTOGRAPHY WAS GOING digital well before graphics began to appear in force on the Internet, but the Internet has certainly accelerated the process.

Many of us believe that photography records the world the way it really is—that photographs don't lie. Most photographers know better, even traditional photographic methods offered plenty of opportunity for a photographer to subtly reduce or enhance an object's importance in the frame. Indeed, "framing" something means to eliminate its surroundings, which is what makes photography more art than science.

Digital techniques have given photographers even more power. The clean, digital keyboard and mouse, with their ability to "undo," with electronic magic wands can pluck an object from its surroundings, then place it seamlessly in a strange place.

The Internet has room for all schools of photography—"straight" photography with little image modification; digital retouching, which enhances but does not change the composition of an image; and digital manipulation in which the original photograph is often a minor starting point.

Photo Perspectives

 http://www.i3tele.com/photoperspectives/

Figure 13.1

American Ballet soloist Keith Roberts. Photograph by Nancy Ellison.

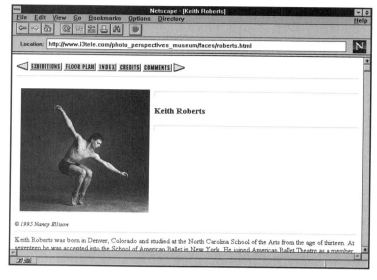

http://www.i3tele.com/photo_perspectives_museum/faces/
roberts.html

Figure 13.2

An impromptu portrait of actress Sharon Stone.

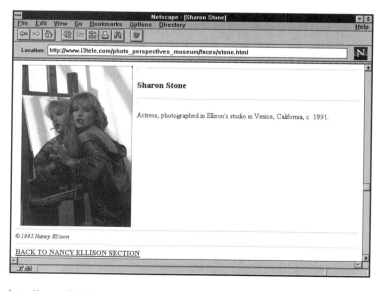

http://www.i3tele.com/photo_perspectives_museum/faces/stone.html

PHOTO PERSPECTIVES bills itself as "a forum for the exchange of cultural and educational ideas, and socio-political commentary."

If what we found when we got there is any example, it is fulfilling that mandate exceptionally well, with an eclectic collection of photographs that celebrate beauty, mourn war, and record rare and endangered species of animals.

On our visit, the gallery featured Nancy Ellison's photos of the American Ballet Theater, an exhibit on Yugoslavia, and a section on endangered animals.

If we had one beef with this site, it is the size of the images, which are quite small.

Ellison's images of the principals, soloists, and corps de ballet of the American Ballet Theater show the art of ballet in the physical grace and flexibility of these portraits.

You'll also find another section of Ellison's work here, with photos of five celebrities: Mick Jagger, Sharon Stone, Grace Jones, Robby Rosa (of music group Menudo), and Jeff Bridges.

For a complete change of pace, we turn to Faces of Sorrow, a photographic record of the tragic disintegration of the former Yugoslavia. It featured 50 photographs by 35 photojournalists from 14 countries, and covered six major sections: Ethnic Cleansing, Combatants, Prisoners, Siege Of Sarajevo, Refugees and Faces of Rape. These are high-quality, powerful images that show war not in its technical glory, or its gory results, but primarily in the faces of the innocent. Most viewers will not fail to be deeply moved by these pictures.

The Ethnic Cleansing section shows the confusion, pain and petty triumphs of the conflict, against the background of the destruction of their physical environment and families.

The Combatants section shows both sides of the conflict, victors and vanquished, acting their parts in the terrible drama of war, while the Prisoners section shows the wasted bodies of those who have not only lost the battle, but are starving to death in prison camps.

In the siege of Sarajevo, life goes on, somehow, while buildings crumble, family members disappear or are dismembered, and bodies litter the streets.

The Faces of Rape section shows the humiliation, trauma, and pain of a tactic deliberately employed in this war as a tool of intimidation and vengeance. ▲

Figure 13.3

A man pleads for his life as the enemy occupies his town.

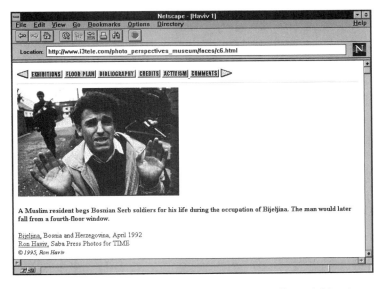

A Muslim resident begs Bosnian Serb soldiers for his life during the occupation of Bijeljina. The man would later fall from a fourth-floor window.

Bijeljina, Bosnia and Herzegovina, April 1992
Ron Haviv, Saba Press Photos for TIME
© 1995, Ron Haviv

http://www.i3tele.com/photo_perspectives_museum/faces/c6.html

Figure 13.4

Starving prisoners in a Serb concentration camp.

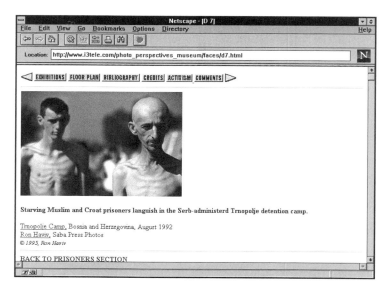

Starving Muslim and Croat prisoners languish in the Serb-administerd Trnopolje detention camp.

Trnopolje Camp, Bosnia and Herzegovina, August 1992
Ron Haviv, Saba Press Photos
© 1995, Ron Haviv

BACK TO PRISONERS SECTION

http://www.i3tele.com/photo_perspectives_museum/faces/d7.html

American Memory

 http://rs6.loc.gov/

IF YOU'RE LOOKING for historical photographs from the United States, you may as well stop searching. This is the place.

Associated with the Library of Congress, the American Memory project is putting many thousands of historical images and even movies on the Internet, and providing users with reasonably effective tools to locate them. (Other sections at this site also cover important manuscripts and audio history.)

The photographic collections, when we looked, included Carl Van Vechten photographs, 1932-1964, primarily portraits of literary figures, artists, and celebrities; scenic views, mostly in the Northeast; color photographs from the Farm Security Administration and the Office of War Information, between 1938-1944, depicting rural and small town America and scenes of the defense and war mobilization effort; 25,000 photographs of turn-of-the-century America from the Detroit Publishing Company; and selected Civil War photographs from the Library of Congress, depicting Civil War encampments, battlefields, and portraits as captured by Mathew Brady and his staff of photographers.

And the movies collection included early films of San Francisco, 1897-1916; William McKinley and the Pan-American Exposition, 1901; and early films of New York, 1898-1906.

The Detroit Publishing Company collection is not only large, but includes many images by William Henry Jackson, one of the most famous photographers of the American West around the turn of the century.

The Farm Security Administration and Office of War Information collection currently includes only color images, so we are talking a mere 1,600 pictures (color was in its infancy at the time they were taken). The Farm Security Administration's more famous

Figure 13.5

Two horses pull a large load of logs, in this photo from 1908.

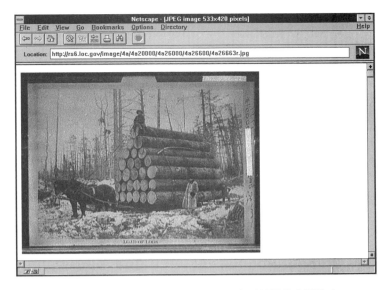

http://rs6.loc.gov/image/4a/4a20000/4a26000/4a26600/4a26663r.jpg

Figure 13.6

President Lincoln's funeral procession on Pennsylvania Avenue. From the Civil War collection.

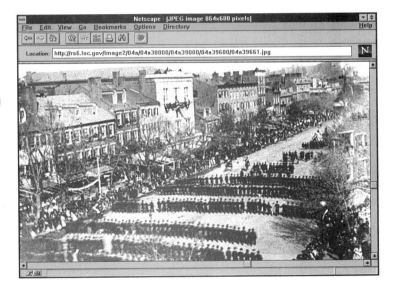

http://rs6.loc.gov/image2/04a/04a30000/04a39000/04a39600/
04a39661.jpg

black and white photography project includes more than 100,000 images and is scheduled to be released on the Internet in 1996.

The Civil War section includes more than 1,100 photographs, which you can search as a time line. Clicking on the time line link brings you to the Civil War by year. Clicking on a year brings up a list of major engagements or events that occurred during that year. No pictures are available of some, but others are links to whole galleries of images on a particular topic. Most images at this level have long titles, and

you can click on "next" or "previous" buttons to keep moving through the images on a topic. Clicking on an image brings up a full screen version.

Many of the images are

large and detailed. Although photographs that are more than a century old may not have the detail and range of modern images, the scans are very well done.

Good navigational tools are essential with collections of this size, and this site does a superb job of providing them. It's easy to find what you want, quickly. All of these sections let you conduct a database search by entering keywords, but most also give you an alternative, which may be easier or faster in some cases.

The massive Detroit Publishing Company collection can be searched alphabetically by subject as well as through the database. For the casual browser, the alphabetical listings may be more interesting. At the first level, you'll get alphabetical ranges, that is the link titled Camels—Canada, covers every alphabetical subject between Camels and Canada, including "camping," "campaigns and battles," and "can industry." Clicking on any one of those words will bring up all the photos with that subject, which can be in the hundreds in many cases.

The Detroit Publishing Company collection is not limited to American scenes, but includes pictures from Europe, Canada, Cuba, and other places, although many of these images are related in some way to the American scene. For example there's a picture of Algiers in here—a picture of an American warship in the harbor, with Algiers barely visible in the background.

The FSA-OWI collection has a similar system of organization, although because it is a much smaller collection, you see the subject headings at the first level of alphabetical listings.

The movie sections will be problematic for many people. Stored in AVI format, which can be played on both Macs and Windows PCs, the films are very large. A film of the aftermath of the San Francisco earthquake runs for 13 minutes and is 133 megabytes in size, which will take a day or two to download at 14,400 bits per second, and could take more than half on hour even on fast Internet connections. Even short clips run in the five megabyte range.

If you want it badly and can't download it, you can collect the call number and order a print from the Library of Congress. This goes for still photos as well as movies.

The San Francisco archive includes 26 films, the McKinley section 28, and the New York section 45 films. Every film selection shows several frames from the film, giving you some idea of what it would look like if you download it.

By the way, you'll find some interesting text files describing the technology and the film or photographic industry at the time.

Figure 13.7

A gun at the naval shipyards in Washington, D.C. around 1901.

http://rs6.loc.gov/image/4a/4a10000/4a15000/4a15000/4a15032r.jpg

Figure 13.8

A new A-20 attack bomber is brought for a test hop. Photo from the Office of War Information collection.

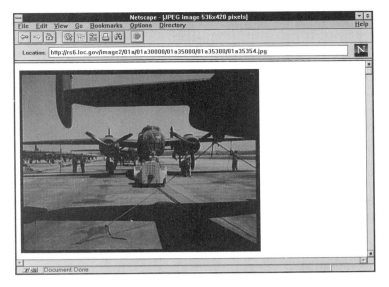

http://rs6.loc.gov/image2/01a/01a30000/01a35000/01a35300/
01a35354.jpg

Figure 13.9

Horse-drawn street cars on New York's Broadway and Union Square in 1901.

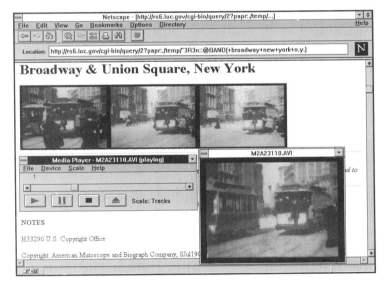

http://rs6.loc.gov/cgi-bin/

This very ambitious undertaking is far from over. Other photo and video collections that will be provided over the next few years include the American Variety stage between 1870 and 1920; Daguerreotype photographs from 1839 to 1850; architectural photographs of New York and other cities between 1920 and 1950; panoramic photographs of American cities and landscapes between 1900 and 1930; photos of San Francisco's Chinatown before the 1906 earthquake; photos of artists and celebrities of the 1920s and 1930s; and views of foreign countries and their transportation systems, taken in 1894. ▲

GRAPHICS SITES REVIEWED IN CH 20

In addition to this chapter's best of the best, read about these sites in Ch 20.

Alan Dorow Gallery

http://www.picture.com/Alan-Dorow.html

Professional photographer Alan Dorow has a sharp eye for people and their surroundings, and a whimsical sense of humor that makes this site a browser's delight.

Allen Rose

http://www.metronet.com/~arose/

News photographer Rose puts his daily work online each day, and shows a portfolio of his best material.

Ansel Adams Home Page

http://bookweb.cwis.uci.edu:8042/AdamsHome.html

A site devoted to the work of this photographic master, primarily his images of the University of California, although a collection of his better-known pieces is also available.

Arthole

http://www.mcs.com/~wallach/arthole.html

Insightful and funny work from a photographer who has mastered that simplest and most difficult of cameras, the pinhole camera.

Atlanta Photography Group

http://www.mindspring.com/~baird/apg/index.html

Exhibits from a photographic collective in Atlanta.

Atlanta Photojournalism Seminar

http://www.mindspring.com/~frankn/atlanta/

Winning photos from a regional photography contest that has become internationally known.

California Museum of Photography

http://cmp1.ucr.edu/

Thoughts, but not many photos, from a museum with a large collection.

Hot Pictures: Russian Photography

http://www.kiae.su/www/wtr/hotpictures/gallery.html

Current work from Russian photographers and artists.

Impact Studio

http://www.netaxs.com/~impact/index.html

What some of the most skilled people in the photography and advertising business are capable of doing with digital tools and good imaginations, for demanding, but paying clients.

Kodak

http://www.kodak.com/

A gallery of more than 80 dramatic images online, all taken by Kodak employees.

Michigan Press Photographers

http://www.cris.com/~Mppa/

An extremely well-designed gallery with the emphasis on news and feature photography.

13

Mythago

http://www.umich.edu/~cjericks/gallery/gallery.html

A gallery specializing in figure studies and landscapes.

Pearl Street Online Gallery

http://antics.com/pearl.html

Landscape photos of the American west and some excellent nature photography, some photos straight and some digitally enhanced.

The Photojournalist's Coffee House

http://www.intac.com/~jdeck/index2.html

A site for photojournalism documentaries, including Covington's Homeless.

Virtual Portfolio (London)

http://www.dircon.co.uk/maushaus/folio.html

An Internet showcase for the work of some of London's top photographers.

Virtual Gallery (Korea)

http://203.248.135.66/gallery/index.html

Photography by Koreans, both art and documentary work, on a well-designed site.

14

Science & Nature

THE INTERNET began as a way for research laboratories to exchange information, so it's not surprising to find many scientific sites on it.

Many of these sites are quite technical. Wander into some of them and you'll get knocked over by scientific jargon, mathematical formulas, and acronyms you've never seen before.

However, several organizations are beginning to use the Internet as a teaching tool, or as an extension of their public education outreach, and that means they use graphics to illustrate basic scientific principles.

This chapter will take you to one of the best of these, then suggest some other places you can go. Be sure to also check Chapters 2, "Animals," 16, "Space," and 17, "Transportation," for additional sites that have a scientific bent to them.

Exploratorium

 http://www.exploratorium.edu/

Figure 14.1

A simple mirror is all it takes to make interesting images at the Exploratorium.

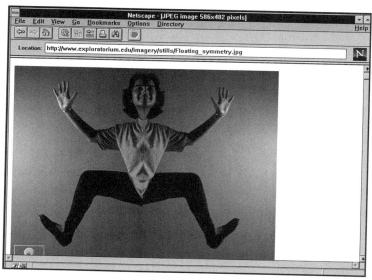

http://www.exploratorium.edu/imagery/stills/Floating_symmetry.jpg

THIS SCIENCE and nature gallery illustrates basic science principles in a fun and educational manner. It's based on San Francisco's Exploratorium, a science exploration and education center with an attached arts center. That makes it of particular interest to the artist or viewer who is turned on by the beauty and patterns of nature. This gallery has gone to great lengths to not only explain science, but to instill a sense of awe and marvel in the sheer visual beauty of natural images and natural forces.

Simple physics and chemistry principles are translated into some wonderful art here. Those patterns of color that form on soap bubbles; the fiery, fluorescent glow of electrical plasma; the effects of flowing wind on water or sand; all have inspired artists who have visited the Exploratorium.

You won't find Great Masters here, but you'll find plenty of thought-provoking ways of looking at the world, and examples of how nature has inspired other artists.

In fact, the Exploratorium is so serious about the beauty of science that it has an "artist-in-residence" program so that artists can use scientific imagery as an inspiration, and perhaps help visitors look at science in new ways.

You'll need to do some digging here, but you won't go far to find some fascinating images. Click on the Learning Studio link at the top, and among other things on the menu you'll find a selection of online exhibits. Many are strongly visual, and illustrate experiments about visual perception.

Teachers will love this area. Students can view material directly online, or you can follow several links to instructions on how to build similar exhibits for the classroom.

For a track which really focuses on images, try the "Digital Library" link from the home page.

Here's where you'll find images from many of the Exploratorium's exhibits, from its Artists-in-Residence program, and a section simply called "Other Interesting Images."

In the Exhibit Pictures section you'll find images from some of the actual exhibits in the Exploratorium. These are innovative experiments designed to help people understand fundamental optical and visual principles such as color and perspective.

Figure 14.2

"Quiet Lightning" is a piece of plasma sculpture by artist Bill Parker.

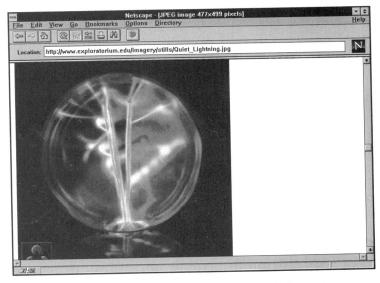

http://www.exploratorium.edu/imagery/stills/Quiet_Lightning.jpg

Figure 14.3

Children express wonder at the "Kinetic Light" exhibit prepared by artist Christian Scheiss.

http://www.exploratorium.edu/imagery/stills/Kinetic_Light.jpg

The real gallery has 650 of these, and what you see online are some good photos illustrating the basic idea. It is difficult to get the full effect over the Internet, but these folks have some excellent photographs here that often convey the gist of an idea.

Also worth checking out is the Exploratorium's section on electronic versions of some of its exhibits (under "Exhibit Images"). The Exploratorium has a section on Genetic Mutation, for example, in which genetic differences in fruit flies cause different colors, shapes, and wing or leg development.

The "Exhibits" area in the Digital Library also contains

some strong visual experiments under its Electronic Exhibits link. These are sections and images specifically constructed for Internet visitors. For example, you find a clever experiment on how we perceive things when they're upside down and a suggestion that you try it with your own face. (They used the Mona Lisa, but we're sure you're prettier.) ▲

Figure 14.4
Light bounces and refracts through a prism.

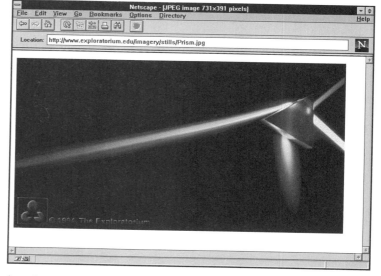

http://www.exploratorium.edu/imagery/stills/Prism.jpg

Figure 14.5
A series of lenses transmit your face 20 feet from your head at Image Relay.

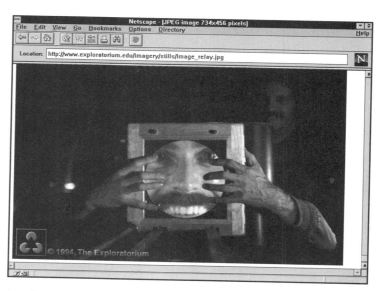

http://www.exploratorium.edu/imagery/stills/Image_relay.jpg

Visible Human

 http://www.nlm.nih.gov/extramural_research.dir/visible_human.html

Figure 14.6

Logo of the Visible Human Project.

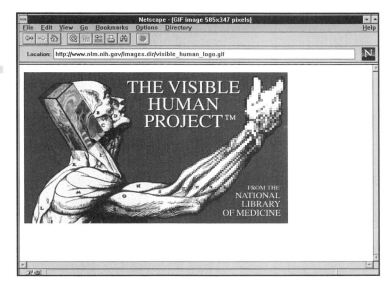

http://www.nlm.nih.gov/images.dir/visible_human_logo.gif

IMAGINE THAT YOU could take the human body and examine its structure slice by slice.

Well, it may not appeal to all of us, but it would be great for anyone interested in human anatomy. And it's becoming available now on the Internet, as part of the Visible Human project. The project is still under development, but you can see the preliminary results already.

The idea is to take male and female cadavers and, using three different types of imaging—computerized tomography (a CAT scan), magnetic resonance imaging, and physically slicing the frozen cadaver a millimeter at a time—develop a highly detailed picture of the human body.

Eventually the three types of images will be combined in a computer, creating a Virtual Human that scientists can examine from any angle at any level of detail, using either or all of these three observation methods.

Only serious researchers will want to download some of the high resolution images from this site: many of the cross sections run into the seven-megabyte range. However, you can click on a link to see some sample image slices of the cadaver, as MRI images, CAT scans, or frozen cadaver images.

If you want to get an idea of how the Virtual Human will work, take the link to the Caltech Interactive Volume Browser, which has assembled the data for part of the cadaver and will let you "zoom" through the body or change your angle of view.

This is a site that really leverages the power of the Internet. There's a huge amount of data here: the images of the male cadaver total 15 gigabytes of data. It would be impossible to publish a book showing all the possible cross sections, since there are an infinite number of them. The beauty of the project is that once all the data is in the computer, it will let you "cut" the cadaver at any point, and at any angle, that you want. Scientists will be able to look at organs, relationships and structures in ways that were not possible before. ▲

Figure 14.7

Zooming in on the Virtual Human shows the structure and some of the organs of the chest cavity.

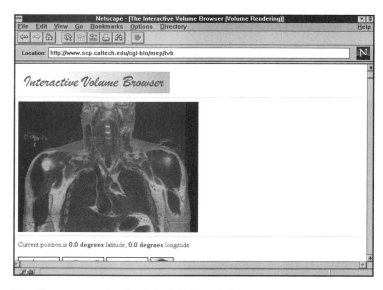

http://www.scp.caltech.edu/cgi-bin/mep/ivb

GRAPHICS SITES REVIEWED IN CH 20

In addition to this chapter's best of the best, read about these sites in Ch 20.

Atlanta Reproductive Health Centre

http://www.mindspring.com/~mperloe/gallery.html

Photos of human reproductive systems, eggs, and embryos.

Berkeley Museum of Paleontology

http://ucmp1.berkeley.edu/

Take the Web Geological Time Machine to learn more about the prehistoric life on Planet Earth.

Biological Sciences Database

http://www.calpoly.edu/delta.html

A database of information about various species, with an emphasis on marine biology.

Centre for Visual Science

http://cvs.anu.edu.au/

A site exploring how we (and other creatures) see and perceive.

Charlotte, The Vermont Whale

http://www.uvm.edu/whale/whalehome.html

How a whale ended up in land-locked Vermont, and what that tells us about glaciers, ice ages, and land formation.

Field Museum of Natural History

http://www.bvis.uic.edu:80/museum/Home.html

Similar to the Exploratorium, the Field Museum of Natural History has special online sections devoted to the evolution of land animals and to bats, with still photos and movies.

FINS (Fish Information Service)

http://www.actwin.com/fish/index.html

A complete information service for aquarium owners, both fresh and salt water. It contains photos of all the common species of aquarium fish.

Franklin Institute Science Museum

http://sln.fi.edu/

An education-oriented site with excellent material on Benjamin Franklin's inventions and the human heart.

Graphics Visualization Laboratory

http://www.lerc.nasa.gov/Other_Groups/GVIS/gvis.html

A laboratory specializing in scientific visualization of invisible phenomena, such as airflow over surfaces, pressure gradients, and mapping of data.

Interactive Frog Dissection

http://curry.edschool.Virginia.EDU:80/~insttech/frog/

You keep your hands on a mouse and dissect a frog online.

National Library of Medicine

http://www.nlm.nih.gov/hmd.dir/oli.dir/

Nearly 60,000 images related to the history of medicine on a laser disk, for retrieval over the World Wide Web.

Ocean Planet

http://seawifs.gsfc.nasa.gov/ocean_planet.html

An exhibition about the ocean, conservation, and the people who depend on the sea, sponsored by the Smithsonian Institution.

Smithsonian Photographs Online

http://photo2.si.edu/

Photos of coral reefs and fish from the Caribbean, and sea turtles and the rain forest in Costa Rica.

CHAPTER 15

Science Fiction

KEEPING UP WITH science fiction is no easy task these days, no easier than science itself. Writers of sci-fi have long dreamed that something like the Internet would one day embed itself into the affairs of humans. Likewise science fiction has embedded itself into the Net.

Web sites dedicated to science fiction are numerous. From classic film, television, and books to the latest extraterrestrial craze, you can visit multiple visions of the future, each with its own concept of what the future holds for humankind.

The search for science fiction graphics leads mainly to the movies and television shows that defined the generation that now runs rampant over, under, and across the Internet.

The Sci-Fi Channel: The Dominion

 http://www.scifi.com

Figure 15.1

One of the several science fiction landscapes offered on the list of images in the FreeZone.

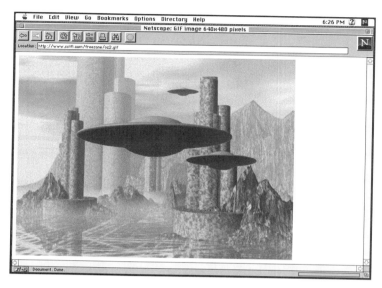

http://www.scifi.com/freezone/oz2.gif

THE SAVIOR OF science fiction, The Sci-Fi Channel, has given sci-fi fandom a new breath with its home page, The Dominion. Here, you can find graphics and videos, and science-fiction oriented online discussions and news articles. The Dominion's presentation is pretty slick, too, as if you're watching a special effects screen on some late night television program.

The prime location for graphics in The Dominion is in the FreeZone. There, browsers can download video, sounds, and images. The video clips are samples from the Sci-Fi Channel promos, but we enjoyed them nonetheless.

The image file (all .gifs) contains a variety of images: alien landscapes, posters from a few television shows, some scenes from *Space:1999* and *Tank Girl*, and a couple of miscellaneous stills. The file sizes range from 60Kb to 213Kb, which is nice to know, since there are no preview files. About half of the filenames are understandable, while the rest are oblique (for

example, Angelique.gif—who's Angelique?).

We happily linked over to the page dedicated to *The Prisoner*, which contains an image map of the compound where protagonist "Number 6" was trapped during the 1960s television show. Clicking on the map's different locations takes you to one or two stills, each from the television show. As a special bonus, clicking on the Town Hall location links you to an image of the underground control room, plus one random photograph of "what Number 6 is doing right now."

The Tekno Nation link delivered us to Mickey Spillane's *Mike Danger* Sunday Comic

Strips. When we visited, the 1994 Sunday comic was running its 20+ episodes, one week at a time. Following the link through, you can view previous weeks or the current week. Each week's strip is broken down panel by panel, for easy reading.

There are other graphics available on the Tekno Nation page. When we visited, the short list of "Publications" included cover art from several other sources, including Gene Roddenberry's *Xander in Lost Universe #0* and Neil Gaiman's *Mr. Hero—The Newmatic Man #9*.

The Sci-Fi Entertainment links you through to a list of

Figure 15.2

One of the panels from the Mike Danger comic strip in The Dominion's Tekno Nation section.

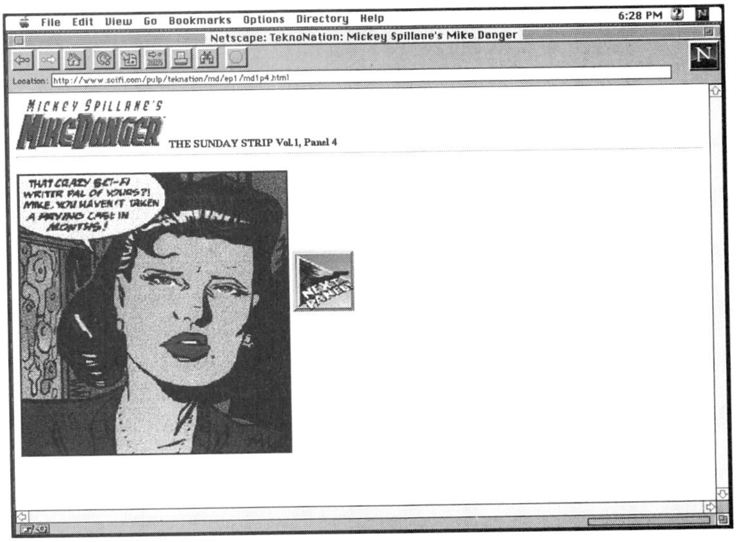

http://www.scifi.com/pulp/teknation/md/ep1/md1p4.html

Figure 15.3

The movie poster from the B&W science fiction movie The Day The Earth Stood Still in The Dominion's FreeZone section.

http://www.scifi.com/freezone/earthstoodstill.gif

current articles, each of which contains at least one graphic. We were able to find decent photographs of Judge Dredd (the film version), the creature from the movie *Species*, and a manly shot of Batman.

Fortunately, the newer versions of Netscape allow you capture all the fun title images on The Dominion. Don't miss

the hip computer art on the FTL Newsfeed page inside the Sci-Fi Originals list. We attempted to browse though "clnet central" and try "the

world's first interactive, on-air, online showcase for computers, multimedia, and digital technology," but couldn't seem to get past the first screen. With time, (and added bandwidth) these problems should vanish.

Before you leave The Dominion, be sure to check out the science-fiction links in Orbit. We found links to a plethora of science fiction movies, television shows, and other resources.

The only problem we had with The Dominion was that it was difficult to reach. We had to try for several hours before we were able to access the Sci-Fi Channel's home page, and found that that didn't always guarantee we were going to be able to reach all of the available files. Visitors might want to check out this site during non-peak times, if there is such a thing. ▲

Babylon 5 Pictures Directory

 http://www.hyperion.com/b5/

Figure 15.4

One of the images from the "Effects" file of the Babylon 5 Pictures Directory.

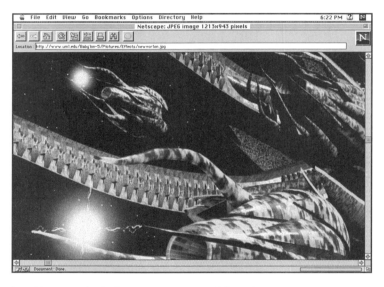

http://www.uml.edu/Babylon-5/Pictures/Effects/newvorlon.jpg

THE TELEVISION SHOW *Babylon 5* is visibly the product of the modern age, with its emphasis on high-quality special effects and a sophisticated viewing audience. The show is steeped in political intrigue, war, and, best of all, good looking set designs, aliens, and space ships.

Since such a complicated script is difficult to catch up with if you haven't been watching the series from day one, this site and its associated links will update you as fast as you can read. By following the link to the top-level *Babylon 5* directory, you'll find links to plot summaries, interviews, and production notes.

Nonetheless, you don't have to know anything about *Babylon 5* to get caught up in the extensive picture files provided through this site. Many visitors will start at the Lurker's Guide (one link away), but this page—the Pictures Directory— is really where you should start if you're looking for graphics.

Figure 15.5

Alien ambassadors Londo, G'Kar, Kosh, and Delenn in a promotional shot, from the Characters subdirectory.

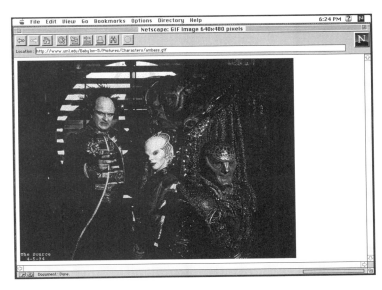

http://www.uml.edu/Babylon-5/Pictures/Characters/ambass.gif

Under Multimedia resources/software, the link to "the pictures directory" takes you to a short list: Characters, Effects, Misc, and Scenes. Each of these is home to extensive collections of images, which can be viewed in either preview or non-preview format. Use the "alternative interface" if you have the bandwidth or the time for the preview images to download. If you choose the non-preview format, you'll find the filenames to be brisk, but understandable, such as approach3.jpg or cockpit.gif.

The index.jpg in each of the four picture files allow you to view the file's entire catalog at once in thumbnail form, in either preview or non-preview mode. Loading up the index.jpg takes much less time than allowing the preview images to be drawn one by

one. There are more than enough smaller images (less than 40Kb), but a majority of the images in these files are very large. Many are over 100Kb.

More photographs of the principal cast members can be found by linking up to the Lurker's Guide, selecting the "setting" link and then the "season one" and the resulting "season two" links. Both seasons provide thumbnail (read: small) headshots of the characters, along with their descriptions.

Following the link to "sound and video clips" leads to a well-annotated list of Microsoft Video .avi files. X users can

download "XAnim" from this site, also, which allows them to play the .avi and QuickTime files (there was only one QuickTime movie when we visited).

Technically-oriented browsers should check out the link to the 3D models of some of the show's spacecrafts. The models appear to be a bit dark and missing the brilliance of their final, on-screen look. Most of the images are in Amiga "Imagine" format.

We attempted several times to try out the Babylon 5 Interactive demo from our Macintosh, but received only a very long page of random code. ▲

Figure 15.6

Babylon 5 Commander Jeffrey Sinclair being interrogated by the Grey Council during the episode "And the Sky Full of Stars."

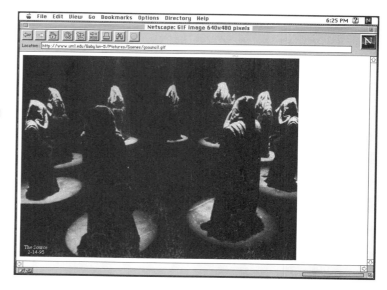

http://www.uml.edu/Babylon-5/Pictures/Scenes/gcouncil.gif

2019: Off-World (A Blade Runner Page)

 http://kzsu.stanford.edu/uwi/br/off-world.html

Figure 15.7

The megatropolis of Blade Runner's future, reflected in the eye of Blade Runner Holden. Holden is later replaced by Harrison Ford's character Decker when he gets too close to finding a renegade android replicant.

BEFORE EXPLORING THE Blade Runner Home Page, we purchased the new Vangelis version of the movie soundtrack, slid the CD into the player, turned it up loud, and set our Netscape machine for the journey to Off-World.

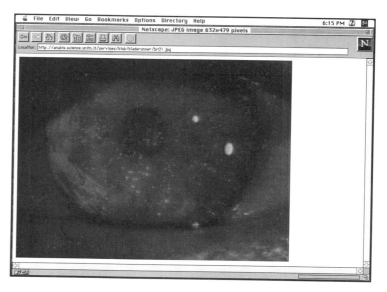

http://anubis.science.unitn.it/services/blob/bladerunner/br01.jpg

Figure 15.8

The image of replicant Zhora is found by Decker, using his 'esper' machine to examine a photograph pixel by pixel. He later tracks Zhora down by her snake tattoo.

http://www.smartdocs.com:80/~migre.v/Bladerunner/photo1.jpg

Blade Runner, now at cult status after its release in 1983, is well represented on the Internet, as it should be. Life with protagonist Decker is integrated with computers, images, sounds, and atmosphere. The two images contained on the top of the Off-World page reflect this vision of the future: Tyrell's pollution-drenched pyramid-like tower, home of the android replicants who have returned to Earth to find the key to life and steal it for themselves before their four-year life cycle counts down; and Decker examining the monitor of his home computer (or 'esper' machine).

The first of two Blade Runner FAQ links includes a subdirectory of images, which, while not containing a particularly alarming number of scans of scenes from the movie, did have the scene of Decker (Harrison Ford) visiting the unfortunate Holden in the hospital, a scene not shown in the original release of the movie. (Finding the same rare image at another site indicated the intense interest in the movie on the Internet.)

From the Blade Runner FAQ, we also followed the next link to "a large collection of Blade Runner images" and found, indeed, a large collection. But these pictures are fuzzy and not done very well, appearing as poorly scanned VHS screen captures. While there might be some sort of 'film noir' look about the scan lines over the images, we didn't spend too much time downloading the images.

The Blade Runner FAQ also linked to a handful of .mpeg and .avi video sequences, and notes on six of the seven different versions of the film. The link to collectibles and resources, though, contained only a few images and the listing of other Blade Runner WWW pages needed updating.

There are several other repositories of images from the film, also. Blob's Image Archives has many good-looking scans that aren't too big and they download quickly. The images aren't titled very well (*blade01* through *blade24* and *br01* through *br04*), so if you are a *Blade Runner* neophyte, you might not know much about the images' backgrounds until you've seen the movie eight or nine more times.

As long as you're here, you can read the FAQs or even the movie script. Another layer of insight can be found on the link to the site dedicated to Philip K. Dick. PKD wrote the book *Do Androids Dream of Electric Sheep?*, from which *Blade Runner* was adapted. You can also find photos of PKD with Ridley Scott, who directed (and interpreted the original story into) the film.

A few of the links were nonfunctioning, but the others met our needs. With a bit of housekeeping, these links will probably be updated soon. (We were sad that we were never able to link to the online version of the Souvenir Book. We didn't even know there was one.)

Visitors are also able to link to the home page for Vangelis, who wrote the original score for the film and has released his own version of the soundtrack. You should be able to download sounds from *Blade Runner*, cuts from other Vangelis projects, and have access to several more *Blade Runner* clips in .avi format. ▲

Graphics Sites Reviewed in Ch 20

In addition to this chapter's best of the best, read about these sites in Ch 20.

The Acceleration Chamber

http://www-usacs.rutgers.edu/fun-stuff/tv/quantum-leap/

Images and information for fans of the television show *Quantum Leap*.

Alien

http://dutial.twi.tudelft.nl/~alien/alien.html

Contains photographs, art, and links to other home pages dedicated to the *Alien* movies.

Danny's X-Files Home Page

http://www.stack.urc.tue.nl/~danny/x-files.html

An extensive collection of scenes from the *X Files* television show.

Dystopian Visions Image Galleries

http://underground.net/~koganuts/Galleries/index.html

The home page for *Star Trek* fans of all generations.

The Purdue Star Wars Picture Archive

http://www.mgmt.purdue.edu/~vkoser/starwars/pics.html

Files and more files from the movie *Star Wars*.

The Star Wars Home Page

http://force.stwing.upenn.edu:8001/~jruspini/starwars.html

A resource for finding images and information about the science fiction epic *Star Wars*.

15

16

Space

FEW FIELDS INVOLVE technology as much as space exploration and travel, so it shouldn't be surprising to find space well represented on the Internet.

Astronomers have always taken pictures by the thousands, but they haven't always been accessible to the public. Now, thanks to image archives available on the Internet, you can access images of virtually any point in space.

The new technology also makes it possible for people anywhere in the world to see space programs in action: to watch launches almost as they happen, observe astronauts in space, and pull in images from space exploration vehicles.

Two events have reshaped the images available from and about space in recent years, and the Internet provides access to both.

The Hubble Space Telescope, whose orbit takes it completely out of Earth's atmosphere, provided astronomers—and you—with images of unprecedented quality.

And the impact of the comet Shoemaker-Levy 9 on Jupiter created a huge demand for images, animations, charts, and other graphical information.

We'll look at the major sites on the Internet devoted to astronomy and space, show you some tools you can use to view, via the Internet, almost any location in the sky, and point you to some of the best places to see those comet impact pictures. As always, you will find loads of pointers to other sites when you visit some of these.

Some of these sites, by the way, are fairly technical, while others have public education clearly in mind, and a few present space images for their sheer beauty and impact.

Whether you're into the technical side of astronomy or not, you can still enjoy the beauty of the images. Even to the non-astronomer, the night sky will never look exactly the same after you have seen the drama of space on the Internet. ▲

NASA (National Aeronautics and Space Administration)

 http://www.jpl.nasa.gov

Figure 16.1

The Hubble Space Telescope has revolutionized astronomy and created a treasure of visual space images.

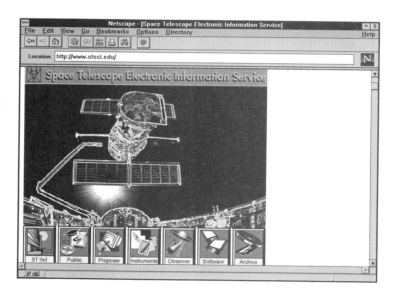

http://www.stsci.edu/

NASA IS THE world's largest, oldest, and most active space agency, and it has moved rapidly in the last year to put its resources on line. The result is a network of Web sites so comprehensive that you can spend many days in it without ever crossing your own tracks.

Since few aspects of the American space program don't involve NASA, chances are good that you'll run across NASA even when don't expect it.

The best place for the drop-in public to go when you get to NASA's home page, at http://www.gsfc.nasa.gov, is the Hot Topics button.

Figure 16.2

NASA's home page has links to NASA labs across the U.S.

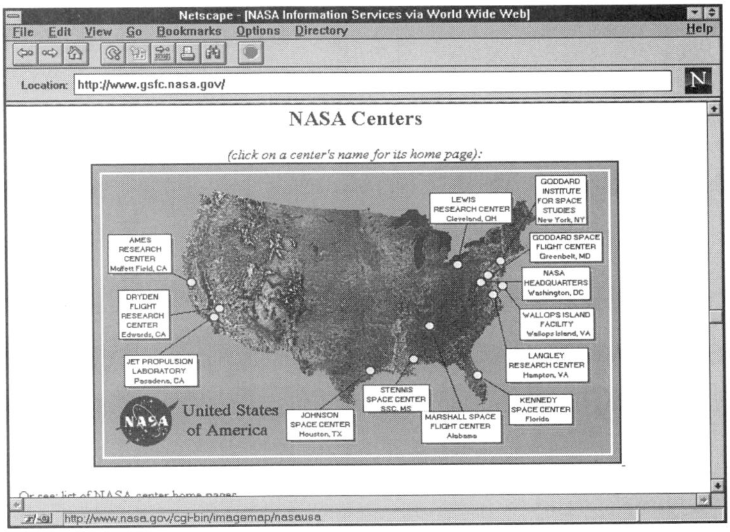

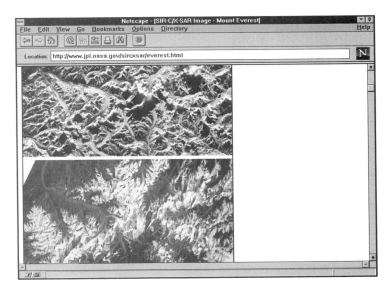

http://www.gsfc.nasa.gov/

Figure 16.3

A radar image from NASA (top) shows more detail about snow conditions around Mt. Everest than a visual photo taken from the Space Shuttle.

http://www.jpl.nasa.gov/sircxsar/everest.html

The first place to look here is Today at NASA. What you'll get will vary from day to day, of course, but this page usually includes a Pick of the Pix section with links to NASA's most popular image sites.

It was well hidden when we looked, but some of the links in the text on this page go to http://shuttle.nasa.gov/ntv/, NASA Television. This is a very cool site, where every minute during a major event or mission, a frame is grabbed from NASA television and posted.

NASA also feeds data to the Internet on CU-SeeMe, a free program you can download from Cornell University (at ftp://gated.cornell.edu/pub/video) to exchange video across the Internet. You don't need to hook a video camera to your computer to take advantage of this. You can use CU-SeeMe's receive mode to see "slow-scan" images on your computer.

Figure 16.4

During a mission or major event, the image on this page will be updated every minute by NASA television.

http://shuttle.nasa.gov/ntv/

The Space Shuttle

If there's a major shuttle mission in the works (and there usually is), you can link to information and images about that mission, either from Today at NASA, or from the Hot Topics page.

These shuttle pages provide an impressive amount of visual information about the upcoming launch. They tend to be most active about a week before a launch date. (If you're not sure of the dates, you'll find a link to Upcoming Shuttle Missions at the bottom of the Hot Topics page.)

We visited the launch countdown site just before the launch of the Atlantis Shuttle, on a mission to dock with the Russian Space station Mir.

By clicking on the Photos section, you'll get images related to the mission, such as pictures of the crew, the special patch that is designed for each mission, and photos related to whatever experiments or payloads are going up on that particular launch. Many of these images are shot by the special IMAX camera, which sits in the shuttle's cargo bay, and they are outstanding images.

The videos button will bring out video shot on the mission. In the pre-launch phase, about the best you might get are pictures of the crew walking about in their uniforms, but as the mission progresses, NASA posts video from the flight itself, organized by each day

of the flight. These videos are typically in the MPEG format, viewable with the MPEG software described in Chapter 24.

Photo Archives

NASA, as you might expect, has a huge supply of photographs, and there are hundreds of ways to get to them. Every home page in the organization usually has a link of some kind to the image data maintained at that location.

To begin, go to the image gallery at the National Space Science Data Center. You'll find a good selection of images from every planet, comets and asteroids, images from Hubble, pictures of spacecraft themselves, and links to other sites. ▲

Figure 16.5

Click on buttons on the Launch Countdown page to see what's going on

http://shuttle.nasa.gov/

Figure 16.6

The Russian Space Station Mir, photographed by the IMAX camera in the space shuttle.

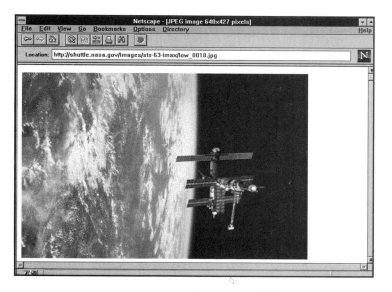

http://shuttle.nasa.gov/images/sts-63-imax/low_0010.jpg

Figure 16.7

A computer-generated image showing a feature on the planet Venus, based on NASA images of the planet.

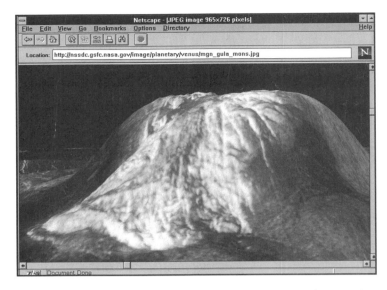

http://nssdc.gsfc.nasa.gov/image/planetary/venus/mgn_gula_mons.jpg

Students for the Exploration and Development of Space (SEDS)

 http://www.seds.org/

Figure 16.8

The Galaxy Page at SEDS offers links to images from the universe.

THEY'RE NOT NASA, but the students who are members of SEDS are keen and they do know how to design a Web page. Furthermore, while NASA displays proper scientific caution about space and technology, Students for the Exploration and Development of Space is not afraid to dream a bit.

http://www.seds.org/other.html

At this site, you'll find a lot of top-notch image and information galleries based on pictures taken in and of space. Click on Galaxy of Images Information to go to its Galaxy Page, where you can jump in a variety of directions.

The students don't have the resources to actually maintain the images themselves. This site is, instead, a great starting point to go elsewhere on the Net. Links are not only listed, but are organized in a clear and understandable way.

In the search for space images you should click on the Astro FTP link. This brings up a page of FTP sites that have large collections of astronomical information, including pictures and images. ▲

GRAPHICS SITES REVIEWED IN CH 20

In addition to this chapter's best of the best, read about these sites in Ch 20.

Comet Shoemaker-Levy Home Page

http://newproducts.jpl.nasa.gov/sl9/sl9.html

A very comprehensive and well-maintained site with many images of the comet impact on Jupiter and links to many other sites devoted to the comet's impact.

Hubble Space Telescope

http://www.stsci.edu/top.html

The best of Hubble and many other startling images from space.

International Space Station

http://issa-www.jsc.nasa.gov/ss2/SpaceStation_homepage.html

Images and information about this international effort to create a permanent space station.

Jet Propulsion Laboratory

http://www.jpl.nasa.gov/

The premier laboratory for space exploration has a vast collection of images about space.

SkyView

http://skyview.gsfc.nasa.gov/skyview.html

Your own deep space telescope offering instant views of almost any portion of the sky, through many different types of telescopes. Fill in a form to get an image back.

Space Movie Archive

http://www.univ-rennes1.fr/ASTRO/anim-e.html

About half a gigabyte's worth of movies and animations, of solar eclipses, the weather from space, Shoemaker-Levy, and, of course, a bit of science fiction and *Star Trek* thrown in for good measure.

Space Shuttle Earth Observations Project

http://ersaf.jsc.nasa.gov/sn5.html

Photos of the earth's surface, taken by cameras on the space shuttle.

Views of the Solar System

http://www.c3.lanl.gov/~cjhamil/SolarSystem/homepage.html

A guided tour of the Sun, planets, asteroids, comets, and meteors.

Transportation

IF THERE IS anything the Internet has taken away from daily life, it's travel. Used to be, you'd have to gear up the family vehicle and head out across the land to see the sights beyond your yard, your office building, or the store down the street. With the advent of the Internet, and specifically WWW browsers, you can travel anywhere in the world and see the photographs of people, places, and things, right at your fingertips.

That doesn't mean transportation is any less important in our lives. You still have to drive to work, you still want to get away from in front of a computer monitor and stir up the dirt somewhere other than home.

There was no lack of illustrated information for all sorts of travel. Trains, automobiles, boats, motorcycles…all modes of transportation are represented on the Internet. And that's what the Internet gives back: more traveling than you ever thought you'd do.

Trains—Harris Mountaintop

 http://mtmis1.mis.semi.harris.com/trains.html

Figure 17.1

The CR Dash8-40CW #6099 at Solomon's Gap near Mountaintop, Pennsylvania from the Trains home page hosted by Harris Semiconductor.

http://mtmis1.mis.semi.harris.com/tr_cr6099.jpg

IT'S ONLY APPROPRIATE that this excellent train site is hosted by Harris Semiconductor, which owns one of the world's renowned collections of engineers. They may not be conductors, but they are certainly well versed in train enthusiast etiquette. That is, lots of pictures and lots of links to other places that specialize in trains.

When visiting this site, there were five colorful images of modern trains labeled as "From the Area" at the top of the home page. Following those were three short descriptions of images that linked to B&W photographs of vintage trains from the RIP Track home page.

We jaunted over to the RIP page (another must-see site),

but had a very difficult time with the link. While researching the topic, it became almost a requirement to wait for long periods of time while train-oriented sites were either down or too busy to connect. But, as it is in real life, waiting for the trains is part of the experience, and the images are well worth the wait.

The RIP link contains a modest collection of classic photographs of steam locomotives, images from places such as the Illinois Railway Museum and other photos changed at the siteowner's fancy.

Web visitors can link through train photographs depicting the Steamtown Grand opening, and from other local Pennsylvania areas, including Wilkes-Barre and Scranton. The link to Scranton provides an overview and a history of the area, clueing in the reader as to why there's so much train activity in mid-Pennsylvania—coal. If you need visuals of the area, you can check out maps of Mountaintop, Luzerne County, and Pennsylvania by following the appropriate links under the Wilkes-Barre and Surrounding Areas home page.

Figure 17.2

Crowds busily make their way around the fleet of trains during the Steamtown Grand Opening. Photo copyright Paul R. Tupaczewski.

http://www.mcs.net/~dsdawdy/Parlor/steamtwn/steam6.jpg

A barrage of high-quality train photographs welcomes visitors to the Steamtown Grand Opening link. The author details the event with prose and a very large collection of preview-sized images that can be displayed full size. Visitors can peruse other files on Steamtown's National Historic site and articles focusing on "Local Coal Breakers" and "Area Engine Facilities." The link to the Baltimore Railroad Museum also contains a handful of color images of more vintage trains, including one of the last two Alleghenys, the heaviest and most powerful of steam locomotives made in the United States.

The section "Railroad Photos" lists 15 different train types, with each type linking to about 10 images of representative trains. We were disappointed that there wasn't much text to explain the significance of the various brands or styles of trains. It was the same story with the "Other" categories, which features photographs of other types of train cars, equipment, and roundhouses (where trains are stored and repaired). Although the top of all Harris pages instructs visi-

tors to "turn off images" in order to read the descriptions of the images, we couldn't figure out how to do that without turning off our Netscape session. Instead, we found two work-arounds: when you "mail" the contents of the home page, you can "quote the document," which will include all the text, including the descriptions. Visitors can also reload the page and, before any images are loaded, immediately click on the stop button, forcing the page to reload just the text and the descriptions.

Several of the Railroad Photos collections also linked to the Norfolk and Western Image Collection, which is included in the list of Photo Archive links near the bottom of the home page. Norfolk, listed as an FTP site, features

images of classic railroad advertisements, railroad bridges, and locomotives, all of which visitors link through one by one. The image descriptions are slightly less sketchy than the Railroad Photos, but concentrate mainly on identifying the trains' series numbers. There is no detail as to file size or type.

As we mentioned previously, train enthusiasts can link to many more photo archives from the Harris site, as well as to links at Yahoo and links to model railroad information and companies.

As any Internet visitor would expect, the images of trains don't stop with Harris, but it's a recommended place to start. The engineers at Harris may work on semiconductors, but they deserve full conductor status. ▲

The 4X4 Web Page

 http://www.indirect.com/www/a4x4/4x4.html

Figure 17.3

Four-wheeling through the Rubicon Trail. One of the few images of 4x4 vehicles not covered in mud.

http://www.indirect.com/www/a4x4/images/watersfj.jpg

EVEN IF YOU DON'T know anything about 4×4 vehicles— except that they take up ALL of your review mirror—you can participate in the sheer joy that 4×4 owners take in their vehicles through the 4×4 Web Page.

Not only did we find several valuable image caches of oversized vehicles at this site, but almost every photograph is annotated with gracious detail discussing the vehicle in question. Most of the images are labeled with file size and type, for easy downloading.

The Feature Vehicles link contains short, inventory-like descriptions of various 4×4 vehicles, each complimented by a collection of home photographs of the vehicles in action. When we visited, we caught glimpses of a Range Rover, Ford Bronco, Jeep CJ5, Chevy Blazer, Dodge Powerwagon, Ford Explorer, and a Toyota FJ-40.

4×4 owners looking for a place to romp their oversized wheels can access the link to a short list of 4×4 Trails and a longer list of Trip Reports. The trails are reviews of specific sites, such as Northern California's Rubicon, Dusy-Ershim, and Deer Valley trails, written either by the siteowner or by other enthusiasts, as are the trip reports. The trip reports describe the full impact of the 4×4's experience: rocky and muddy.

When we visited, about half of the Travels & Trails submissions contained photographs of the writers' vehicles plowing through muddy streams, muddy roads, and muddy rocks. Fortunately, the images themselves were clean (although sometimes slightly crooked), and gave us a better understanding of life atop tall tires.

The Travels & Trails link also linked to the California State Vehicular Recreation Areas home page that contained another handful of reviews of California vehicle-based parks. These reviews, as part of the California Department of Parks and Recreation, also spell out exactly which vehicles are allowed where and when. Plus, each park home page contains at least one photograph of the park, usually with an off-road vehicle speeding through it.

Figure 17.4

A steamy photograph of a 1982 Pink Pearl Toyota FJ-40 from one of the many featured vehicles found on the 4x4 home page.

http://www.indirect.com/www/a4x4/images/wahfj.jpg

Figure 17.5

Stuck in the mud near British Columbia's Placer Lake.

http://www.indirect.com/www/a4x4/images/whip7.jpg

At the bottom of the home page are links to what could be the meatiest section of this site, nonchalantly labeled, "And pages dedicated to your favorite 4×4!" If your favorite vehicle is a Toyota or Jeep, you're in luck. The Toyota page contains a gracious collection of photographs of numerous Toyota-brand vehicles, each with a full paragraph of description and miscellaneous facts. There's also a sublink to "more Land Cruiser pictures," which is also not to be missed if you have any interest in the

Toyota flagship. Ford and Suzuki contained very little when we visited, and Chevy and Isuzu did not have active links. Still, these topics might be more complete when you visit.

The Jeep home page also has images, with photographs of "Jeeps in India" and "Early Jeeps," the latter containing some wonderful historical entries. The Jeep page also links to a short but excellent

QuickTime movie (550Kb) of a white Jeep passing two convoy trucks on the dirt shoulder of a thin, Indian road. "Typical Ladakhi driving," comments the photographer in the notes.

The rest of the 4×4 site is dedicated to links to FAQs, upcoming events, club and product information, a classified ad section, and the prerequisite "Other links…" in case you haven't seen enough mud on the Internet. ▲

17

Motorcycle Online

 http://motorcycle.com/motorcycle.html

Figure 17.6

Motorcycles keep heading your way on the Motorcycle Online Photo Archive.

http://motorcycle.com/mo/mcphotos/mcnelson/nelson11.jpg

WE BARELY ESCAPED from Motorcycle Online. Once we logged into the site, we spent hours roaming from link to link. We felt like we were on the Internet's open road, free of the cramped construction of many sites that usually offer large collections of images, particularly FTP and gopher sites that contain only long lists of file names.

Here are a few suggestions if you plan to visit this site. First, be prepared to spend some time at this site if you're interested in downloading some quality images of motorcycles. There are many links at this site that will bog down a slow modem or a slow computer, so beware.

Also, race down to the Photo Archives before you look anyplace else for images of motorcycle madness. Most of the images here are high quality, good looking, and capture the essence of bearing down on the highway, your knees to the tarmac, bugs popping up on your helmet visor, etc.

If that's not graphic enough for you, link over to the Video Archive and enjoy the short, flipbook-type animation at the top of the page. After that, you can cruise through the small collection of video clips (.avi and .mpeg formats only). In case you haven't loaded your computer for real-time action, the archive is supported with direct links to video-playing software for Windows, UNIX, OS/2, and Macintosh.

And finally, when you're finished looking at pictures, take a ride through the links to Daily News, Feature Articles, The Virtual Museum, Nuts & Bolts, and the rest of the prose-based links. Almost every link is accompanied with more and more photographs that illustrate life with a motorcycle.

There were 13 feature articles, all them with photographs, when we swung through the link. We read reviews and checked out pictures of BMWs, Triumphs, Kawasakis, and read about racing experiences in "A Photo Tour of the Isle of Man" and "Off-Road, Nevada Motorcycle Adventures." (Even the interviews were illustrated!)

When visitors link to Virtual World, they can tour articles and images of motorcycle trips through Rome, Yellowstone National Park, and Mexico. Each of these articles contained very descriptive photographs of both the motorcycles and the sights along the way.

Figure 17.7

Two dirt bikes, looking over the Nevada backlands. From the off-road editor at Motorcycle Online.

http://motorcycle.com/mo/mcdirt/mcphotos/rainrut.jpg

Don't go so fast through Motorcycle Online that you miss the Virtual Museum, which linked to eight articles (when we visited) covering topics such as "A Brief History of Indian Motorcycles" and "If you think modern race sanctioning bodies are problematic, read about the 1913 FAM convention!" Every article contained images illustrating the history of motorcycles, including some vintage photographs that shouldn't be missed, even for non-motorcycle fans.

We were very impressed with the Parts & Accessories link. The two sublinks to Graves Motorsports and Mike Corbin's Saddles both were well stocked with images of motorcycles, motorcycle parts, and motorcycle apparel, all of which visitors are able to order online, not to mention the downloadable images. Corbin specializes in selling actual motorcycles, such as Triumphs and Warbirds, and customized equipment. Graves Motorsports focuses more on motorcycle parts, such as handlebar kits and fairing brackets.

The link to Graves Motorsports also contains a small number of images of racing champion Chuck Graves, including a 2Mb .avi video clip of Chuck racing at the Marlboro Roberts YZR500s at Pocono International Race-way. There's also a 3Mb .avi video clip from Motorcycle Suspension Tuning by Chuck Graves.

Just when we thought we'd found everything we needed, we followed the link to the Skeptics Society, which led to sublinks to press kits that contained scans of the technical information and blueprint drawings of up-and-coming motorcycle models. The Skeptics link advertised "high-resolution, copyright-free photos," and while we didn't see any, there might be in the future.

On the open road of the Internet, Motorcycle Online is a promising reststop. ▲

GRAPHICS SITES REVIEWED IN CH 20

In addition to this chapter's best of the best, read about these sites in Ch 20.

Automobile Pictures Archive

http://dutoc74.io.tudelft.nl/voitures/archive.htm

An extensive collection of old-fashioned, experimental, rare, and specialized automobiles.

Mark Rosenstein's Sailing Page—America's Cup On-Line

http://community.bellcore.com/mbr/sailing-page.html
http://www.ac95.org/

Two sites dedicated to life on the sea. Photographs, news, and racing information.

NASA Dryden Research Aircraft Photo Archive

http://www.dfrf.nasa.gov/PhotoServer/photoServer.html

A virtual library of NASA's space and flight programs.

The Pickup Truck Home Page

http://www.rtd.com/~mlevine/pickup.html

A community-type home page for those who love their trucks, and love to show other people their trucks.

PM Zone (Popular Mechanics)

http://popularmechanics.com/homepage.html

An online version of *Popular Mechanics* magazine, with pages dedicated to new automobiles, best buys, and more.

18

Travel & Geography

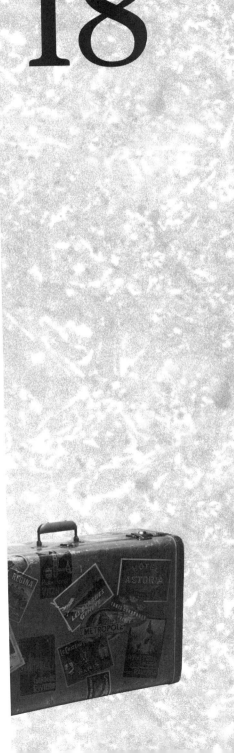

THE INTERNET CAN be a great way to get tourist, travel, or weather information, and sometimes real-time pictures, of an area before you travel there. It's far quicker than writing to the local Chamber of Commerce and waiting for some brochures to arrive by snail mail. In fact, local Chambers of Commerce or tourist bureaus often manage Internet sites and put all the information available in their brochures into their online effort, where it can be updated seasonally and distributed quickly.

Another contribution to Internet travel is the travel journal. An individual will make a trip, keep a journal, and take some photos. The Net is a great way to do something with those photos in addition to putting them in a photo album or worse, stacking them in envelopes in your bedroom closet. They're online where you, your friends, and interested strangers can view them.

With a few exceptions, we're not going to cover specific locations here, because there are just too many. If you're interested in a particular place, use one of the major search engines and type in its name. We'll also tell you in our alphabetical section about special search engines devoted just to travel. One way or the other, we'll bet you get a positive response of some kind for most locations of any size or popularity in the world.

Web Travel Review

 http://www-swiss.ai.mit.edu/webtravel/

Figure 18.1

The Icefields Parkway in Canada's Rocky Mountains.

http://www-swiss.ai.mit.edu/samantha/icefields-parkway-top.jpg

THIS IS THE kind of site that makes us feel sorry for people who don't have computers. They can't read about Phil Greenspun's trips across the U.S. and Canada, or to Costa Rica or New Zealand, because his marvelous travel writing and great photography can only be viewed on the Net.

One section of this site won a Best of the Web award in 1994, and you won't have trouble figuring out why. It's easy to spend hours here.

Even though it is mostly a one-man project, this is not a small site. When we visited, it had 600 pages of text and 2,000 photographs.

The content here consists of illustrated travel stories by Greenspun, a Boston programmer and graduate student who is an exceptionally fine photographer and writer.

His best-known effort in this genre is called Travels with Samantha. Samantha is an Apple PowerBook, the machine on which Greenspun records his travel adventures and reflections.

With more than 200 pages of text and 250 photographs, Greenspun's journey starts in Boston, heads across Canada via Quebec and Montreal to upper Michigan and then across the northern states and through Canada to the Alaska Highway. Back by boat to Seattle, the trip dips briefly north to catch Vancouver, B.C. and Victoria, around the Olympic Peninsula, before heading back east through Idaho, Utah, Colorado, Kansas, and Ohio.

The site also has Footsteps, a sequel to Travels with Samantha, in which Greenspun travels through the American south.

Greenspun also tackles

subjects closer to home with his camera and computer. His New York City Vignettes includes a picture of an obscenely thick deli sandwich, with a brief detour to record a misguided police bust on the street.

A photo essay on New Mexico is, Greenspun admits, a combination of great photos and weird commentary.

Just to show that he's not one of those travel writers who will only go to places most people have never heard of, Greenspun tackles Disneyland too. Of course, after Greenspun's commentary on his choice between "wimp rides" and decapitation,

Figure 18.2

Alaskan Brown Bears park at the top of a falls during the salmon run.

http://www-swiss.ai.mit.edu/samantha/snag-and-watch.jpg

Figure 18.3

A scene from New York Vignettes.

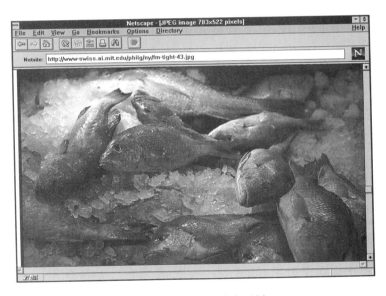

http://www-swiss.ai.mit.edu/philg/ny/fm-tight-43.jpg

Disney wished Greenspun had never heard of them. Too late.

A trip to Berlin and Prague generated some great stories, less exciting images. He also has a trip to Costa Rica, one to the Cayman Islands, and a tour of Australia and New Zealand here.

Greenspun's writing is an ever-spinning mix of the philosophical, the practical, and the amusing that is worth downloading and reading or sharing at leisure.

Most of the sites simply mix text and photos, but Travels with Samantha gives you several options. You can read the whole journal, which will take some time. You can also download it, but then it won't have the photos.

If you're not interested in reading Travels with Samantha and would like to simply look quickly at the pictures, the table of contents has a link to two types of slide shows. The Dynamic Slide Show, recommended only for those with fast Internet connections,

Figure 18.4

Rafting down Costa Rica's Pacuare River.

http://www-swiss.ai.mit.edu/cr/pacuare-11.jpg

Figure 18.5

A Costa Rican parrot tucks its head into its feathers.

http://www-swiss.ai.mit.edu/cr/pj-folded-24.jpg

brings up a four-frame window and slowly changes pictures in each of the windows.

The regular slide show contains the same photos that appear in the text, minus most of the text (read: just captions). It's probably the best way for the casual browser to explore this site, although the large number of thumbnails (a dozen or more for each section, each in the 20Kb range) will take a while to come in on a modem connection.

Finally, you can access a particular part of the slide show by page number. It consists of 20 pages, each labeled by the part of the journey it covers.

You'll also find links at this site to a diversion by Greenspun into the world of politically correct revisionism, under the innocuous title Heather Has Two Mommies. It's the story of a trip to the zoo, where one is not sure whether the strangest animals are inside the cage or outside. The photos are great, in either case.

Figure 18.6

A polar bear ponders life. From Heather Has Two Mommies.

http://www-swiss.ai.mit.edu/zoo/polar-bear-slumped.jpg

You'll also find links at this site to a diversion by Greenspun called Heather Has Two Mommies. It's the story of a trip to the zoo, and the photos are great.

All the images here were digitized by Kodak's Photo CD technology, and while crediting the photographer with a great eye, the images are technically superb, with great color and tonality. Most can be blown up to full screen size or, if you like, to larger than full screen if you click on a [BIG] icon next to each photo. ▲

GRAPHICS SITES REVIEWED IN CH 20

In addition to this chapter's best of the best, read about these sites in Ch 20.

China News Digest

http://www.cnd.org/Scenery/
Keywords: travel and geography, news

An archive with the top scenic sites of China, as well as news-related photos about the Tienanmen Square protest.

CIA World Factbook

http://www.odci.gov/94fact/fb94toc/fb94toc.html

This is the CIA fact book, with extensive detail on more than 260 countries and up-to-date maps, lists, and information on various international organizations, the text of international environmental agreements, time zone maps, and more.

Global Network Navigator Travel Features

http://gnn.com/gnn/meta/travel/features/features.html

On-the-road illustrated reports from various travelers.

Grand Canyon

http://www.kbt.com/gc/

Travel and background geological information on the Grand Canyon, with photos from many parts of the canyon.

Grand Canyon River Running

http://www.tucson.ihs.gov:3001/

A virtual tour down the Colorado River through the Grand Canyon.

Loma Prieta Earthquake Photos

http://wrgis.wr.usgs.gov/docs/geologic/ca/dds-29/photocd.html

Images from a CD-ROM on the earthquake that rocked the Bay Area on October 17, 1989.

Lonely Planet

http://www.lonelyplanet.com/

A strong travel site, with many images from Lonely Planet Publishing's popular travel books.

Multiworld

http://www.jnw.com/mw/iss01/index.html

A bilingual English and Chinese magazine, well illustrated, with some oriental art and illustrated travel features.

Perry-Castañeda Library Map Collection

http://rowan.lib.utexas.edu/Libs/PCL/Map_collection/Map_collection.html

The Perry-Castañeda Library Map Collection holds more than 230,000 maps covering every area of the world.

Russia By Pictures

http://www.cs.toronto.edu/~mes/russia/photo.html

Extensive and well-organized links to places, many in Russia itself, which have photos and information about Russia.

Space Shuttle Earth Observations

http://ersaf.jsc.nasa.gov/sn5.html

Photos of the earth's surface, taken by cameras on the space shuttle.

UK Guide

http://www.cs.ucl.ac.uk/misc/uk/intro.html

A clickable map drops you into the scenic regions and cities of the United Kingdom.

Vietnam Pictures Archive

http://sunsite.unc.edu/vietnam/

A different view of Vietnam: its wonderful scenery and peaceful farmers and fisherfolk.

Virtual Hawaii

http://www.rspac.ivv.nasa.gov/space/hawaii/index_mirror.html

A comprehensive tour of the Hawaiian Islands, with photos taken from the ground, from the air, and from satellites.

Xerox PARC Map Viewer

http://pubweb.parc.xerox.com/map

A very powerful, fast and useful "map on demand" interactive server. Click on the spot you want to see and the Map Viewer draws a map on the fly.

CHAPTER 19

XYZ

THE INTERNET is not about computers or routers or software, as anyone who spends any time on it should quickly discover.

It's about people: about what people like, don't like, their passions, their libidos, their relaxation, their hobbies, their work, their obsessions, their families, travels, dogs, cats, and iguanas.

As a result, not everything on the Internet is going to fit into neat categories. Indeed, that's really the beauty of the Web, and the joy of surfing. You go to that site because you're looking for information about Shakespeare, which takes you to a rare book site, which takes you to the rare-book-site Webmaster's hotlist, which takes you to The Whole Tomato, which leads to a section on earth-berm houses, which leads to…

And no two people will have the same experience on the Net, because within a very short time they'll find themselves taking very different paths.

That's what this chapter is about: the stuff that either doesn't fit neatly into any category, or that seems to crop up in almost every category.

Pathfinder

 http://www.pathfinder.com/

Figure 19.1

The Pathfinder main menu changes constantly as sections are updated.

http://www.pathfinder.com/

THIS IS ONE of those sites that we just keep coming back to again and again, because it's so huge and so good.

Overall, it's not specifically a graphics site. But if you know where to look you'll find more graphics here than on most other sites. Furthermore, you'll find some graphics that are hard to find on other sites. And the quality of both graphics and Web design here is always very high.

Pathfinder is part of the Time-Warner enterprise, the folks who publish *Time, Life, Sports Illustrated, Fortune,* and *People,* among other magazines. The neat thing about this site is that while so many companies and commercial sites view the Internet as a kind of teaser to give you a glimpse of their products, Time Warner has a no-holds-barred, give-'em-everything approach.

News and Hot Topics

The Time-Warner tradition has always been graphically rich. *Time* magazine has always billed itself as an illustrated magazine, and *Life*, its sister publication, virtually defined photojournalism between the 1930s and the 1970s.

You can get the text and some photos from the current issues of their magazines here, which makes this one of the best sites for hot topics in any of the dozens of areas in which they publish magazines. If you want to see images of a hot or current topic, you'll probably find it faster here than almost anywhere else on the Net. The focus of this site, however, is text, rather than graphics, so you're not going to find the graphics you want everywhere you look. We'll point you to areas where you'll find the
most graphics.

To navigate through this huge site, you can click on the image map that appears at the top of the home page, or scroll down and click on the names of the magazines and news sections that are part of this site. We found the latter strategy easier and less confusing.

A few of the latest news stories are listed at the top of this list. These are from Time Daily, a section which is more current than the weekly magazine on the newsstand and contains a brief summary of top stories.

Each summary of the top three or four stories is accompanied by a photo or two

Figure 19.2
A Time cover from Pathfinder.

http://www.pathfinder.com/@@IDHIBAAAAAAAAB0S/time/magazine/
domestic/covers/950731.coverdom.jpg

that can be clicked on for enlargement. You'll also find links to stories on the subject that appeared in previous editions of *Time*. Unfortunately, these earlier stories aren't illustrated. You can, however, look at *Time* covers, which means that sooner or later all of the world's most important people will probably end up here. Previous covers of *Time* are also available, along with text from previous issues of the magazine.

Another place with plenty of graphics is *Life* magazine. Here you'll find a Photo of the Day and a Photo Essay. Also browse through other sections of the magazine; many are photographic in content, even though the titles may not tell you that.

You'll also find a strong collection of links to various photo galleries, including some classics from *Time* and *Life* in the Virtual Photo Gallery (see our profile of this gallery in Chapter 20, under Time-Life Photo Gallery).

Some other sites near the top here may or may not be illustrated. The Election '96 link had a significant photo essay on Newt Gingrich when we visited, for example.

Photo Galleries

Next you'll want to try an important link on the Pathfinder home page called Time Life's Photo Sight.

You'll find links to many of the same locations available through Life, but you'll also find a "photo picks" section. This section features photos requested by users of the system. If there's a photo you'd really like to see, you can fill in a form and send in the request to Time Life. Every week they post a new collection of images requested by their readers.

Clicking on one of those choices produces not only the image, but also a little quiz, which, if you get the correct answer, brings up another photo of the subject. Since you get to try again, no one really loses.

Many of the other publications that are part of Pathfinder are graphics intensive. For example, the section for Time-Warner's urban music and culture magazine, *Vibe*, has a large selection of clips from popular music videos. Also, if you click on the Meta-Index at the top of the video section, you'll get a list of links to the stars whose work is online. Clicking on a star's name brings up not only a list of videos, but also a photo of the star. Click on the More About link and you'll get another photo and bio of the star. There's also an illustrated fashion section here, called Style.

People and *Entertainment Weekly* are other places you'll find pictures of the hottest stars (see our profile of these sites in Chapter 20).

Figure 19.3

A Picture of the Day from Life.

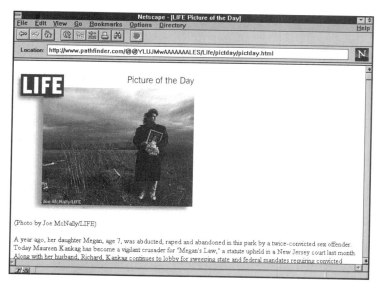

http://www.pathfinder.com/@@YLUJMwAAAAAALES/Life/pictday/
pictday.html

Figure 19.4

*Newt Gingrich takes the gavel
on the day he became Speaker
of the House.*

http://www.pathfinder.com/@@YLUJMwAAAAAALES/pathfinder/
politics/newt/bigday4.gif

Figure 19.5
*The Stealth Bomber, a reader's
pick for the week.*

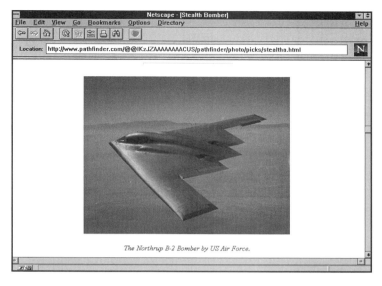

http://www.pathfinder.com/@@7JKNogAAAAAAACgS/pathfinder/
photo/picks/stealtha.html

Figure 19.6
*Sandra Bullock at home, from a
recent feature in People.*

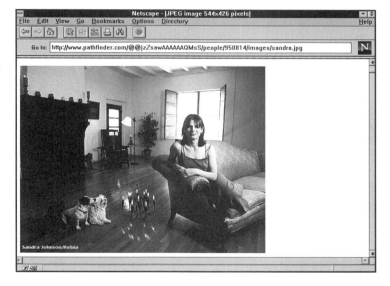

http://www.pathfinder.com/@@jXKKMgAAAAAAABYS/people/950814/
images/sandra.jpg

Figure 19.7

Motley Crue, in the Elektra
Records section of Pathfinder.

http://www.pathfinder.com/@@joNEewAAAAAAQC0S/elektra/artists/
motley/motley.jpg

Figure 19.8

Scene from a computer game,
Conqueror: A.D. 1086, from
Time-Warner Interactive.

http://www.pathfinder.com/@@02vfBAAAAAAACwS/twi/conqdir/
bttlewin.gif

Figure 19.9

From Artslink, a metal sculpture by Tsai Wen-ying called "Square Tops."

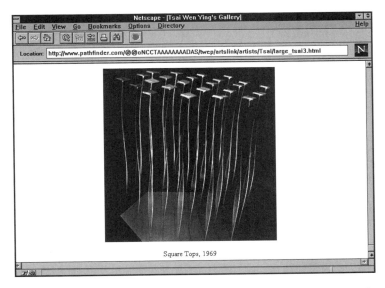

Square Tops, 1969

http://www.pathfinder.com/@@oNCCTAAAAAAAADAS/twep/artslink/artists/Tsai/large_tsai3.html

More Than Magazines

The Time-Warner empire is not limited to magazines. You'll find a link here to Elektra Records, where you'll find photos—often several of them—of recording artists on this label. You can also download video and sound clips.

If you're looking for something from the silver screen, try the Pathfinder's Reviews link, which takes you to movie reviews, including a photo from the flick, from any Time-Warner publications.

Another entertainment project is Grooves, a combo Internet/CD project, which features little-known up-and-comers in the music world. This is really a music and text site, but there is a picture of every artist.

If you want to get an advance look at some upcoming computer games and CD-ROMs, you can check out Time Warner Interactive, where you'll see screen shots of the company's latest products, and some that haven't hit the market yet.

Pathfinder also has an online art gallery of its own, called Artslink. This gallery is part of the section called Time-Warner Electronic publishing.

When we looked, the gallery featured about a half-dozen artists. Some works were shown in virtual galleries, where the images are "hung" on virtual walls and you click your way through the gallery, turning corners and looking down corridors to get to the pictures. If you can fight your way through this, you'll get a look at some exceptional images.

The Virtual Garden

One of the most popular destinations on the Internet is the Virtual Garden, a part of Pathfinder with so much depth it's scary.

You'll find gardening articles, usually well illustrated and photographed, from *Sunset Magazine*, which circulates in the American West, and from *Southern Living*, a southern regional publication.

Many of these articles have photos or diagrams of the flowers or gardening techniques they are discussing, although in general, we found the magazine sites rather stingy with photos.

Maybe photos aren't that essential, however, because a few clicks away you'll find the Time Life Electronic Gardening Encyclopedia, which has photos and information on about 3,000 plants. It has a search engine as well: Type in a common name and the encyclopedia delivers a list of all the plants with that in their name or description.

Entering the search term "rose" produced 60 hits, some with several entries beneath them. For example, clicking on tea roses brought up a list of nine such roses.

The House Plant pavilion contains two separate directories, one for foliage plants and the other for flowering plants. The directories list only the names, but clicking on a name brings up a color picture of the flower. With more than 200 plants listed, it's a valuable resource for the indoor gardener.

Finally, you'll also find an illustrated Project Directory here with illustrated guides to performing basic and advanced gardening tasks in both landscaping and basic gardening. The landscaping files are in Adobe Acrobat format, which the Webmaster notes provides superior illustration capabilities, and can also be taken to a job site. The basic gardening series are available as both Adobe Acrobat files or as standard HTML, which you can view directly with your Web browser. ▲

Graphics Sites Reviewed in Ch 20

In addition to this chapter's best of the best, read about these sites in Ch 20.

ArtServe

http://rubens.anu.edu.au/

A vast database of architecture and ruins from ancient Greek and Roman sites, European prints from 1400 to 1900, prehistoric British ritual monuments, Islamic architecture, the entire text of a book on Diocletian's residence at Split, and some views of modern Hong Kong architecture.

Babes On The Web

http://www.tyrell.net/~robtoups/BABE.html

A listing of good-looking women who have pictures of themselves on their Web pages.

Babes On The Web II

http://ucsub.colorado.edu/~kritzber/new/babes.html

A listing of good-looking men who have pictures of themselves on their Web pages.

Dead Sea Scrolls

http://sunsite.unc.edu/expo/deadsea.scrolls.exhibit/intro.html

Images from the Dead Sea Scrolls and from the community that wrote and preserved them.

DIVA

http://www.monash.edu.au/visarts/diva/diva.html

DIVA stands for Digital Images from the Visual Arts Library at Monash University, in Melbourne Australia, and it is a treasure trove of visual images in the arts, architecture, aboriginal art, video, and garden and landscape design.

Electric Postcards

http://postcards.www.media.mit.edu:80/Postcards/

Want to send a postcard to your friends over the Net? Pick out a card from here, enter their e-mail addresses and they'll get a notice that they can pick up a postcard from this site.

FUNET

ftp://pictures@ftp.funet.fi/pub/pics/

A general, all-purpose directory with thousands of files and images under various categories. If you're accessing it from outside Scandinavia, it requires that you use this URL (don't put http:// in front of it), and it will ask you for a password. Fill in your e-mail address as the password.

Jon's Image Archive

http://lynx.uio.no/jon/gif/

A reasonably well-organized archive of images from many sources and on many topics. Strong on animals and Nordic scenery.

Missing Children Database

http://www.scubed.com:8001/public_service/listing.html

Pictures of missing children from around the world, and in the U.S., by state.

NetCam

http://www-white.media.mit.edu/~steve/netcam.html

This guy wears a camera on his head. The results go on the Internet.

On-line Visual Literacy

http://www.pomona.claremont.edu/visual-lit/intro/intro.html

An excellent exploration of how we see and how artists work, liberally illustrated with some QuickTime movies to add to the effect.

Rob's Multimedia Lab (RML)

http://www.acm.uiuc.edu/rml/

A huge collection of movies, fractals, pictures, sounds, and other multimedia resources. One of the best on the Net.

Smithsonian FTP Site

ftp://photo1.si.edu/images/gif89a/

Miscellaneous images of air and space technology, Afro American Art from the National Museum of Art, science and technology, including animals, and technology history.

SUNET

ftp://ftp.sunet.se/pub/pictures/

A huge, general archive of photographs, art, and other images.

Web Voyeur

http://www.eskimo.com/%7Eirving/web-voyeur/

Links to cameras that are connected to the Internet.

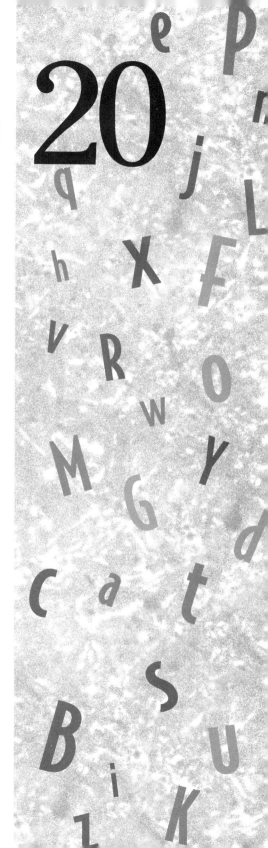

Graphics Sites from A to Z

GRAPHICS IS WHAT this book is about: how you can find pictures and images on the Internet that can increase your enjoyment, understanding, and who knows, maybe even your income. For example,

▼ You can download screensavers directly from some sites on the Internet or convert the images into screensavers or decorative wallpaper for your computer screen.

▼ The Net is loaded with hundreds of images from the world's finest painters, photographers, and other artists. It's the largest showcase of art, both contemporary and classic, that you're ever likely to have in your home or office.

▼ The Internet may have the perfect graphics—a map or clip art—for your newsletter or business presentation. All you have to do is save the image to your disk.

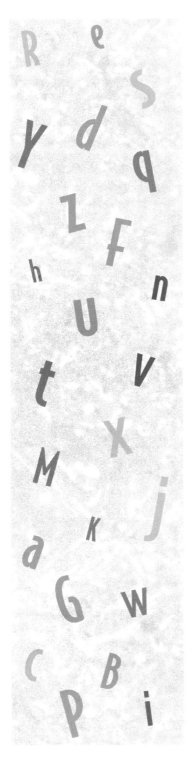

We have visited over 3,000 of the better-known graphics sites on the Internet to come up with this hotlist of some of the best graphics sites. In choosing these sites, we considered the following:

▼ Does the site have enough images to warrant a visit from someone interested in seeing graphics? Are the graphics well chosen, unique, or particularly striking?

▼ Is the graphics quality high, with clean, well-cropped, and properly sized images, good color, and sharpness?

▼ Is this site well designed? Can you identify the contents easily, and quickly jump to the section you want? Is it easy to move around in the site? Are the links up-to-date? Do sections or items have understandable names? Are sections divided into manageable chunks and organized well?

▼ Are images well sized, neither so small that detail is lost, nor so large that you can't fit them on you screen?

▼ Is the site modem-aware? Does it use logos, thumbnails, and other graphical devices efficiently for those on slower connections to the Net? Does it tell visitors the size of larger images so they can tell in advance how long it might take to download the images?

@Art

SEE RELATED SITES:

Ch 6 ART IN CYBERSPACE
Ch 13 PHOTOGRAPHY

@ART IS A SPARE, lean exhibit site on the Net with a great deal of intelligence and careful selection behind it.

The focus of the site is what the curators call the "second generation" of digital art, a more mature phase of computer-generated or computer-modified art where the computer and associated technology has begun to disappear and art is emerging in which the computer is often invisible. At the same time, the exhibit acknowledges the reality and presence of the new digital world and the new forms of human interaction which it brings.

Rebeca Bollinger's "Online Dance Hall Girls" is perhaps the most direct demonstration. Images of women's faces, pulled off the Net from who-knows-what newsgroup (we were afraid to ask) are arranged in collages that look at female identity in the "invisible social spaces of communication technologies," says Bollinger.

Another artist, Gloria DeFilipps Brush, combines images from household spaces, knick-knacks, and architectural features into new, often troubling designs and spaces where perspectives and relative sizes are twisted in

An image from Gloria DeFilipps Brush at @Art.

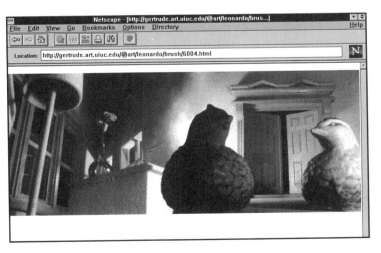

http://gertrude.art.uiuc.edu/@art/leonardo/brush/6004.html

ways that we don't normally see. Though modified with a computer, the images are seamless and photographic.

With about a half-dozen artists represented in all, the exhibit touches many other bases, including science, personal histories, and modern mythologies, such as the effects and memories of the Holocaust.

Clicking on the Archive link brings up a few more galleries of artists whose work has been featured in the past, and some of their images, which you can view. ▲

3D Strange Attractors and Similar Objects

 http://ccrma-www.stanford.edu/~stilti/images/chaotic_attractors/nav.html

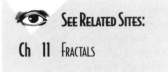

SEE RELATED SITES:

Ch 11 FRACTALS

TIM STILSON'S PAGE on "strange attractors" demonstrates the truly weird and wonderful stuff that can come out of fractals.

This site not only has a large number of fractals, but Stilson's standards of quality are very high. He takes the fractal form and applies techniques like ray-tracing, which give the images shadows and highlights, image manipulation with Photoshop, and out-of-focus backgrounds to create powerful and striking images.

Strange attractors are a type of fractal formula that can create solid-looking, three-dimensional objects. It's hard to describe these objects because they are purely imaginary, but when fixed up with a ray tracing formula and set against a photographic background they become powerful, nuanced works of art.

They have the look and texture of steel or wood sculpture, sometimes with solid blocks, other times with delicate traceries.

On the home page you'll see a few sample images from each group, and a More of These link. Clicking on More of These brings up another page with images related, stylistically and mathematical, to that group on the home page.

Here's what you'll find in some of the groups:

The "polynomial strange attractors" create strongly curved planes and solids, and resemble sculptures cut from metal.

Stilson's "fsh" attractors often create more delicate curved forms, and some have an almost liquid quality to them. Stilson uses special ray-tracing techniques to deliver the three-dimensional look of these images.

The small collection of "Chaos game objects" shows how fractals can generate regular geometric shapes, based on triangles and squares. Building these up and putting them into various shapes and colors creates cubes and pyramids. ▲

This gallery of "polynomial strange attractors" pushes fractal design clearly into the world of art.

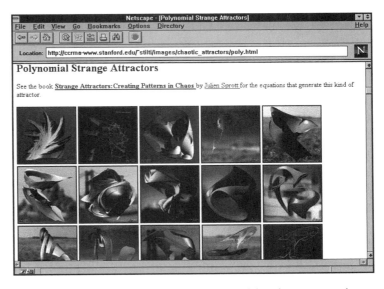

http://ccrma-www.stanford.edu/~stilti/images/chaotic_attractors/poly.html

911 Gallery

 http://www.iquest.net/911/iq_911.html

See Related Sites:

Ch 5 Art Galleries
Ch 10 Computer-Generated Art

KEYWORDS: ART GALLERIES, computer-generated art

911 is a real art gallery in Indianapolis (named after its street number, not the emergency telephone number) that specializes in electronic media and computer-generated art.

It has a real presence as well as a site on the Net, so its work is shown in both physical and virtual galleries: on walls in its physical gallery for non-digital viewers to get a look at what digital artists are doing, and on the Net for networked people to view.

There's a lot of art on this site, and it's top notch stuff: digital art good enough to hang on a wall.

The site has a Current Show with several images visible and a statement about the artist.

Going into the Previous Shows area brings up several collections featured here earlier. Within each collection you'll find a half-dozen images, of which only one or two can be clicked on to view and enlarge. But the thumbnails are large enough to give a good look at the images in the exhibition.

When we visited, seven previous exhibitions were available for viewing, which makes a rich feast for the digital connoisseur.

"Tracks Through a Pulp Forest"
by David Herrold.

http://www.iquest.net/911/tracktre.jpg

The artists here use a variety of digital techniques. Some use photo manipulation to create photographic manipulations. Others use the computer as a drawing tool with which they create original art.

In the Print Gallery link you'll find a section with prints from yet another artist.

Then there's a Traveling Exhibits gallery, which shows the work of digital artists from elsewhere whose work is visible at the 911 gallery.

One artist, Walter Wright, uses digital manipulation in connection with video to produce digital videos, clips of which can be downloaded from the Web site. ▲

alt.binaries.pictures.fractals

See Related Sites:

Ch 11 Fractals

Fans of the fractal art form will want to check out this newsgroup occasionally to catch up on the most innovative fractal work being done on the Net.

As a newsgroup you'll find this far less static than the galleries on the Web. This newsgroup is so popular, in fact, that serious fractal collectors make sure someone

downloads new images for them while they are on vacation, so they won't miss any. There's currently no archive site where you can find messages and images that have been posted in the past.

This newsgroup's main purpose is to let people who design and generate fractals share their work with others. You'll also find pointers to

A fractal downloaded from the alt.binaries.pictures.fractals newsgroup.

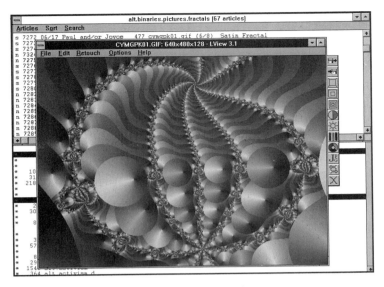

CYMGPK01.GIF, in alt.binaries.pictures.fractals

other sites on the Internet that specialize in fractals, tips on using the very popular Fractint program, included on the CD-ROM included with this book, and parameter files that are used to create specific fractal images.

This is not the only newgroup devoted to fractals. There are a few others you might check out:

▼ sci.fractals has a more scientific approach so you'll find more heavy-duty math here than pictures.

▼ alt.fractals, but it is often empty.

▼ alt.fractals.pictures, which tends to have fewer images and less action than alt.binaries.pictures.fractals.

As is usual with newsgroups, you'll need to know the basics about downloading images from newsgroups to use this one. The images do not appear directly in the newsgroups, but are specially encoded files that must be decoded before you can view them. Check Chapter 23, "Getting Graphics from the Net," for more information downloading files from newsgroups.

One problem with any newsgroup in the alt.binaries area is that because binary (computer-readable, as opposed to human-readable) files are so large, and because this is such a popular area for sexually-explicit material, some service providers may not provide this newsgroup. That's unfortunate, because this group has some great material in it. ▲

Acanthus Virtual Gallery

 http://cad9.cadlab.umanitoba.ca/Virtual_Gallery.html

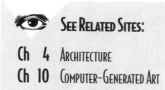

SEE RELATED SITES:

Ch 4 ARCHITECTURE
Ch 10 COMPUTER-GENERATED ART

MANY WEB SITES related to architecture come from architectural schools or universities where designing architectural models is part of the course, and if they're a little extreme, well, no one will ever have to live or work in your model.

The models at Acanthus are different: they are the work of real architects who get paid to design and supervise the construction of real buildings that real people live and work in.

The site is run by a university computer-aided design laboratory to demonstrate how architects actually use the technology in their daily work.

Computers have affected not only the design and drafting side of the profession, but the nature of architectural collaboration, as you will discover when you visit some of the working Canadian architects featured at this site.

Barry Pendergast and Carman Bennett work together, but only digitally speaking: their working spaces are linked by a network, as they work on projects that emphasize housing, community planning and churches, and government offices. A recent assignment, for a demanding government client, involved designing an electronic prototype for a long-term care hospital room.

Electronic prototype of a long-term care room.

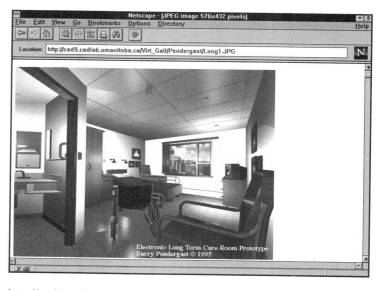

http://cad9.cadlab.umanitoba.ca/Virt_Gall/Pendergast/Long1.JPG

Saskatchewan architect Derek Kindrachuk shows work done on some public buildings and private residences. Winnipeg-based Michael Boreskie has designed many churches and religious spaces and is a member of the North American Church Planning Resource Centre. One of his major commissions was development of the altar for a papal mass held in Winnipeg in 1984. ▲

Papal mass site designed by Michael Boreskie.

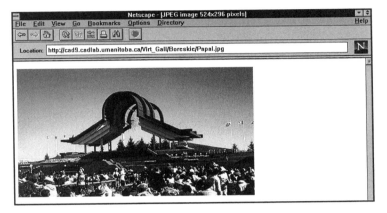

http://cad9.cadlab.umanitoba.ca/Virt_Gall/Boreskie/Papal.jpg

African Art, National Museum of

 http://www.si.edu/organiza/museums/africart/homepage/nmafa.htm

 **See Related Sites:**

Ch 7 Art Museums

As this site demonstrates, Africa has a rich artistic heritage that was expressed in not only ritual and decorative objects, but in everyday affairs.

The site specializes in African art from south of the Sahara. Like many of the Smithsonian's Web sites, this one hints at far more than it delivers. The number of images visible from the Net comes nowhere near close to representing the museum's actual collection.

Those that are here, though excellent quality, are not large, even when you click on them. Images are used primarily to illustrate key points in the text, rather than as information points themselves.

The exhibits on the Net correspond to actual exhibitions in the museum. When we looked, they included:
▼ Images of Power and Identity
▼ Pottery as a Woman's Art in Central Africa
▼ The Art of the Personal Object

- ▼ Point of View Gallery
- ▼ The Ancient Nubian City of Kerma
- ▼ The Ancient West African City of Benin

The exhibits showed the richness of decorative and craft arts in Africa, and also the daily attention to beauty. The "personal objects" exhibit, for example, has a simple headrest elaborately carved in the shape of an animal.

In the women's pottery section you see that everyday cooking and storage vessels were often carefully decorated and pigmented.

The Point of View Gallery includes some work done by photographer Eliot Elisofon, but don't go there expecting to see a portfolio of Africa: the Net version shows only two images from this great photographer, which is disappointing, given that the museum's photo collection consists of more than 250,000 color slides and black and white photos. As one of very few sites covering this subject matter now, this site is useful, but the Museum of African Art would be even more useful if we actually got to see more African art. ▲

A terra cotta equestrian figure from Mali.

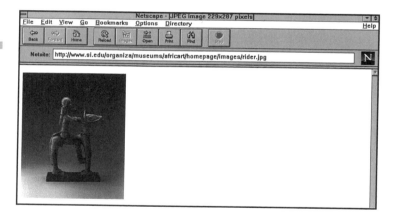

http://www.si.edu/organiza/museums/africart/homepage/images/
rider.jpg

Akira Picture Archive

http://www.informatik.tu-muenchen.de/cgi-bin/nph-gateway/hphalle8/~rehrl/
Akira.archive.html

See Related Sites:

Ch 3 Animation & Cartoons
Ch 15 Science Fiction

AKIRA IS THE MOST ambitious of epic Japanese anime, and perhaps one of the finest of any form of animation. We cheered to find that the Akira Picture Archive contains a large sampling of .jpgs and GIFs from both the animated movie and comic book.

With the exception of a small graphic at the top of the site, the Akira Picture Archive doesn't preview any images from the anime, and the index doesn't provide the size of the files.

For the *Akira*-novice, it's potluck as to what the graphic will look like and how long it might take to transfer. We downloaded a few of the files, and found no predictability to the file size (29Kb to over 200Kb!).

The anime images are mostly color single frames, while the manga list contained both single and multiple-panel images scanned from the original B&W version of the comic book. Because the anime images were captured from the video, they're slightly fuzzy and look like they could use a wash through a Photoshop "sharpen" filter. (See Chapter 24, "Viewing & Using Graphics from the Net," for more information on enhancing graphics.) ▲

Akira's protagonist, Kaneda, downloaded from the Akira manga images.

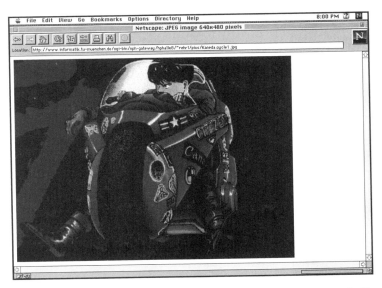

http://www.informatik.tu-muenchen.de/cgi-bin/nph-gateway/hphalle8/
~rehrl/Akira.archive.html

Alias/Wavefront

 http://www.alias.com/

 See Related Sites:

Ch 3 Animation & Cartoons
Ch 10 Computer-Generated Art

Morphing, explosions, weird animals and mutants, strange landscapes. Few companies are as intimately involved with these things as Alias Research, Wavefront, and Silicon Graphics. The first two are software companies whose code can create all these special effects, either as straight animation or mixing them with live action.

The third makes the best animation workstations in the world, on which the Hollywood studios and major video companies depend to move artificial worlds at real-life speed or faster.

You may not be able to afford what these companies produce, but at this site you can at least window shop. It's studded with images and animations that show off what these people can do.

When you get to the site you'll have a couple of image-laden options. Clicking on Overview of Alias/Wavefront products will put you into a gallery describing the software products. These galleries are peppered with images and animations, but if you want the images and animations without the heavy advertising, plow through a few welcome screens from the home page until you get to a link to Alien Nation. Click on the Welcome link, and you'll find access to an images gallery, an animation gallery and an Alias Sketch gallery.

These galleries display the best work of some of the people who use Alias/Wavefront products to create computer and video games and television special effects, in the form of still images and MPEG movies.

The MPEGs depict way-out stuff like fantasy creatures and explosions, or a disembodied hand drumming its fingers on a table, but also subtle real-world effects such as snow falling past a street lantern, hair waving in the wind, smoke billowing from a smoke stack. None of them are monstrous in size, and some come in small and large sizes, so it's not impossible for someone with a modem connection to download animations. ▲

Mysterious faces, with a marble-like skin, drawn by Gil Bruvel.

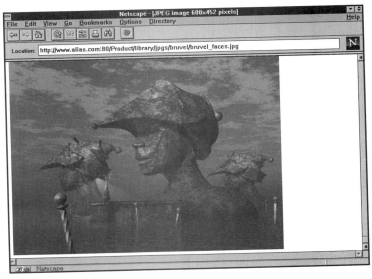

http://www.alias.com:80/Product/library/jpgs/bruvel/bruvel_faces.jpg

Alien

 http://dutial.twi.tudelft.nl/~alien/alien.html

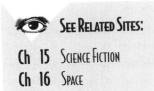 **See Related Sites:**

Ch 15 Science Fiction
Ch 16 Space

THE MOVIE *Alien* and its counterparts made an indelible mark on the quality of science fiction movies. Following the vision of Swiss-born H.R. Giger, the film's images continue to haunt the Internet, much as the movie itself lingers in the minds of its viewers.

Visitors to this site will find high-quality scans from all three movies (*Alien, Aliens,* and *Alien 3*), sounds, other

A photograph of the incredibly moody alien queen.

http://dutial.twi.tudelft.nl/~alien/pics/queen05.gif

Giger art, background information, breakdowns and images of the futuristic weapons, and intimate detail (and more photos) of the alien lifecycle. And don't rush off without looking at Roman's Collection, photographs of a true alienphile.

The Giger index contains B&W sketches, scans of various cover art, and photographs of his work, himself, his family, and a few of his friends. If you link over to the Giger page, you can download images of a bar in Tokyo fitted to Giger's design, and pictures taken from a Giger/Swatch project.

The life and death of one of the fallen marines in *Aliens* is also documented, through a link to Wierzbowski Hunters. You can download the movie clip of his death, and follow step-by-step the few scenes in which he appears.

The images from the Jaguar Alien Game are low-resolution. We were much more excited by the scenes from the Alien version of Doom. You, the player, are caught in the dark tunnels, armed with only a handgun as the sound of scraping claws against metal pumps the last vestiges of adrenaline through your system.

Don't worry. On the Internet, no one can here you scream (unless they have the sound files, which are also available here). ▲

Robert Altman's Photography Gallery

 http://www.cea.edu/robert/x.index.html

 SEE RELATED SITES:

Ch 8 CELEBRITIES & ENTERTAINMENT

Ch 13 PHOTOGRAPHY

FOR MANY YEARS the chief photographer for *Rolling Stone* magazine, Robert Altman has gone digital, to the everlasting thanks of baby boomers whose era he helped define photographically.

Altman was not merely an observer of the American popular scene, but in some ways a key participant in shaping public perceptions of these artists and times.

His most famous and enduring work chronicles the '60s, and it may bring tears to the eyes of some baby boomers to visit a site that celebrates the music and the sensitivities of that time. You'll find the great movements of the era here: anti-war marches, city kids pushing plows as part of the back-to-the-land movement, confrontations with police.

You'll also see portraits of important players, such as Timothy Leary, Jane Fonda, Caesar Chavez, Dennis Hopper, and Ken Kesey.

But *Rolling Stone* was primarily about music, and that side of Altman's work that dominates this site.

There's a special gallery of The Rolling Stones (the group, not the magazine) pictures, and a pantheon of other famous artists: Jim Morrisson at The Fillmore East, Janis Joplin at the Avelon Ballroom in San Francisco, and folks like Boz Scaggs, Iggy Pop, Joe Cocker, Grace Slick, Chuck Berry, and Bo Didley, and the infamous Tina Turner cover of *Rolling Stone*.

The images from the '60s and '70s are often shots of live performances or recording sessions. In the Woman gallery, you'll find more reflective portraits of friends and models.

Most images are in black and white, which is the medium that Altman used during his career with *Rolling Stone*. Don't let that stop you: Altman, like many other top photographers of that day, used black and white's power very effectively to create shapes and define textures. ▲

Altman's photo of Janis Joplin has become the definitive view of the gritty vocalist.

http://www.cea.edu/robert/JanisJoplin.jpeg

Alternative Virtual Biennial

 http://www.interport.net/avb/

Ch 6 ART IN CYBERSPACE

CHAPTER 6, "Art in Cyberspace," explains how the Internet has given exposure to artists who may have been turned down by snooty museums.

We've never met anyone from the Whitney Museum in New York, so have no reason to believe their taste is anything but impeccable, but the people at Alternative Virtual Biennial have a different view. They bill this site as a site for artists to "work with new aesthetics that are not recognized by the Whitney Museum of New York."

Those aesthetics, according to the essay that you will get when you head for the exhibition pages, are a reaction to the "low-culture," confrontational art that seems to be so popular today. By connecting their art to the visual vocabulary of the past, of the Renaissance and traditional sacred art, for example, they want to speak a "language of humanism" that puts the weight of tradition and our common symbol systems behind modern art. The goal is not to resurrect the art of the past, but to use its visual language to address today's situations, the essay says.

Since this is the Internet, you get to play curator by visiting this site.

Amy Ernst, granddaughter of surrealist painter Max Ernst, displays what she calls "Renaissance Surrealism" in which the styles of Renaissance painting are used in compositions where fragments of reality are juxtaposed in a very modern way.

Vincent Romaniello's paintings have classical compositions and perspectives, and are based on materials used during the Renaissance, but deal with modern intellectual dilemmas.

Paul Warren and Catsua Watanabe look at religious icons, painting saintlike faces in new settings and contexts, often using computers to produce digital effects.

John Wellington's style is classical and realistic, but he places his subjects in modern landscapes, often in urban settings where the buildings of our time take on a kind of ethereal perfection. ▲

"Sleeping Worker" by John Wellington.

http://www.interport.net:80/avb/JWIMG1.jpeg

Art Metal

 http://wuarchive.wustl.edu/edu/arts/metal/Gallery/Gallery.html

SEE RELATED SITES:

Ch 5 ART GALLERIES

THEY PROUDLY CALL themselves blacksmiths, but these forgers of metal have more in mind than making plows and shoeing horses.

This site shows off the work of a group of artists who all work in some way with metal. Depending on the technology or the materials they work with, they come under names as diverse as blacksmiths, "whitesmiths," jewelers, sculptors, and blade-smiths.

The techniques, materials, and styles of the artists shown here are varied.

Enrique Vega specializes in forged metals, creating metal accents, sculptures, and installations designed to complement residential, business, or commercial spaces. His pieces range in size from small accent pieces to a 12-foot high sundial placed in a mall.

Hank Kaminsky works with sand-matrix techniques to produce smaller items such as jewelry, small sculptures, and decanters, while David Hoffman creates fantastic shapes out of forged metals.

Nol Putnam is a blacksmith who works primarily with wrought iron, producing gates, banisters, and other architectural features out of a metal most of us consider hard and unforgiving, but which this blacksmith calls "fluid, strong and delicate at the same time."

Each artist provides thumbnails of art that you can click on to get a larger image. Vega's selection is so extensive that it is divided into subgalleries to help you navigate around it. He also shows some of the CAD drawings that he relies on to design and develop many of his pieces. ▲

A metal child's mask by Enrique Vega, a la a certain cartoon woodpecker.

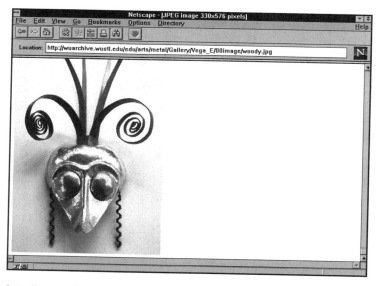

http://wuarchive.wustl.edu/edu/arts/metal/Gallery/Vega_E/00image/Woody.jpg

Anecdote

 http://anecdote.com/

See Related Sites:

Ch 6 Art in Cyberspace

THE ANECDOTE IS an underground club in Ann Arbor, Michigan, that provides space on its walls for local artists. That art is also posted on the club's Internet site.

The Internet site tends to be limited to the current exhibition in the club, which means the number of images is low, but they will change on a regular basis. The site also promises to add more art in the future.

To see the art, go to the Art Gallery section from the home page. When we were there, two artists were represented, one with eight images, another with 16. The listing for each

artist will take you to that artist's individual page. The gallery helpfully tells you not only how many thumbnails you'll find in the gallery, but their total size, which is helpful for those on modem connections who'd like an idea of how long they might have to wait.

When we were there, one of the featured artists was Julia Gardiner, who works with latex on canvas. Her images show a bold, casual style with rather downbeat themes—Guilt and Shame, Demons, Rack of Lamb, Eaten Alive, and so on.

The other artist was Saint Ryan whose models probably count among the smallest ever used by an artist: protozoa and diatoms (that's what you get for working in a university town). It turns out that these tiny plants and animals have rather fantastic shapes, which Saint Ryan uses as an inspiration to develop a gallery of "microscopic angels and devils."

A final, but memorable feature of this gallery is its Ann Arbor Classic Cards, which in the true spirit of university life, feature photos of nude women interacting with everyday crowds in Ann Arbor's business district. ▲

"Communal Diatomaceous Pirana Wannabe." Saint Ryan's work is inspired by microscopic protozoa, some of which look like monsters or angels.

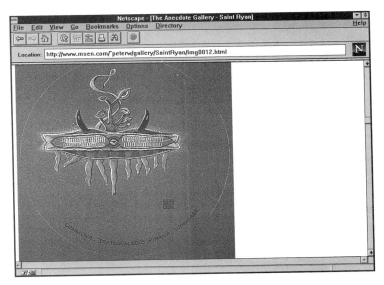

http://www.msen.com/~peterw/gallery/SaintRyan/img0012.html

Ansel Adams Home Page

 http://bookweb.cwis.uci.edu:8042/AdamsHome.html

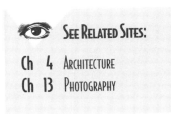 **SEE RELATED SITES:**

Ch 4 ARCHITECTURE
Ch 13 PHOTOGRAPHY

ANSEL ADAMS DOMINATED American landscape photography in the 1950s and 1960s with memorable images of mountain and desert scenery that are still extremely popular.

This site shows off the work of this photographic master, although not necessarily in the way we would like.

A computer screen is not the best way to view Adams' images. His famous Zone System for photography enabled him to photograph landscapes with dramatic highlights and shadows, which maintained subtle gradations of detail. Only the best printing comes close to reproducing what Adams achieved on photographic prints.

The bulk of the photographs at this site are from a major commercial assignment that Adams undertook in the late 1960s to photograph the campuses of the University of California.

Possibly because Adams permanently re-defined the black and white landscape, the images may look rather conventional, but they bear the marks of Adams' impeccable craftsmanship as a photographer, even if university campuses aren't at the top of your list of favorite photographic subjects. The exhibit also has photos of some of the faculty members and the research they were working on at the time.

And if you do want to look at California architecture, you'll find few sites that show its public architecture as well, from a distance and in detail.

Some of the more pictorial photographs contain AU sound files in which Adams describes how he took the photograph.

If you want to see the work for which Adams is better known, take the link to the Exhibition Bookstore link, and find your way to the Museum Graphic Note Cards. That will link you to a display of all of Adams most famous images.

Unfortunately, since these are scanned off the postcards, the image quality is much lower than the University of California campus pictures. ▲

Adams could hold both shadow and highlight detail even in the harsh desert sun, as in this photo of a trip to Joshua Tree National Monument.

http://bookweb.cwis.uci.edu:8042/AdamsFull/038.gif

ArtServe

http://rubens.anu.edu.au/

👁 **See Related Sites:**

Ch 4 Architecture
Ch 7 Art Museums

This Australian National University collection may be the largest single collection of images on the Net.

Winner of a 1994 Best of the Net award, its database contains more than 13,000 images. Not all of them will interest everyone, of course. It helps to be particularly interested in ancient Mediterranean architecture because more than 8,500 of these images cover hundreds of sites in Egypt, Turkey, Greece, Italy, and elsewhere.

For those interested in European art, the site has about 2,800 images of European prints, from the 15th to the end of the 19th century.

For the scholar or student, the site offers database searches to help navigate through it all. You can select images from the Mediterranean architecture database by archeological or geographic location, by type, and by name.

The database of prints can similarly be searched by artist, period, type of work, or subject.

The quality of some of these images could use some work, but many are available as both full views and more detailed closeups. Most of the prints and architectural photos are in black and white.

Another link adds access to another 3,281 images on laserdisc covering classical and medieval architecture.

The site also includes an essay, photographs and historical prints of Diocletian's palace at Split, a quick overview of important archeological sites in Turkey, many pictures of Islamic architecture and, for a change of pace, pictures of modern Hong Kong architecture.

Webmaster Michael Greenhalgh, professor of art history at the Australian National University, has also put an entire book about *The Greek & Roman Cities of Western Turkey* online here. Oddly, it is not illustrated and has no links to illustrations in the database. Given the amount of work it takes to simply get the database online and all the images properly cataloged, we can hope illustrations will be coming in the future. ▲

20

"1831-1903 Church and Farm at Eragny," an 1890 print by Camille Pissarro.

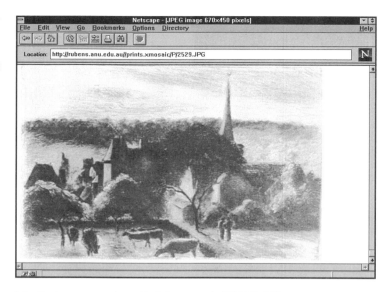

http://rubens.anu.edu.au//prints.xmosaic/P/2529.JPG

Court of the Myrtles at the Alhambra, Granada

http://rubens.anu.edu.au/islam/pics/100/068.JPG

Art.Online

 http://bighorn.terra.net/artonline/

See Related Sites:

Ch 5 Art Galleries

ART.ONLINE OFFERS commercial artists a serious chance to get their work on the Internet.

Few of the images at this site will raise many eyebrows in the critical art world, but for those looking for a rest from digital gimmickry, bizarre juxtapositions, seizure-inducing color schemes and the like, Art.Online will be a true oasis.

The art at this site is scenic, positive, and quietly powerful or inspiring.

Artists represented here cover topics such as wildlife art, African American art, nautical art, Southwestern, Western, and Native American art, and rock & roll art. In some cases, (for example, wildlife art and nautical art), only one artist is represented, but you may find a dozen or more images to view. In other cases

(African American art), you'll find a dozen artists, each represented by one or two images.

The home page has some good-sized thumbnails on it that can help you gauge the style of the artist or section. Clicking on that brings you to the artist's galleries where, again, you can click on an image to enlarge it.

The section on Western, Southwestern, and Native American Artists offers some of both: many of the artists here have several images showcasing their work.

This site isn't snobbish when in comes to prices, either. Most of the images are available as posters or prints at prices under $100. For those looking for something they can both hang in their home or office without apology, and still afford, this might be a good place to start. ▲

"Cousins by the Dozens," by Paul Goodnight.

http://bighorn.terra.net/artonline/images/cousin.gif

Atlanta Photography Group

 http://www.mindspring.com/~baird/apg/index.html

 **See Related Sites:**

Ch 6 Art in Cyberspace
Ch 13 Photography

The Atlanta Photography Group is a collection of 350 photographers in Georgia who share both physical and virtual gallery space.

In both cases, exhibits change quite frequently, so you'll want to visit this gallery every so often to see what these people are up to.

Each month the current exhibit changes, but the previous month's exhibit is accessible through another link.

When we were there, the site had some excellent black and white landscapes by Matt Lennert, and some strong, posterized figure studies by

Comer Jennings, plus a black and white documentary on people who attend a site of religious visions in Georgia.

To further showcase the work of its members, the gallery has a Push Pin page. Clicking on any of the images there (five when we visited) brings up a larger gallery of work on that or similar themes by a particular photographer. Some include an artist's statement and all have an e-mail address for responding to the artist.

It's important to keep clicking as you go through the Push Pin section. What appears to be thumbnails are in many cases merely buttons or icons that access a completely different image. Those on modem connections, in particular should not be tempted to leave it at the thumbnails, because they'll miss much of the meat of this section.

We saw some exceptional and thoughtful work at this site, both in the featured exhibitions and the Push Pin gallery. Craig Scogin's montages and Laura Reilein's moving essay on childhood, family, and control were particularly strong. ▲

An image from Comer Jennings Lennert at the Atlanta Photography Group.

http://www.mindspring.com/~baird/apg/pages.html/index.page/Artist2/comer5.JPG

Atlanta Photojournalism Seminar

 http://www.mindspring.com/~frankn/atlanta/

 **See Related Sites:**

Ch 12 News, Weather, & Sports

Ch 13 Photography

The Atlanta Photojournalism Seminar began as a regional event, as its name implies, but has become a major photojournalism event.

For those interested in the state of the art in photojournalism, this site has the winning photos, plus thumbnails of many runners up, from its prestigious photojournalism competition.

When we visited, the best way to view the photographs was to click on the link to the previous year's (the seminars are typically held in late November or early December) winners. There you'll find the winning photographs in more than a dozen categories. You'll also be able to click on a link that will take you to a contact sheet (thumbnails) of the runners up in each category.

One disorienting feature about this site is that, when we looked, very few of the photos had captions, so you sometimes have to guess what the

20

subject of the picture is or the circumstances under which it was taken.

In spite of its international reputation, the APS is still a predominantly southern show, with most of the participants and winners being from Dixie newspapers or schools.

This is a site that should become more valuable over the years. While it has lists of previous year's winners, going back to the 1970s, only this year's winners have links to their winning photos, online. If they keep doing this however, the site should become a valuable resource for those interested in photojournalism as time goes by. ▲

Intensity in the face of an athlete in this image from the Atlanta Photojournalism Seminar site.

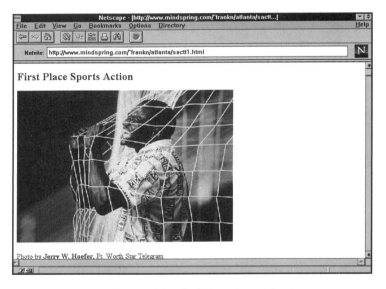

http://www.mindspring.com/~frankn/atlanta/sactt1.html

ArchiGopher

 gopher://libra.arch.umich.edu:70/11

ArchiGopher was one of the earlier efforts to encourage cooperation among architects on the Internet, by offering images, architectural models, and other forms of inspiration. Its directories are a rather quirky collection of material, which is what makes it a fun place to visit.

However, the text documentation is uneven and missing completely in some cases, and the whole site would benefit from a tune-up. Many of the images are smaller than we would like to see, as well.

Directories here cover a variety of architectural and artistic themes: Greek architecture, Italian Classical Architecture, 3D Computer-Aided Design Models, the painter Kandinsky, Renaissance architect Andrea Palladio, and most intriguing, a section on Lunar Architecture, that is, structures built on the moon.

The most image intensive area is under the Greek Architecture section, where you'll find some good color photography of important sites of Greek architecture, such as the Acropolis, Delphi, Mycenae, Olympia, and the Temple of Apollo.

The Images of 3D CAD models includes a section on a CAD model of a Volvo and, more interesting to non-Volvo owners, about 25 examples of student work involving computer-aided design.

The section on Lunar Architecture, though speculative at this point, pokes fun at early conceptions of lunar settlement as glass-shielded pods on the surface of the moon and argues that the Babylonian Ziggurat makes more sense, since radiation shielding alone would require that lunar settlements be covered by at least 10 feet of moon soil. You'll find here a couple of pictures of old ideas as well as some speculative designs for massive (everything weighs much less on the moon, so it's easier to build this way) structures for humans. ▲

By the light of the silvery Earth…

gopher://libra.caup.umich.edu:70/I9/LunarArchitecture/slide03.gif

Atlanta Reproductive Health Centre

 http://www.mindspring.com/~mperloe/gallery.html

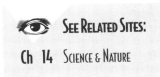 **SEE RELATED SITES:**

Ch 14 SCIENCE & NATURE

THE ATLANTA REPRODUCTIVE Health Centre is a clinic that has put a large amount of information about infertility on the Web, including an entire book on the subject.

For those looking for images, they'll find a picture gallery at this site that illustrates some of the issues involving both healthy reproductive systems and diseases that can affect fertility.

Most of these images are quite clinical, many of them taken using a laparoscope, a tiny viewing device that is inserted through a small incision in the abdomen to view the inside of the body.

The images include several pictures of normal ovaries and ovarian functions, as well as diseases of the ovary and uterus.

You'll also find pictures of human eggs, from the point of fertilization to the stage of the blastocyst, an early stage of pre-embryonic development.

It's not difficult to find the images on this site, although there's no link directly to the photo gallery from the home page.

Click on the Infertility icon, and you'll see there a link to the Image Gallery.

The gallery is divided into four sections, dealing with normal functions of pelvic organs, pelvic pain and endometriosis, fertilization and implantation of eggs using advanced reproductive technology, and abnormalities of the pelvis, uterus, and ovaries. Within each section, you'll find three to 10 inline images, which can be clicked on and enlarged.

Anyone with questions about fertility and some of the basic female organs involved in reproduction will find this an excellent site, both in its text and images, to get more information. It also has links to many other sites that address fertility, safe sex, and other issues. ▲

A fluid-filled follicle on the ovary is about to burst and release an egg.

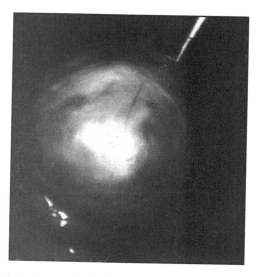

http://www.mindspring.com/~mperloe/fol.jpg

Allen Rose

WWW **http://www.metronet.com/~arose/home.html**

SEE RELATED SITES:

Ch 13 PHOTOGRAPHY

As YOU SURF the Internet, you'll notice a lot of pages that don't get updated when they should.

But Allen Rose is a very brave soul. He puts his work on his Internet home page every day. Not just his best work, but his daily work.

Fortunately for him, and for the rest of us, Rose is an outstanding daily news photographer, and we didn't find anything that looked like a dud.

When you get to the home page here and click on the Today's Work link, you'll discover the option to look at up to two weeks' worth of Rose's work. You can click on a day of the week (Sunday through Thursday), or on the Today icon to see the latest. Another icon takes you to the previous week.

Each day's selection may show the results from several photo assignments that he had that day. You'll also find a photo of the week on the daily work page. Clicking on the image brings that up, or you can click on the text link, which takes you to all the images shot that day, and some text to provide a context for the picture of the week.

As a newspaper photographer, his work requires versatility and speed. Quality is nice, but *a picture* is sometimes more important than *the picture*. On occasion, Rose offers two alternatives and suggests that viewers send him e-mail indicating which one they would choose if they were the photo editor.

The home page also has a link to a portfolio, showing selected images from feature, sports, and news assignments that Rose has done. ▲

Dallas Cowboys vie for a pass during training camp.

http://www.metronet.com/~arose/today/M/pass.jpg

Arthole

 http://www.mcs.com/~wallach/arthole.html

HARLAN WALLACH is not one of those photographers who likes to carry a small camera store around in a khaki vest with 31 pockets.

His specialty is the pinhole camera, an instrument at once so simple and so difficult to master that it disappeared from the serious photographic scene sometime in the last century.

But Wallach has something else going for him: penetrating insight into modern culture that will have you laughing and crying at the same time when you visit this Internet site.

He typically combines an image from his pinhole camera on a postcard style frame with another photo or image using more standard equipment. The two images may clash or complement each other, presenting the viewer with a visual puzzle to unravel.

Wallach's style is minimalist in both his photographs and his excellent writing about them. You won't find one of those complicated and dull manifestos here: just journals of his adventures, with his photographs as a brilliant counterpart.

The photographs are uncomplicated and direct, although the ideas they convey are often powerful, wry, or provocative.

The New York Postcards section at this site is an illustrated travelogue, with pinhole compositions accompanying Wallach's often amusing writing about his trip to New York.

Roadside Attractions is a bizarre roadie's album, with pictures of tortured automobiles and roadkill. The automobile photos are usually accompanied by some automobile manufacturer's slogan used in a context the manufacturer may not appreciate.

Another section, called Chicago Murder Sites, superimposes pictures of locations where murders occurred with newspaper clippings describing what happened. These are not forensic photos with body parts laying around, but simply photos of where the murders occurred. The pinhole camera's strong perspective gives the images a sense of fateful doom.

In Firenze, Wallach combines a short tale about a day in Florence with his trademark pinhole photos. It's an adventure to click on a link in the text and see what comes up. ▲

An image from Harlan Wallach's Roadside Attractions series.

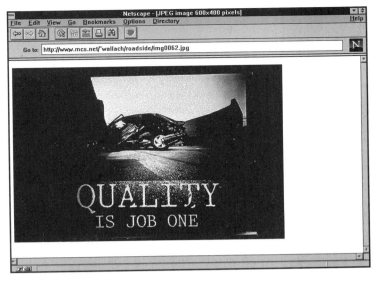

http://www.mcs.net/~wallach/roadside/img0062.jpg

Artix Gallery

 http://www.artix.com/biz/artix/

SEE RELATED SITES:

Ch 5 ART GALLERIES

THE ARTIX GALLERY is where you're going to find commercial work by people who are at the head of the line in the world of commercial art.

Let's be honest about a lot of the art on the Net. It has energy; it has imagination; but it doesn't have maturity and refinement. A lot of rough edges still show.

The artists in the galleries featured on Artix are rarely cyber-artists. They work with more traditional artistic media—clay, brush, pen—and their years of experience and familiarity with their craft means that they produce exactly what they see in their mind's eye. There's a comforting maturity, discipline, and quality in these works, without it becoming stale or predictable.

It has Web pages for many of the top Manhattan galleries, such as Paolo Baldacci, Sandra Gering, Nancy Hoffman, the Malborough Gallery, and Allan Stone.

These galleries are very selective in the artists they display, so you won't find great gobs of images online, but those that you do find are going to be of superb quality.

When we looked at the Hoffman gallery, for example, we found only one artist there,

Carolyn Brady, but 11 of her exquisite watercolors were viewable from the Net.

Only two items from a single artist were visible in the Paolo Baldacci gallery, which was rather disappointing, particularly since the artist was a sculptor and there wasn't much chance that anyone would somehow duplicate this image after downloading a JPEG image of it.

The Sandra Gering gallery, on the other hand, had ten artists listed, and on checking some of their directories, we found one or two pictures in each. Because this gallery had more artists, it also had more breadth and took more chances. Images ranged from artist William Anastasi's puzzling juxtaposition of a broken television and video camera, to Richard Estes' photo-realistic paintings. ▲

"La Chaise de Marie Antoinette" by Carolyn Brady.

http://www.artix.com/biz/artix/181.html

ArtScene

 http://artscenecal.com/index.html

 See Related Sites:

Ch 5 Art Galleries

ArtScene is a monthly magazine that covers the art museums and art galleries of Southern California.

The Web site is an online version of that guide, complete with maps to the galleries, listings of galleries and upcoming exhibitions, and the like.

To look at the Southern California art scene from the Internet you'll want to click into the image bank section of this site.

You'll see a listing for galleries, but few of the galleries listed here put more than one image in their section.

Your best option is the Artworks Inventory by Artist Names link, which takes you to an alphabetical listing of artists who have images in the image bank. When we looked, the image bank contained about 50 images from 40 artists.

The links are actually not to the artist, but to the artist's work. In other words if an artist has three images at ArtScene, you'll see the artist's name and three links, with the titles of the images, underneath that.

Unfortunately there are no thumbnails here, so you're going to have to simply browse through the collection by artist.

What happens when you click on those links will also vary. Sometimes you'll get a full-sized image, but other times you'll get only a small image that is part of an article or column in *ArtScene* magazine. Since many of these are only in black and white, they aren't as lovely to look at as a regular digital image of the picture. And some would qualify as only thumbnails on most sites.

Nevertheless, the articles do provide an important context for these works and show the images themselves. ▲

Martha Alf's "Yellow Rose with Red Background."

http://artscenecal.com/Alf1.html#Yellow

Texas Tech ASCII Art

gopher://gopher.cs.ttu.edu:70/11/Art%20and%20Images/
ClipArt%20%28ASCII%29

As anyone who has spent much time on the Internet soon realizes, you haven't arrived until you have a cool sig.

A sig, which is short for signature, is automatically appended to every e-mail message you send, and to newsgroup postings, if your software allows it.

Sigs can contain profound or clever sayings, your name and address (your e-mail address alone usually doesn't say much about you), or it can have a drawing. But the drawings have to be made up of standard ASCII characters or they won't make it through text-only gateways on the Internet.

For those who don't feel skilled or creative enough to come up with their own ASCII art, Texas Tech's Gopher archive is the place to begin.

It's also a testament to human creativity with even the crudest of tools. Would you believe that some folks actually come up with 3D images using this stuff?

One section is devoted to ASCII fonts, that is, letters made up of ASCII characters letters to create large three-dimensional, shadowed, or unusual letters, which you can cut and paste to create your own words.

You can also click on the Other ASCII Collections button to see what some other artists have done. Under the Scarecrow directory, you'll find some large files that contain more than 400 images each. ▲

CAUTION ASCII art has its place, but that place isn't always at the end of every message you send on the Internet. Good netiquette requires that you don't send people a lot of useless information. Lengthy sigs are particularly unwelcome in Internet newsgroups and on mailing lists or listservs. As a rule of thumb, sigs should be no longer than five lines of text.

A cityscape in 3D ASCII Art. Look at the image a bit cross-eyed and it will appear three-dimensional.

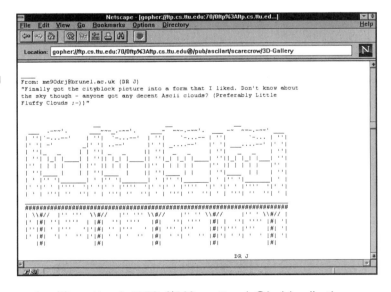

gopher://ftp.cs.ttu.edu:70/0ftp%3Aftp.cs.ttu.edu@/pub/asciiart/
scarecrow/3D-Gallery

Astarte Gallery

WWW http://www.icl.co.uk/Astarte/Images/a11.gif

👁 **SEE RELATED SITES:**

Ch 5 ART GALLERIES

WE HAVE A feeling that the artisans who crafted ancient fertility figures or mummified Egyptian falcons didn't anticipate cyberspace, but their works live there now.

The Astarte Gallery is a London shop that specializes in such figures from antiquity, from all parts of the world.

Clicking on the Antiquities link brings up a list of regions where antiquities are found. Depending on what's in stock and what has been photographed and scanned for the Net, you'll see a link to that particular region. When we were there for example, the gallery had no American or British antiquities viewable on the Net, but Egyptian and Far Eastern antiquities were well represented, with a few pieces from Greece, Western Asia, and the Middle East.

The Egypt section had a mummified falcon, jewelry, pots, and part of a sarcophagus. The Western Asia section included a couple of fertility goddess figures and the Far East section had some Han and Tang pots and figures.

No thumbnails are shown at the main menus, and the images are all fairly large GIFs (100Kb or larger), so it could take some time to browse through this gallery on a modem connection. Clicking on a link to an area brings up a list of all the current items in that section, and clicking on an item brings up a thumbnail and description of that item. You can then click on the image to get a reasonably large and detailed picture.

If you're interested in owning some of this art, by the way, you might be surprised by the prices. ▲

A circular lamp filler, with a boar's head spout, from Southern Italy around the second century B.C.

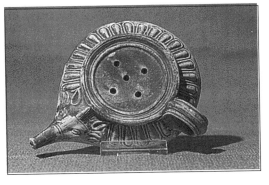

http://www.icl.co.uk/Astarte/Images/a23.gif

Automobile Pictures Archive

  **http://dutoc74.io.tudelft.nl/voitures/archive.htm**

👁 **See Related Sites:**

Ch 13 Photography
Ch 17 Transportation

People love cars. We build them and take them apart, we tinker with them, show them to our friends, we drive them around town for no good reason, and we take pictures of them. In tribute, the Automobile Pictures Archive brings to the Internet all those cars that most humans don't have the chance to experience.

The site opens with an image of the Car of the Week, and following the link, visitors can sort through an archive of previously selected cars.

The bulk of the archive is eclectically categorized by country (French, English, American, and Italian) and by a few random topics, such as Bugatties, prototypes, racing cars, movies, and "nice motorcycles." The automobile selection within the sites is composed primarily of classic cars and prototypes of vehicles we were unfamiliar with, which made the site even more valuable. For American cars, for example, we'd neither seen nor heard of the Stutz, the Miller, or the Cunninham. Even the list owner wasn't sure about the DMC brand, asking, "Or was it Irish?"

The links to racing and new-and-not-categorized cars are FTP-like sites, the former containing an extensive list of .jpg and GIF images. If you're not well-versed in automobile history, you might feel a bit lost in the FTP directories, with only the file names to guide you.

Since the site owner also hosts a home page dedicated to fans of the Bugatti automobile, the link to Bugatti is deeper and more detailed than the other categories, with images from the vintage 1920s through the modern 1990s racing machines.

The archive has two downsides. We would have liked to have more background information on the various automobiles and their makers, and the sites' location in the Netherlands proved for some long download times. We experienced quite a bit of overseas lag when paging through the files. Still, the wealth of vintage automobile images makes the archive a classic in its own time. ▲

The Viper GTS Coupe, one of the former "Cars of The Week" in the Automobile Pictures Archive.

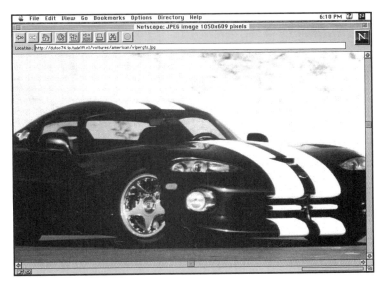

http://dutoc74.io.tudelft.nl/voitures/american/vipergts.jpg

A 1947 French Bugatti 73A prototype, designed and shown in Paris by Ettore Bugatti just prior to his death.

http://dutoc74.io.tudelft.nl/voitures/bugatti/t73a.jpg

Avatar Archives

 ftp://avatar.snc.edu/pub/furry/misc/

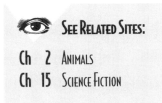 See Related Sites:

Ch 2 Animals
Ch 15 Science Fiction

The folks who inhabit the Internet are big fans of science fiction and fantasy. One of the most popular manifestations of that is the "furry," a kind of animal-human hybrid. Sometimes it's a raccoon with clothes, or a squirrel with breasts, or a nearly-human form with a lion's fangs or claws.

Some folks take this so seriously that they call themselves furries and develop role-playing characters, which they draw in various poses, situations, and clothes.

The Avatar Archives is devoted to the art of the furry, with hundreds of images of furries posted on its site.

This site has so many images that good organization is important. You can download a 400Kb master file if you like, but this site is exhaustively indexed by date, or by the first letter of the file name. If you're accessing this through a graphical browser, click on an index section (for example, index-by-name.b.html) and you'll get a list showing every file that begins with the letter b, along with the file size, its dimensions in pixels, the number of colors, and a brief description. ▲

"Nitro-coon," depicted at the Avatar Archives.

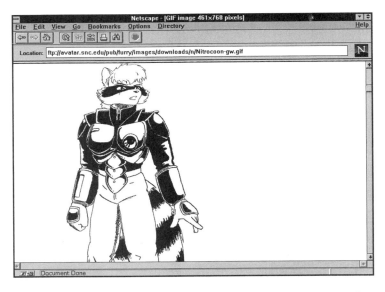

ftp://avatar.snc.edu/pub/furry/images/downloads/n/Nitrocoon-gw.gif

Furries

Just what *is* a furry, anyway?

A document on furries at the ftp://avatar.snc.edu/ site explains:

"Simply enough, a furry is a funny animal taken seriously. Roger Rabbit, Bugs Bunny, and Mickey Mouse are funny animals; they are anthropomorphic, mostly behave like people, and are pretty much the cartoon equivalent of character actors. Usagi Yojimbo, Omaha the Cat Dancer, and the original Teenage Mutant Ninja Turtles are furries (even though turtles don't have fur); they are even more anthropomorphic in appearance than the funny animals are, but behave like crosses between humans and animals. They are sapient, and just as much "people" as any fictional character, but they aren't presented as animals for laughs. Most furries tend towards their human aspects, their "species" not all that important."

Biological Sciences Database

 http://www.calpoly.edu/delta.html

 **SEE RELATED SITES:**

Ch 2 ANIMALS
Ch 14 SCIENCE & NATURE

ALTHOUGH ITS NAME suggests a general interest in biology, this site actually specializes in marine biology.

Although it was clearly under construction when we looked, We're looking forward to going back when the collection has been refined and updated. That's because unlike some scientific sites that are intended to give you the feeling of an academic library, making your way through this site is fast and intuitive.

Click on Select a Group of Organisms and you get a selection of general marine categories, such as birds, fishes, mammals, or reptiles.

It's logically organized, and common names are used for all the examples. If you want the scientific name, that's available when you select an individual animal, along with information about its habitat, food, and so on.

Most selections will have several photos of the animal you've chosen, many even have QuickTime movies showing the animal in its natural habitat.

You'll find that the fish category has the largest number of images, although birds are well represented.

One powerful feature of this database is its search engine. Click on the Search this Database button and you'll get a form to fill in. Enter a word that appears anywhere in the text of the database, and links to any items that match it will come up.

A search using the word "California" for instance turned up 17 items, across all the various categories, including fish, birds, plants, and mollusks. ▲

A hammerhead shark floats by, in the Biological Sciences Database.

http://www.calpoly.edu:8010/db/marine-biology/Fishes/
Scalloped_hammerhead/photos/72321_Hamhead_shark.DN.jpg

Berkeley Museum of Paleontology

 http://ucmp1.berkeley.edu/

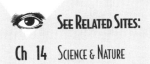 SEE RELATED SITES:

Ch 14 SCIENCE & NATURE

THE MUSEUM OF Paleontology at Berkeley is a good site for the amateurs among us. There aren't a huge number of images at the moment, but it's clearly under construction and will be an excellent resource in the future.

The site has excellent navigational tools. When we looked it was still under construction, and the museum very helpfully indicated which sections weren't complete.

From the opening screen, click on exhibits, then scroll down to the invitation to Take the Web Geological Time Machine. This shows a list of periods of geological history. If you're interested in dinosaurs, be aware that there weren't any before the Mesozoic period. If you click on a time period, then click the Ride the Web Geological Time Machine button at the bottom, you'll go to an explanatory page about that particular period. There you'll see a Fossils of This Time button, which will take you to galleries of images.

Pterodons, whose remains have been found in Egypt, confront an ancestor of the rhinoceros, an Arsinoitherium.

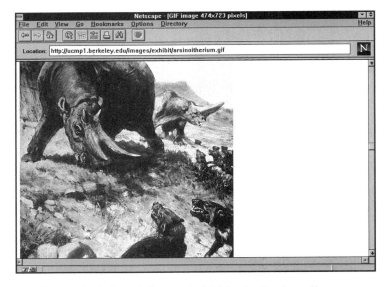

http://ucmp1.berkeley.edu/images/exhibit/arsinoitherium.gif

If you see a link to the dinosaurs, you can also take that directly. It takes you to a Hall of Dinosaurs (http://ucmp1.berkeley.edu/exhibittext/cladecham.html) where you can either click on an image map or on text links below to see more about that time. ▲

Babes on the Web

 http://www.tyrell.net/~robtoups/BABE.html

Babes on the Web II

 http://ucsub.colorado.edu/~kritzber/new/babes.html

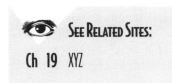

👁 **See Related Sites:**

Ch 19 XYZ

IF YOU EVER needed evidence that cyberspace has its own reality, this is probably it.

Babes on the Web is a collection of photos of women who have home pages on the World Wide Web. Babes on the Web II is a collection of photos of men who have home pages on the World Wide Web.

Most of the photos are quite ordinary, but that hasn't stopped Babes on the Web Webmaster Rob Toups. He's rated the photos on a four-babe scale, from Babe-o-rama (four) to Babe-o-matic (one).

Now, Toups claims that his primary interest is in the HTML skills of these women (he probably also buys Playboy for the articles). Toups is no slouch at HTML himself, so he actually is in a position to make some judgment about that. His selection of babes is, however, entirely personal.

None of the photos is actually stored at Toups' site. In all cases, clicking on a Webmistress's name actually takes you to her site.

Needless to say, BOTW has been controversial, and problematic for some of his nominees. One, with a topless picture on her home page, announced that only the thumbnails would be visible after getting 21,000 hits in one eight hour period and incurring the wrath of her service provider.

Babes on the Web II is a response by Blake Kritzberg, a female whose site is arguably an even deadlier shot in the gender wars. BOTW II rates the men whose pictures appear on Web pages. We consider this deadlier because many fragile male egos have proven unable to handle not finding themselves listed as at least "cuddly," if not "dangerous" or downright "steamy," the three ratings category at Kritzberg's site. She does give Toups credit for one thing: it's one of the best places for women to find the relatively few other women on the Internet. ▲

Home page for Babes on the Web.

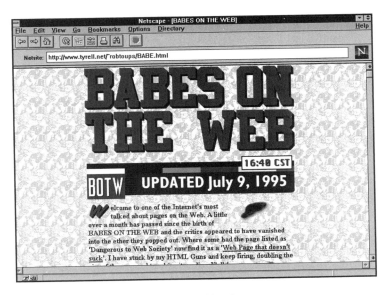

http://www.tyrell.net/~robtoups/BABE.html

British Library

 http://portico.bl.uk/

See Related Sites:

Ch 7 Art Museums

The British Library is one of the most famous intellectual centers in the world, and home to many of the world's cultural treasures.

Now it's online, with a growing number of special exhibits and permanent displays.

When we visited, menus and links were not organized or labeled very well, which made it difficult to find the good stuff. Try clicking on Current Portico Highlights to make sure you can find out what's new.

From there we found we could get to their latest exhibition, to the British Library Treasures section, and to the electronic *Beowulf*, an effort to digitize this ancient manuscript for scholarly study.

The latest exhibition happened to be on the Art of the Mapmaker, although you couldn't know that unless you followed the links to the current exhibition.

At any rate, this exhibit had pictures of some very famous maps, including Ptolemy's 150 A.D. map of the world.

From the top menu we couldn't find our way at all to the Permanent Exhibition area (try the current exhibition link and then go to the bottom to find a link to the Permanent Exhibitions).

Ptolemy's World Map, c. 150 A.D.

http://portico.bl.uk/exhibitions/maps/ptolemy.html

The special exhibitions are not necessarily graphical. If you're a Keats or Purcell lover, you'll appreciate reading about the work of these geniuses, but it's not a pictorial display.

However, click on the On Permanent Exhibition link and you'll get to a section on famous manuscripts, including the first, dated example of printing in China nearly 600 years before Gutenberg invented moveable type.

Considering that the Museum has already developed several CD-ROMs and has a collection of 10,000 slides of its holdings, however, we expect to see more of this famous and important collection online, and easier to get to, in the future. ▲

Black Star

 http://www.blackstar.com/Welcome.html

 SEE RELATED SITES:

Ch 13 PHOTOGRAPHY

BLACK STAR IS one of the oldest and most successful stock photo agencies, and now has a site on the Internet.

As is typical with stock photo agencies, you're not going to get much for free, nor should you (photographers need to eat, too). Black Star doesn't exactly cripple their site, but their approach is to make it impossible for you to get exactly what you want from their stock library of four million photographs while still letting you see what they can do.

From the main menu you'll see a link to take a random tour of Black Star's photos. Click it and you'll see about six thumbnail images, with captions. You can keep clicking on a button to get more photos, but they can't be enlarged past the thumbnail stage. Black Star says it has 40,000

images online, which is easier to comprehend when you realize the thumbnails are only about 6Kb, and they're coming off a CD-ROM attached to the server. It also means you can click until your mouse or wrist wears out before you'll see the complete collection.

However, Black Star doesn't leave you completely squinting at thumbnails. Clicking on the Photo Resources link on the home page takes you to a selection of ten Black Star photo stories. These are short documentary or feature pieces with a small amount of text and about a dozen images each, which can be clicked on to get a reasonably sized image.

Again, you can't access specific images that you want, but if you want to see samples of some good work by leading

A nun demonstrates her martial arts skills in a story about a group of nuns in New York.

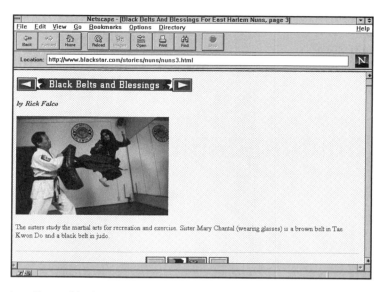

http://www.blackstar.com/stories/nuns/nuns3.html

photojournalists, you'll find it here.

From this photo-stories page we could also link to Blackstar WorldWide, where we found a list of about ten regular Black Star photographers. Clicking on their names brings up links to particular images or to photo stories they have done, which you can click through using a "next" arrow. ▲

Books That Work

 http://www.btw.com/

SEE RELATED SITES:

Ch 17 XYZ

BOOKS THAT WORK publishes Windows software that helps klutzes and computer nerds actually do something useful, like build a deck, paint a room, and the like.

They also have a Web site to show off and demonstrate their products, and you might want to dip in there occasion-ally for graphics and anima-tions on home improvement, gardening, and auto-repair topics.

The company's Web site contains images and anima-tions from its half-dozen CD-ROMs on these and other topics. Naturally they are trying to sell CD-ROMs, but they provide the Internet surfer with free samples of images and animations from the CD-ROMs, which can be useful.

When we visited, they had a home improvement tip of the month, a gardening tip of the month, and a section on designing and installing sprinkler systems (this was in the middle of summer, about the time when the joy of moving the sprinkler around manually was beginning to lose its luster).

The home improvement tip dealt with choosing brushes, and showed some still frames from animations demonstrating how to determine brush quality. The gardening tips involved the selection of plants for hot sunny areas and showed several digital pages from one of the company's CD-ROMs with photos of plants that are good for such environments. A complete, but unillustrated guide to lawn care was also online.

To play the animations, which run about 150Kb, you'll need a Macromedia player, which you can download from the site.

Some other useful tidbits at the site include a fill-in form for calculating how much paint you need to paint a room. ▲

Animations provide additional information about home-improvement and other subjects.

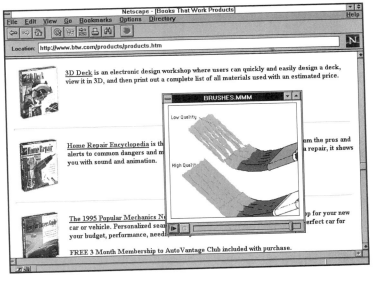

http://www.btw.com/products/products.htm

Buena Vista's Movie Plex

 http://www.disney.com/BVPM/index.html

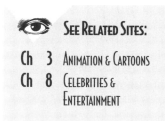 **SEE RELATED SITES:**

Ch 3 ANIMATION & CARTOONS

Ch 8 CELEBRITIES & ENTERTAINMENT

MOVIE DISTRIBUTION HOUSES are giving ordinary folk access to the background material—press kits, stills, and video clips—which have heretofore been reserved for the entertainment media. Now they just put it on a Web site, and anyone can come in and get it.

Buena Vista's movie plex is one such example. Anyone visiting this site can grab the press kit with the press stills (black and white, several to a page, not that clear), plus color stills (downloadable gifs and jpegs, much better), plus the movie trailer and dozens of smaller video clips from the movie, about the movie, from the actors, and about the actors.

If you're a fan of a particular star in a Buena Vista film, this site can be a gold mine. Not only can you download color pics of your idol or flame, but you can grab QuickTime videos of the actors, directors, and producers talking about the film and their roles. These will be a great addition to the true fan's collection of memorabilia.

It is intriguing to hear Mia Farrow talking about family relationships (in an interview from the set of *Miami Rhapsody*), or director Robert Redford talking about television and the American dream,

A marquee-style menu guides users to the movie files at Buena Vista's Movie Plex.

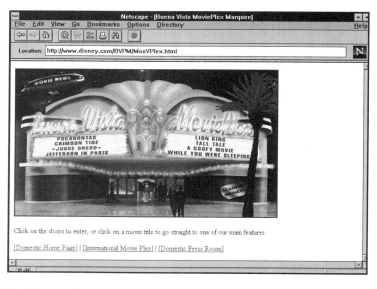

http://www.disney.com/BVPM/MooVPlex.html

in relation to his film *Quiz Show*.

At Buena Vista's site, in connection with one single show, we counted more than 70 megabytes of QuickTime trailers, clips, and interviews in 41 separate files, ranging in size from 200Kb to 9Mb.

Because QuickTime files are large, you can either grab the full trailer (preview), which tends to run between five and eight megabytes and which is only practical for those on fast Internet connections, or you can download the smaller promotional clips, which are about one megabyte. Whether downloading that on a modem connection is worth the 30 seconds or so of jerky animation that you'll see, only you can decide.

Buena Vista distributes Walt Disney films, so there's something for young folk here. You can download black-and-white line drawings from the film to use as a coloring book. ▲

Children can get line drawings to color from Buena Vista's Movie Plex.

http://www.disney.com/media/BVPM/LionKing/Pictures/CB-Poster.jpg

The Calvin and Hobbes Archive

http://www.eng.hawaii.edu/Contribs/justin/Archive/Index.html

👁 **SEE RELATED SITES:**

Ch 3 ANIMATION & CARTOONS

Ch 8 CELEBRITIES & ENTERTAINMENT

WITH COPYRIGHT LAWS in the balance, leave it to fans of the *Calvin and Hobbes* comic strip to upload a dumptruck's worth of Calvin and Hobbes art on the Internet for WWW and FTP access.

When visitors click on the link to any of the available pictures, they're warned that Bill Watterson owns the copyright to the material and that the images are only "samples" to encourage people to buy *Calvin and Hobbes* books. In the spirit of Calvin, gobs of downloadable GIFs follow immediately.

Another flair of chutzpah is the list of visitors who have probably downloaded the files.

There are links to 18 other pages that contain *Calvin and Hobbes* material (including a few in other languages). Our favorite is the link to the animation of the "flip book" strip. It takes a long time to load, but it's definitely worth it.

We felt cheated that we couldn't reach the server that held the *Calvin and Hobbes* cards (Magic the Gathering), but were mollified that all the FTP sites were up and running when we stopped by. Each of

One of many Calvin and Hobbes images available at the archive site.

http://www.eng.hawaii.edu/Contribs/justin/Archive/Color-Strips/Calvin24.gif

the three sites (two in other countries) is filled to the gills with downloadable images.

There are also links to alt.binaries.pictures.cartoons, rec.arts.ascii, and alt.ascii-art, where visitors can probably find even more art (sans copyright warnings).

This site was the "Cool Site of the Day" on September 21, 1994 and probably still is. ▲

Grand Canyon

 http://www.kbt.com/gc/

 SEE RELATED SITES:

Ch 2 ANIMALS
Ch 14 SCIENCE & NATURE
Ch 18 TRAVEL & GEOGRAPHY

ONE EXPERIENCE THAT will take a while to duplicate in cyberspace is the experience of standing at the rim of the Grand Canyon and looking across miles of open air and steep canyon walls.

But this will have to do for now: a well-done site on the Grand Canyon, offering photographs of its trails, vistas, and wildlife.

This site is not a National Parks Service site but is maintained by Bob Ribokas, who has done an amazing job as an unpaid individual putting together information on the Grand Canyon.

You'll find photographs almost everywhere you go on this site, and a rich set of hypertext links to take you to even more.

The most image-rich areas come under the Guided Tours link and the Photo Gallery.

Click on Guided Tours and you'll find well-illustrated synopses of the South Rim's South and East Entrances and the North Rim.

The photo gallery is divided into several sections: rocks and water, wildlife, and flora. By default you'll get the text version of the list, but you can click on a link to view thumbnails, which are fairly small and should come up well even on a modem connection.

Rocks and water covers both the big, spectacular scenery and some of the falls and detailed rock formations in the canyon. There's a small selection of animal photos, and a larger collection of photos showing the main plants of the Grand Canyon.

If you're thinking of visiting the Grand Canyon, another link on the home page takes you to maps of the area and of many of its trails. You'll also find links to a page on running the Grand Canyon by boat.

Many of the images are available as both partial-screen GIFs and as larger, full-screen JPEGs. ▲

Lone Pinon Pine and Zoroaster Temple, seen from Yaki Point.

http://www.kbt.com/gc/pinyon.jpg

Charlotte, The Vermont Whale

 http://www.uvm.edu/whale/whalehome.html

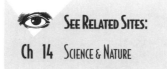

SEE RELATED SITES:

Ch 14 SCIENCE & NATURE

NOW YOU WOULDN'T think that a Web page about Charlotte would lead you to paleoclimatology, glaciers, ancient seas, and a railroad construction project, but then you never know what you'll find on the Internet.

This site is a simple, straightforward use of the Internet as a teaching tool. It's an illustrated, hypertext story about a whale skeleton that was unearthed near Charlotte, Vermont in 1849 by railroad workers.

Parts of the skeleton were destroyed by the workers, who figured the bones came from an old horse, but enough remained for a naturalist of the time to identify the bones as

those of a Beluga whale that died or was washed up in Vermont during the Ice Ages when Lake Champlain was an arm of an ancient sea.

The site is organized in a simple-to-navigate manner, designed to answer basic questions about the whale.

Click on How Did a Whale Get in Vermont? and you go to a section that shows photos of glaciers, and images of the Champlain Basin during the last Ice Age.

The site is a mixture of drawings, diagrams, maps, and photographs that explain natural features and processes related to the origin and discovery of the whale.

Some links will take you to photos and information about beluga whales, which is the kind of whale Charlotte was, and the laboratory and field research required to learn more about the whale and Vermont geology. ▲

A drawing explains how the whale skeleton was preserved for thousands of years.

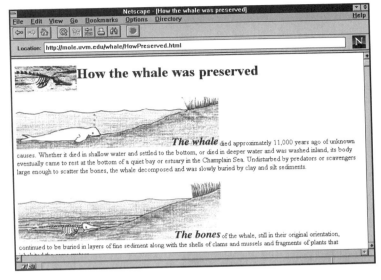

http://mole.uvm.edu/whale/HowPreserved.html

CineMaven Online

 http://www.uspan.com/maven/

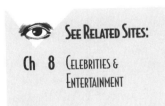

See Related Sites:

Ch 8 Celebrities & Entertainment

FILM REVIEWERS GET press kit after press kit of photos from the movie studios, and before long, the kits and the photos and the press releases are blocking all the light, filling every flat space and overflowing the file cabinets.

Then, one day, the cleaning lady comes along and throws everything away, and all the people who could never part with all those important pictures say "well, we can always get more."

Doug Thomas, a Seattle movie reviewer and video store owner has a better idea: put them on the Internet.

You'll find at CineMaven Online a large collection of pictures from top movies.

These are the black-and-white promotional photos which the studios hand out, so they frequently have several photos ganged onto a single image. They also tend to be a bit small, at least on a super VGA screen, but because these photos are intended to survive newspaper reproduction, they do reasonably well from a Web browser.

From the opening page, go to The Gallery, where you can either pick movies by the first letter of their name, or simply browse the whole collection. It's a fairly extensive collection, with images from more than 65 films, including some oldies, such as *Dr. Zhivago*. As time goes on, this should become an important archive for movie buffs. ▲

A scene from Bad Boys, on CineMaven Online

http://www.uspan.com/maven/pics/badboys.jpg

California Museum of Photography

 http://cmp1.ucr.edu/

See Related Sites:

Ch 13 Photography

WE'RE INCLUDING THIS site because it is an important site, although its potential when we visited was far from realized.

While the site has many online exhibits, and the museum has a huge collection of photographs and photography materials, the site has three drawbacks: first, it bends over backwards to avoid putting any photography on the Net; second, it can be stultifyingly boring; and third, it is seriously disorganized.

To deal with the last point first, it has both a title page, and a home page. They're not the same. We've given you the URL of the title page, which has a link to the home page, which does little except link you to categories of exhibition: historical photographs, art projects, current exhibitions, children's projects, stereographs, and cameras.

Just to make sure you'll never figure this out, some links further down call the title page the home page, and links to some exhibits appear in numerous places while others are well hidden.

Your best bet is to go to the title page, see what you like there, then click on the table of contents to see if there's anything you missed, then click on the home page and see if there's anything else that wasn't covered by the other two indexes. After the first page, however, most people will be far too bored to continue.

Ironically, the most popular medium at the Museum of Photography is text. Virtually every exhibit or exercise listed here has a few snapshots—it would be stretching things to call any of it photography—and a lengthy, often self-indulgent, academic essay.

The most interesting parts of this site are the historical photographs, which consist of small collections (a few dozen images each) of old photos of Los Angeles, San Francisco, Japan, and Russia.

Most disappointing is that the Museum has an extensive collection of original photographs (18,000 matted prints and 50,000 negatives, plus other items) from virtually all the world's great photographers, and we could find only two of them online. Only a tiny fraction of its 350,000 stereographs appear, and you won't find any photos of its 8,000-strong collection of cameras and other photographic technology. ▲

An image from Jim Pomeroy's Seeing Double exhibit.

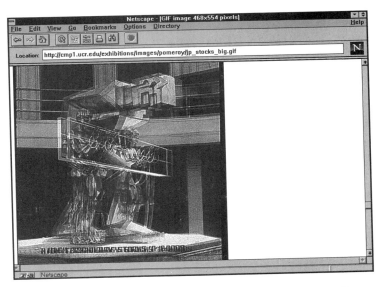

http://cmp1.ucr.edu/exhibitions/images/pomeroy/jp_stocks_big.gif

Comics 'n Stuff

 http://www.phlab.missouri.edu/~c617145/comix.html

SEE RELATED SITES:

Ch 3 ANIMATION & CARTOONS

THE COMICS 'N STUFF site is more a resource for finding comics on the Internet than it is a storage for graphics, but we couldn't resist telling you about it. The Comics on the Web is about as complete a listing of daily, weekly, and monthly comics as you'll find anywhere.

Most of these strips are displayed for only Internet folk, but there's also a healthy dose of syndicated strips listed, from *Alley Oop* to *Doonesbury* to *Too Much Coffee Man*.

One of the innovations of this site is access to the Comics 'n Stuff WebChat Room, available to visitors using Netscape 1.1. Click on the WebChat icon and follow the link to enter the Comics 'n Stuff Chatroom. The interactive interface provides a fairly friendly way for people to talk back and forth.

This site also links to Point Sites, a home page devoted to reviewing and rating Internet comics, plus a few other pages. ▲

One of the comics-oriented resource pages on the Internet.

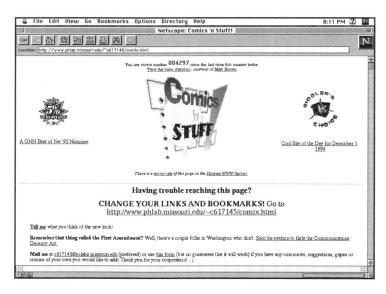

http://www.phlab.missouri.edu/~c617145/comix.html

Art Crimes

http://www.gatech.edu/desoto/graf/Index.Art_Crimes.html

See Related Sites:

Ch 6   Art in Cyberspace

EVERYTHING IS FREE: shady characters, anonymity, all-night sessions, hints of illegality, and challenges to authority.

Although that sounds like the qualities of some people on the Internet, it is actually the description of Art Crimes, which unquestionably is one of the coolest sites on the Net.

Art Crimes is devoted to graffiti, and the Internet is quite possibly the most appropriate gallery to show art that:

▼ is often illegal

▼ disappears in three days or less

▼ is anonymous

▼ is wild, crazy, bursting with energy, anger, and pride
(Sounds like some of those alt newsgroups, doesn't it?)

An International Art

The Art Crimes Webmakers love great graffiti, and they've collected photos of graffiti from all around the world. That's a good thing, because the lifespan of this art can be only a few days: long enough for a rival artist, a city cleaning crew or a wrecker's ball to turn it into memories.

Graffiti images may have the same abstract qualities as the art sitting on many gallery walls.

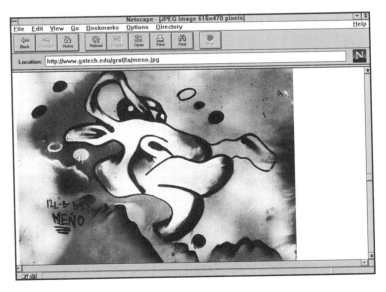

http://www.gatech.edu/graf/la/meno.jpg

Graffiti, in the average person's mind, is a phone number on a toilet stall (graffiti experts now call this "latrinalia," by the way) or the work of inner-city vandals, but the Art Crimes site, which organizes graffiti by country and city, will quickly change your mind. Art Crimes is not a tongue-in-cheek Web site, but it takes this art form as seriously as do many of its artists.

Many are dedicated and skilled artists, in contrast to the usual gang image. If you want to compare serious graffiti with gangland stuff, check out the El Paso 2 gallery (under the El Paso heading) for examples of the simple, rushed style of gang graffiti, which is used to mark territorial boundaries.

Art Crimes has collected examples of graffiti from North and South America, Europe, and Australia. Most major American cities are represented here, and some, such as Los Angeles, are represented by more than a dozen different sub-galleries.

On the international scene, there's graffiti from Australia, France, Canada, the Netherlands, Germany, and Czechoslovakia, among others.

A special gallery is devoted to that favorite vehicle of the graffiti "writer," trains. It's not just the New York subway that is marked. You'll see how Europeans, too, can grace trains with unofficial paint jobs.

The official paint job of a European train has been transformed by the more dynamic vision of a graffiti writer

http://www.gatech.edu/graf/trains/train1.jpg

This vivacious female drawn by John Howard is named "Maezona" ("Big Mother") in Sao Paulo, Brazil.

http://www.gatech.edu/graf/sao/maezona.jpg

American Graffiti

Art Crimes shows that graffiti artists are a very international club, who are influenced by each others' work, and particularly by American work.

But you'll find as much variation among the American graffiti writers of Boston, New York, Atlanta, Los Angeles, El Paso, and other American cities as you do between them and artists in other countries. In other words, good graffiti tends to be original and dynamic work.

In the Sao Paulo section you'll see the work of transplanted Californian John Howard, whose playful figures have adorned the city for 25 years (and 40 arrests).

Ron English

A special section is devoted to Ron English, an iconoclastic artist whose most famous work consists of revisions to standard billboard advertising. Cigarette companies, in particular, wake up one morning to find the space previously occupied by their official ad now touts the cancer-causing capabilities of their product.

In other, non-graffiti images here English pokes fun and raises questions about major symbols of our time and culture.

If you don't have access to a graphical web browser, you can still download the images at Art Crimes from a couple of ftp sites: ftp.aql.gatech.edu (in the /pub/art/graf directory)

and **ftp.gatech.edu** (in the /pub/desoto/graf directory). For quick viewing download the small gifs, and for the full picture, download the jpg images. ▲

Even other artists are not sacred for Ron English, who metamorphoses a famous pop artist into his own image, in a picture called "Anti-Warhol."

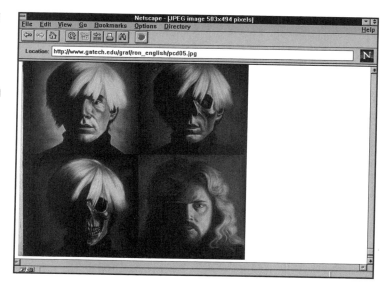

http://www.gatech.edu/graf/ron_english/pcd05.jpg

Covered Bridges of Southeastern Pennsylvania

 http://william-king.www.drexel.edu/top/bridge/CB1.html

SEE RELATED SITES:

Ch 4 ARCHITECTURE
Ch 18 TRAVEL & GEOGRAPHY

THE COVERED BRIDGE is a disappearing symbol of rural America, and this Web site is devoted to preserving that memory.

Although covered bridges exist in many states, this site concentrates on the southeastern Pennsylvania area, covering 46 bridges in Pennsylvania, Delaware, Maryland, and New Jersey. There's a link to a related area that looks at covered bridges in Oregon, whose heritage in the area of covered bridges is not nearly as well known, but which was building covered bridges after their construction had stopped elsewhere. (No, there are no images here of the bridges of Madison County.)

You have several ways to look at the bridges. You can view a list by county, by structural type (about six different truss designs were used to build the bridges), or you can take a "driving tour" of the bridges in a particular area. They are actually instructions for those with real cars to follow in Pennsylvania, but if you're coming over the Net, you can click on links for each bridge in the tour to see its picture.

Another way to look at the bridges is by season. Some bridges were photographed in different seasons, and the images are accessible that way. The pictures here are not calendar quality, but they are certainly good enough for you to get a clear idea of the bridge and its setting.

The images of each bridge typically include several shots, including pictures of details of the bridge, or more scenic shots taken some distance away. Each bridge also has a narrative describing it and a technical description of its span, construction, and other details. ▲

White Rock Bridge in Pennsylvania's Lancaster County.

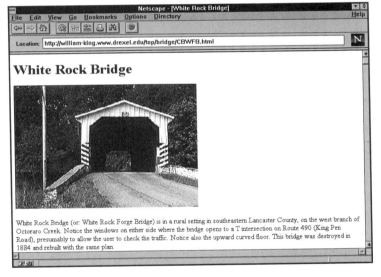

http://william-king.www.drexel.edu/top/bridge/CBWFB.html

Centre for Visual Science, Australian National University

 http://cvs.anu.edu.au/

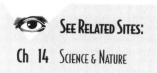
SEE RELATED SITES:

Ch 14 SCIENCE & NATURE

THE CENTRE FOR Visual Science studies factors that influence the way we see things, and has put several tantalizing puzzles online related to vision and perception.

The most famous part of this site goes by the name of B-EYE.

You may already know that bees have compound eyes with hundreds of lenses, all looking in slightly different directions. What can you see out of an eye like that?

Giger sets out to show you, with a well-illustrated collec-tion of sample images, how they would be projected onto a bee's retina, and how the lenses on a bee's eye would show the image.

You can look at some pre-created sample images, which show patterns, such as crosses, concentric circles, or more subtle variations of gray scales and how they would look to a bee. You can also see what something a bee might actu-ally care about, such as a spi-der or a spider's web, would look like through a bee's eye.

An enlargement of a bee's eye, and how it might see an image of an ant.

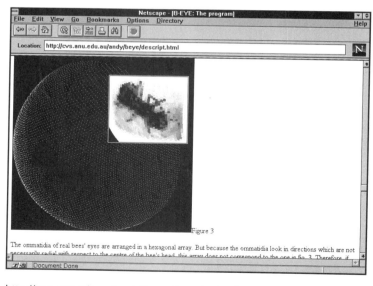

http://cvs.anu.edu.au/andy/beye/descript.html

Another option is to "hover" like a bee in front of a pattern and see how it changes as you change angle and distance.

The final choice gives the viewer a choice of patterns, angles, and distances. The computer will retrieve an image of what a bee might see based on the values that the user plugs in.

Another section covers single-image stereograms, those strange looking images that, if you cross your eyes just right, provide you with a hidden three-dimensional view of something. In addition to samples, Giger has a riddle to solve: you must resolve the three-dimensional image in a series of single-image stereograms for clues that guide you from one image to another through a virtual maze. ▲

Cyberia

 http://www.easynet.co.uk/pages/cafe/cafe.htm

See Related Sites:

Ch 6 Art in Cyberspace

CYBERIA IS A site that is part of a cyber cafe, a real food and drink joint that has computers online as well. (If you want to know more about cyber cafes, there's a document here describing what they're like.)

Part of Cyberia is an online art gallery. When we were there, they featured a special exhibit by Fay Stephens, who has built some large digital compositions and collages around the subject of radiation. Title: Chain Reaction.

Cyberia also has a permanent gallery area for artists and photographers to show their work.

Alex Berka's section shows the work of a digital artist who has mastered the medium, no longer needs to play with the toys, and has moved on to real pictures. The pictures are a gas, and so is the text that accompanies them, although we're afraid he might actually be serious.

His basic premise is that primordial urges, filtered by the modern rational mind, cause strange things to happen. His goal is to "model the collision between science and the glut of urges that nature has supplied us with."

Martin Gardner's Ministry of Hope series has a similar paradoxical vein, in which beautiful "viruses" (viruses always look beautiful with the right ray-tracing algorithm and color choices) are the subject of mock warning posters. The idea is that beauty and peril, propaganda, deception, and truth get mixed up when art and technology meet.

Jeremy Gaywood works with the visual vocabulary of the computer to produce sight gags for the moderately computer literate. Will we ever forget Mrs. Pac Man telling Junior "Yes, Junior, dots again" (for supper)? He also knows why computers crash (same reason that people do, it turns out).

The images at this gallery are large and luscious, with decent-sized thumbnails that will save you downloading the full image if you're on a slow connection, although it may take a while for each gallery to come up initially. ▲

"Hungry for Love" is the title of this Alex Berka piece.

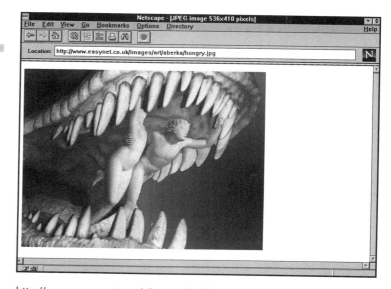

http://www.easynet.co.uk/images/art/aberka/hungry.jpg

Daniel's Icon Archive

 http://www.jsc.nasa.gov/~mccoy/Icons/index.html

 See Related Sites:

Ch 9 Clip Art & Icons

So you've started to write some HTML to make yourself a little home page, even if it's just a file on your computer, but it doesn't look anything like the pro's pages, or the last 16 cool sites of the day you've looked at. You are in despair, afraid to launch yourself into cyberspace on such a sorry vessel.

Let us give you some advice: pop over to this archive of ready-made icons, lines, and symbols, pull a few down, and go to town.

This site is a treasure chest of icons from the classy to the campy, plus lines of all kinds to turn that dull page into a masterpiece of high World Wide Web art (or a mess, but at least a colorful mess rather than a dull one).

At this site you'll find those cool, marble-textured buttons and arrows, all those little "under construction" signs that make the Internet look like the Interstate freeway system at the height of vacation season, those colorful little buttons with their cute highlights, and a long, long list of shaded and textured lines that you can use to create a spine-chilling home page.

They're organized a couple of ways: by type of element—icons, buttons, bullets, lines, and miscellaneous—and by source. The source listings show all the icons used at a particular site. Next to the gallery of icons from a source is a link to the source itself, so you can see how a particular set of icons gives a site its overall look and style.

While there appear to be some duplicates in these files, it's very well organized, considering how much data it contains (there are at least 1,300 icons, buttons, and lines here).

Clicking on an element or source will bring you to a page where you can elect to view a contact sheet of all the icons in that area, or view them one by one. The contact sheets range in size from about 50Kb to 150Kb. The icons themselves tend to be in the 500 to 5,000-byte range. Even your modem connection will seem fast at this page!

The icons here range from simple block figures to the full photographs, which have been reduced to icons at the Planet Earth site. You'll find lines with graduated fills, lines with rainbow gradations, and lines with

20

figures or creatures romping on them. *Simpsons* fans and Trekkers will find a few elements here as well.

You'll find balls in marble and granite, fuzzy balls with soft highlights, sharp balls with strong highlights, and more. Virtually all of these are transparent GIFs, designed so that when a round or irregular object sits on a page, it doesn't show up as a square image, but instead allows the background to show through around the edges of the icon itself, preserving its round shape.

If you like the set of icons in a particular section, you can download a compressed UNIX or PKZip file containing all of them.

From the main home page you can also download a compressed file containing all the icons and lines in all of the sections.

Keep in mind that the ZIP file with all the icons is a UNIX archive that, when exploded, tries to create long directory and file names that were illegal in DOS before Windows 95. You'll still get a lot of the files, but your decompression utility will probably protest. Also tell your decompression utility to unzip directory names as well as files. With PKZip, for example, you would use the command pkunzip icons. zip -d to get the icons to go into their correct directories.

A huge collection of WWW page-makeup elements doesn't

The Planet Earth collection uses photographs to create icons.

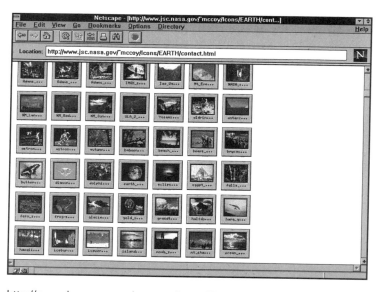

http://www.jsc.nasa.gov/~mccoy/Icons/EARTH/contact.html

A collection of lines for Web pages.

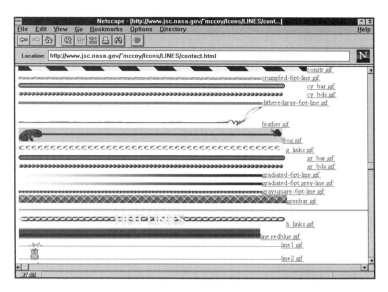

http://www.jsc.nasa.gov/~mccoy/Icons/LINES/contact.htm

exhaust the resources of this page.

Click on one link here, and the site will generate a custom ball for you on the fly, wrapping a fresh-from-the-floating-point fractal around a sphere to create a "planet" effect.

For the more technical, or perhaps just the fatally curious, the site also has links to important documents about creating transparent GIFs, using GIFs and JPEGs on your home page and creating backgrounds. Finally, you'll find a few well-chosen links to other icon and background collections. ▲

Digital Collage

 http://www.csulb.edu/Collage/index.html

 **See Related Sites:**

Ch 6 Art in Cyberspace

UNIVERSITIES ARE IN an exceptional position with regard to art and the Internet: it's a great way to display art to a wide audience; new artists and student artists don't have many opportunities to display their work; and universities usually have excellent Internet connections already in place.

Given those circumstances, putting student work on the Internet is a great solution to a young artist's lack of exposure.

This gallery, from California State University Long Beach, features work from students and faculty. It's not a completely open gallery—only work from CSULB students and faculty will be shown here—but it has some excellent work on display.

Clicking on the Enter the Gallery link brings you to a collection of thumbnails from each of the artists who are currently exhibiting (six when we visited).

The art work had a strong slant toward commercial illustration, such as logos and packaging. If you're looking for a commercial illustrator, this is one of the few places we've seen that kind of work on display, and if you are a commercial illustrator, maybe you'd better see what those kids are coming up with today.

The fine arts program at CSLUB also includes some digital video, so you may run across the odd QuickTime clip here as well.

A special exhibit, on view when we visited, is worth a mention. Titled Black and Blue (for oil and water, among other things), it is a visual essay about Long Beach, an important oil center in the Los Angeles area. ▲

"The Reaching," by Richard Bell.

http://www.csulb.edu/Collage/Black_Blue/Images/BellRichard/reaching.jpg

Digital Photography (Peoria)

 http://www.bradley.edu/exhibit/index.html

SEE RELATED SITES:

Ch 6 ART IN CYBERSPACE
Ch 13 PHOTOGRAPHY

DIGITAL PHOTOGRAPHY IS a juried art exhibition that defines its specialty as "any two-dimensional image that had its origin in a lens-imaging camera device and was brought to completion within a computer."

Images here run the gamut between camera and computer. In some, the role of the computer is all but invisible. In others, it is the camera that has disappeared.

The site actually consists of two sites, one for the 1994

"Lone Tree," from the Digital Photography '94 exhibit, by Dan Looper.

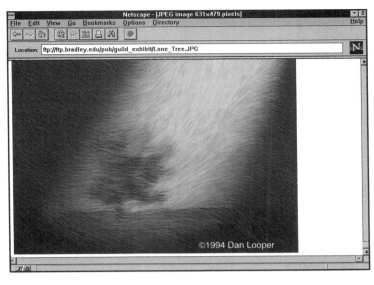

ftp://ftp.bradley.edu/pub/guild_exhibit/Lone_Tree.JPG

competition and another for the 1995 competition. Since this is an annual exhibition and the sites are linked, we've given you the URL for Digital Photography '94, so you can start at the beginning in a nice linear fashion.

The 1994 exhibit has five "walls," each of which has five pictures on it. The images vary from slightly altered photographs, to heavy use of plug-in filters to get special effects, to collages that combine images from several photos.

On the opening page there's also an MPEG movie showing the opening of the exhibit,

which you can probably skip unless you really need to see a quick pan of the gallery and some close-ups of the hors d'oeuvres.

The 1995 exhibit is slightly larger, with 10 walls to see, but only three images per wall, and a longer movie, complete with some cool transitions. (You don't get to see much of the hors d'oeuvres, however.)

The exhibit shows that computer modifications can generate virtually any style of two-dimensional art, from photography to oils to water color, that the artist has in mind. ▲

Digital Art Endeavors and Other Artistic Experiences

 http://ziris.syr.edu/home.html

SEE RELATED SITES:

Ch 6 ART IN CYBERSPACE

DIGITAL ART ENDEAVORS is a university-sponsored gallery that uses the Internet as one of its most important tools.

In some of the galleries here you'll find art that is the result of collaborations over the Internet, and if you're so inclined, you can take part by contributing an image, text, or sound to the art already visible.

Collaboration can be complicated and frankly you'll find yourself scratching your head to figure out how some of these projects work.

In Diversified Paths, participants start with a "parent image," then modify it in some way. The modified version is placed back into the "path," and succeeding artists will use the "child" image to create yet additional variations. The original images can be selected by picking one of the images out of a visual chart, or from a text list. On some occasions there's a vague resemblance between the parent image and the text (for example, the parent image of

"Elvis is Everywhere" is a picture of Elvis), but in other cases ("Catching Flies"), a viewer could be excused for seeing only the dimmest connection between the image and the text version.

Never mind, it's great fun to see how a single image can evolve, dissolve, and concatenate over time.

The Chain Art Project involved images being shipped around via ftp, being modified each time to create an image that was, eventually, the work of dozens of people. Diagrams show how the image evolved as it moved from site to site.

Digital Journeys similarly involves collaboration among artists. An illustrated essay starts off the idea and others are expected to send their reactions to the theme.

While you're at the site, check out some of the grad student and undergraduate sections to see what the Next Generation is up to, if you dare. ▲

The parent image, the iris of an eye, became this image in the next iteration, by a contributor to Diversified Paths.

http://www-cgr.syr.edu:80/~path/GroupB/1clgr.jpg

The Dilbert Zone

 http://www.unitedmedia.com/comics/dilbert/

SEE RELATED SITES:

Ch 3 ANIMATION & CARTOONS
Ch 8 CELEBRITIES & ENTERTAINMENT

DILBERT, THE SOUL of the corporate machine, resides fully on the Internet, the happy hunting ground for full-time employees seeking solace from the work-a-day life. Sitting like a prize in the middle of this site is an archive of two weeks worth of Dilbert and a miscellaneous assortment of "Prehistory of Dilbert—early rejections."

The daily Dilbert strips are regularly updated GIFs that run slightly behind the syndicated newspaper publishing date. The page devoted to character descriptions contains clean, color graphics of the principal Dilbert characters that are also downloadable.

Aside from the graphics, this site is as corporate as they come, which shouldn't be surprising because business is, after all, business. There are

links to merchandise, licensed vendors, newsletter subscriptions, and so on.

Interestingly, Adams uses the site to blast a shot at "blatant commercialism" with a link to an interactive form where visitors can let Dogbert (Dilbert's dog) know what you think of Dilbert products now on the market.

According to Dogbert: "I'm offering you a chance to comment on the type of Dilbert and Dogbert-related crapola you think you can't live without. If there's a strong demand for something in particular, I'll see about having it made and offering it directly on the Web."

If Dilbert's Internet account is anywhere as popular as the syndicated version, we're sure to see even more Dilbert on the Internet soon. ▲

20

DIVA

 http://www.monash.edu.au/visarts/diva/diva.html

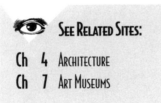

See Related Sites:

Ch 4 Architecture
Ch 7 Art Museums

DIVA STANDS FOR Digital Images from the Visual Arts Library at Monash University, in Melbourne Australia, and it is a treasure trove of visual images in the arts, architecture, aboriginal art, video, and garden and landscape design.

Aussies are big players on the Internet, with one of the highest penetrations of computer ownership in the world, but they are so distant from North American and European art centers that their artistic heritage is not well known. Thanks to the Internet and DIVA, however, that has been repaired. It provides a thorough and fascinating overview of the state of the visual arts in Australia.

It may be far away geographically, but DIVA demonstrates that the themes of Australian art are as sharp and contemporary as those anywhere else.

At the home page here, you'll get a link to Australian art in general, or for a more focused look, under Australian Painters and Sculptors, at each artist.

The gallery of Australian art demonstrates great variety. There are striking contrasts and qualities, ranging from the powerful abstracts of the late Roger Kemp, to the provocative landscapes of Arthur Boyd,

"Bathers, Shoalhaven Riverbank and Clouds" by Arthur Boyd.

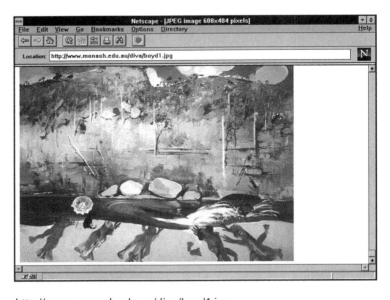

http://www.monash.edu.au/diva/boyd1.jpg

http://www.monash.edu.au/visarts/diva/tillers4.jpg

who works Australian images into a much larger canvas.

Davida Allen and Jenny Watson deal with feminine themes and their own experience.

A section on performance art illustrates with still pictures the work of Jill Orr and Linda Sproul, whose work explores issues such as pain, male and female stereotypes, and other issues.

Orr is part photographer, part performance artist. She uses her own body as the central figure in photographs that look at ecological and feminist issues.

Sproul confronts audiences with their own sexual and social stereotypes in her performances.

Because DIVA is at Monash University, which is in Melbourne, most of the archi-tectural sections here focus on Melbourne. There is one section, however, with some photos of the famous opera house in Sydney.

The section on gardens and landscape design harbors a surprise: the images do not depict Australian gardens but rather the gardens of Renaissance Italy, in historical drawings and pictures and contemporary photos. A special treat is a section with 15 images from Claude Monet's (huge) garden in Giverny. Fans of Monet will want to look through this one for the inspirations for Monet's work. (While marveling at Monet's work, we can now wonder how in the world he managed to get any painting done while keeping up such a huge garden.)

We were disappointed to find that a section on

Jill Orr lies on the ground in her mother's wedding dress, covered with bread and fish, as part of a performance piece called "Lunch with the Birds."

http://www.monash.edu.au/visarts/diva/1perf19.jpg

aboriginal art was under construction when we looked, but if it reaches the caliber of the other sections of this site, it should make a good visit in the future. Also under construction was a virtual exhibition space, and a section on young Australian artists, both of which may showcase the work of addi-

tional Australian artists in the future.

These pages are masterfully done, easy to navigate, well illustrated, and have plenty of explanatory notes about the artists. You will find some pages with large numbers of thumbnails, which can take some time to download. ▲

A house design by Australian architect Max May.

Netscape - [JPEG image 716×460 pixels]

File Edit View Go Bookmarks Options Directory Help

Location: http://www.monash.edu.au/visarts/diva/may.jpg

http://www.monash.edu.au/visarts/diva/may.jpg

Alan Dorow Picture Gallery

 http://www.picture.com/Alan-Dorow.html

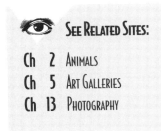

SEE RELATED SITES:

Ch 2 ANIMALS
Ch 5 ART GALLERIES
Ch 13 PHOTOGRAPHY

PROFESSIONAL PHOTOGRAPHER ALAN Dorow has a sharp eye for people and their surroundings, and a whimsical sense of humor that makes this site a browser's delight.

It's divided into several sections, each of which will bring up a gallery of thumbnails you can click on to get a larger picture.

In the most amusing section, Animal Crackers, Dorow uses digital manipulation to put animals—and sometimes people—in unusual situations: a sunbather dreams on, ignorant of the polar bear sniffing about his feet; two people converse inside the monkey cage as a tiger, hyena, and

zebras peer at them from the outside; a gorilla shares a quiet moment in his cage with a picnicking family.

Under Assignment work, you'll find the bread and butter of the commercial photographer: business portraits and a few lifestyle or business illustrations.

The Border States gallery contains black-and-white images along the U.S. Mexican border, with some powerful compositions that show the blend of history, tradition, cultural and ethnic mixes, and the new western economy. This constitutes work in progress for a book Dorow has planned.

20

An image from Alan Dorow's Boardwalk U.S.A. series.

http://www.picture.com/gallery/Alan-Dorow/Boardwalks/5001.jpeg

Dorow's fascination and rapport with people really comes through in the section on Boardwalk U.S.A, a collection of images from boardwalks on the U.S. East coast. Dorow has the eye of a master, and apparently casual photographs show careful attention to detail from edge to edge.

The technical quality here is also outstanding, although we wish the images were a bit larger. All were scanned for a maximum size of 400 pixels, which makes horizontal images quite small on a browser screen.

If you really like these images, you can order copies of original prints from Dorow as well. ▲

Durham Cathedral

  http://www.dur.ac.uk/~dla0www/c_tour/tour1.html

 See Related Sites:

Ch 4 Architecture
Ch 18 Travel & Geography

Durham Castle and Cathedral, recently recognized as a UNESCO World heritage site, is one of those places that was destined to be a fortress and church.

To medieval architects and planners the rocky promontory that was nearly an island, surrounded by the waters of the River Wear was impossible to resist. Perched on the hill, both the fort and the Romanesque towers of the Cathedral can be seen from far in the distance.

This World Wide Web site now offers a photographic tour of this 900-year-old cathedral (the castle has become part of the local university).

From the top menu you can elect to take a guided tour of the peninsula (a promontory around which the River Wear takes a hairpin turn) or a guided tour of the cathedral itself.

Selecting a tour of the peninsula brings up a map of the peninsula. Numbered dots on the map are keyed to photos

A photo shows the enormous length of central nave of Durham Cathedral.

http://www.dur.ac.uk/~dla0www/c_tour/choir.gif

below, which will bring up high-quality photographic views of the cathedral, castle, or the surrounding areas.

Selecting a tour of the cathedral brings up a plan of the cathedral, in the classic medi-eval cross pattern, with key spots marked and numbered with dots. The dots correspond to links further down on the page, most of them with photos, which show the interior detail and views of the cathedral. ▲

NASA Dryden Research Aircraft Photo Archive

http://www.dfrf.nasa.gov/PhotoServer/photoServer.html

SEE RELATED SITES:

Ch 13 PHOTOGRAPHY
Ch 17 TRANSPORTATION

THE BULK OF Dryden's photograph archive is devoted to the experimental aircraft that drive the imagination of both enthusiasts and non-enthusiasts, such as The Stealth Bomber, the Space Shuttle, and the X series.

There are so many images in this archive that even graphics gluttons may feel intimidated. Dryden's home page site manager has taken extensive steps to control the bloat by labeling each collection by aircraft type, as well as warning how many images are con-tained in the collection. Each link begins with a photo index, which previews all of the images and gives the file names. More information can usually be found within each link, noted at the top of the individual collections.

Additionally, each photograph is provided in 1280×1024 and 602×480 resolution, depending on how much time you want to commit to downloading. File sizes are given for each resolution. The only

20

An HL-10 being serviced on a lakebed testing ground in 1969 with a B-52 flying overhead.

http://www.dfrf.nasa.gov/PhotoServer/HL-10/Small/EC-2203.jpg

Post-impact fireball of a controlled impact demonstration crash in 1984 of an ECN-31808.

http://www.dfrf.nasa.gov/PhotoServer/CID/Small/ECN-31808.jpg

shortcoming of the archive is the brief file descriptions, such as "F-16 AFTI in banked flight."

For visitors who are too overwhelmed by the size of the archive to know where to start, the site provides the Top Ten Downloads from the Dryden WWW Photo server, categorized by month. The number one photograph in June 1995 was downloaded more than

2,700 times (AD-1 in flight at 60 degree wing sweep), and represents only a small percent of the 71,080 total images downloaded during that month.

There are also links to Other Dryden Images, such as photographs of the EVA (extra-vehicular activity) spacewalk that repaired the Hubble Telescope; and to Other NASA Image Archives. While the aircraft featured at this site are experimental, the Dryden is definitely a success. ▲

Dead Sea Scrolls

 http://sunsite.unc.edu/expo/deadsea.scrolls.exhibit/intro.html

SEE RELATED SITES:

Ch 7 ART MUSEUMS

WHEN THE DEAD Sea Scrolls were discovered in caves in the Judean desert in 1947, the scholarly world was abuzz with excitement.

However, that excitement was dulled over several decades by the fact that few scholars were given access to the scrolls and the numerous fragments. Finally, an unofficial version of the scrolls was assembled, without permission of the authorities, from the parts that had been released.

Now, thanks to the Internet, anyone can look at them.

Old pieces of parchment with ancient Hebrew written on them may not make the most exciting images on the Internet, but this site does demonstrate the power of the Internet to offer access, through graphics, to documents whose meaning and context is still under debate.

You'll probably appreciate the detail and care that goes into working with documents as old as these, as well, after viewing the tiny, ragged-edged pieces of parchment that scholars have been working with.

For those of us who can't read Hebrew (and probably for many who do but can't make out the faint writing on these extremely old documents) translations are provided for all the documents.

The original exhibit at the Library of Congress had nearly 100 objects in it. A decent subset—12 scroll fragments and 29 other objects—appears in the online exhibit.

The other objects are taken from the Qmran community, the group which is believed to be responsible for writing and saving the Dead Sea Scrolls, and include coins, pottery, vases, phylacteries, cups, and other objects.

Some Torah Precepts from the Dead Sea Scrolls.

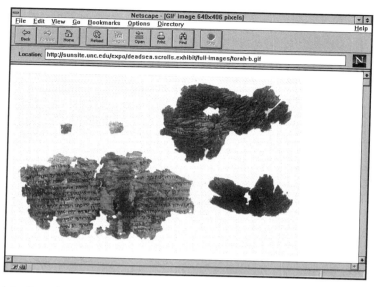

http://sunsite.unc.edu/expo/deadsea.scrolls.exhibit/full-images/
torah-b.gif

Desktop Cinema

 http://www.iac.net:80/~flypba/TRAILERS/index.html

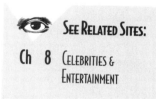

See Related Sites:

Ch 8 Celebrities & Entertainment

EVER HAVE THE experience of seeing a preview of a movie, deciding you just had to go, then realizing that the preview contained all the good parts? You could have saved yourself eight bucks, parking, babysitting, and popcorn down your shirt if you had just watched the preview instead of the movie. Well, folks, Desktop Cinema is for you.

Desktop Cinema is a site where you'll only see the trailers. This site is actually the home page of a small airline (perhaps their routes aren't long enough to show the whole movie), but it looks professionally done.

From the home page, click on the alphabetical index, and you'll see a list of letters. Click the first letter of the film whose trailer you want to see, and you can download it.

This site thoughtfully has two icons for every movie. One is to download the movie itself, and the other, if it's there, will take you to the site of the movie's production company or distributor, where you can often find still photos from the movie, additional video clips, background information, and so on.

If you click on QuickTime links from the home page, you'll get to a list of links to film studios and distributors. It also includes links to other QuickTime sites and clips from many popular television shows as well, such as television comedies and sci-fi dramas like *Earth2, Hercules, SeaQuest, Star Trek Voyager,* and *The X-Files.*

You'll need a QuickTime viewer to get the information off here, because that's what the movie studios use for most of their files. If you don't have one, there's a link to Apple, which can help you get a copy of the viewer. ▲

A moment of terror in a trailer of the film Species.

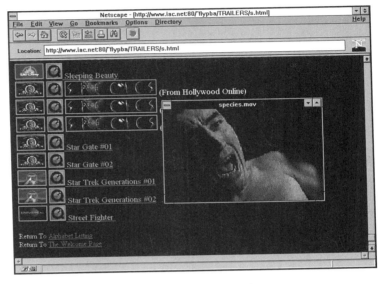

http://www.iac.net:80/~flypba/TRAILERS/s.html

Elliott Brown Gallery

 http://www.ftgi.com/iar/1.html

 SEE RELATED SITES:

Ch 5 ART GALLERIES

THE WORLD OF artistic glass is not a large one, given the difficulties of working with the medium. If you're interested in seeing what can be done with glass, you'll want to check out this gallery.

The number of images per artist is not large, but this gallery represents a large number of artists working in that medium, so you'll get a chance to compare styles and products (and prices, gulp).

The best way to get into this gallery is near the bottom of the home page, where you'll see a section called Artists Represented.

Little camera icons indicate which artists have images associated with their information. Clicking on any one of those artists will bring up a small subgallery devoted to that artists, with a brief biography and a couple of thumbnails that can be clicked on and enlarged.

At the bottom of that subgallery you'll find a list of other artists with images online. Clicking any name will get you to a subgallery with expandable thumbnails from that artist.

You'll see how some artists work with highly geometric or abstract creations, exploiting the translucence of glass, while others experiment with form, creating realistic objects such as human figures or plants.

Others focus on blending colors in glass in relatively simple objects such as bowls or vases to get colorful objects where the liquid quality of glass adds a special dimension to the color blends. ▲

"Forest/Fire Chaos II, 1995" in glass by Toots Zynsky, The Netherlands.

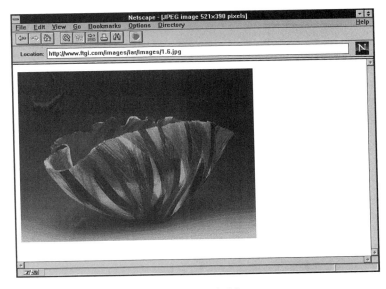

http://www.ftgi.com/images/iar/images/1.6.jpg

Electric Postcards

 http://postcards.www.media.mit.edu:80/Postcards/

 **SEE RELATED SITES:**

Ch 19 XYZ

IT MIGHT SEEM difficult to replace the postcard or greeting experience online until you visit the Electric Postcards site.

The Electric Postcards site isn't an exact duplicate of real-world postcards, but it has its advantages:

▼ The postcard gets home before you do.
▼ You don't need a stamp and you don't have to write sideways to get everything on the card.

The text of the card appears below the card at the Electric Postcard.

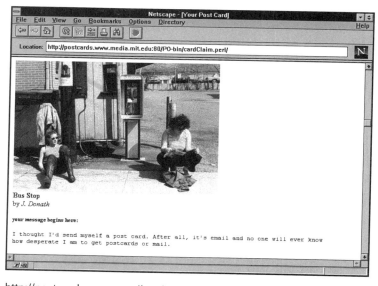

http://postcards.www.media.mit.edu:80/PO-bin/cardClaim.perl/

Here's how it works:

You go to the URL, then head for the postcard rack to pick out a post card. You have a fairly wide selection here and just as in a real postcard store, you can pick out images that fit with the message you want to say.

If the world is exploding around you, a nice Kandinsky might be appropriate. If you're finding the accommodations below par, you can try an image from New York's Lower East side. We chose an exciting bus stop scene to show you what a thrill it is to travel.

Fill in your name and your e-mail address and the recipient's e-mail address, then type away in the text box, saying whatever you like. You can even put HTML code, such as a link to a site on the Internet, here. Then hit the send button.

The recipient receives e-mail with a special code saying that there is a postcard waiting at this site. They fire up their Web browser and come to this site. They go to the pickup window, enter their code, and view their card. ▲

Electronic Frontier Foundation Graphics Archive

 http://www.eff.org/pub/Graphics/

 **See Related Sites:**

Ch 9 Clip Art & Icons

THE ELECTRONIC FRONTIER Foundation is an important organization for maintaining sanity in cyberspace.

Dedicated to the cause of effective public computer networks, it has also stepped in with intelligent interventions in public policy debates on the Net.

If you're looking for some graphic ammunition for similar causes, either on your own Web site, for bumper stickers and emblems, t-shirts, and the like, you'll want to check out this site.

There are a few photos of EFF staff here, but the graphics that will be most attractive for people visiting this site will be those related to using the Net to empower people, preventing government from exercising too heavy a hand, and a few neat information highway stickers. Several are scans of EFF bumper stickers that could probably be printed and stuck to your own vehicle.

Click on the EFF Icons Archive link and you'll find yourself in an icon directory with more than 500 GIF icons

in it, as well as a few JPEGs. These are general-purpose icons for use on Web pages, not just EFF-related subjects. The icon archive includes dozens of arrows, VCR-style control buttons, cartoon characters like Asterix and Bill the Cat, some very cool lines used to separate sections of your Web page, and some backgrounds that can be tiled to make a background.

The icons are in an FTP directory, alphabetized by name, but if you want to quickly look at a range of icons, you can click on some index links in the library. A link to Icons F-H will bring up all the icons whose names begin with the letters F-H.

Unfortunately, once you see an icon you like here you'll still have to figure out which one it is in the FTP directory, because only a few of the icons that show up in the index are a link to the actual icon. Most are inline graphics, which shows you what's available, but doesn't tell you what its name is. ▲

20

Detail of an anti-Clipper Chip poster from the Electronic Frontier Foundation.

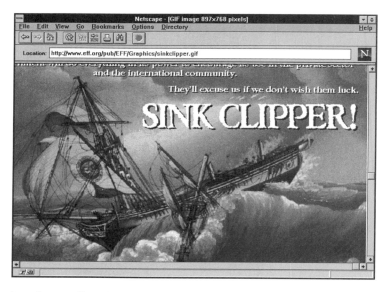

http://www.eff.org/pub/EFF/Graphics/sinkclipper.gif

Age of Enlightenment

 http://dmf.culture.fr/files/imaginary_exhibition.html

SEE RELATED SITES:

Ch 7 ART MUSEUMS

THE ENLIGHTENMENT, a period of liberal thought which led to the French and American revolutions, was also a time of artistic ferment.

This was a time when France, both prosperous, yet groaning under the extravagance of its monarchs, had money for art and was exploring grand philosophical and social themes. The French Ministry of Culture has gathered representative images of that period at one Web site.

If you remember that this art represents what Europe was thinking just before the great revolutions overturned established aristocracies in North America and Europe, you'll find the themes of many of the paintings intriguing. They are also grand paintings, finished in a sweeping, salon painting style.

At first glance this seems like yet another of those Internet museums that is long on words, short on visual product, because only one image from each artist is presented here. But the French artistic heritage from the Enlightenment is so rich that even with only one picture from each artist (including the prolific "Anonymous," who is also

"Jesus Driving the Merchants out of the Temple" by Jean-Germain Drouais.

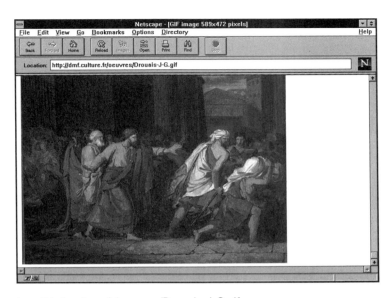

http://dmf.culture.fr/oeuvres/Drouais-J-G.gif

restricted to one painting) this exhibit contains more than 100 paintings.

Unfortunately, the exhibit has no thumbnails, so you either have to know what these images are, or spend a good deal of time browsing through them.

Of some help are the links you'll find in several text documents defining the period and offering some background information on the Enlightenment, but your best bet is the Index of Artists, which brings up an alphabetical list showing the name of the artist, the title of the work on display, and the city and museum where the original painting is now located. ▲

Space Shuttle Earth Observations Project

 http://ersaf.jsc.nasa.gov/sn5.html

YOU KNOW, when you get right down to it, there's no place like home. Especially when you're about 125 miles up, after being hurled into space by a barely-controlled explosion, and getting home means a fiery re-entry into the atmosphere.

Even if you're not a shuttle astronaut, it can be interesting to see what the old homestead looks like from a few hundred miles up.

The Space Shuttle Earth Observations Project, part of NASA's Earth Sciences Branch, uses one of the simpler space technologies around: astronauts take a camera, point it out the window, and shoot pictures.

But that low-tech approach has enabled them to capture images of great parts of the Earth's surface on their missions around the world.

When you first hit this site you'll see some of the better images the astronauts have taken. There's an impressive photo of Hurricane Elena, shot in 1985; images of ocean currents; pollution in the Soviet Union; and a clear shot of the huge area covered by an exploding volcano in the South Pacific.

But the chances are good that if you don't live at the North Pole or Tierra del Fuego or some other location where shuttles don't pass over frequently, the astronauts have taken a picture of your hometown.

At the bottom of this site is a link to a map of the world that you can click on. You have your choice of a great screen-filling, half-megabyte monster that will let you choose your site carefully, or a smaller map where you can only choose a general area.

Simply click on the area you want to see, and the host computer will come back with a list of images you can see. The list includes the latitude and longitude of the photo and a short description of the subject matter. Each photo is accompanied by a text description that provides more

The Rabaul volcano, on the east end of the island of New Britain, spreads ash over a vast area of the Pacific Ocean in 1994.

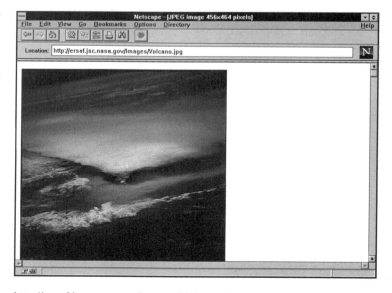

http://ersaf.jsc.nasa.gov/Images/Volcano.jpg

Click on the map at the Earth Observation Laboratory to see photos taken from the space shuttle.

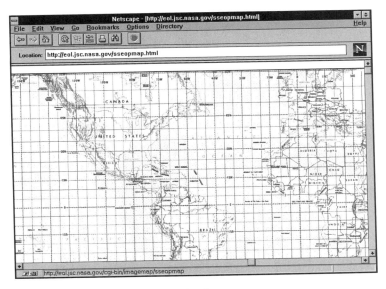

http://eol.jsc.nasa.gov/sseopmap.html

precise information about the angle from which the picture was taken, the height of the shuttle and the time, and the latitude and longitude of the center of the picture.

Even without graphical browsers you can still get at the image database by telneting to **photos@sseop.jsc.nasa.gov.** By using a standard character interface you can retrieve pictures of the area you want. ▲

The Essential Escher

 http://www.umich.edu/~mransfrd/escher/

SEE RELATED SITES:

Ch 7 ART MUSEUMS

M.C. ESCHER'S DELIGHTFUL visual puzzles—a school of fish that turns into a flock of geese, stairs that go up and down at the same time, and other tricks—seem to never lose their appeal. If anything, they are enjoying a revival. They are especially suited to the techno-logical mindset of the Internet, where Escher's work has al-ways been appreciated for its mathematical precision and the questions it raises about the way we perceive the world. Some have argued that Escher was the first artist of the 20th century to incorporate the science of the 20th century, such as relativity and modern psychology.

At this site you'll find about 200 of Escher's images. You have several options in accessing the work. You can view his pictures by year, to follow Escher's own artistic and intellectual growth; by title; or by looking at a gallery of the most popular work.

If you want to understand Escher better and understand some of the principles he was exploring, you can click on the Mathematical Analysis button on the home page. It's actually a very readable summary of some of the mathematical issues with which Escher dealt, prepared by Webmaster Matt Ransford. It has links to all the images that it mentions, so it's an excellent guided tour through Escher's later work (the essay covers his art with a mathematical context after 1937). The essay is based on a book by Bruno Ernst and divides Escher's work into easily digestible portions. ▲

"Three spheres II," drawn in 1946, explores a theme popular with today's ray-tracing computer software.

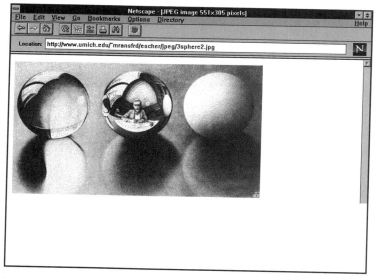

http://www.umich.edu/~mransfrd/escher/jpeg/3sphere2.jpg

Electronic Visualization Laboratory

 http://www.ncsa.uiuc.edu/EVL/docs/html/gallery.html

 SEE RELATED SITES:

Ch 10 COMPUTER-GENERATED ART

THE ELECTRONIC VISUALIZATION Laboratory is one of those rare places that offers advanced degrees for both engineers and artists in the same location.

Computers can be used to visualize invisible scientific phenomena or to create a visual representation of scientific or statistical data. Scientific data or mathematical formulas can also be used as tools for the artist.

The artists at EVL have access to some of the most powerful computers in the world, at nearby Argonne National Laboratory and the National Center for Supercomputing Applications.

From the home page, clicking on the Electronic Gallery brings you face to face with this dichotomy: your choices are the art/design gallery or the science/technology gallery.

The most prolific artist here is Tom Coffin, who works with abstract, computer-generated images, although he gives them names suggesting a theme. Under Yantra, for example you'll find images inspired by Tibetan mandalas.

Soldlikemeat involves complex mixtures of pure-color video, which make dazzling images. The Extended series adds geometric overlays to the Soldlikemeat collection.

Jason Leigh shows some graphics developed for games, as well as scientific images.

Tom Nawara uses images captured from video as his raw material, creating overlays and filters that modify the original and create new art.

The Scientific gallery is not as extensive. It has a collection of miscellaneous images, but displays them as only small inline images, without captions, which is more or less a waste of bandwidth.

You'll find a bit more in the scientific area under Carolina Cruz-Neira's gallery, which has some models of biochemical processes and has even applied computer graphics to the area of investment portfolio management. Of greatest long-term interest, although you can't see much over the Internet, may be her work with CAVE, Cave Automatic Virtual Environment. This room-sized virtual-reality effort is pictured and described online. ▲

EVL artist Deb Lowman uses an object transformer program to generate sensuous shapes.

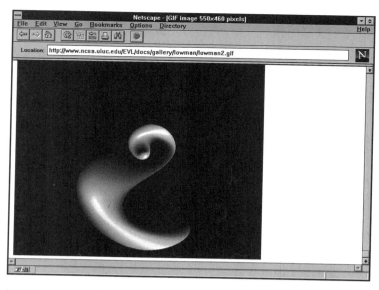

http://www.ncsa.uiuc.edu/EVL/docs/gallery/lowman/lowman2.gif

Entertainment Weekly

 http://www.pathfinder.com/

SEE RELATED SITES:

Ch 8 CELEBRITIES & ENTERTAINMENT

PHOTOS AREN'T THE main focus of this site, but it is nevertheless lavishly illustrated everywhere you look. Since it's about the entertainment industry, it's a great place to pick up images of the people who are in the news, or young and upcoming entertainers who are just beginning to make their marks.

As is usual with a news-oriented product, content will change on a weekly basis. But if there's a hot movie that is about to be released, or has just been released, chances are good that EW will have something on it.

Check out the cover story for that week, because it is most likely going to have pictures of stars who are the subjects of stories or interviews. These are superb pictures, too, shot to the standards of Time-Life, and you're not going to find them elsewhere on the Net.

You can also look in the Movie Reviews section, because they all come with photos featuring the stars of the film.

For the latest films, click on the Reviews button and locate the film you're looking for. This section only shows the most recent films reviewed in the magazine, but if you click on the Short Reviews link under the movie reviews for the week, you'll get reviews of all the films currently showing, with at least one photo from each film showing the stars.

At the bottom of the page you'll find the most direct route of all: a searchable database. The default is to search the entire Pathfinder database of Time-Warner magazines, which will produce quite a few hits if you're not careful. ▲

Sandra Bullock, featured in an Entertainment Week interview.

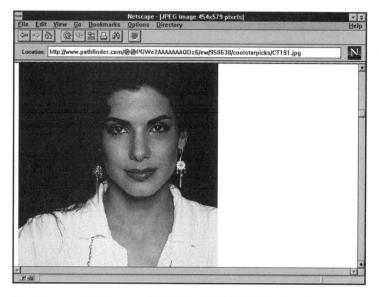

http://www.pathfinder.com/@@PGWe2AAAAAAAQDz6/ew/950630/coolstarpicks/CT191.jpg

Val Kilmer in an Entertainment Weekly interview.

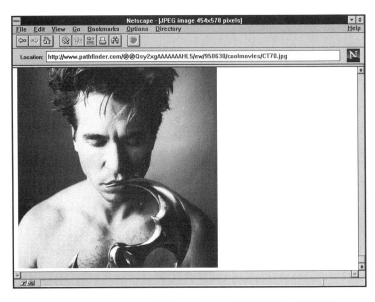

http://www.pathfinder.com/@@Qsy2xgAAAAAAHL5/ew/950630/
coolmovies/CT70.jpg

FineArt Forum Gallery

http://www.msstate.edu/Fineart_Online/gallery.html

SEE RELATED SITES:

Ch 6 ART IN CYBERSPACE

FINEART FORUM is an electronic news service that is available via e-mail, or online Gopher or WWW sites. It also has its own gallery for carrying images of some of the artists who are covered by the news service.

You'll find a variety of art here, from installations to galleries of photographs and artists statements of various kinds. You can also pick up a copy of the newsletter, which has lots of information about other sites and activities on the Internet.

When we were there it had photographs of installations by Australian artist Wendy Mills, who produces interactive sculptures.

A section on Joseph DeLappe showed art dealing to a large extent with the role of the media. It has some delicious composite images, which turned all the anchormen on television into a single smiling, wise-eyed, nodding individual.

Celeste Brignac's photos cover digital images, fashion, portraiture, and fine art photography.

Paul Brown has a multi-layered gallery that covers

A menagerie of images in this digital work by Jay Riskind.

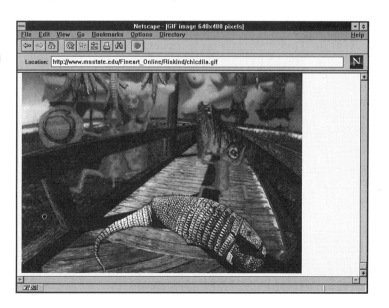

http://www.msstate.edu/Fineart_Online/Riskind/chicdila.gif

several eras of his work, including B.C. (Before Computers). A pioneer in computer-generated art, he displays several images that were at the dawn of technologies such as ray-tracing and shadow generation techniques used in computer-generated art.

Then there's the art by performance artist Stellarc who, because of the nature of his art, shows how he makes it, rather than what it looks like. He's fond of adding a third arm or hand to his body to see what kind of art it makes. He's also fond of some medical procedures to create what he calls "stomach sculpture," and we would prefer, in this case not to see how it's done. ▲

FBI's 10 Most Wanted

 http://www.fbi.gov/toplist.htm

 SEE RELATED SITES:

Ch 8 CELEBRITIES & ENTERTAINMENT
Ch 19 XYZ

EVERY NOW AND then, while focusing on white-collar computer crimes, like stealing passwords and data, it's useful to remember that there are people out there whose potential danger is a lot more personal.

The FBI's 10 Most Wanted List is a long-running part of American culture, having run for more than 45 years. Most of us don't get into the police station enough to get a look at the list, but the FBI now puts it on the Internet.

At this site you'll find photos of the FBI's 10 most wanted fugitives from justice. Actually, it's often more like eight or nine most wanted since there is occasionally a vacancy on the list.

Navigation at this site is simple. You've got a list of names. Click on one to retrieve the picture.

Pictures are accompanied by lengthy descriptions of the fugitives including Social Security numbers used, tattoos and scars, and hobbies or activities they are known to pursue when not engaged in criminal activities. You'll also get a description of the crimes the fugitives are accused of committing.

The FBI warns that citizens should not try to confront anyone they believe to be a fugitive, but should contact the nearest FBI office. There's a link to a list of all the FBI offices at the site.

It will be interesting to see whether the Internet proves a useful supplement to the FBI's publicity campaign. Of the 438 fugitives whose faces have graced the list since it was first posted in 1950, 412 have been located, 129 of them as a result of citizens who identified the fugitives. ▲

One of the FBI's 10 Most Wanted now graces the Internet.

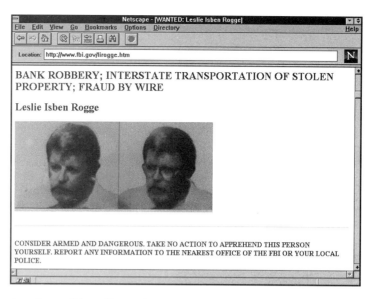

http://www.fbi.gov/lirogge.htm

Field Museum of Natural History

 http://www.bvis.uic.edu:80/museum/Home.html

 **SEE RELATED SITES:**

Ch 14 SCIENCE & NATURE

THE FIELD MUSEUM of Natural History is one of the oldest and most famous of its kind.

Its Web page is a youthful, sprightly look at some of the major exhibits, lavishly illustrated with drawings, photographs, MPEG movies, and sound files.

Clicking on the Exhibits icon on the home page brought us to several major sections of the museum: a section on the evolution of land animals, including reptiles, dinosaurs, and mammals; one on Javanese masks; and another on bats.

If you're the movie type, you could go directly to the media center and watch some very short animations showing dinosaurs eating or running. The same section also includes some interactive games, usually illustrated in some fashion, where you can test your knowledge of the subject.

To see the dinosaur exhibit, you could take a well-marked Quick Tour, which goes, frame by frame, through major features of the exhibit. Side tours show images of related animals or features, but a simple click will get you back on the tour where you left off.

20

A Javanese mask from the Field Museum's collection.

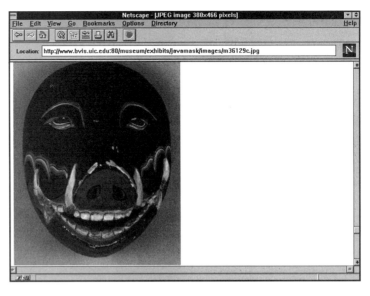

http://www.bvis.uic.edu:80/museum/exhibits/javamask/images/
m36129c.jpg

The Javanese mask collection is an important one, because the 80 masks in the collection were made in the late 1800s and came to Chicago during the World's Colombian Exposition at Chicago in 1893. The large reconstruction of a Javanese village at that exhibition was a big hit at the time.

The bat section has images of the museum's displays on bats, as well as two MPEG movies showing bats eating and hanging upside down. ▲

FINS (Fish Information Service)

http://www.actwin.com/fish/index.html

IF YOU THINK cats, butterflies, and damsels might all frolic in your garden someday, you obviously don't own an aquarium.

FINS is a very complete information service for aquarium owners, both fresh and salt water, that contains photos of all the common species of aquarium fish.

The graphics aren't big, but then neither are the fish.

This site uses common names, the kind you would find in an aquarium or pet store, although the scientific names are listed as well.

When you get to the site,

you can select from either the catalog of marine fish and invertebrates, or the freshwater species. FINS then gives you a bunch of options for searching further. You can sort the collection of more than 200 photos by common name, scientific name, or type of fish. You can also search directly for a fish by typing in any keyword associated with it, by clicking the search button, and filling in the form.

If you want to visually browse the pictures, you can select one of several pictorial guides. These bring up clickable image maps. If you see something you like, or you're trying to identify that unusual fish with the pink stripes you saw in a friend's aquarium, there's a good chance it will turn up in one of these pictorial guides. Click on the fish and you'll get a more thorough explanation. ▲

FINS provides an easy, visual way to identify and choose fish.

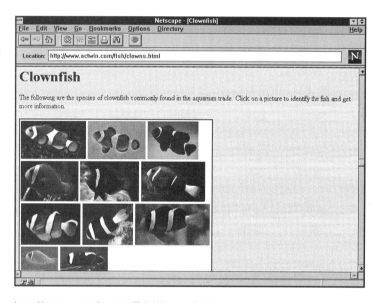

http://www.actwin.com/fish/clowns.html

Franklin Institute Science Museum

 http://sln.fi.edu/

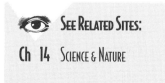
SEE RELATED SITES:

Ch 14 SCIENCE & NATURE

BENJAMIN FRANKLIN WAS one remarkable guy, someone who today we would call a "Renaissance Man" or a "polymath," someone who excelled in many different areas.

He was an astute politician who guided the development of the United States and served as an ambassador. He had an inquiring and scientific mind, and made some important discoveries about electricity. He was practical: families and forests the world over owe him a debt for the Franklin stove, which replaced open fireplaces with a far more efficient and safer cooking device. And he still had enough common sense to write the classic folk wisdom collection *Poor Richard's Almanac*.

The Franklin Science Museum is dedicated to the scientific side of Franklin. On its Web site it offers online exhibits related to Franklin and to basic science.

The museum had two shows in its virtual exhibit area when we visited—one on Benjamin Franklin and another on the human heart.

The exhibit on Ben Franklin includes several movies, including a QuickTime introduction to Franklin, and you can see pictures of Franklin's birthplace, tombstone, printing press, hot air balloons, several of his inventions, such as the Franklin stove and bifocals, and other images associated with the man.

The heart exhibition had QuickTime movies of open heart surgery, an echocardiogram of a beating heart, and tips on how to take your pulse, as well as heart X-rays, animations of the beating heart, an image of arteries and capillaries.

The museum also had a teacher's unit on wind and wind energy, with photos, movies, bibliographies, and links to other sites on the Internet related to wind. ▲

Ben Franklin's bifocals, and a movie of the human heart, at the Franklin Science Museum.

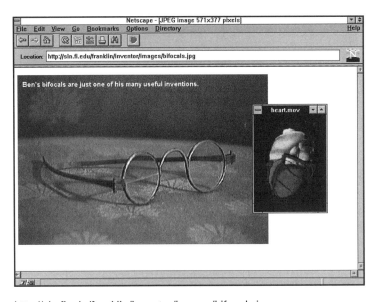

http://sln.fi.edu/franklin/inventor/images/bifocals.jpg

Frank Lloyd Wright in Wisconsin

 http://flw.badgernet.com:2080/

SEE RELATED SITES:

Ch 4 ARCHITECTURE

CONSIDERING HIS IMPORTANCE in architecture, and in American architecture in particular, there are surprisingly few places on the Internet where one can go to look at the work of Frank Lloyd Wright.

Wright was innovative in his designs, but acutely sensitive to local landscapes and materials. Many of his structures have a timeless, classic quality, appearing modern today even though they might have been designed 50 years ago.

This is about as good a site as one can find on the Internet at the moment, even though it covers only Wright's buildings in his home state of Wisconsin, and even then only eight of the 41 structures in Wisconsin that he designed.

You can get at pictures of Wright's work in two ways at this site. One route takes you to an online version of a tour brochure intended to guide those who want to actually visit the buildings. It has pictures and descriptions of each of the buildings, which include Wright's home, offices, a school, churches, a warehouse, and the Seth Peterson cottage (with information about how you, too, can rent a weekend in this cottage).

One of the most important buildings he designed, and the one in which he certainly spent the most time, was his own home, the famous Taliesin (Welsh for "Shining Brow"). While the tour brochure has one picture, the multi-media gallery link takes you to a much more complete look at Taliesin, with three exterior and three interior views. In a video gallery you can download some AVI or QuickTime clips of Wright speaking about architecture. ▲

20

Exterior view of Taliesin.

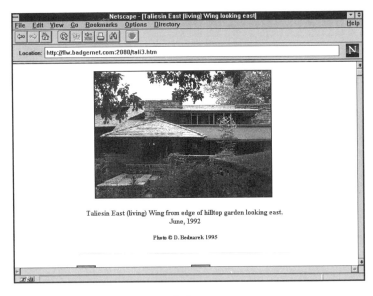

http://flw.badgernet.com:2080/tali3.htm

Fluxus Online

 http://anansi.panix.com:80/fluxus/FluxusMenu.html

 **SEE RELATED SITES:**

Ch 6 ART IN CYBERSPACE

SERIOUS. BIZARRE. BITING social comment. Total waste of time. Best site on the Net. Disgusting.

That pretty well sums up Fluxus in a nutshell. The site has several self-definitions of itself, but they're not much good, and in fact they're not intended to do much good:

"Fluxus is the wry, post-Dada art movement that flourished in New York and Germany in the 1950s and '60s, and influences many contemporary artists. The rest you have to figure out yourself…"

It's hard to write about a site that covers the bleeding edge of art in so many directions:

still images, video, poetry, icons, dance, and the like. This is a site with tremendous depth and breadth, plus plenty of things you've never heard of nor thought of before. One of the less radical contributors here is Yoko Ono, if that tells you anything.

You might also want to download a copy of the Genetic Code Copyright, a legal-looking certificate, complete with gold seal, in which you Do Forever Hereby Copyright Your Unique Genetic Code. Any reproduction thereof is strictly prohibited.

Larry Miller's Genetic Code Certificate.

GENETIC CODE COPYRIGHT

I, _____

Born a natural human being on the _____ day of _____ in the year _____,

In the town, state and country of_____,

Of my mother, _____ and my father, _____,

DO HEREBY FOREVER COPYRIGHT MY UNIQUE GENETIC CODE,
HOWEVER IT MAY BE SCIENTIFICALLY DETERMINED, DESCRIBED OR OTHERWISE EMPIRICALLY EXPRESSED.

Any reproduction, regeneration or facsimile duplication, whether in whole or in part,
whether physically manifested or technologically represented is UNIVERSALLY PROHIBITED.
All rights and permissions are reserved and may only be assigned, in whole or in part,
to a specified agent via legal, written authorization by me or by my legal heirs upon my decease.

Sworn to and subscribed before me as witness
on this _____ day of _____
in the year _____
in the town, state and country of

Sworn and declared by me,
an Original Human,
with fingerprint affixed herein

WITNESS   PROCLAIMER

http://anansi.panix.com:80/fluxus/FLUXUS_ONLINE/FLUXON_ART/
WRITE/Genetic_Code___Certificate/_Larry_Miller3.JPEG

This is a site with plenty of in-your-face, confrontational, rude art that calls into question not only art, but artists and viewers and ultimately the meanings of the symbols and objects they see and use and live with every day. But that's the point. You'll leave this place shaking your head in awe, wonder, and frustration all at the same time.

As a site that uses the latest technology, Fluxus also probes and pokes at technology and the way we think about it. You'll want to see some of the amusing images of the "Techno-Buddha." ▲

The Fractal Gallery

 http://eulero.cineca.it/~strumia/FractalGallery.htm

20

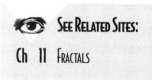

See Related Sites:

Ch 11 Fractals

Alberto Strumia's Fractal Gallery, at the University of Bologna in Italy, is a beautiful exploration of the fractal form.

Strumia has some lovely images here, but this site is really oriented to demonstrating some simple fractal forms and ideas rather than blowing you away with sheer content.

Strumia presents a fair amount of the mathematics of fractals at this site, but in a helpful and useful manner. The basic concepts are clearly illustrated with pictures that show non-mathematicians what's actually happening.

If you're stymied by simple math, but are still curious about how fractals are made, Strumia illustrates the technique with a kind of non-techie guide to fractals, using something called the curve of Van Koch. It shows how you can take a simple line, and by repeatedly replacing each line with a more complex series of lines, produce a more complex image.

By transforming each straight line into a more complex series of straight lines, and repeating the process several times, a more complex image is developed. This is the basic process by which fractals are made.

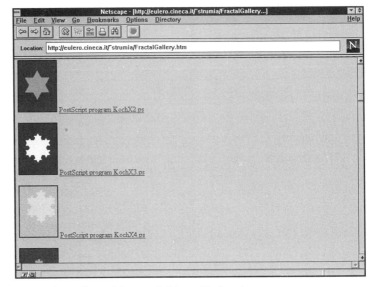

http://eulero.cineca.it/~strumia/FractalGallery.htm

The Fractal Gallery has many illustrations of three-dimensional fractals such as this "Gothic Cathedral" fractal.

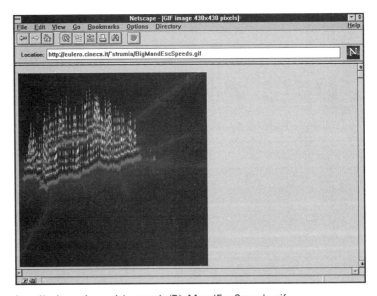

http://eulero.cineca.it/~strumia/BigMandEscSpeeds.gif

Strumia also includes some very simple program code that you can use to generate simple fractals on your own computer.

Strumia looks at three major types of fractals (Mandelbrots, Julias, and images that look like real objects), and often begins with a very simple version of the formula to demonstrate its basic shape and characteristics.

From there you move on to more sophisticated versions or in-depth looks. For example, you'll find the basic Mandelbrot set here, but this site looks at one of its features, "The Seahorse Valley," in detail.

This site also looks at some of the ways in which fractal images can echo real life. You'll find fractals that look like insects, mountain ranges, iced lakes, gothic cathedrals, leaves, and other shapes. ▲

Fractal Movie Archive

 http://www.cnam.fr/fractals.html

👁 SEE RELATED SITES:

Ch 3 ANIMATION
Ch 11 FRACTALS

FRACTAL PICTURES AND Animations, home of the Fractal Movie Archive, is one of those mathematical playgrounds on the Net where the non-mathematical can still play.

It has a good set of mini-galleries showing the work of some of the better fractal artists on the Net, but its main claim to fame is the extensive set of fractal animations in the Fractal Movie Archive.

We're talking about more than 110 animations, and 160 megabytes of "footage," in a variety of common video formats, such as mpegs, QuickTime, .fli, and .flc formats.

You can fly through all kinds of theoretical constructs, such as fractals, solutions to famous mathematical problems, and sets of numbers.

A popular pastime is to do a "deep zoom" on the Mandelbrot set, which, because it is a fractal image, continues to show detail even at huge magnifications.

Slightly more conventional animations can zoom you through the hills north of San Francisco, then down and through the Golden Gate bridge, just above the roadway, then around the end and underneath the bridge before heading back to the hills, all without raising an eyebrow at the Federal Aviation Administration, since it's done entirely with a fractal image.

20

Zooming through the Golden Gate bridge at the Fractal Movie Archive.

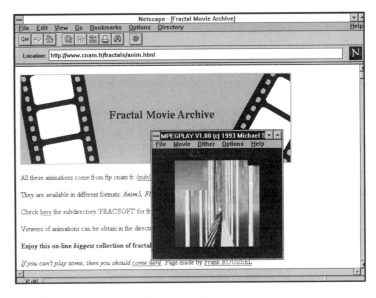

http://www.cnam.fr/fractals/anim.html

Other animations take you through canyons, over deserts, and around mountains.

Many of these images are in the multi-megabyte range, with up to 14 megabytes, but some of the simpler versions are mpegs of a few hundred kilobytes. Our San Francisco trip, for example, is a moderate 181Kb.

Don't forget to stop by some of the galleries on your visit here. One of the best galleries at this site belongs to Jean-Francois Colonna. While many fractal artists try to extract every last photon of vividness out of your computer screen, Colonna shows refreshing restraint and taste.

Check out his autostereograms—images which, if you let your eyes cross and focus in the distance, can display a three-dimensional effect. Results will vary, depending on your computer screen and eyes. Colonna also has some excellent synthesized mountains, clouds, and sunsets. ▲

Jean-Francois Colonna's "Shell in Motion."

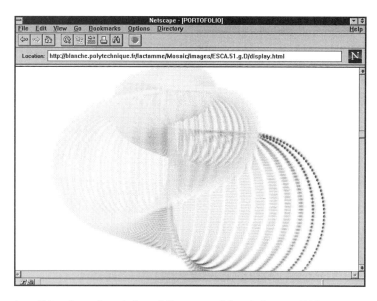

http://blanche.polytechnique.fr/lactamme/Mosaic/images/ESCA.51.g.D/display.html

Interactive Frog Dissection

 http://curry.edschool.Virginia.EDU:80/~insttech/frog/

SEE RELATED SITES:

Ch 2 ANIMALS
Ch 14 SCIENCE & NATURE

DISSECTING ANIMALS IN the laboratory is a powerful teaching tool, but not everyone enjoys the smell of formaldehyde or the thought that some poor animal gave up its life to have its private parts exposed to snotty-nosed students.

Ta-da. To the rescue comes the Interactive Frog Dissection, where you keep your hands on a mouse and disassemble a frog. The authors say it's a great teaching tool, and we've heard that the frogs like it better as well.

The frog is pictured, stage by stage, as it is pinned to a dissection tray and then carefully dissected. But it's not

merely a set of static images. As you scroll through the pictures you learn the fine art of frog dissection, and then it's your turn to play biologist.

If you play the game properly, you actually have to interact with the images on the screen, "putting" the pins in the right place to hold the animal to the dissection tray, making incisions in the right locations, and so on. You do that by clicking on the appropriate points with your mouse.

Each click on an incision point, for example, will elicit a "Sorry, try again" or "That's right" message in return. Once you've identified all the right points, it's time to move to the next step.

Those in a rush can easily navigate to various levels of the tutorial by clicking on the appropriate section at the top.

Photos at the end show the frogs innards in fine scientific detail, with some parts high-lighted to make sure you can identify them.

The site also has QuickTime movies to illustrate various steps of the process. They range from about 1.5 mega-bytes to nearly 7 megabytes, so fast Internet connections are recommended. ▲

Interactive frog dissection.

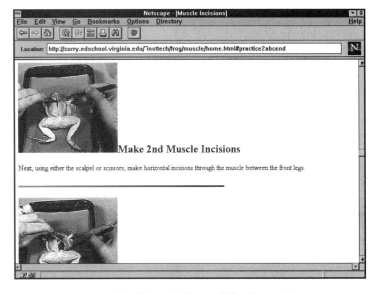

http://curry.edschool.virginia.edu/~insttech/frog/muscle/
home.html#practice2abcend

FUNET

  ftp://pictures@ftp.funet.fi/pub/pics/clipart/

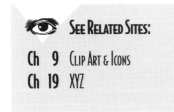

SEE RELATED SITES:

Ch 9 CLIP ART & ICONS
Ch 19 XYZ

LIKE ITS SISTER at SUNET (Swedish University Network) one border over, FUNET (Finnish University Network) is a huge, all purpose archive, with about 40 gigabytes of files on line. Only a portion of those are images, but that still leaves a lot of images.

This site has an extensive clip art collection. Many of the images contain multiple pieces of clip art, so although there are more than 500 files in the pub/pictures/clipart directory, there are more pieces of clip art than that.

Few directories have an index or a readme file identifying the files in the directory, so you have to rely on file names, which are fortunately in English.

We were particularly impressed with the Scenes directory, and its extensive collection of photos from many countries. Some countries may only have a few images, but sometimes when you need something to illustrate a foreign country almost anything typical of that country will do.

The service runs with a line-speed restriction, that is, the download speed is determined by the number of users on the system. If you're on a modem anyway, this may not cause problems, but those with faster connections might experience slower response than they're accustomed to.

There's a trick to logging into this server, because it limits access from outside Europe. Users from outside Nordic Europe who want to access the graphics archives must log in with the username "pictures" and their e-mail address as password. If you are using a World Wide Web browser, use the URL we've listed here. It should ask you for a password. Type in your e-mail address, and you should get in, unless too many people are accessing the archive, in which case you won't be able to access it.

From the main page, click on the pub/ directory, then on graphics/ to get to the picture files. ▲

A German castle image from the FUNET archive.

ftp://pictures@ftp.funet.fi/pub/pics/scenes/Germany/castle.jpg

20

Geometry Center

 http://www.geom.umn.edu/

 **See Related Sites:**

Ch 10 Computer-Generated Art

If they taught geometry back when I went to high school the way the Geometry Center teaches geometry, I probably couldn't keep my hands off the stuff.

Of course, the teacher might have though it doodling, or playing billiards during math class, but at least I'd be prepared to take the chance.

First, if you just want to look at cool images, click on the link to the graphics archive. It grabs a random image from its database of images and pops one on the screen. Every time you access the page you'll see a different image. Or you can click the New Picture button to grab another image out of this archive of images.

Most of the images come with a brief explanation of the geometric principles behind them, but if you already know the basics about "tiling 3-d space by repeated application of rotational symmetries" (their words, not mine), you can always click on the Complete Description link to get a more sophisticated explanation. (Yeah, I thought you'd say

that.)

As nice as the images are, there's more fun in the link for interactive applications. These let you select some basic starting points or values, which the host computer uses to draw new geometric shapes. Your computer doesn't do anything except send some numbers to the host computer. It does all the number crunching and returns the result.

I hate to get practical here, but quiltmakers would go crazy over the Quasi-Tiler application, which comes up with all kinds of elaborate, colored patterns based on input from the user. The Kali draws patterns of lines, while orbifold pinball traces the pattern of a rolling ball on a weird surface (you determine the angle at which the ball starts rolling).

Cyberview lets you rotate three-dimensional objects by clicking on their surfaces.

By the way, teachers can retrieve course materials related to what happens here to use in their own geometry classes. ▲

An image retrieved at random from the Graphics Center archive.

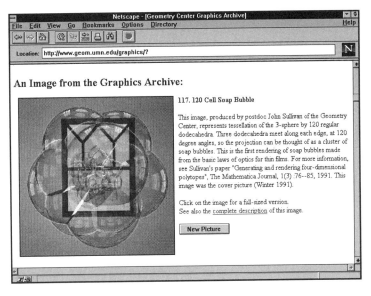

http://www.geom.umn.edu/graphics/?

Glensheen

http://www.d.umn.edu/glensheen/

MAYBE YOU CAN solve a mystery for me. Today, if you want any really fancy wooden ornament for your home, you have to get it in plastic. No one makes finely detailed wood decorations anymore, and if they do, I can't afford it.

Yet, before the age of power tools, mansions were built with room after room of exquisitely detailed finishing, moldings and panels, all done by hand or with very crude hand-cranked tools.

Those are the thoughts that come to mind while wandering through Glensheen, a splendid English-style manor in Duluth. It was completed in 1908, after three years of construction and $800,000, for Chester Adgate Congdon, a local attorney and millionaire.

This is the kind of home that has not only a dining room, but also a breakfast room, with a built-in fountain. Then there's the 10-head shower stall, for that total cleansing experience.

Restored to pristine condition, Glensheen was lovingly photographed by Doug Frisk, who has organized the pictures into a tour of the building and grounds.

You can view this site as though you were a visitor dropping in through the front door. Frisk provides links to the right, left, up the stairs, wherever, to get you around the huge home.

Or you can browse through images of the house in more or less random order, by selecting the "rolls" of film with pictures on them.

If you select the calendar option, you can see some historical, as well as current photos of the house.

In addition to showing the rooms, Frisk shows details that should be of interest to archi-tects, decorators, and people wondering how they made all that fancy stuff without power tools. And, there's a small glossary that covers some of the terms used in the tour, with hyperlinks to the text of the tour.

Antique collectors, decora-tors, and interior designers will love this site, since it shows much of the exquisite period furniture in the mansion, wall coverings, and other details. ▲

Glensheen's grand staircase.

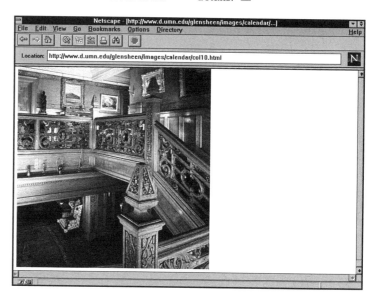

http://www.d.umn.edu/glensheen/images/calendar/col10.html

Grotesk

 http://www.zynet.com/~grotesk/

 **See Related Sites:**

Ch 19 XYZ

You MAY THINK what you wish, after you read about Dan's Gallery of the Grotesque, but in pursuit of the variety of graph-ics sites on the Internet, we felt we could not ignore this fa-mous gallery. You may wish to, however. It is graphic indeed. These images will stay with you for a long time, probably longer than you would like.

Its specialty is *forensic*

photography, the pictures that the police take of the scene of an accident, before anything is moved or disturbed. Added to that are images of dead people and animals, mutations, and so on, always accompanied by flippant commentary and bad puns.

The only good thing about this gallery may come from the Webmaster, who says the gallery depicts how our threshold of disgust has been raised, and our lust for new and bizarre stimuli has increased.

"In your relentless pursuit of even more intensely aberrant stimulation, where will you go from here?"

This gallery is divided into several sections: Necrotica, America's Least Wanted, The Dead Files, and Tasteless Treasures contributed by patrons of the Gallery of the Grotesque.

The Necrotica gallery contains images of dead animals and people, and we're not talking about polite funeral masks, but on-the-scene images of people killed in bizarre accidents. This is the stuff they only show the jury.

In America's Least Wanted section, we have John Bobbitt's penis while not connected to John Bobbitt, and an image of the location where the organ used to be; a grisly scene from the Nicole Brown Simpson household; a final view of Kurt Cobain, and one or two other ghastly images.

The Dead Files contains images of war, such as what happens to a human body when a large grenade or mine explodes directly beneath it, or when it gets in the way of a flame thrower, tank, or automatic machine gun. ▲

Kurt Cobain's death certificate.

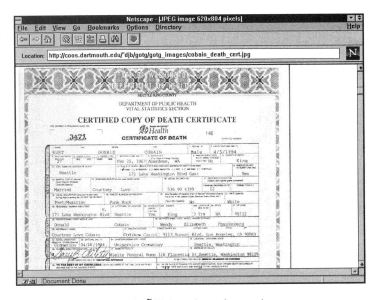

http://coos.dartmouth.edu/~djb/gotg/gotg_images/
cobain_death_cert.jpg

Grotesque in Art

http://www.ugcs.caltech.edu/~werdna/grotesque/grotesque.html

SEE RELATED SITES:

Ch 6 ART IN CYBERSPACE

THIS SITE IS billed as one that explores the "principle anxieties of modern man." It is undeniably a dark site, one with powerful, often troubling or paradoxical images.

Not recommended for children, the site is neither pornographic nor deliberately bizarre. Much of its strength, in fact, comes from the reputations of the artists who are represented here. The images include important and seminal images from artists like Edward Munch's "Scream," Goya's "Incantation," William Blake's "Urizen," and others.

By this selection, the anxieties of "modern man" were seen or experienced by artists more than 200 years ago.

The agony of the artist is seen here, as troublesome themes are wrestled with in paintings, drawings, and sculptures.

The gallery is divided into sections, depending on the particular anxiety you want to examine: Fear, Religion, Paranoia, Madness, Torture, Sex, Death or War. Some sections have a half-dozen or more images while others have only a few.

Our main concern about this site, which is on many of the hotlists on the Internet, is that it hasn't been updated for some time. The overall quality of the site is good, however, and worth a visit by anyone interested in observing how artists wrestled with great questions of their times. ▲

George Tooker's "The Subway" in the paranoia section of Grotesque in Art.

http://www.ugcs.caltech.edu/~werdna/grotesque/plates/plate26.jpg

Gallery Sight

http://www.webcom.com/~zume/

SEE RELATED SITES:

Ch 6 ART IN CYBERSPACE
Ch 13 PHOTOGRAPHY
Ch 18 TRAVEL & GEOGRAPHY

PHOTOGRAPHS CAN OFTEN tell a story, or at least leave an impression, all by themselves.

Gallery Sight is run by several professional photographers who use it as a place to put up photo essays on topics or places that interest them. You're free to download and use the images for personal use.

This is a well-organized, good-looking site that doesn't severely penalize those with modem connections. Each sequence of images or collection of images on a topic is organized as a page of small (usually less than 4Kb) thumbnails and a description of the occasion or setting. Clicking

on a thumbnail or a text link will bring up the photos.

On our visit, six photo essays were in place. Rajiv Mehta contributed two, one an affectionate look at a small-town hairstyling salon and its customers, the other a review of Woodstock '94.

Photographer Said Nuseibeh contributed an outstanding collection from the Dome of the Rock, a Christian, Jewish, and Muslim holy site in Jerusalem. In a few photos, Nuseibeh captures the site's exterior and interior views, and details.

Karen Preuss contributed photos of the Mojave desert, contrasting the beauty of the

An image from Rajiv Mehta's photo-essay on Woodstock '94.

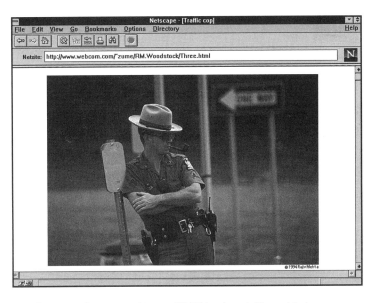

http://www.webcom.com/~zume/RM.Woodstock/Three.html

desert in the spring with some of its harsh impact on signs of human habitation.

John Watson had an essay on the passengers and vehicles of San Francisco's bus line, and Marco Rigonatti posted photos from his continuing expeditions to capture the light and the people of Brazil.

The display and photos at this site are outstanding, with attention to detail, rich colors, and technically superior photographs. ▲

Graphics and Visualization Laboratory

http://www.lerc.nasa.gov/Other_Groups/GVIS/gvis.html

See Related Sites:
Ch 14 Science & Nature

One of the most powerful applications for computers is to simulate the real world.

Some things can't be seen or measured accurately, safely, or cheaply: the flow of air around the turbine blades of a jet engine or in the inside of a tornado, or how a new car crumples up when it hits a brick wall. However, engineers can create mathematical models and have a computer calculate things like air speed or impact stress.

NASA's Graphics and Visualization Laboratory specializes in developing graphical models for such simulations, and they make some dramatic and intriguing images.

The images at this site are divided into two areas: Images and Animations.

In the Images section you'll find pictures of airflow around aircraft structures, pictures of microscopic structures, and the interaction of fluids or gases. You don't have to know anything about this stuff to marvel at the beauty and complexity of the images, and you might even learn something, like how complicated the air or water flow is around a simple shape.

In fact, that's the point: scientists can generate a lot of data and theories about what happens, but the calculations are so complicated and the amount of data is so huge, that it's very difficult to get the big picture. These images are not merely pretty pictures, but techniques for reducing mind-numbing calculations and data in ways that make it easy to see what's actually happening.

For a simple and usable example, download the MPEG file labeled Wing Animation in the animations section. It's less than 40Kb, and all it does is show how the airflow around a wing goes from smooth to complex and turbulent as the wing bites into the air at a steeper angle. You may or may not want to think about this the next time you fly in an airplane. ▲

Analysis of airflow around a prop fan.

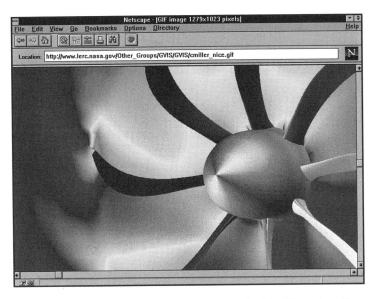

http://www.lerc.nasa.gov/Other_Groups/GVIS/GVIS/cmiller_nice.gif

Hot Pictures: Russian Photography

http://www.kiae.su/www/wtr/hotpictures/gallery.html

H

 SEE RELATED SITES:

Ch 13 PHOTOGRAPHY

THIS SITE FEATURES the work of about a dozen Russian photographers and artists, most of them as individuals and some others under collective names.

These artists may be unfamiliar to most Westerners, so the site offers some insight into the new work coming out of the new Russia. Many of them are in their 30s, have been trained under the Communist regime, and are now enjoying relative artistic freedom.

The photographer who goes by the name FENSO (it's actually a troika of three people) has an exhibit of some oddly-dressed folk enacting some kind of fictional combat in the forest.

Then there's Alexander Kholopov's series of apparently fake postage stamps featuring manhole covers, which proves that bizarre humor isn't an American stronghold.

Boris Mikhailov's specialty is snapshots taken on city streets, which place his subjects in odd juxtaposition to the buildings around them.

Avdei Ter-Oganian proves that the East is as decadent as the West with his exhibition of pornographic playing cards. Alexander Revizorov does a bit of computer manipulation; and Alexander Slyusarev presents cityscapes, some scenic, others empty or threatening.

In general, we're not sure what we learned about the Russian photography scene from this exhibit except that technical standards seem to be rather low and artistic choices are perplexing.

The choice of ways to display images on the Web is also rather curious. Some of these galleries feature 50Kb thumbnails, which expand into nearly 400Kb, 1600-pixel-square images. Modem users will find it tough slogging, and most people will find 1600×1600 pixel images far too large to view. In some cases, the images start to break up at this magnification, suggesting that they could be much smaller without losing detail. ▲

Russian poster warning of computer viruses, by Alexander Revizorov.

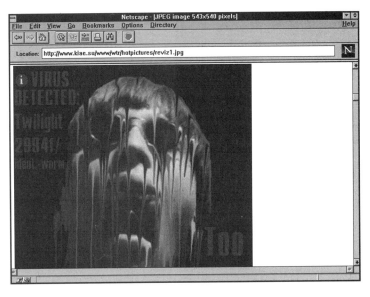

http://www.kiae.su/www/wtr/hotpictures/reviz1.jpg

Hubble Space Telescope

 http://stsci.edu/top.html

http://stsci.edu/pubinfo/BestOfHST95.html

THE HUBBLE SPACE Telescope has had an extra-ordinary impact on our understanding of space, and it has been a boon for those who want high-quality images from the stars and planets.

The Space Telescope Science Institute runs this Web site, where you'll learn all you need to know about the telescope and view some of the most startling images ever seen in space.

Hubble's images reveal space not as stars twinkling quaintly in the night, but as a violent and strange place, where entire galaxies collide, collapse, explode, and otherwise wreak mayhem across vast expanses of space. In revealing phenomena that could not be seen by Earthbound telescopes, Hubble has got scientists scratching for explanations and re-examining old theories about the universe.

The quickest way to access this is to click on the Public button on the home page, and then access the Hubble Space Telescope's Greatest Hits page.

These 10 images are some of the most remarkable images

the telescope has created. Clicking on one brings up another section where several versions of the images are available, along with comprehensive notes, and in some cases MPEG animations.

From the Public section at this site, you can also go to an FTP archive (http://www.stsci.edu/ftp/pubinfo/) of Hubble images. It is organized by type of image (GIFS, JPEGS, and MPEGS, among others) and by subject (Comet Shoemaker-Levy 9, the Hubble Space Telescope itself, and educational material). This directory also contains some larger and higher resolution (up to one megabyte) TIFF images. ▲

Never before observed, these bright jets of gas are firing from new stars. The bottom jet is three trillion miles long.

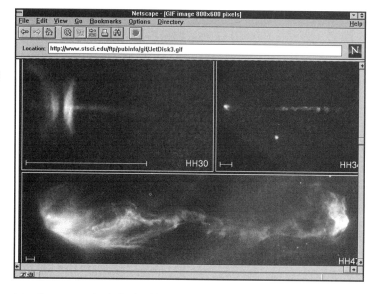

http://www.stsci.edu/ftp/pubinfo/gif/JetDisk3.gif

Hydra

 http://reality.sgi.com/employees/rck/index.html

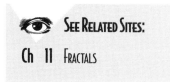

RICK KELLER'S FRACTAL explorer is one of the most sophisticated of its type on the Net.

Fractal explorers are interactive sites that display a basic fractal image, and let you click on it. Since fractals are images that display mathematical values, the values at the location you click are used to start a new fractal image, and that new image is sent back over the Net for you.

It sounds more complicated than it is. To put it simply, if you can click on a picture, you can use this site. Now, that's not too hard, is it?

For the most dramatic results, click on boundary areas in the original picture, areas where different shapes and colors are changing rapidly.

You don't need any special software on your computer, other than a graphical browser like Mosaic or Netscape. All the hard work is done by the host computer on the Internet, which creates a new image file based on your choices, then sends that new image file over the Net to you.

Hydra allows you to choose not only a location, colors, zoom rate, and a Mandelbrot or Julia variation, but two-dimensional or three-dimensional images. Three-dimensional techniques are often used by fractal artists to create realistic-looking landscapes such as mountains or valleys.

All these choices can be confusing, so check out the Cool Examples page for some pictures that show how one image can be derived from part of another, or how changing from 2D to 3D affects the picture.

When you're done with that, try the Image Gallery section for hundreds of images developed by Keller's fractal explorer. They'll show up on your screen as large image maps containing more than 150 images each, and clicking on an image will produce a full-screen version. All told, it represents one of the largest galleries of fractal images on the Net. ▲

These images, many of which are simply variations on the same location of a single fractal, demonstrate the variety possible with Robert Keller's 2D and 3D fractal explorer.

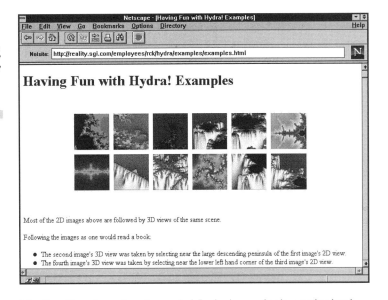

http://reality.sgi.com/employees/rck/hydra/examples/examples.html

Interactive Genetic Art

 http://robocop.modmath.cs.cmu.edu:8001/

SEE RELATED SITES:

Ch 10 COMPUTER-GENERATED ART

ONE OF THE most popular games in the early days of computing was a simple game called Life.

The idea was to take a pattern of dots, and apply a formula to them. Depending on how many other dots a dot touched, it either lived or died the next time the image was generated.

The Interactive Genetic Art site works on something of the same principle. The images are generated by a mathematical formula and voters (that's you and anyone else who comes to this site with a graphical browser) can vote on whether they like them or not.

The computer takes the votes generated this way and develops new images or new variations. Eventually the process is stopped and the result is fixed as a final image.

When we visited the site had three galleries, the first called International Interactive Genetic Art, the second International Interactive Genetic Art II, and the third called Genetic Movies.

The first gallery shows some fragments or basic building blocks of pieces, while the second gallery shows more complete images. Clicking on the images will produce the mathematical formula used to create them. The second gallery also has a link to a slide show, where you can watch as images from the gallery are pulled up at random and displayed on your screen.

The movies are fascinating to watch, and not particularly large (we grabbed one at about 80Kb). The movies show the colors and shapes changing smoothly over time.

You'll also find a winner's gallery here, where you can look at images created by previous runs of the programs and the voting. ▲

"Detail from Filament," an interactive art production.

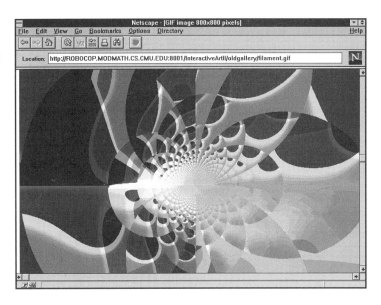

http://ROBOCOP.MODMATH.CS.CMU.EDU:8001/InteractiveArtII/
oldgallery/filament.gif

Impala Gallery

  http://www.thegroup.net/impala/imphome.htm

SEE RELATED SITES:

Ch 5 ART GALLERIES

THE IMPALA GALLERY specializes in the arts and crafts of Asia, Egypt, and West Africa.

The site is divided into four sections: Asian, Egyptian, African, and stoneware pottery.

You'll get some lessons in art here, as the images are usually accompanied by text describing how the various objects at this site are used. Because the items pictured here are actually hand-crafted by native artisans, there's a warning that what you see in the picture may not be identical to what you get if you decide to order a piece.

In some cases the art is simply a replica of some famous piece. For example, in the Egyptian section you'll find replicas of pyramids or items found in the tomb of Tutankhamen.

We wouldn't mind seeing more pictures at this site, but we've included this site because it's going to give you a look at some things that aren't found in many other places on the Internet.

The quality of photography at this site could use some improvement, and the images are not particularly large, even

20

when taken to their largest size. In some cases, the enlarged image is only moderately larger than the thumbnail previously visible on the page.

Fortunately, the thumbnails are large enough to give you a good idea of what the object looks like. ▲

A Djimbay drum, made of wood covered with cowhide, and found in several West African countries.

http://www.thegroup.net/impala/031a.gif

Impact Studio

 http://www.netaxs.com/~impact/index.html

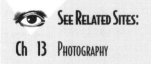

See Related Sites:

Ch 13 Photography

WANT TO KNOW whether people will ever pay any money for this digital graphics malarkey?

Try this site. With its super-quality advertising images and superb digital manipulation it shows what some of the most skilled people in the business are capable of doing with digital tools and good imaginations, for demanding, but paying clients.

The site actually houses two enterprises, both of them owned by the same folks. On one side you have a photography studio that does a lot of advertising and editorial photography. On the other side is a production studio that specializes in digital manipulation. Don't bother with the distinction, however. Visit both.

Your first stop should be the link called Impact 100% Digital's Ad Book, where the company shows off some of its concept work and pieces from actual ad campaigns. We found the hamburger shots ordinary but some of the others show the attention to detail and quality of very fussy studio photographers. These are top-quality images on a well-designed and managed site.

One member of the photography team has done extensive photography for AIDS awareness and other sexual equality issues, and has a personal gallery of images done for these projects as part of this site as well. They illustrate some dance events and other themes related to gay, lesbian, and AIDS awareness.

Andrew Hendricksen is the computer graphics whiz part of the team, and his small gallery at this site also has some classy, top-of-the-line images. ▲

"Language Arts" from Impact Studios.

http://www.netaxs.com/~impact/LanguageArts-big.jpg

Implicate Beauty

http://www.vanderbilt.edu/VUCC/Misc/Art1/Beauty.html

BRIAN EVANS BILLS his site's focus as "computational art." Using various mathematical processes, he builds some striking and powerful images and animations.

Evans is most concerned about beauty and art, both visual and in sound, so while there's some high-powered mathematics and rendering going on in the background, the view from the front looks quite friendly and accessible.

This site also has some neat interactive opportunities that let visitors create some fanciful tracings, by applying simple geometric mathematics. Actually that makes it sound tough. Can you pick a number between 0 and 6.28? I thought so.

Evans focuses not only on static images, with a small but impressive series of fractals, but on the way they can evolve and change mathematically, a process he calls color chording. He has several QuickTime movies in which a single

20

mathematical process not only draws a changing abstract image, slowly modifying both its shape and colors, but also generates accompanying sound.

If you're set up for QuickTime, and can download files in the 2-3 megabyte range, you can head for the screening room to get copies of the animations. If you're not, go to the color explorations section, where you can see frames from the animation. You can look at a storyboard image, which has frames from the animation. They can give you an idea of the changes that occur in the animations.

And, if you're feeling play-ful, head for the Do-It-Yourself section, where you plug values into an electronic spirograph and Evans' computer sends back the result. Once you get something simple, try changing the values slowly. You'll be surprised at how much differ-ence an apparently small change can cause.

You can choose from draw-ing trochoid curves (the tech-nical name for spirographs) or henon maps (another math-ematical function). Unless you're the henonistic type, you'll probably like the tro-choids much better. The latter can create elaborate symmetri-cal loops, while the former look vaguely like topographi-cal maps. ▲

A simple cone mathematically evolves into a complex series of images.

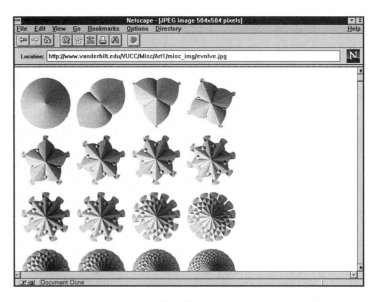

http://www.vanderbilt.edu/VUCC/Misc/Art1/misc_img/evolve.jpg

Interactive Media Technology Center

 http://www.oip.gatech.edu/mmtltop.html

 SEE RELATED SITES:

Ch 3 ANIMATION & CARTOONS
Ch 10 COMPUTER-GENERATED ART

COMPUTERS PLAYED A big role in landing the city of Atlanta one of the world's most prestigious prizes: the 1996 Olympic games.

The Interactive Media Technology Center at Georgia developed presentations and animations that showed what the city had in mind, and that let the Olympic organizing committee interact with computer models of the city and the site.

Now you can access some of that material on the Web. While you may or may not be hugely interested in some of the graphics images here, it's a great site for those who are interested in doing presentations and animations. You'll get a good look at what it takes to put together convincing and crowd-pleasing graphics.

From the home page, go to the IMTC projects link, where you'll find various sections covering the work that the IMTC is working on, including animations, computer graphics, biomedical simulations, emerging technology, multimedia presentations, and sports technology.

Under Animation and Computer Graphics you'll find, among other things, examples from the city's Olympic presentations. IMTC created fly-bys, fly-throughs, and architectural visualization of proposed buildings. You can download some of their movies in QuickTime format.

The animations sections also includes some video produced for the 1992 Earth Summit in Brazil and a teaching video about the Galapagos Islands, used for a youth education project.

Under Multimedia project, you'll find a batch of interactive and video projects, including several employing Apple's new QuickTime VR software, such as a virtual reality tour of an art museum and some art objects.

Our main beef with this site is its stinginess with still images. Many are very small. In one case, the image we got when we clicked on a thumbnail was actually smaller than the thumbnail. ▲

http://www.oip.gatech.edu/images/pda.gif

Isaacs/Inuit Gallery

 http://www.novator.com/UC-Catalog/Isaacs-Catalog/Isaacs-Internet.html

ONE OF THE harshest artistic environments in the world must be the Canadian far north. We're talking about an area so far north that trees never grow. Obviously artisans can't work with wood, or much else, because most of the year the landscape is covered by snow and ice.

However, northern shorelines contain some beautiful, workable stone, and, in the past, native artisans could use ivory from walruses and narwhals, some leather from seals, and further south, some grasses and rushes for baskets.

Out of this meager set of artistic materials one of the most popular forms of primitive art, Inuit (Eskimo) carving and art has arisen.

Using mainly the stones found in their spartan landscape during the short summer months, Inuit carvers create animals of images and people of tremendous simplicity and power. Their sculptures are full and rounded, immanent with the spirits that the carvers believe the animals and even the stones of the region harbor.

Exploited initially by "southern" art experts who found ready markets for these works of totemic power, Inuit artists have since formed cooperatives to market their work for them, and this gallery is one of them.

An Inuit stone sculpture from Northern Canada.

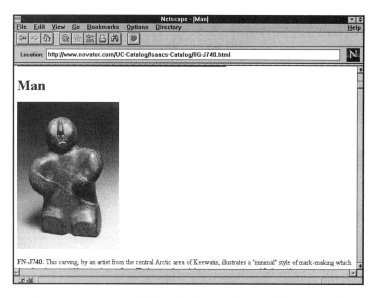

Man

FN-J740. This carving, by an artist from the central Arctic area of Keewatin, illustrates a "minimal" style of mark-making which

http://www.novator.com/UC-Catalog/Isaacs-Catalog/IIG-J740.html

This site lacks depth—for most artists you'll find only one or two pieces depicted online—and the graphics are rather small. However, it is the best place on the Internet to see this genre of art, and it represents artists from many different northern communities, each of which has its own artistic style and symbols.

You've got a couple of ways to get into this gallery, and you might try both of them, just for fun.

On the one hand, you can select the art by medium— sculptures, prints and drawings, wall hangings. The stone sculpture area is by far the largest (we saw 21 pieces when we visited), but you'll find other choices under bronze sculptures, drawings and prints, wall hangings, and baskets.

The other choice is to select art by community. Each of these communities has its distinct artistic tradition and emphasis, so by visiting one community after another you'll begin to get a sense of that. A tip: Baker Lake and Cape Dorset are the oldest and most prolific producers of native art, so you may want to start there. ▲

International Space Station

 http://issa-www.jsc.nasa.gov/ss2/SpaceStation_homepage.html

SEE RELATED SITES:

Ch 15 SCIENCE & NATURE

Ch 16 SPACE

WHILE THE HUBBLE Space Telescope and Comet Shoemaker/Levy 9 grab the spotlight, a program with great potential for the future is perking along: the $17 billion International Space Station, with contributions from the United States, Canada, Japan, Russia, and the nations of the European Space Agency (including Belgium, Denmark, France, Germany, Italy, The Netherlands, Norway, Spain, and the United Kingdom).

Most movies about space have a space station or two in them, but so far the Spacelab, which fell back to Earth, and the small Russian Mir space station are the only real-life projects. The chance to look at a real space station, one that will grow and be a major center for many types of research, is a great opportunity.

The ISS home page is a great way to get a visual look at this project. At the rather crowded opening graphic, you can click on program overview to get to a page of information about the project.

Near the bottom, you'll find a large graphic of the space station itself. It's a rather ungainly thing, looking vaguely like some giant insect, because it will be brought up into space in pieces and assembled there.

A view of the proposed space station in an early phase.

http://issa-www.jsc.nasa.gov/ss/prgview/sspicts/smallphase2.gif

The picture is actually a clickable map, however. Click on any part of the space station and you'll get a definition of the part.

These definitions could be much more informative than they are. Learning that we have clicked on the Research Modules (RM) and the RSA Docking Module, for example, doesn't exactly sate our curiosity. As the project gets a higher profile, we can hope for better things.

The page includes several "fly-around" animations of the space station, and also an animation of a docking sequence with the space shuttle.

Also on the page are some still images showing the space station in a relatively simple, early configuration, and a couple of views of the space station docked with the space shuttle. ▲

JAAM

 http://www.iNTERspace.com/art/jaam/jaam.html

SEE RELATED SITES:

Ch 5 ART GALLERIES

JAAM IS A native art gallery on the Internet, this time specializing in the work of the Indians of the Pacific Northwest and the coast of British Columbia.

You'll find some very classy masks, bracelets, pendants, and rings here, although you may want to hold on to your wallet. Some of these items, particularly the masks, have hefty price tags. Fortunately, this is the Internet, so you can wear your jeans in the gallery and not worry about how expensive things are.

This site has a strong religious and traditional culture emphasis, with heavy use of the totems, the spirits, which figured so prominently in Northwest Indian culture.

In fact, one of the navigational tools at this site is the ability to search the collection of items by spirit: Bear, Bookwus (the wild man of the forest), D'zonokwa (the wild woman of the forest), Eagle, Grouse, Hummingbird, Salmon, Sun, Moon, Whale, or Yagis (the great sea serpent whose movement causes the tide).

Each of these totems has its particular role and strengths in

A mask depicting Bookwus, the wild male spirit of the forest.

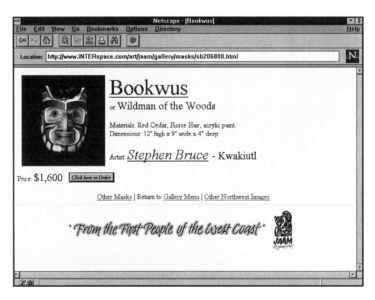

http://www.iNTERspace.com/art/jaam/gallery/masks/sb206800.html

the natural order, and totem poles (none on display here when we looked) display these totems in sequences that have meanings to the natives who carved and displayed them.

In the cultural spotlight section you'll find a list of the artists at the site, and you can click on the objects they have created to view them. ▲

Jon's Image Archive

 http://lynx.uio.no/jon/gif/

 SEE RELATED SITES:

Ch 2 ANIMALS
Ch 14 SCIENCE & NATURE

THIS ARCHIVE IS a valiant effort to bring some order to the wide variety of images on the Internet. Like many such galleries it has its strong points and other places where the effort is more interesting than the result.

The strengths include a good collection of aircraft pictures, mostly from World War II, and a good gallery of animal pictures.

Particularly outstanding is the Cat gallery, which has one of the best collections we've seen of wild cat images.

The archive also contains an extremely popular section on girls. The images meet the standards of dress one commonly finds on European beaches (the Web site is based in Norway), which is to say

many of these one-piece bathing suits don't cover anything above the waist, and we're not sure which piece some of the other one-piece suits are supposed to be covering.

Because the traffic to this section is so popular, the Webmaster urges some restraint in downloading, particular during Norwegian working hours.

There's a fiction section with images from mythology, Hollywood, and literature.

In the WWWNat section, you'll find a good selection of original landscape photographs, showing primarily mountain scenes and forests. The nature section includes images of nature, such as famous mountains, taken from elsewhere on the Net. ▲

20

This tiger cubs image is part of the comprehensive cat collection at Jon's Image Archive.

http://lynx.uio.no/jon/gif/cats/tigercubs.jpg

Jet Propulsion Laboratory

 http://www.jpl.nasa.gov/

 **SEE RELATED SITES:**

Ch 14 SCIENCE & NATURE

THE JET PROPULSION Laboratory has been synonymous with American space exploration since the days of Sputnik, when it was formed.

Specializing in the construction of space craft for exploring the solar system and planets, JPL has acquired an enviable collection of space and astronomy images taken by its spacecraft.

When you get to JPL's home page you might first have a look at the News Flashes, which will contain images collected over the last few months that have not yet found their way into the archives.

But the main area of interest will be under the Image/

Information archives, which contain hundreds of images about and from most of the missions undertaken by JPL.

This is a great repository about space, because it includes more than just pictures of the stars. It includes photos and diagrams of JPL satellites, and pictures of satellite launches as well as pictures of stars, planets, and Earth.

Early JPL missions, such as the Mariner spacecraft, are represented by a small section of the gallery.

One of the most famous inter-planetary journeys was undertaken by the Voyager probes, and their pictures of the outer planets are well represented here.

There are also some cool renderings of future or in-progress space programs. Gallileo is heading for a lengthy rendezvous with Jupiter, and you can see some of the images from that voyage now.

Even though a mission to Pluto has yet to be launched, you can see artist's renderings of the spacecraft and its encounter with the distant planet, and diagrams showing its tiny size compared to that of other space probes.

JPL was involved in developing the Wide Field and Planetary Camera, which was added to the Hubble Space Telescope in 1993, so this archive includes some spectacular images of stars and galaxies that have been shot through the telescope.

You'll also find photos of the Shoemaker-Levy 9 comet's impact with Jupiter here. While the Hubble Space Telescope could not see the impact directly (because the comet hit Jupiter just over the horizon from Earth's view), you can see huge clouds rising over Jupiter's horizon just after several of the impacts, as well as the dark holes that were visible as the impact sites rotated into view.

One of JPL's major missions has turned out to be what it calls the mission to Planet Earth. Turning JPL's technology and high-powered cameras on ourselves has resulted in some remarkable visual data taken from space.

From the top level of the Images/Information Archive menu you'll see a listing for the TOPEX/Poseidon data files. This extensive collection of weather images contains colorful charts that plot ocean

Venus, as pictured by the JPL Magellan probe.

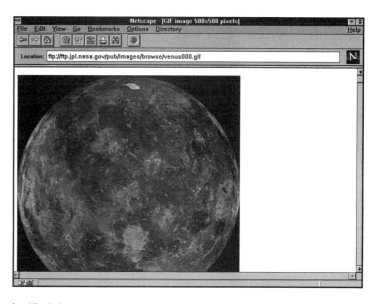

ftp://ftp.jpl.nasa.gov/pub/images/browse/venus000.gif

Tropical storm Gale sits off the coast of Florida, while high winds hit the Pacific Northwest and Newfoundland, according to this JPL map of oceanic wind speeds.

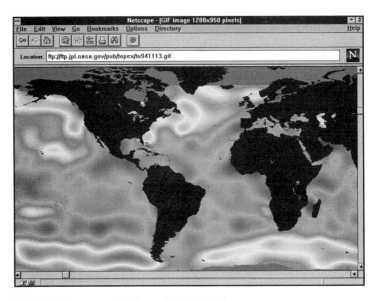

ftp://ftp.jpl.nasa.gov/pub/topex/tu941113.gif

weather, every three days. The maps show wave height, wind speed, and other variables that affect the ocean.

For some of the highest resolution images on the Internet you can turn to the high resolution image gallery, also available from the Images/Information Archive.

These images are taken by the SIR-C radar satellite. Since radar cuts through clouds, it can depict Earth's surface at any time of day or night and in any kind of weather. Many of these images are black and white, but some have been fixed up with "false color" to show the type of vegetation or altitude of the subject. Others represent interesting combinations of data, such as views of major volcanoes where radar imaging has been combined with ground-based maps to provide highly detailed infor-

mation about an area.

Be warned, however, that when JPL says high resolution, they mean it. Some of these images are so huge that only those with the fastest Internet connections could pull them down in a reasonable time. They would also require a good chunk of hard drive space, and lots of RAM to be able to store and display them.

Images of New York and Mount Everest, for example, hit the 70 megabyte range.

Whether your town is covered by SIR-C appears to depend largely on whether you've had a volcano eruption recently, or whether you live in a city where one of the project's contractors, some of them European, are from. In other words, don't count on being able to download a high-resolution image of your town.

San Franciscans are out of

luck, for example. There are no images listed here of the Bay Area. On the other hand, major metropoli like Flevoland, in The Netherlands; Oberpfaffenhofen, Germany; and Oetztal, Austria, have received the SIR-C high resolution treatment. ▲

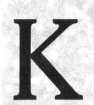

Kodak

 http://www.kodak.com/

SEE RELATED SITES:

Ch 13 PHOTOGRAPHY

AS THE COMPANY that basically invented the consumer photography industry, Kodak is a necessary stop for anyone interested in images on the Internet.

The company points out that it is not really an image company. It makes products so that you can make images. Nevertheless it has a gallery of more than 80 dramatic images online here, all taken by Kodak employees.

You can view them online as JPEG images or, if you have the right software and a fast connection, you can down-load them in Kodak's Photo-CD Image Pac format. A warning: the latter are in the four megabyte range, and use Kodak's compression engine. When unpacked, this can produce a full-color 2000 × 3000 pixel image in the 18 megabyte range, which not all image manipulation programs and computers can handle.

To get to the pictures, click on the digital images link, which will bring up a list of seven galleries, each containing a dozen images. When you go into a gallery, you'll also see a link to Photo-CD Enabled

Crater Lake in winter.

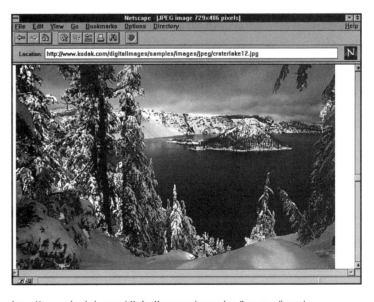

http://www.kodak.com/digitalImages/samples/images/jpeg/
craterlake12.jpg

Software, which has a list of software that supports the Image Pac format. You might want to see if you have anything on that list before downloading an image you can't view or use.

The galleries cover close-ups, primarily of nature; cityscapes, showing key views of major cities, such as New York, London, Paris, Hong Kong, Sydney, and Venice; existing light, with some dramatic pictures of fireworks, neon signs, a laser light show, and luminescent jellyfish; landscapes, mostly of American mountains and parks, with a Bora Bora jungle river and a couple images of the Swiss Alps; man-made patterns covers signs, building facades, hot-air balloons, a quilt, and a couple of stained-glass windows; natural patterns has some nice cloud and water effects, along with grasses and animals in groups; and the variety section has some animal and nature pictures, among other things.

The images here were taken by Kodak employees who, not surprisingly, have very high standards of quality. At this site you're probably looking at about the best images you can see on the Internet, given the state of the art: the original pictures are top notch and the scanning on a special Kodak workstation is also superb. ▲

Kaleidospace

 http://kspace.com/

 SEE RELATED SITES:

Ch 5 ART GALLERIES

KALEIDOSPACE WAS ONE of the first Net-based galleries to open, and has assembled an impressive collection of nearly 90 artists in various media—literature, graphics, video, and music—who offer their work for sale here.

At the opening page you'll see a wheel marking the various sections of the gallery. You can click on the center of the wheel to get a list of the artists and the type of work they do, or click on a general section, such as Art Studio, Screening Room, Tool Shop, Music Kiosk, or Interactive Arena, among others.

Clicking on Art brings us to a page that lists what's on Kaleidospace by gallery, medium, subject, or links to other areas.

The galleries, in this case, are not online galleries, but real art galleries that list their offerings on Kaleidospace.

When we looked, Kaleidospace had 14 artists listed in its arts section alone, with a wide variety of styles and subjects.

20

The artists represented here are offering real, not digital works for sale. You can order art directly from the artists here, for shipment to your home or office.

In general, because the art here is intended for sale to collectors or individuals, it's not terribly radical, and some of it is quite conventional. These are people who need to make a living from their art, and Kaleidospace provides them with an opportunity to put their art where the world can see it.

One of the strengths of the online format is the depth of information you can get about the artists. Most studios might offer a small card or brochure, if the studio or artist can afford it, but at Kaleidospace, clicking on an artist's name can produce extensive background information, a list of previous exhibitions, a list of owners of the artist's work, and even a QuickTime movie or two that shows an exhibition or an interview with the artist. ▲

"Portrait of Nofretete," metal work by Vitold Kosir.

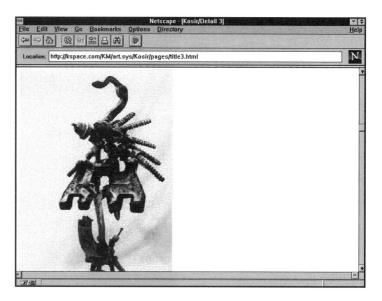

http://kspace.com/KM/art.sys/Kosir/pages/title3.html

Key West

http://rossi.arc.miami.edu/mmedia/

 SEE RELATED SITES:

Ch 4 ARCHITECTURE
Ch 18 TRAVEL & GEOGRAPHY

THIS EXPERIMENTAL EFFORT to bring a city on to the World Wide Web makes use of clickable image maps and other techniques to show off Key West, Florida.

Unlike many travel sites on the Internet, this is not a glossy Chamber of Commerce effort, but a project developed by architecture students at the University of Miami. As a result, its focus is an effort to understand and explain Key West rather than attract tourists. If you're looking for historical and background information, it's great. If you're looking for a hotel, keep looking.

You'll find more than usual historic and geographic information about the city and its development over the years. Some of this, only an architect or planner could love, such as a series of maps tracing lot and road development in Key West.

You can follow the history of the city through several text screens with links to pictures, in many cases.

The architectural details section has some of the quaint Victoria and Southern architectural details, but no comment to describe them.

A section on the city's ecosystem, more interesting than most, shows some of the plant and animal communities and discusses the geology of the city.

Under Points of Interest, you will see a map of the downtown part of the city with key sites marked in red. Clicking on a dot brings up a photo and description.

The site also has some videos showing aspects of construction and architecture in Key West.

The site is generally well organized, although a needlessly large (260Kb) image map used to access details of the architecture in Key West will definitely slow down those with modem connections. ▲

20

Sponges for sale and the site marking the southernmost point of the United States, in Key West.

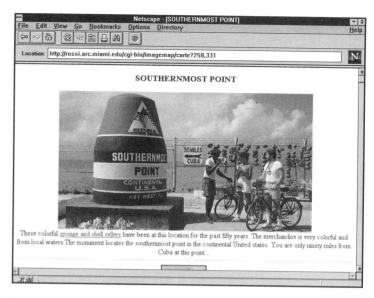

http://rossi.arc.miami.edu/cgi-bin/imagemap/

Los Angeles Architecture

http://info.cardiff.ac.uk:80/uwcc/archi/jonesmd/la/

See Related Sites:

Ch 4 Architecture

With apologies to those Angelenos who consider their city to be a paragon of architectural refinement, Los Angeles is better known for buildings that have only fronts, for a kind of make-believe architecture.

But there's nothing like a fresh pair of eyes, and this site is Los Angeles architecture through the eyes of an unjaded newcomer, Matt Jones, an architecture student from Wales.

Working from an analysis of Los Angeles by another commentator, Jones divides the architecture of the region into Surfurbia, architecture and buildings related to L.A.'s ocean setting; the downtown core, which has changed significantly in recent years; the residential foothills; and the famous "autopia," Los Angeles' freeway system.

He marvels at everything from shopping malls with chain link palm trees to private residences and offices.

Jones compares the newer architecture of Los Angeles with buildings constructed earlier, often through links in his text commentary. Among other things, he illustrates

Edgemar Shopping Mall, Venice, designed by Frank O. Gehry & Associates.

http://www.cf.ac.uk/uwcc/archi/jonesmd/la/surf/edgemar.html

today's emphasis on window-less walls on the street side of a home, and high security gates, compared with the openness and welcoming feel of older homes such as Frank Lloyd Wright's Ennis-Brown House in Hollywood Hills. You'll also see photos of Gamble House in Pasadena, a 1908 "winter cottage" with exquisite detail, and with both informality and elegance.

Jones, who got around Los Angeles by bus to get his photographs, doesn't have a great deal to say about autopia, except that some of the advertising structures aimed at drivers may influence American architecture in the same way that train stations influenced British architects. ▲

Los Angeles County Museum of Art

 http://www.lacma.org/

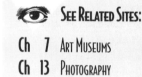

See Related Sites:

Ch 7 Art Museums
Ch 13 Photography

THIS MUSEUM'S ONLINE gallery is kind of like those diet tips you always read about: You don't need to eat everything; just take a taste.

LACMA's approach to an online gallery is to show off the breadth rather than the depth of its collection.

Within each category you'll only find one work from each artist, so you're not going to get anything more than a taste of the styles around.

The most stunning evidence that can work is the relatively new Photography Los Angeles Now exhibit, which shows off the work of 65 photographers from the Los Angeles area, usually with one or two online pieces. The sheer breadth of this exhibit gives new meaning to the term photography and to the ways in which artists are using photography as an artistic process.

This exhibition is particularly well designed for the Internet: after clicking on an image to view it full-screen, Internet visitors can comment on the work, read about the artist, and even send comments to the artist via e-mail.

In other sections at LACMA, you'll find a wide variety of types of art represented: traditional and pre-modern American art; ancient figurines and art; costumes, textiles, furniture; old masters from Europe; art from the China and Japan, India, and other Southeast Asian countries; photography, print, and drawings, and some 20th century art.

Some sections, such as its photography and decorative arts section, are reasonably unusual to find in a regular art museum.

Being Los Angeles, the Far Eastern and Asian sections are very strong as well.

The photography section (not part of the P.L.A.N. exhibit) has many of the major names in the art of photography, such as Minor White, Edward Weston, Aaron Siskind, Robert Frank, and Alfred Stieglitz.

There's also a QuickTime movie on the home page that gives you a quick tour of the museum. ▲

Betty Lee, Documented Memory I, from the Photography Los Angeles Now exhibit.

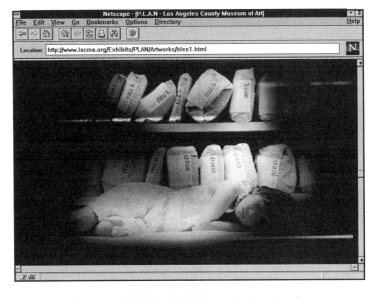

http://www.lacma.org/Exhibits/PLAN/Artworks/blee1.html

LensWork

 http://www.teleport.com/~lenswork/gag9.htm

 **See Related Sites:**

Ch 13 Photography

LensWork is a Portland-based Web site that shows some of the finest work done by photographers in the U.S. Northwest.

Special exhibitions are placed online, as are Web versions of photographic books and of portfolios that are published in a quarterly photographic magazine of the same name.

An exhibit online when we visited was a collection of photos by Oliver Gagliani. Austere and sometimes abstract, these black and white photos were technically superb, although not particularly moving in content. Gagliani sees the world as texture and values of light. A decrepit old home, with its peeling paint and bare boards is a veritable paradise for Gagliani's camera.

Another project online, from photographer Barry Peril, looked at the residents of a low-income housing project, where residents have come together to reduce crime and improve their quality of life.

Brooks Jensen had a photographic study of machine shops, garages, and the men who work in them, under the name Men of Steel. This exhibition is also available as high-quality folios, which sell for $250, but the photos shown online are also available for $10 on diskette for those who use modem connections and many not want to spend the time online.

The gallery also has a section called the Portland Photographer's Forum, where other work can be shown. When we visited it had another show by Peril, this one on the Vietnamese community.

The site tends to show very high quality work. In many cases the photographs represent a Web version of work that has been made into a book, or a preview of a project about to be published as a book. ▲

"Three Drills," from the Men of Steel exhibit.

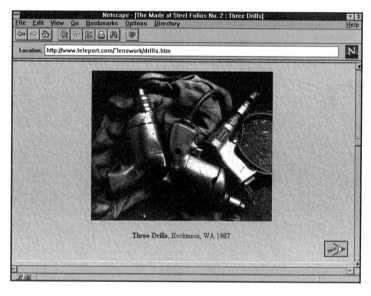

http://www.teleport.com/~lenswork/drills.htm

Bill's Lighthouse Getaway

 http://gopher.lib.utk.edu:70/lights.html

 SEE RELATED SITES:

Ch 4 ARCHITECTURE
Ch 18 TRAVEL & GEOGRAPHY

AS YOU'RE POUNDING away on your computer keyboard, have you ever said a kind word for that old manual typewriter it might have replaced?

That's the situation lighthouses are in: new technologies such as global positioning satellites, superior radio navigation, and automated, unattended beacons are reducing the requirement for lighthouses, particularly the picturesque manned versions that saved so many lives and prevented so many accidents over several centuries of seafaring.

William A. Britten, Systems Librarian at the University of Tennessee in Knoxville, Tennessee has assembled a web page with a comprehensive collection of these lights. Usually located on rocky outposts, the sites and the buildings themselves are picturesque and appealing.

The home page comes up with thumbnails indicating that pictures are available from lighthouses in Maine, Massachusetts, Rhode Island, the Mid-Atlantic region, the Outer Banks, the South Atlantic coast of the U.S., and California.

Clicking on an image or link on the home page brings you to a short text file describing the lights, with embedded links to specific lighthouses. Click on a link and a gallery of pictures with further description of that lighthouse comes up.

If you're in a rush, the bottom of the home page has a link to Image Files. Clicking here brings up a list of all the lighthouses, and all the images. It's an impressive collection: when we looked it had 128 pictures, covering 52 lighthouses. ▲

Assateague lighthouse at sunrise.

http://www.lib.utk.edu:70/I/Other-Internet-Resources/pictures/lights/astg4.gif

Merike Lugas

http://www.eagle.ca/~roda/RodMerArts/ArtGalIntro.html

SEE RELATED SITES:

Ch 5 ART GALLERIES

MANY ARTISTS ARE clamoring to get their galleries on the Net, but we find that many don't use it well. However, Merike Lugas is one artist who lives and works out of the artistic mainstream, in rural Ontario, but uses the Web to put her art, and her work, front and center.

This is an extensive gallery of work from an artist whose images show her passion for life and her love for the practice of art.

Lugas works largely with female forms in both her painting and sculpture, but she has a rich, consistent style and ties her work to social and emotional themes.

Lugas gives the viewer several ways to see her work. The way you select will depend to a large extent on the speed of your Internet connection.

The Painting and Sculpture Wings have larger thumbnails that make it easier to see what an item looks like without having to really click on the thumbnail to see anything. Then there's the Sculpture Garden, which shows a number of pieces not shown in the sculpture wing.

Lugas not only encourages downloading of her images to viewers' hard drives for later viewing, she provides instructions on how to do it. ▲

"Vulnerable Angel," by Merike Lugas.

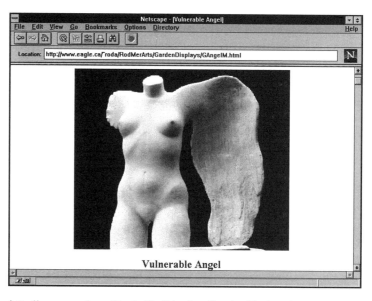

http://www.eagle.ca/~roda/RodMerArts/GardenDisplays/
GAngelM.html

Missing Children Database

 http://www.scubed.com:8001/public_service/listing.html

 SEE RELATED SITES:

Ch 19 XYZ

TELEVISION HAS BEEN enlisted in the cause of crime fighting through programs that publicize unsolved crimes and provide the public a number to call. In some cases, a long-sought perpetrator is captured within minutes of the airing of the television segment.

The Missing Children Database brings that power to the Internet. Photographs and text descriptions of children, and the circumstances under which they disappeared, are stored at this site where anyone can view them.

Many of these cases involve actual or suspected family abductions, while others may involve abductions by strangers.

The images are divided up by the location (region and then state) where the child was living at the time he or she disappeared, which may or may not be helpful when trying to determine whether a child was abducted. No thumbnails are provided, so you'll have to browse these images one by one, which could be time-consuming. At the time we looked, for example, the California directory alone had 123 pictures in it.

In cases involving children abducted some time ago, the National Center for Missing and Exploited Children does an "age-progression" image, showing the child as he or she is expected to look today, based on normal aging patterns.

The Center also provides a telephone number to call, just in case you do happen to see someone who you suspect might be a missing child.

The Center does ask that the images not be widely distributed on the Internet (we asked permission to use the one photo that you see here). ▲

20

A photo of a missing child (left) with an age-progression version (right).

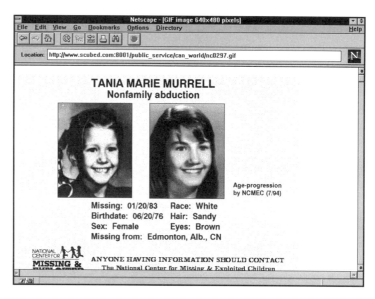

File   Edit   View   Go   Bookmarks   Options   Directory

Help

Location: http://www.scubed.com:8001/public_service/can_world/nc0297.gif

TANIA MARIE MURRELL
Nonfamily abduction

Age-progression
by NCMEC (7/94)

Missing: 01/20/83   Race: White
Birthdate: 06/20/76   Hair: Sandy
Sex: Female   Eyes: Brown
Missing from: Edmonton, Alb., CN

NATIONAL
CENTER FOR
MISSING &

ANYONE HAVING INFORMATION SHOULD CONTACT
The National Center for Missing & Exploited Children

http://www.scubed.com:8001/public_service/can_world/nc0297.gif

MPEG Movie Archive

  http://w3.eeb.ele.tue.nl/mpeg/index.html

Ch 19   XYZ

MOVIES ON COMPUTERS are still "under development," to put it kindly. They're best suited for those with very fast Internet connections, and fast workstations that can do a decent job of showing the video or animation when you do get it.

MPEG is a movie format that is particularly well suited for the Internet because it does such a good job of compressing video, making it relatively compact for transmitting. You'll need to download an MPEG viewer, or use the MPEG player on the CD with this book, to view these clips.

This site collects movie clips from a variety of sources, and organizes them into several sections: Supermodels, Animations, Music, R-Rated Clips, Racing, Movies & Television, and Space.

Don't expect full-length films here. Some of the smaller clips will run for about five seconds, and very few of these movies will run for more than a minute. Running time depends on the size of the frame, how many frames per second the movie was developed for and the like, but a one-megabyte MPEG about 300 pixels square at 15 frames per second will run for perhaps 25 seconds.

The Supermodels section features lovely ladies like Cindy Crawford, Christie Brinkley, Kim Basinger, and

Pamela Anderson working out, participating in photo shoots, and generally looking beautiful. You'll find one or two clips here under 60Kb, but most range between 200Kb and a megabyte.

The Animations section contains entertainment animations such as scenes from *The Simpsons*, animated logos from companies and universities, plus many scientific animations of robots and fly-throughs of buildings and universities.

The music video section has a few clips from Michael Jackson, plus one each from Janet Jackson, Eric Clapton, and a few other entertainers and groups.

The R-Rated section contains pictures of more seductive activities: hot young women, strippers, and scenes from erotic movies, such as the ever-popular Teri Hatcher clips from *Cool Surface*.

The Racing section specializes in Formula One clips, and in particular scenes of cars hitting walls and each other.

The Space section features several movies related to the Shoemaker-Levy 9 impact on Jupiter, some rocket launches, the Hubble Space Telescope repair, and some shots from American landings on the moon.

The Movies & Television section has a small number of clips from action movies like *Under Siege*, *Airwolf*, and *Raiders of the Lost Ark*.

This is an extremely busy site, and places restrictions on what can be downloaded from it, and when. It gets about 1,200 downloads a day, and moves about a gigabyte, or more than a CD-ROM's worth,

Mika Hakkinen's car hits the wall during the Hockenheim Grand Prix.

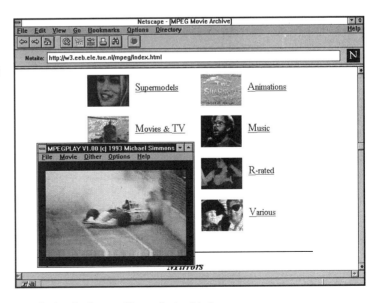

http://w3.eeb.ele.tue.nl/mpeg/index.html

of data across the Internet every day.

It has numerous mirror sites in other locations that carry all or most of the same films. If you find that you can't access the site or you get time-outs, you should try accessing the mirror site close to you. ▲

Michigan Press Photographers Association

 http://www.cris.com/~Mppa/

SEE RELATED SITES:

Ch 13   PHOTOGRAPHY

THE MICHIGAN PRESS Photographers Association is a determined and hard-working bunch who turn out one of the best Web sites devoted to news photography.

This nicely-done site features the winners and runners up in their annual photo contests (starting with the 1993 contest), and also information about the CD-ROM that they churn out every year.

The site includes QuickTime movies and audio clips related to photos, such as the comments of judges about each photo, as well as the photographs themselves.

On the home page you'll find buttons right up front for the portfolios for each year's winning photographs.

Clicking on one of the Winners buttons brings you to a page where you can elect to view the photographs by category (18 categories, of which a few honor individuals and don't have photos associated with them), by newspaper or by photographer.

Most people (except the mothers of Michigan news photographers) will probably want to view the photos by category. Within each category you'll find thumbnails of the photo that took first place in that year's contest, plus thumbnails of a half-dozen or so honorable mentions. Clicking on a photo enlarges it and provides additional caption information. A handy "next" arrow on the bottom of the page takes you directly to the next picture if you're looking at full-sized images, or the next category if you're looking at thumbnails.

The pictures at this site are truly excellent: dramatic, well-lit, technically sound, and the site makes it easy to find your way around. We know several Webmasters who should be taking lessons from these people. ▲

A family expresses concern about a child believed to be caught in a fire.

Netscape - [http://www.cris.com/~Mppa/1994/spot1.html]

File Edit View Go Bookmarks Options Directory   Help

Location: http://www.cris.com/~Mppa/1994/spot1.html

Click here to download a sound (AIFF) file of judge's comments recorded during the selection of this photo.
Family members and friends gather for support as they await word about a child feared trapped inside the burning house. The child was later found elsewhere.

http://www.cris.com/~Mppa/1994/spot1.html

The Masters' Collection

 http://www.portal.com:80/~jdoll/joes/masters/

 **SEE RELATED SITES:**

Ch 5 ART GALLERIES
Ch 7 ART MUSEUMS

SO YOU'VE BEEN to the WebMuseum and now you want your own Monet.

You've come to the right place. The Masters' Collection takes original works of art and makes high quality duplicates of them, complete with brushwork, fancy frame, and matting.

When you get to this site, you can choose to view selections from some of the most famous paintings in various categories, such as the Impressionist work of Benson, Monet, Renoir, Wendel, or Van Gogh; florals from Monet, O'Keeffe, Renoir, Roesen, or Van Gogh; landscapes from Bierstadt, Farquharson, or Thompson;

groups and figures from Koehler, Riviere, and Trumbull; plus country scenes, children, animals, nautical paintings, hunting and sports, southwest and western art, and religious art from da Vinci and Michelangelo.

The company claims that its process, which chemically bonds paint-like material with a photographic image and applies it to a canvas makes the painting indistinguishable from a real oil painting.

Your friends could get suspicious if you insisted that the painting really was the $2 million original of some masterpiece (and your insurance agent might like to know

20

about it as well), but if you'd like a good reproduction of a famous painting for your wall, this is one way to get it.

Prices vary, and the site has price lists available, which match codes on the displayed paintings.

The company plans to put its full catalog on the Net at some point, but for now you have two choices: you can look at the brochure, which has a few samples, or you can go to the Top Favorites from the catalog.

The emphasis here is on popular works, so you won't find anything terribly avant-garde or downbeat. ▲

"Two Young Girls At The Piano," by Pierre Auguste Renoir.

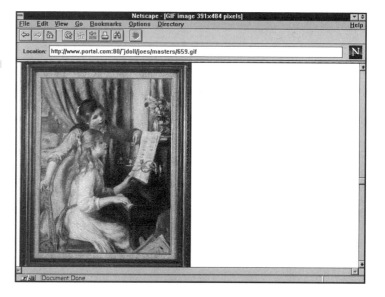

http://www.portal.com:80/~jdoll/joes/masters/659.gif

Marthart.com

 http://www.wri.com/~mathart/

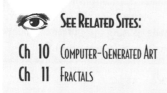

👁 **See Related Sites:**

Ch 10   Computer-Generated Art
Ch 11   Fractals

Stewart Dickson wears a bundle of hats, from sculptor to systems manager, and his Internet site reflects his eclectic set of graphical interests.

Under Topological Slide you'll find a virtual reality playground on a mathematically generated object. With a virtual reality helmet, the viewer can move through and around this theoretical space. Marthart.com has no virtual reality viewer at this point but by clicking on the link, you can see a series of frames that depict what a ride through virtual reality would look like.

Go to Mathematical Visualizations to see some intriguing three-dimensional objects created by mathematical formulas, and then enhanced by computer rendering.

In a rather clever move, Dickson includes stereoscopic images of some of these creations at his Web site. By crossing your eyes a bit as you stare at them, you can actually see them in three dimensions.

Mathart.com also features some figure studies done completely digitally. The images were captured with an electronic camera, and the model could view herself on the monitor while posing, to get the best pose. The images were enhanced to get a posterized effect, dropping out subtle gradations in favor of strong graphics.

Dickson's experiments with three-dimensional fractals are more experimental than

visually appealing. Fractal fans might appreciate a series of images that depict four different views of a three-dimensional Julia set from different directions.

For pictures of musical instruments that most musicians have never imagined, try the Acoustical Works section of Mathart.com.

In Works in Carved Metal you'll find images designed on a computer and created by a computer-controlled milling machine. Dickson entered some in a juried art show, even though they had not been made yet, on the strength of digital pictures of the sculptures that the jury thought were real photographs.

Under 3D Books you'll find pictures of sculptures made up of thin sheets of translucent material. The images on the Net are simply photos of those objects, but they do hint at intriguing possibilities for artists. ▲

A virtual reality ride through an imaginary mathematical image.

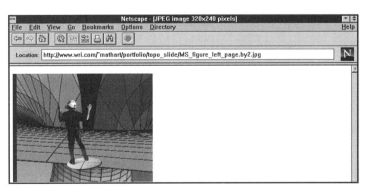

http://www.wri.com/~mathart/portfolio/topo_slide/
MS_figure_left_page.by2.jpg

MTV

 http://mtv.com/

SEE RELATED SITES:

Ch 3 ANIMATION & CARTOONS
Ch 8 CELEBRITIES & ENTERTAINMENT

MTV IS THE brash young face of American culture: impolite, unrestrained, fast-moving, and weird. And very, very proud of it.

The music television station has lent its name to a whole generation of young people, so it's probably worth your while to visit its Web site to see what's coming down the pike, even if you're not really one of the MTV generation.

Like it or not, MTV has had a seminal role in defining the "look," not only in clothing and music, but in graphics design and fonts as well, so it's a site of some interest to any-one involved in graphics.

What you'll find here is a well-done site that still retains MTV's gritty energy. It doesn't try to be pretty or coy. If you want Beavis and Butt-head, get 'em here. If not, no one asked you to visit.

The chief focus of this site, from a graphics point of view is the famous pair who have re-written the laws of couth, plus some newer and less-well known animation figures such as The Maxx and The Head.

To find them, head for the MTV Oddities Page when you get to the site. You can choose to head into a section devoted to The Maxx, a strange-looking, muscle-bound mutant, or to a

Beavis and Butt-head at the lingerie store.

http://mtvoddities.viacom.com/images/BNB01.JPG

section for The Head, who has overdeveloped that part of his body, and we mean overdeveloped.

Within each of these sections, you'll find a Sight and Sounds link. Here you'll find single frames from the animations, plus QuickTime movies and some audio files.

The B&B animations, in particular, should be favorites among those who collect the wisdom of this pair of sages. Some of their great moments are recorded here, for those who appreciate them. ▲

MultiWorld

 http://www.jnw.com/mw/index.html

 **SEE RELATED SITES:**

Ch 13 PHOTOGRAPHY
Ch 18 TRAVEL & GEOGRAPHY

MULTIWORLD IS A bilingual (Chinese and English) magazine distributed via the Web. It isn't a pictorial magazine in particular, but most of its articles are illustrated with great images, some of them from out-of-the-way places.

Of course, we're basing all of this on one issue, which is dangerous, but that issue looked so good we thought this thing might turn out to be a strong, well-illustrated product.

Stories are written and published in either Chinese or English, and there's no translation. However, you can look at the pictures even if the story is in Chinese.

The inaugural issue had travel photos from Poland, China, Newfoundland, Tibet, and Antarctica, and the magazine is inviting submissions for art and stories about nature, travel, and other subjects that can take readers on a "virtual journey."

The photographs accompany the text, and some stories are more profusely or better illustrated than others. The photos are taken by the writers, so you're not going to get plastic or airbrushed travel photos from the local tourist agencies. In many cases these images reflect the experiences of the writer.

The initial issue also had some computer art work intended to look like Chinese calligraphic painting. Computers have yet to master the subtleties of Chinese brushwork, it appears. ▲

20

Glaciers of Antarctica from "To the Bottom of the Earth," a story in MultiWorld.

http://www.jnw.com/mw/iss01/image/gl3-3.jpg

Mythago

 http://www.umich.edu/~cjericks/gallery/gallery.html

SEE RELATED SITES:

Ch 13 PHOTOGRAPHY

MYTHAGO IS A gallery specializing in nudes. In spite of all you're heard about pornography on the Internet (and this is not a pornography site), nudes are rare on the World Wide Web. The moment the word gets around (which takes anywhere from 30 to 45 seconds) that you can see pictures of naked ladies for free, the site is typically swamped and the Webmaster starts to get nasty e-mail from his or her Internet access provider.

That said, it's good to find a few sites, at least, that offer some insight into figure photography, because it has always played an important role in photography, as it has in other visual arts.

This site pays homage to variations on classic figure study themes, with the shape and smoothness of the human body used as a compositional element.

This site features the work of several photographers. The Skinkisses gallery is studies of light, texture, and meaning in photographs by Jody Schiesser. Figures are contrasted with grasses, bark, and other natural textures.

Siempre Bella (Forever Beautiful) is the title of Edward L. LaBane's section. He works with the shape and contours of landscape, matching them with the figures, tiny against the buttes, ridges, and folds of the Southwest landscape.

In the section called Living Rock Willton Jones' nudes echo the landscape they are set in: folded rock, fluid stream, ridged mountains. Samuel Claiborne's Experimental Acoustics work falls more into the field of portraiture. Christopher Erickson works with the social context of nudity and sexuality, in words as much as in images.

Most of these images are in black and white, which is particularly good for making links between body and nature. Flesh tones match the natural surrounds, while the play of light over the human form and differences in texture tend to stand out. ▲

"Treehug" by Jody Schiesser.

http://www.umich.edu/~cjericks/gallery/graphics/treehug.jpg

National Library of Medicine

 http://www.nlm.nih.gov/hmd.dir/oli.dir/

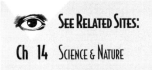 **SEE RELATED SITES:**

Ch 14 SCIENCE & NATURE

THE NATIONAL LIBRARY of Medicine has put nearly 60,000 images related to the history of medicine on a laser disk, for retrieval over the World Wide Web.

You can search through this massive database of images by using a simple fill-in form, which lets you specify words in the text, title, or abstract, and to specify a starting and ending year to limit the retrieved images to a particular time. You can also select by continent, oceanic region, or state.

We tried a few runs through the database. A search for "diabetes" garnered 40 hits, many of them posters of the sort that one would find in doctors' offices or clinics, plus several images related to insulin and management of diabetes. A search on "infant" turned up 287 matches.

Once it has retrieved a set of images, you can direct the system to show you images in groups of anywhere from five to 40 at a time. Clicking on the image enlarges it, while clicking on the title produces the collection record, which often has additional information about the image.

An immunization photo from the National Library of Medicine's Online Images database.

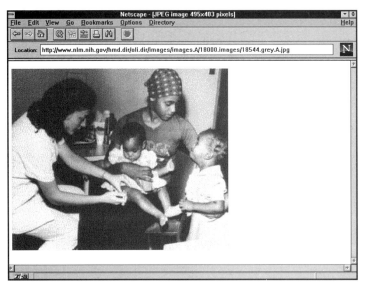

http://www.nlm.nih.gov/hmd.dir/oli.dir/images/images.A/18000.images/ 18544.grey.A.jpg

Images that are copyrighted have a bar through them. The library says that as it conducts further research on copyright issues, the bar may be taken off many of the images. We found that at least half the images had the diagonal bars across them, meaning that if you wanted to use one you would have to contact the library and order a print from them, paying any copyright fees that applied in your case.

This database would be particularly useful to anyone doing historical research, since it includes many images from past centuries. ▲

Norton Gallery of Art

 http://www.icsi.com/ics/norton/

 **SEE RELATED SITES:**

Ch 5 ART GALLERIES

OUR GENERAL EXPERIENCE with art museums on the Internet is rather underwhelming. They'll tell you what hours they're open (which isn't very useful to someone 5,000 miles away), and show you lovely pictures of their building, but when it comes to putting actual images on the Internet for visitors to view, they stumble, sometimes offering only one image per major museum category.

The Norton Gallery of Art does better than that. Its Web site still lacks the depth we'd like to see, but it's better than most at displaying both special exhibitions and images from its permanent collection.

The museum usually puts two to three images from upcoming special exhibitions on its Web site. When we visited, this list included displays of some major artists, including Mark Rothko, Edward Hopper, and Andrew Wyeth.

This section of the gallery does not use thumbnails. Instead, it displays several nearly full-sized images of the pictures, which means this could be slow going for those with modem connections. You'll be downloading two to three images, ranging from 20Kb to 150Kb each, each time you move into one of these sections.

The Norton Gallery also offers a reasonably generous look at the images in its permanent collection, which specializes in French and American Impressionists and Post-Impressionists. A few pictures from each of the permanent galleries are presented on the home page in a very viewable size. Below that you'll find the permanent galleries, which display about a half-dozen major pieces from each of the museum's major collections. ▲

20

"Braids," from Andrew Wyeth's Helga series.

"Braids", 1979
Tempera. 16 1/2" x 20 1/2"
Private Collection

http://www.icsi.com/ics/norton/wyeth.html

National Press Photographers Association

 http://sunsite.unc.edu/nppa/

See Related Sites:

Ch 13 Photography

The National Press Photographers Association is the largest group for press photographers in the United States, and provides educational services, special courses, and other services to its members.

Its online Web site does a great job of getting information on the organization to its members, but those interested in looking at their photos may have some difficulty. We found that the site did have photos on it, many of them excellent quality, but it was far too difficult to get to the image galleries.

Places where you might expect to find them, such as Pictures of the Year or the monthly still clip contest, where photographers send in clippings of their best published pictures, were only text files.

We started to hit paydirt under the Electronic Photojournalism Workshop area. The NPPA is doing a great job in teaching its members and newspapers how to move to a digital world, which is very important for news folks who have to move images from one part of the world to another to meet daily deadlines.

We went to the section under Surf the Results of the last Electronic Photojournalism workshop, where clicking on Pages from Workshop Story

Assignments brought up 30 different photo essays, with from one to five photos each, on stories from member photographers. The NPPA is a big fan of Adobe Acrobat, so if you have an Acrobat viewer, you can also see a print-style layout of the images, instead of the HTML layout that most of the essays also have.

The images on these pages are larger than thumbnails, smaller than full screen, so on a modem connection it could be slow going: you will in many cases be loading three or four 90Kb images. ▲

Image of a Siberian Tiger in a photo essay by Teresa Hawkins.

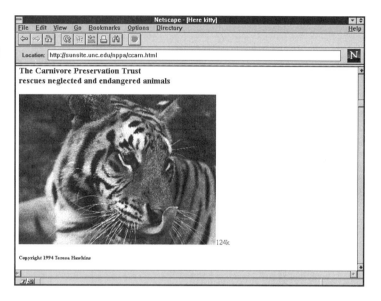

http://sunsite.unc.edu/nppa/ccarn.html

Net@Works Exhibition

http://www.interlog.com/~steev/exhibition.html

👁 **SEE RELATED SITES:**

Ch 6 ART IN CYBERSPACE

YOU'VE HEARD THE one about "a prophet has no honor in his own country." Well, welcome to Mexico—and a survey of Canadian art. Canadians are among the world's experts on holograms, so there's a section of them in here.

There aren't a huge number of graphics at this site, partly because much of the art here is the kind that requires installation. Such art requires special lighting and you need to see it in three dimensions, so it doesn't play well on the Internet. You should get the idea from one display in which, as you approach what appears to be a pothole and

20

peer in, a frog appears in a stream and the sounds of the street are replaced by sounds of nature.

This exhibit was under construction when we looked, however, so we're hoping that by the time you look there will be much more to see. They are also planning to add QuickTime movies and some audio files.

You can navigate by clicking on any of the artist's names, and from there, you can simply click on Next Artist at the bottom of each page to go to the next one. ▲

An image from Rondo, a performance and holographic installations by Mary Alton.

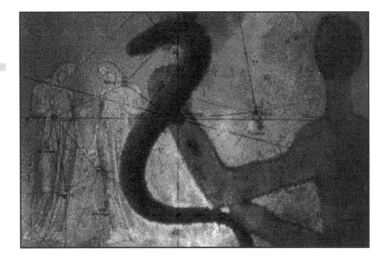

http://www.solect.com/exhibition/gallery/Memory_mirror.gif

On-Line Visual Literacy Project

http://www.pomona.claremont.edu/visual-lit/intro/intro.html

 SEE RELATED SITES:

Ch 17 XYZ

LIKE EVERY OTHER site you'll find discussed in this book, this site has graphics. More important, however, is that it is about graphics, about how artists, advertisers, filmmakers, and others use the most basic visual elements to create images and mental associations.

The idea here is to present you with a primer on the elements of graphics: dots, lines, shapes, dimension, hue, direction, value, motion, and so on.

This site uses hypertext very effectively to guide visitors through the ideas presented here, and makes intelligent use of images, both classic and new, to demonstrate how artists and photographers apply basic visual techniques to create images that we interpret as "real."

The extensively illustrated text here is serious and comprehensive, but not dry or academic. The authors of this piece (actually a project from a class at Pomona College) do an excellent job of matching ideas in the text with real life examples.

For example to illustrate the use of scale and depth, they show still images from several scenes in *Citizen Kane*. Director Orson Welles used the placement of his characters, and the resulting effect that it had on their scale (those close to the camera are large, those farther away are small) to chart the changing relationships of the characters as the film progresses.

QuickTime movies are also used judiciously to illustrate key points about visual graphics, such as how a series of dots becomes a line, and creates motion and direction.

Subtle effects from classic images, such as the Mona Lisa, are explained and illustrated. You'll also see how movie makers use color to create emotional effects in viewers, and how advertising images use visual techniques to create impressions of their products. ▲

Edward Munch's "Scream" gets much of its disturbing power from the way directional lines flow and compete.

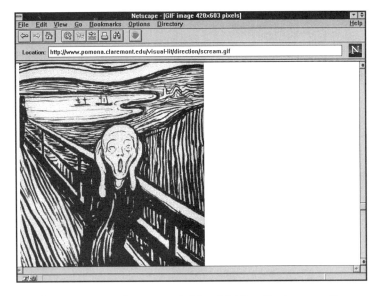

http://www.pomona.claremont.edu/visual-lit/direction/scream.gif

Ocean Planet

 http://seawifs.gsfc.nasa.gov/ocean_planet.html

 **SEE RELATED SITES:**

Ch 2 ANIMALS
Ch 14 SCIENCE & NATURE

OCEAN PLANET IS an exhibition sponsored by the Smithsonian, and is the Web counterpart of an exhibition that started traveling across the United States in 1995, and will still be on the road in the year 2000.

It's a stupendous achievement as a Web site: rich in graphics, easy to navigate, with lots of images and movies.

You can access the components of the exhibit by clicking on its floor plan. You'll get a photo of the room, and you can click on any item in it or click on text below for more information on the topics covered in the room.

Each room has a theme, such as people of the sea, the environmental dangers facing the oceans, ocean science endeavors, and the like. In each room you'll find dozens of illustrated exhibits. You can download a theme film in sections (each of which is from 1 to 1.5 megabytes). The animation takes you from outer space to a splashdown near Hawaii, and then into the Mariana Trench, the deepest spot on Earth, before surfacing and leaving Earth again.

Another way to access the material in this exhibit is to fill

An animation takes viewers from space to the deepest part of the ocean.

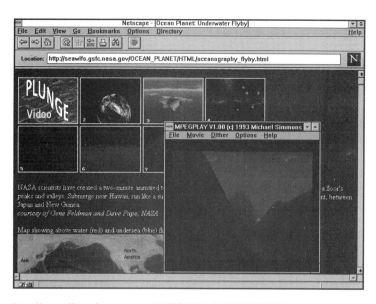

http://seawifs.gsfc.nasa.gov:80/OCEAN_PLANET/HTML/
oceanography_flyby.html

in a form that will search the exhibit database for related information. You can choose to look for photographs, illustrations, or objects associated with your search, and almost everything found will come up with an image and accompanying text.

The results can be surprising. A search on the word "birds," for example, turned up cuttlefish bones (used to give pet birds more calcium), a primitive South Sea compass, a fishing charm, an otter killed by oil pollution, a White ibis,

and an item about damage to habitat from boating.

One section has photos of people who are working to save the oceans, and another section covers the role of women in exploration, fishing, and other oceanic topics.

An ocean science room has images of animals and features only discovered in the last few years. One can discover that no one identified a tiny crustacean that lives in the surf until now, but one of the newly discovered creatures is a type of whale. ▲

Orthodox Christian Page

 http://www.ocf.org:80/OrthodoxPage/

See Related Sites:

Ch 9 Clip Art & Icons
Ch 19 XYZ

RELIGIOUS FOLK ARE major consumers of clip art for brochures and church bulletins, but there aren't many clip art sites on the Internet to serve them.

This site, which has a good collection of both black-and-white clip art and full-color images, is a good source on the Net for such images.

The images here vary considerably in quality and size. Not all can be blamed on the site, which appears to make an effort to keep quality high. Some of these images represent very old icons that have not weathered the years well.

Clicking on the Icons icon takes you to the icons area, as it should. You can look at the clip art section or the miscellaneous icons section in either text or with inline images. Those connecting via modem may want to go the text route, because each of these galleries has an extensive collection of images that will take some time to download, even as thumbnails.

As might be expected, the images have an Orthodox theme, and show Orthodox-style crosses, Orthodox saints, and Orthodox churches. In the clip art section you'll also find some banners and borders with faintly religious themes to them, suitable for both religious and secular publications.

Many images are very large:

A 16th century icon of Jesus, from the monastery of St. Catherine, Sinai.

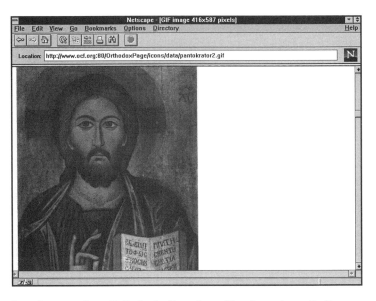

http://www.ocf.org:80/OrthodoxPage/icons/data/pantokrator2.gif

larger than they really have to be for an Internet browser. While some are less than 100Kb, most are 200Kb or larger, with some hitting more than a megabyte. All sizes are marked, however, so you know what you're getting before you decide to download it. ▲

OTIS (Operative Term is Stimulate)

 http://sunsite.unc.edu/otis/otis.html

 See Related Sites:

Ch 5 Art Galleries
Ch 11 Fractals
Ch 13 Photography

It's DIFFICULT TO describe OTIS, other than as the largest visual arts gallery on the Internet. OTIS is, to put it briefly, an Internet art gallery where anyone can contribute and anyone can look. When we looked it had 231 artists on board, some with only a few pictures, some with many dozens of contributions.

It accepts any kind of visual art, in any medium that can be made visible on the Internet. The list of media includes "photos, drawings, ray-tracings, video stills, paintings, computer-assisted renderings, photos of sculpture/3D pieces or performances, photocopier art, record/CD covers, quilts, tattoos, pyrotechnic displays, and any other type of image-based expression."

Some media not found in many other places are ASCII art and executable art, such as self-running Macromedia programs that you download and run (a potentially risky art form that could include viruses, so beware).

OTIS has a light-hearted, light-headed feel to it, but that doesn't mean it's messy or chaotic. You can get at the art you want by selecting a medium or content, such as landscapes, portraits, nudes, animals, political art, and other subjects. You can also click on the links to all the artists from its lengthy list of them.

As you might expect, the art on OTIS varies widely, since it offers exposure for folks who might not get past the jaundiced eye of an art gallery owner, a juried exhibit, or a museum curator. But our perusal of this gallery showed that there is some exceptionally fine work on board.

OTIS doesn't offer any index pages that might present lots of thumbnails you can choose from, but every image has a description, a name and a size, so you can determine whether you want to take the time to view it.

OTIS also has a few "only in cyberspace" wrinkles. The Randomized Infinite Grid is one. Various artists contribute their art to a 4×4 grid, and the computer randomly selects the art that appears in each cell.

The result is a collage that will appear different each time you access it.

OTIS also sponsors regular grids, in which artists use Internet Relay Chat to collaborate collectively on a grid. Sometimes the grids may have a theme, sometimes not. ▲

An OTIS grid project represents the work of several artists communicating over the Internet.

http://sunsite.unc.edu/otis/ftp/SYNERGY/GRID/trode-grid.jpg

Pattern Land

 http://www.netcreations.com/patternland/index.html

P

👁 **SEE RELATED SITES:**

Ch 9 CLIP ART & ICONS

NO COOL WEB site these days would be complete without a background of some kind of color, pattern, or theme that says something about you or your page.

Visiting Pattern Land is not unlike visiting a fabric store, looking for the texture, color, and feel that says "This is me!"

With more than 500 patterns on display here, chances are good you'll find something to your liking.

You have two primary ways to view the patterns here. You can browse through the archive from beginning to end, with about eight backgrounds at a time showing up on your screen. Clicking on a background makes it the background for your entire screen. Click the back button on your browser to go back where you were.

The other approach is to view the archive by name (when you browse the first method, the name shows up as text on the screen, so if you decide you want it, you can easily locate it from the name archive).

If you're the subtle type, you'll find elegant, delicate pastels with only moderate textures that give your page the feel of fine parchment. Some have an embossed quality to them, while others have a reflections-on-water waviness. If your name is Macintosh, you might try finding the appropriate tartan pattern. (There's nothing like a loud tartan to ensure that people spend a long time on your home page trying to read the type.)

For the extrovert and flashy home page, try something like neontrip or cheetah.

If you've got a specific theme to your home page, you may find a great background here: filmstrips for a movies page, honeycombs for bee-keeping, or daisies for a gardener. ▲

A tiled pattern turned into a Netscape background at Pattern Land.

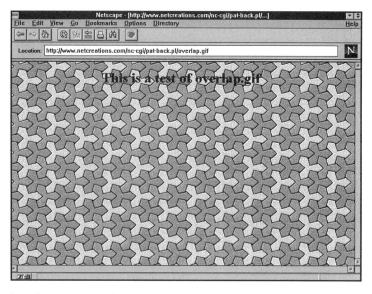

http://www.netcreations.com/nc-cgi/pat-back.pl/overlap.gif

Pearl Street Online Gallery

 http://antics.com/pearl.html

The Pearl Street Gallery, located in Boulder, Colorado, specializes in evocative images of Western landscapes, primarily in the southwest deserts and Colorado.

Most images begin as black-and-white photographs and are then sepia toned or hand colored. Sepia toning is usually reserved for pictures of the plains and ranch buildings, where it adds a natural richness to the images. Hand coloring is applied to landscapes with stronger visual elements, or to buildings. The hand coloring can range from subtle to strange and startling to dazzling false-color creations with a poster effect.

Most of the landscape images are by the same photographer, C.A. Merriman, who has a clean, strong style well suited to the wide open spaces and the visual planes of the American west. The technical quality of both the images and the digital scans is first class.

Most of the images show the deserts and plains, but the photographer has also traveled to the Northwest U.S., so you'll find a few picturesque images of harbors and a small gallery of color images from the Hoh rain forest in Washington State. Merriman also has a couple of lovely sunset images from the Indian Peaks area of Colorado.

One section worth dipping into here is the Colorado wildflowers gallery with pictures by Steven P. Cone. These are lovely, sharp, carefully composed pictures of wildflowers and mushrooms.

The site could be slow-going for modem users, with many thumbnails in the 35Kb range. Be patient. It's worth it. ▲

San Luis Valley, Colorado.

http://antics.com/pearl/site.jpg

Pet Pages

 http://www.dynamo.net/dynamo/pets/pets.html

Ch 2 Animals

"HI, MY NAME is Chloe, I'm a happy goat. That's because I have a nice warm barn and straw to sleep on through these cold winter nights. It's my first winter here in Montana and I don't like to get my feet wet so I stay inside as much as I can."

Yes, talking animals on the Internet. You'll find it at Pet Pages, a site that will put an image of your very own Chloe, Fido, Fluffy, or Tweety on the Internet. Some are accompanied by sounds as well, just in case you're yearning to hear a dog bark or a cat meow.

Pet Pages is the kind of site you'll either love or hate. Those who think the Internet should be only for "Important Stuff" will probably hate it.

Pet Pages is kind of a vanity site for people who want to be able to brag that their parakeet now has a Web site, which is just a bit of an exaggeration.

Also if you're a pet owner, and want to read other people's stories about their dogs and cats, or put your own pictures and stories on the Internet, the Pet Pages is a good place to do it. In addition, it has links to other pages about pets.

Image quality varies, from excellent to hardly recognizable (some people seem to take the notion of a black cat in a coal bin literally). Since the site limits pictures to 20Kb or less, most will come up fast, even on slow connections.

Some of the text is touching, some of it is boring, and some of it will make those of you who are not pet owners, gag. It's all supplied by the pet owners themselves, so don't blame the Webmaster at this site. ▲

Chloe, the happy goat.

http://www.dynamo.net/dynamo/pets/misc/jpg/chloe.jpg

Photo Antiquities

 http://deskshop.lm.com/photo.antiquities/index.html

SEE RELATED SITES:

Ch 13 PHOTOGRAPHY

PHOTO ANTIQUITIES SPECIALIZES in original photographs from the early days of the medium, when flash powder, darkrooms in tents, and 10 minute exposures were the state of the art.

The images here can be grouped into a couple of categories: historical photos of famous people or situations, photos of everyday life in the good old days before computers, and photographic novelties that explored the potential of the medium. Most of these items are for sale.

Although this gallery is generous in showing its images, there are many more: the total collection is said to number more than 100,000 items.

Got an old stereoscope around? You can pick up some stereograms for it, and view them here. The view shows one of the images in a large size and the stereo pair as an inset, so if you like to stare at your computer screen for a long time you can try to view the stereo image on screen.

Some sections show only one image each, while others are better furnished. It has a special section on the Civil War, the first American war in which photographic technology was developed to the point to be useful. The Civil War section is particularly well populated with images of Abe and Mrs. Lincoln, assorted Civil War generals, and pictures of Harriet Beecher Stowe, author of *Uncle Tom's Cabin*, and abolitionist Henry Ward Beecher. Many of the Civil War images are signed on the back by famous photographers, such as Matthew Brady.

The Native Americans and the West section also had a large group of pictures of native chiefs and braves, stagecoaches, wagon trains, and Indian villages, all taken in the 1860s by a Salt Lake City photographer. ▲

Photo of Cheyenne wigwams by G.W. Carter of Salt Lake City, Utah circa 1860s.

http://deskshop.lm.com/photo.antiquities/images/p527i.jpg

The Pickup Truck Home Page

 http://www.rtd.com/~mlevine/pickup.html

THE OLD-FASHIONED concept of a "truck" as a utility vehicle is quietly eroding, as a large majority of urban truck owners specialize in form over function. Fittingly, plugged-in pickup truck owners flaunt their wheels on this home page.

A majority of the space at this site is devoted to scans of new pickups, most likely from information brochures. For example, in Pickup Truck Profiles, visitors are witness to glossy photographs of brand new vehicles, each captured with their individual charm. The gloss on the showroom

20

One of the few "street trucks" in the Custom Sport Truck category on The Pickup Truck Home Page.

http://www.rtd.com/~mlevine/Pickup_Images/SPORT2.JPG

paint seems to shimmer against the radical blue and white background that dominates all the links connected to The Pickup Truck Home Page.

Also in Pickup Truck Profiles, American vehicles dominate (under the wavy American Flag set in motion by liberal use of a blur filter). Each of the American categories (Chevrolet, GMC, Ford, and Dodge) provide extensive overviews, technical and financial information, and photographs of each brand of pickup. Foreign pickup truck categories (Toyota, Nissan, Mazda, and Isuzu) are also informative and illustrated, but not to the same extent. Toyota's coverage is devoted to the larger T-100 series, considered to be "mid-size" as opposed to most American "full-size" pickups. Nissan and Mazda are provided a much lighter fare, and the Isuzu link was "under construction" when we visited.

The site owner recognizes his bias, however, pointing out that he prefers Chevrolets and American trucks. In recognition that people do drive pickup trucks in other parts of the world, he is working on a new link, Pickups Around the World. That link was under construction also.

The largest single collection of photographs at this site is available in the On The Fly link to the current pickup truck news, where new and future models are displayed and discussed.

For the Internet community, browsers can check out the Truck of the Week, which featured (when we visited) one photo of the truck and the one-question Pickup Truck of the Week FAQ: "How do I send a picture of my truck to The Pickup Truck Home Page?"

Links to other categories such as Off-Road Racing provided only one or two images, but we're sure this site will gain in both popularity and size, as The Pickup Truck Home Page was awarded Cool Site of the Day for July 26, 1995, and boasted over 150,000 page access between July 6-23. ▲

Pavilion Internet Gallery

 http://www.pavilion.co.uk/PIG/

THIS ONLINE GALLERY that cheerfully brands itself with the acronym PIG, collects a versatile collection of work, including poetry, photography, painting, and wire sculpture.

Matthew Dales is a photographer whose detailed landscapes and natural close-ups are so sharp you're not sure whether you're looking at a mountain or a molehill. His work shows patterns of nature through erosion and other natural forces.

Linda King is a painter who is moving on to her next medium, skin, as a tattoo artist. What we saw when we looked however, were works from the time when she still worked with paper and canvas.

Vivienne Prince and Fidel Garcia work with wire to produce small sculptures of people or animals, and Dettmer E. Otto shows off a bold style in a gallery of commercial and editorial illustrations.

And then there's Shot, a gallery sponsored by the Festival of Women Photographers, where the viewer is the target. We won't say much about this adults-only gallery except its concluding thought: "Shot has put you in its sights, has aimed at your PC, has played with your triggers, has satisfied a need to come at the request of a call." Yes, indeed.

Navigation at this gallery is obvious and straightforward.

"Detail of The Arrow, Not the Archer" by Linda King.

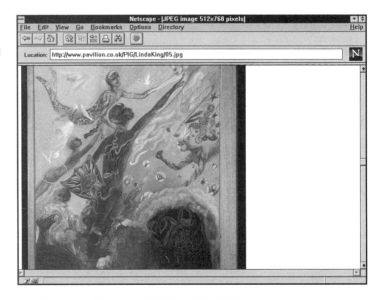

http://www.pavilion.co.uk/PIG/LindaKing/05.jpg

Each artist has a thumbnail that takes you to a gallery of images that you can enlarge for viewing. The thumbnails here are fairly large, in some cases more than 40Kb, so those on modem connections may find themselves waiting on occasion. ▲

The Photojournalist's Coffee House

 http://www.intac.com/~jdeck/index2.html

SEE RELATED SITES:

Ch 13 PHOTOGRAPHY

ONE OF THE big problems with being a newspaper photojournalist is that weeks of work may result in one day's publication. And then your output is used to wrap fish.

The Photojournalist's Coffee House not only provides permanence to stories that can afford to be told many times, but it offers world-wide exposure to documentary photography.

This site houses several documentary photo series, most by Webmaster John Decker. His best known project is Covington's Homeless, a sympathetic, yet detached series of photos depicting homeless people who live on the streets and in the riverside "hooches" of Covington, Kentucky.

Decker's careful photojournalism presents strong graphics that don't obscure the story behind these people's lives.

Another exhibit here by Decker covers carnies, the workers who set up and take down traveling carnivals. Decker shows the people against the struts, wires, and tracks of their trade, and also conveys the "if this is Tuesday it must be Circleville" grind, with its brief moments of relaxation and levity.

Decker proves a master of managing available light, in a situation where the people could be lost in the glare of neon.

A series on circus clowns focuses on their backstage life, practicing, waiting for their act to begin, preparing their costume.

Also on the site are two documentary shoots by Tahra Makinson-Sander, one on teen pregnancy and another on a Croatian soldier struggling to rebuild his life in Ohio. The latter is a warm, affectionate portrait of a man who has lost everything except an irrepressible desire to not only live, but to enjoy life to the fullest.

The site offers two ways to navigate through these photo essays. You can click on a thumbnails link to see all the photos in thumbnail versions, or you can use next and previous buttons to move through the exhibits. The thumbnails are quickest for those

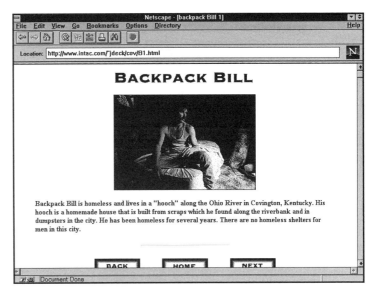

http://www.intac.com/~jdeck/cov/B1.html

concerned about purely photographic issues, but use the next and previous buttons if you want the story behind the photos, which we would advise. ▲

Pompeii Forum Project

 http://jefferson.village.virginia.edu/pompeii/page-1.html

SEE RELATED SITES:

Ch 4 ARCHITECTURE

A DEVASTATING EARTHQUAKE hit the city in 62 A.D., destroying many buildings and homes. Seventeen years later, a nearby volcano erupted, completely covering the city and most of its inhabitants with ash and lava.

The devastation of Pompeii, however, was a boon for architects, and the Pompeii Forum Project records some of the important archaeological features of a site that, because of the disasters that befell it in the first century, survived until the 19th century without the usual erosion, destruction, and rebuilding that faced every other ancient Mediterranean site.

Architects and historians love the site because it not only shows the Roman architecture of the time, but because of the earthquake and subsequent reconstruction, many parts of the site represent the latest architectural and building theories of that time.

20

A photo of the current state of the Imperial Cult building in Pompeii, along with an animation showing how it might have looked.

http://jefferson.village.virginia.edu/pompeii/icb-g1.jpg

From the home page, clicking on the link to go directly to the forum brings you to a large, clickable map of the town for which images are available. You can either click on one of the numbers, or scroll down to a list of the buildings and click on one of those links. Up will pop a plan view of the building you selected, with small camera icons on it. Clicking on a camera brings up a photo of the area, and often some explanatory text. A link in the section on the Imperial Cult Building brings up a study of how the room and roof might have been constructed, along with several fly-around animations of the structure as it might have looked.

This is an excellent site for anyone who wants some insight into how archaeologists, historians, and architects do their work. The high-quality photographs show Pompeii as it is today, while the text and background computer graphics demonstrate the experts' reaction to it. ▲

PM Zone (Popular Mechanics)

 http://popularmechanics.com/homepage.html

SEE RELATED SITES:

Ch 12 NEWS, WEATHER, & SPORTS

Ch 13 PHOTOGRAPHY

Ch 17 TRANSPORTATION

POPULAR MECHANICS HAS been publishing since the earliest days of motor vehicles, and it's guaranteed a slot in the future with its own WWW home page. The magazine launched itself into the Internet with PM Zone, bringing with it the encyclopedia-level of mechanical information that's been a *Popular Mechanics* staple since 1902.

Following the Automotive link ("Where The Rubber Meets The Road On The Information Superhighway"), visitors can browse through more than 200 illustrated 1995 New Car and Truck Profiles. While there, they can read through the Incentive Watch link for the latest information on which automobile maker is offering what kind of cash-back deal. PM backs up its current vehicle data with Owners Reports that tell the automobile's real story by those who do the buying and the driving.

One of our favorite spots at the PM Zone is the Movie of the Week and its associated PM Movie Archive. When we stopped by, the movie of the week was a MH-53J Pave Low 3E Helicopter executing "a night attack on a target." The archive netted us 25 more defense-oriented video clips, each of them about 2Mb or more. All of the videos are in

Progress Dude, the poster child of Popular Mechanic's PM Zone Internet home page.

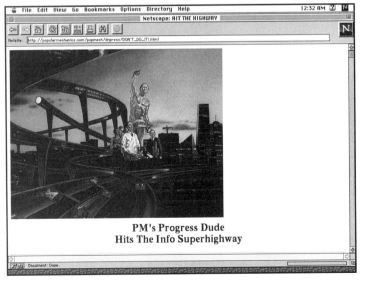

http://popularmechanics.com/popmech/dnpress/DON'T_DO_IT!.html

.mov format. At first, we wondered why all the videos were military operations, then realized that they were captured from PM's American's New War Machines video (which you can order from PM). We didn't mind. A video clip is a video clip.

Photographs illustrate all of the article-based links, too. Tech Update Of The Day focuses on a short update from current headlines, and links to PM's archive of Updates. The Features Of The Month are longer articles with more illustrations, but are updated only monthly.

PM's Time Machine archives features and illustrations from 1902 through 1960. In the Do Not Press link, PM compares and contrasts historical inventions with modern inventions, such as car alarms, in-line skates, and snowmobiles, all of them with images from the original magazine.

The PM Zone claims that subscribing to *Popular Mechanics* magazine is cheaper than a monthly bill from your Internet provider, but we're sure you'll get your money's worth here. ▲

Persistence of Vision (POV)

 http://www.povray.org/

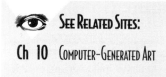

See Related Sites:

Ch 10 Computer-Generated Art

POV-Ray is a copyrighted, but freely available ray-tracing program that has become a passionate hobby for many people.

Hackers use it for fun; scientists use it to create stunning graphic images of molecules, microscopic surfaces, and star systems; and artists use it to create powerful, expressive images that look too good to be true.

This site shows off some of the best work done in this medium, and also holds a monthly contest, whose results you can review at this site.

Navigation at this site is straightforward. On the home page you'll find a ray-tracing image of the month, and below that, a list of links. You'll also find ray-tracing images in two sections.

The Hall of Fame is an FTP directory loaded with some of the best ray-tracing images that hobbyists and professionals have put on the Internet. You'll find scenery, strange insects and dragons, marbled porticos, and common household objects here. If you're on a slow connection, you might want to download the text file (it has the same file name as the image, but a .txt extension), which accompanies many of the images. You may be able to determine from that whether you want to download an image or not.

An entry from John Hooper on the topic "Science" in the monthly comp.graphics.raytracing competition. It took 32.5 hours to render on a 90 MHz Pentium computer.

ftp://ftp.povray.org/pub/competition/competition-Jun-95/electric.jpg

In spite of the computing time required to make them, these images are not particularly huge. Some come in at under 100Kb, and few are larger than 400Kb.

All the images are stored here as GIF and JPEG images, making it easy for most people to view them.

Because ray-tracing does such wonderful work with reflections, randomly mottled surfaces, and shadows, you'll probably notice that almost everything in most of these scenes has a glossy or reflective glossy surface—sometimes even insects and animals. That's mainly because the image creators like to show off the ability of ray-tracing software to keep track of the way light bounces off reflective surfaces.

The second section where you'll find images is under the monthly comp.graphics.raytracing competition. In this competition, someone comes up with a topic and all the ray-tracers out there try to illustrate it in some way.

The topics are quite general, which leaves plenty of room for ray-tracers to exercise their creative imaginations. Some of the images are almost abstract or conceptual, while others depict everyday objects.

The topic for June 1995, for example, was science. Some contributors worked with laboratory instruments, such as microscopes and beakers, while others worked on models of molecules or pictures of laboratories or experiments gone awry. The quality of the work varies here, from experts to first-time novices.

Most images also come with a text file describing the image

and how long it took the computer to fully "render" it. There's also a source code file, so if you've downloaded POV for your computer, you can run this code through the program to generate a similar image.

The software itself is available for download from this site, with versions for Amiga, IBM-compatible, Macintosh, UNIX, and Linux systems (be sure to read the README file first, to make sure you get all the files). ▲

Eric G. Suchanek, Ph.D, used a Silicon Graphics computer to render this image of DNA sequences under a bell jar.

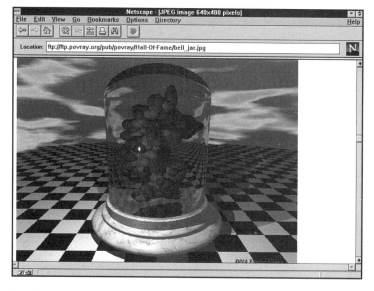

ftp://ftp.povray.org/pub/povray/Hall-Of-Fame/bell_jar.jpg

People Magazine

 http://www.pathfinder.com/

SEE RELATED SITES:

Ch 8 CELEBRITIES & ENTERTAINMENT

YOU WANT PICTURES of the stars, celebrities, and ordinary people who make the news? This is the magazine that moved gossip upscale, and with its Time-Life photography standards, it's a great place to get the latest images of people in the news.

Since the URL changes every week, depending on the issue of the magazine, we're pointing you to the general Pathfinder URL, which holds all the Time-Warner publications.

By the same token, the content changes every week, so if you're starstruck, you'll want to dip in here every week to see if some of your favorite people are featured and pictured here. However, if you can't find what you want, you

Nicole Kidman, from a People Magazine interview.

File Edit View Go Bookmarks Options Directory   Help

Location: http://www.pathfinder.com/@@kzi66wAAAAAAgD76/people/950703/images/nicole2.jpg

http://www.pathfinder.com/@@kzi66wAAAAAAgD76/people/950703/
images/nicole2.jpg

can always click the Last Week's People button and page down through previous issues.

The cover story is your best bet to pick up good graphics of people in the news.

When we visited, for example, it had a cover story on stars before they were stars, which included early photos of Jerry Seinfeld, Nicole Kidman (both before and after stardom), David Caruso, Demi Moore, and Sharon Stone.

The picture count on cover stories will vary from issue to issue. Occasionally, you'll find only one. Other times, you'll hit a jackpot of photos.

Another good place to look in *People* is the Picks and Pans section, which covers the best and worst for the week in movies, television, and music. The images here may appear tiny, but you can click to open the full story, and click again there to get a full-screen version of the image. ▲

Paramount Pictures

 http://www.paramount.com

See Related Sites:

Ch 8 Celebrities & Entertainment

WHEN THE BIG boys move onto the Web—the motion picture companies with their $100-million plus filming budgets—you can count on top notch graphics.

This site shows off the latest from Paramount Pictures, so it is necessarily selective about the graphics it shows, which includes only current Paramount pictures.

But if you're looking for images of some of the top stars, and those stars are in a Paramount picture, you'll want to have a look at this site.

This site is one of the most creative sites on the Web, with out-of-the-ordinary navigational tools. They may not be easier to use than the standard fare, but they do add a lot of spice to an already hot site.

When we visited, it featured three just-released movies, and three new television shows from Paramount. As you might expect from a site like this, you'll find photos of the stars and the action all over the place.

Many of the films include a photo gallery or images database, which in this case is a list of about two dozen images from the film. The film's main advertising poster, all the major actors, and many of the minor players show up in these pictures from the film.

Paramount helpfully includes two tracks into the images database, one for those with fast Internet connections and one for those on modems. The graphics-lite version is mostly text, and when you want to see an image you click on the text-based link, while the faster version has a large bitmap on the opening page, and thumbnails of all the graphics in the database.

Each film has its own images database, so to get there, click on the film's name first. That gets you to a description of the film, with small inline graphics. At the bottom of the description you'll see a link for more information about the film (here's where you make your choice of fast or slow connections) and from there you can pop over to the images database or photo gallery.

You can also download QuickTime movie clips from the films. Again, Paramount will deliver the 5 to 8 megabyte file, made to run at 15 frames per second for up to several minutes for those with fast connections. But if you're coming in on a modem, you can download a smaller (and slower, more like 5 frames per second) 1 megabyte clip of part of the preview, which will run for about 30 seconds.

Poster from the film Congo, on the Paramount Web site.

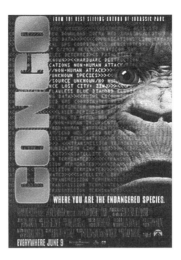

http://www.paramount.com/images/COPOSTER.GIF

Paramount is also into television production, and the television show sections provide extensive background information on the shows, as well as GIFs of every member of the cast and pictures from production. This will vary from show to show.

Paramount is doing more than recycling press kits here: They make an effort to go beyond the ordinary, adding special wrinkles for their movies and television shows. ▲

ProArts

 http://www.lanminds.com/local/proarts.html

SEE RELATED SITES:

Ch 6 ART IN CYBERSPACE

PROARTS IS THE cyber version of an innovative operation in the East Bay area across the water from San Francisco.

For a few days more than 300 artists in the area open their doors to the public, offering them a chance to drop in and view the art and studio and talk to the artist.

The Web version isn't quite as complete, with only 100 works from artists participating in the open studios event. On the other hand, you're likely to visit more studios on this site in cyberspace than you are in person over a few weekends. Okay, so it's not as good as visiting the studio, but it sure is easier on the feet.

The site offers a couple of guided tours, in which you can select the medium you'd like to look at or the city. (A Volkswagen van link on the bottom of the page is your tour guide.) In addition, you can

20

view an alphabetical list of the artists.

Unless you're looking for someone in particular, the tour by medium will give you the easiest way to cruise through this gallery. You just get one image from each artist, but hey, there are 100 of them, so this can take a while even at that.

Media include acrylics, ceramics, drawing, glass and jewelry, metal, mixed media, oils, photography, print-making, textiles, and watercolor.

The quality of the photography at this site varies from excellent to marginal, and we do wish the images were a bit larger. Guess we'll have to visit the East Bay next year. ▲

"Texas UFO" by Tad Schock.

http://www.lanminds.com/local/pages/342.html

Pixel Pushers

 http://www.pixelpushers.wis.net//

SEE RELATED SITES:

Ch 5 ART GALLERIES
Ch 6 ART IN CYBERSPACE

PIXEL PUSHERS IS a gallery that specializes in the work of digital artists, that is people who use computers extensively or exclusively to create art.

This site doesn't have great depth—you'll only find one picture from each artist represented—but did have 23 artists when we looked, including some significant names like Buffy St. Marie and Kai Krause (of Kai's Power Tools, a very popular image manipulation add-in for Adobe Photoshop and other graphics programs).

The images in this online gallery were also showing at a Calgary gallery at the time we looked, to provide greater public access to the concept of digital art.

What's exciting about this gallery is the sheer range of styles that it shows. There's everything from simple digital cloning to highly abstract visions.

You can view the work by artist, by pulling in a list of thumbnails associated with each artist (click on the thumbnail to get a larger selection of pictures).

Among the things you can buy here are prints of any of the images, or a CD that contains all the images plus some music composed or selected to accompany them.

You can click into an audio section where you can download some of the music or listen to selected artists talk about their work. These files range in size from 400Kb to more than a megabyte however. ▲

Detail from a downloadable poster at Pixel Pushers that shows the work of all of its artists.

http://www.pixelpushers.wis.net//XPix/PPPoster.JPEG

The Acceleration Chamber

http://www-usacs.rutgers.edu/fun-stuff/tv/quantum-leap/

See Related Sites:

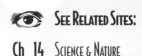

Ch 14 Science & Nature

IF YOU READ through the Leaper's Log near the top of this site, you'll see that *Quantum Leap* never ceased to be popular. The 95-episode series (aired March 26, 1989 to May 5, 1993) is now in syndication by the Sci-Fi Channel and the USA Network. Still, fans insist that they can never get enough.

The list maintainer knows this, and posts: "But no, I don't know anything about plans to bring *Quantum Leap* back. If I ever do, you can be sure I'll post information here about it. Thank you."

The subdirectory Index of GIFs from the Et cetera link brings up a fair number of GIFs available from The Acceleration Chamber; however, in the vein of *Quantum Leap*, appearances can be deceiving—half of the GIFs are merely smaller versions of the full-sized GIFs. While this is nice for visitors with slow modems, it does mean that there are fewer photographs.

The file names for the GIFs at first seem mysterious, but if you flip through the site's Episode Index, you see that the small, thumbnail images accompany a few of the episode summaries, and are named accordingly.

A larger index of images and art can be found on the link to ziggy.cisco.com under the Leaps Elsewhere, which leads to the official *Quantum Leap* anonymous FTP site. At the time of our visit, the FTP archive contained 104 GIF files. A few of these files are for Scott Bakula fans. There are photos from his other acting jobs, such as his role as Peter Hunt on *Murphy Brown*, and from his convention appearances.

There are links to other QL sites newsgroups. We might have seen the last of *Quantum Leap,* the television show, but, if the fans have any say, we haven't seen the last of Sam and Al. ▲

Watched over by the ethereal Al, Sam (Dr. Samuel Beckett) must fill in for a billiards pro to save a small bar from foreclosure in the episode "Pool Hall Blues."

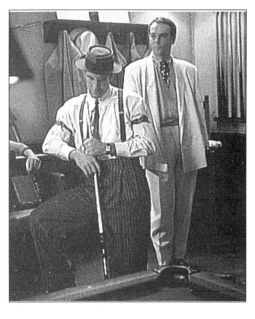

http://www-usacs.rutgers.edu/fun-stuff/tv/quantum-leap/Gifs.dir/pool-hall-blues.gif

Renaissance and Baroque Architecture

http://www.lib.virginia.edu:80/dic/colls/arh102/index.html

SEE RELATED SITES:

Ch 4 ARCHITECTURE

THIS SITE IS actually intended for the use of students studying architectural history at the University of Virginia in Charlottesville.

It illustrates, among other things, a trend among university faculty members to put course materials online. No more faulty projectors, slide trays, or scratched overheads: just enter the URL for today's lecture, and students can look at the images any time they wish.

So we'll look over the professor's shoulder, to mention that this exhibit has a fine collection of images from Italy and many other places around the world where the influence of Italy's Renaissance and Baroque architects has been felt.

That means you'll travel around Europe and the United States among other places. You don't get the lectures (unless you pay tuition), but most of the early images in this set have captions and others are being prepared. As a visual overview of the profound influence that Italian design has had on world architecture, it's a good place to start.

Detail of the Piazza del Duomo, Florence, 11th–19th Centuries.

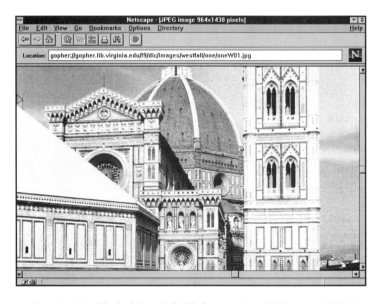

gopher://gopher.lib.virginia.edu/I9/dic/images/westfall/one/oneW01.jpg

You'll have to be patient at this site, even with a fairly fast connection. Each section of the lecture has 20 or more images, all of them shown as thumbnails when you access a lecture session, so the pages can be slow to draw.

The images themselves are large and luscious, with excellent detail. In fact, to view most of them properly you'll have to save the image files and view them with some other program for viewing JPEG images, since you can't generally fit the whole of these images on the screen. ▲

Royal British Columbia Museum

 http://rbcm1.rbcm.gov.bc.ca/

SEE RELATED SITES:

Ch 19 XYZ

ONE OF US actually used to live in Victoria, B.C., and the Royal British Columbia Museum was one of those treasures worth visiting again and again.

Not at all stuffy, it brings history and nature alive in its public display area, so it's a treat to see it once again on-line. It hasn't lost its sense of providing the public with easy access to basic information. The online museum is organized somewhat like the real one.

The museum specializes in building reconstructions of places or objects (old streets, stores, ships, and mills) the way they used to be to give visitors a sense of the scale and richness of historical settings, and this site has many photos of those exhibits.

On the first floor of the online exhibit you'll find a fairly extensive section about first peoples.

Other sections are a bit thinner. The Oceans section is very thin, unfortunate given the fact that this museum is literally a stone's throw from salt water. You'll find some nice images of the animal dioramas in the natural history section. Don't confuse them with photos of live animals. Perhaps the natural looking photo of the mammoth will clue the forgetful in that not all of these are photographs of living animals.

In the modern history gallery you'll find photos of the reconstructed cabin of Captain George Vancouver's Discovery, which charted the west coast of North America extensively in the 1790s.

When we were there, the museum also had a link to a special exhibit on The Heritage of Genghis Khan that looked intriguing. Unfortunately only three images from this exhibit of 200 artifacts were placed online.

The museum was working on a new section, called Dis-

20

Totem poles at the Royal British Columbia Museum.

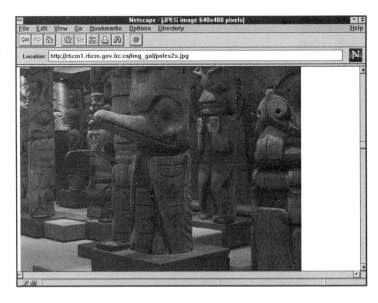

http://rbcm1.rbcm.gov.bc.ca/img_gal/poles2s.jpg

covery, when we visited. This illustrated newsletter about the museum and its exhibits has more images about its most topical exhibits. ▲

Rob's Multimedia Lab

http://www.acm.uiuc.edu/rml/

ROB'S MULTIMEDIA LAB is one of several all-in-one collector sites on the Net, where you'll find a mixed collection of images rather than images organized around a specific theme.

As its name suggests, it's more than just still pictures, however. It has numerous sound, animation, and movie files, and many built-in links to even more multimedia files.

One thing it shares with most other sites is a lack of visual aids to tell you what

you'll see when you download a picture. The site has no thumbnail images, only a few text files describing what a picture contains, and few file descriptions. There's often no way to know what's in a file until you download it. Considering that these files run to 600Kb for still images, and much larger for movies and animations, that's a drawback.

For example, there's a nice section on aircraft here, mostly military, but about the only clue to each file's contents is its name, and that's not always enough. A 324Kb image called PLANES.GIF, for example, is rather large for someone to download to determine what it really contains (one each of the U.S. Air Force's many aircraft on the tarmac at an air base, just in case you're wondering).

But we shouldn't complain. After all, we're getting it free, except for the darned meter that the Internet access provider keeps ticking while we're downloading. We could always volunteer to create an index and upload it (yeah, right), for the Webmaster who's probably got his hands full managing the huge number of files and links at this site just the way they are.

As in many such "collector" sites, as we call them, you're taking potluck when you come here because there's no standard for images that are in many cases contributed by others. Copyright information is not listed with the pictures, and their size varies from barely-better-than-thumbnail to too-large-for-the-screen.

Sections may have incredible strengths in some areas, weaknesses in others. In the Autos section we counted 13 images of 1994 Mustangs, and five images of other cars.

To help you out, here are some of the areas where we noticed some exceptional strengths: lots of *Jurassic Park*

pictures, an excellent section on fractals, a good set of train and aircraft pictures, a strong animals section, 25 images from M.C. Escher, a fair number of cartoon and comic characters, a very large collection (more than 200 images) of fantasy pictures, a strong (more than 200 images) section on landscapes, numerous space pictures, and a special section on Christmas, including a whole subdirectory devoted to the Grinch.

This being a multimedia site, it has an extensive collection of movies. We counted about 160 MPEG movies, plus additional images in the ANIM, AVI, FLI, and QuickTime formats.

Since these files can easily get into the megabyte range it was good to see that at least a few of them have small text files explaining their contents. A real find is a picture of a can of that Internet favorite, Spam, in the advertising section. Rob's Multimedia Lab also has a very extensive set of links to other movie, sound, and image sites.

For example, the U.S. Postal Stamps section links to the U.S. Postal Service where you can view some of its online stamp images (including Elvis).

Then there's a link to the QuickTime clips at Comedy Central, and links to other sites specializing in weather movies, the Fractal Movie Archive, the MPEG Movie Archive, and

20

A selection from the large collection of fantasy pictures.

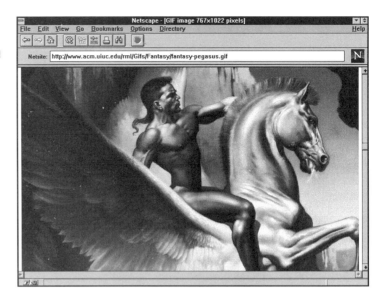

http://www.acm.uiuc.edu/rml/Gifs/Fantasy/fantasy-pegasus.gif

other such sites

There's a good set of links related to sports like hang-gliding, mountain-climbing, kite-flying, sky-diving, and skiing, plus links to some train sites, and to some science fiction and fantasy sites related to *Star Trek* and *Star Wars*.

Other fractal sites also get a mention, and it has links to many of the other big collector sites, like SunSite, SUNET, FINET, and the Digital Image Archive.

These links are helpfully labeled with icons indicating whether they contain still images, movies, or sounds.

Overall, in spite of our concerns about labeling and titles, which is a common problem with a site of this size, this site achieves its goals very well. If you're looking for movies, or still images, there are few sites in the world that are going to give you a better shot at finding what you need than this one. ▲

Mark Rosenstein's Sailing Page America's Cup On-Line

http://community.bellcore.com/mbr/sailing-page.html
http://www.ac95.org/

SAILING ACROSS THE open water reveals facets of the human soul that are rarely seen on dry land. We settled into the rhythm of Mark Rosenstein's Sailing Page for that very reason—we could feel the water spraying across our faces, even as we sat in front of our relatively dry computer monitors.

This page is less an archive of sailing photographs as it is a resource to the plethora of other sailing and boating sites across the Internet; however, Rosenstein does provide a reasonable glimpse of Life at Sea with the images available here. Under Some Local Stuff I've Collected, visitors can breeze through Rosenstein's adventures aboard the *Soren Larsen* and HMS *Rose* vessels.

A much larger archive of sailing photographs can be found at America's Cup On-Line, dedicated to sailboat racing. The link to the America's Cup Photo Album captures a majority of the available images, which is no small feat. The images in On The Water plunge WWW visitors directly into the neck-to-neck races, and On Shore brings home in a few images the feeling of those left behind.

There are seven QuickTime

The crew aloft aboard the Soren Larsen, *a 140-foot brigantine ship.*

http://community.bellcore.com:80/mbr/images/gif/soren-crew.gif

movies stored in the link to video clips, but even the live-action footage is overshadowed by the five individual collections on the Photo Exhibit link.

Another don't-miss collection in the Photo Album is People, featuring a longer list of portraits of those involved in sailing the ships that race for the America's Cup.

Whether for the love of sailing (Rosenstein's Sailing Home Page) or for the love of the sport (America's Cup On-Line), both sites steer visitors on the Internet Superhighway toward an ocean of illustrations. ▲

Salem

 **See Related Sites:**

Ch 4 Architecture

Ch 7 Art Museums

Ch 17 Transportation

Ch 18 Travel & Geography

SALEM, ONE OF the oldest towns in America, was a maritime center whose far-ranging schooners and clippers brought the town prosperity and treasures from distant places. The city's Web site offers many pictorial images of that heritage.

On the home page you'll find links to Salem's architectural heritage, its maritime heritage, and a section about witches. Of course, you'll want to look at the witches stuff first, but it doesn't have many pictures, so get back to the home page and start looking at the architectural and maritime sections.

The maritime heritage area is liberally sprinkled with pictures of the sailing vessels that made and kept Salem prosperous during the era of sail.

The area has links to sections on Salem's early maritime history, between 1776 and 1812, and after 1812, when the age of steam began.

For a page with silhouettes of different ways to rig a sailing vessel, click on any link describing a vessel's general

The interior of Cleopatra's Barge, the first American ocean-going yacht.

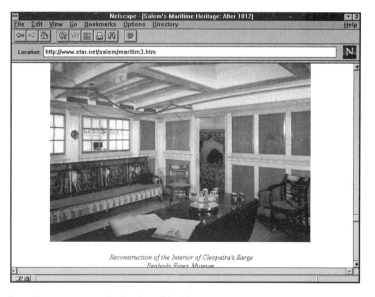

http://www.star.net/salem/maritim3.htm

class, such as "topsail schooners." You'll get silhouettes and descriptions of typical sailing configurations.

The section on Salem architecture describes the classic homes of Salem, some built in the 1600s and still standing.

As you go through the Salem pages, you'll also see links to the Peabody Essex Museum. Follow those links to get into the galleries, small but well done, which illustrate many of the trade articles that the early mariners brought back from China, Japan, and elsewhere.

Salem grew wealthy as its skilled mariners exploited new trade opportunities with China and Japan, and the museum has a significant number of online pages that illustrate the articles of that trade with both China and Japan. ▲

Stanford Computer Graphics Library

 http://www-graphics.stanford.edu/

SEE RELATED SITES:

Ch 10 COMPUTER-GENERATED ART

YOU MAY NOT realize it, but computer games and neat animations often require programmers to solve very complex problems.

How should reflections and shadows appear, especially on uneven surfaces? When morphing two objects—creating a sequence in which one object appears to turn into another, right before your eyes—how do you match all the points so that they move smoothly between the beginning and the end?

The folks at Stanford Computer Graphics Library are working on problems like those, not only for games but for many very powerful tools that might be available for science or the workplace in the future.

They make it real easy to figure out where to go when you get to their site: the main menu has links to boring stuff like technical papers, course outlines, and job openings—and then something called "cool demos."

The demos are cool, indeed, but the descriptions here are highly technical, and it may not always be clear to you and me why being able to paint a virtual bunny is so special. This is a scientific, and not a general public kind of site, however, so the scientifically minded will learn a lot here.

The most interesting material is the link to volume morphs (morphs done in three-dimensions, which are better than the more common two-dimensional morphs). You can watch a human head turn into an orangutan head (and you thought evolution only moved in one direction!), a

The Stanford Computer Graphics Library works with seemingly simple concepts, such as how an object creates reflections on a diffuse surface, with powerful mathematics and computer rendering of images.

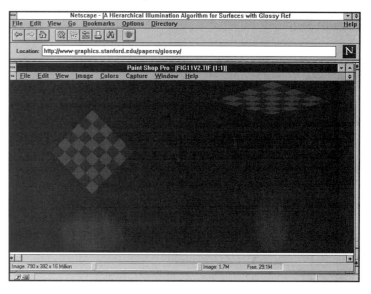

http://www-graphics.stanford.edu/papers/glossy/

dart turn into a jet aircraft, and a lion turn into a horse. The dart-to-aircraft morph is available in a very compact 69Kb file, making it possible for even modem users to download easily, while those with fast connections may want to try the 3.2 megabyte fly-by sequence. ▲

Santa Fe Fine Art

 http://www.sffa.com/index.html

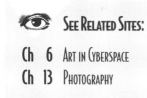

See Related Sites:

Ch 6 Art in Cyberspace
Ch 13 Photography

SANTA FE, NEW Mexico, has quietly built itself a reputation as a major town for people who love art and hate New York or Los Angeles.

This elegantly finished site shows off some of that talent, with distinctly western, yet modern scenes.

The site, when we visited, included a couple of photographers—Edward LaBane's figure studies, and David Hoptman's classy platinum/ palladium prints of landscapes and still lifes.

In LaBane's work, the figure becomes an element of landscape, sometimes blending and echoing the shapes and the fall of light on cliffs, trees, and hills, and other times falling fluidly against harsh rock.

Tom Gavitt's watercolors capture the contours and the sunbaked pastels of the southwest, and he finds endless delight in the geometry of Pueblo architecture.

If you then click in to Stan Berning's gallery of abstract oils, you see that Berning has abstracted the colors and the shapes of the southwest for his cerebral work, where they create the formal elements for abstract painting.

Gail Perazzini's abstracts are more adventurous and rowdy. She plays with texture, blends, and movement in her abstract work, creating complex blends with almost oriental transparency.

In the sculpture section, Ralph Roybal uses patinas to create color and detail on finely detailed sculptures of traditional native scenes and figures.

Robert Garcia's sculpture in bronze and stone is more abstract and streamlined.

AnaMaria Samaniego's prints and monotypes play with the broad sweep of the southwestern landscape, contrasting folding rock with flat planes, and the twisted shapes of plants with the swells and undulations of the eroded hillsides. ▲

"Song of Orpheus" by Gail Perazzini.

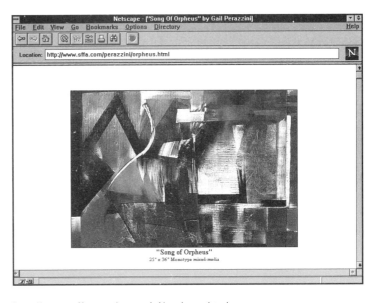

http://www.sffa.com/perazzini/orpheus.html

David Hoptman's "Mop Sensuously."

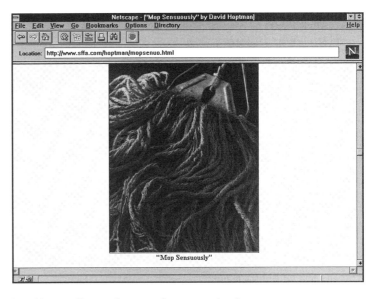

"Mop Sensuously"

http://www.sffa.com/hoptman/mopsenuo.html

Silicon Graphics Silicon Surf

 http://www.sgi.com/

SEE RELATED SITES:

Ch 10 COMPUTER-GENERATED ART
Ch 14 SCIENCE & NATURE

WHEN IT COMES to sheer graphics power, Silicon Graphics is a name you'll frequently hear. Its very fast computers, coupled with ultra-fast video systems, and the ability to perform functions across several computers make the company a darling of Hollywood, leading ad agencies, and large corporations.

This site shows off the company's stuff, and while you may not have the moolah at the moment for an Indy Extreme or Impact, you can always window shop on the Web.

From the home page, you'll immediately spot the link you want called Serious Fun. That

gets you several choices. The Surf Zone exploits a new 3D, virtual reality technology called VRML (Virtual Reality Modeling Language), but standard Web browsers can't use it yet. When we looked it was only ready for a few UNIX platforms and Windows NT. However, you can explore the Surf Zone in 2D with regular Web browsers. The Surf Zone includes a gallery of images done by SGI computers.

Another option under the Serious Fun menu is the Image Gallery. The general graphics section there simply has a few photos supplied by SGI employees or customers. You'll see some scientific images

20

under that section and there's a section showing contest winners from some SGI contests for graphical artists and scientific visualization.

You can download a Jurassic Park theme poster (SGI machines did the animation for the dinosaurs), or drop into several special galleries show-casing images created on SGI machines by their customers or employees.

SGI is naturally showing off the graphics capabilities of its systems, which means this is not a great site for the graphically challenged, such as those with slow modem connections. ▲

Detail of a Silicon Graphics rendering of a Buckyball, an unusual form of carbon with potential as a lubricant or electrical super-conductor.

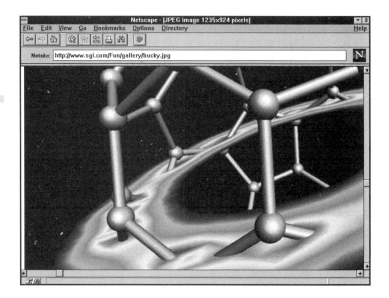

http://www.sgi.com/Fun/gallery/bucky.jpg

Sharky's Art Gallery & House of Graphic Delusions

 http://www.aloha.com/~sharky/artwork.html

SEE RELATED SITES:

Ch 10 COMPUTER-GENERATED ART

THE REAL WORLD is full of light sources, light reflected from surfaces, and surfaces that reflect light or absorb it to some degree. It's difficult to duplicate that completely accurately in art, particularly when you don't have a real model to work from, or you're trying to show surfaces generated by, say, a mathematical formula.

Ray-tracing is one effort around that. The computer is

given information about objects, their relative location, the way their surfaces reflect light, and the light sources themselves. It then begins to calculate every ray of light emerging from the light sources, determining where it will go, and how it will be reflected by other objects in the scene. The result (after, in some cases, days of computer time on a single image) is an image of startling reality and clarity.

Sharky's site shows off this technology, gathering images from around the Internet from some of the best ray-tracing artists around.

It's not a difficult site to navigate in. Page down to the list of individual artists, or just keep paging down to get a description of each artist and each work represented here.

You'll find plenty of images showing the famous reflecting-sphere(s)-hovering-over-a-chess board. In fact, this image, Lesson One for any ray-tracing wannabe, is so popular that ray-tracers had a "non-contest" to see if anyone could come up with any original versions of it. Some of those are displayed here.

Because these images are best viewed in detail, the site has small thumbnails, which you can download (they don't appear automatically) before deciding whether you want to see the whole image. ▲

Not a photograph, this image was generated by Andrey Zmievsky, using a ray-tracing program.

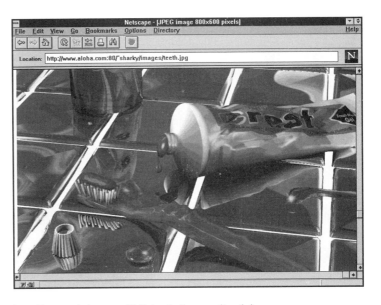

http://www.aloha.com:80/~sharky/images/teeth.jpg

20

The Smithsonian

 ftp://photo1.si.edu/images/

THE SMITHSONIAN INSTITUTION has long had a reputation as a repository of American history and life, and now selections of its extensive collection are in an online photo gallery.

This is a site with many one-of-a-kind products in its image galleries: the original Star-Spangled Banner; the first phonograph; the command module that took the first astronauts to the moon; the first electric motor; the first American satellite, Explorer; the aircraft that the Wright Brother's flew at Kitty Hawk in 1903; Charles Lindbergh's Spirit of St. Louis aircraft; an aircraft flown by Amelia Earhart; and the first aircraft to break the sound barrier.

As you might expect, this is a very mixed collection, a quality that those who have visited the Smithsonian have learned to love. You've got pictures of Native Americans, dinosaur skeletons, modern rocket aircraft, gems, birds, guns, and many images from around Washington, D.C. The Smithsonian has been called "the attic of America," and indeed, it reminds us of stumbling into the attic of some relative whose curiosity and sense of wonder was combined with an inability to throw anything away.

Although FTP is not as visually appealing as Mosaic or Netscape, this site is extraordinarily well organized for those who want to retrieve images. Some pictures are from the associated National Museum of Art, some are from the National Zoo, some are from the Smithsonian Observatory, and many record the technological history of America. This place covers a lot of ground and it has only just begun to put its collection online as retrievable images.

Fortunately, the Smithsonian gives you all kinds of tools to find what you want, if you're looking for something specific. Images are stored as GIFs, JPEGs, and even uuencoded JPEGs, for those who want to send copies of these images through e-mail and other gateways that don't handle binary files.

There's a directory here (/previews-text) that has "contact sheets" of selected images from the collection, as well as captions for all the images. The contact sheets may not be complete at a given time; however, there are more images in the gallery than appear there.

Because you can't view the images before downloading, you might want to browse the captions before browsing the image galleries themselves. When you see something that sounds interesting, you can mark it down and retrieve it later.

To top it all off, you can download small programs for DOS, Mac (a HyperCard Stack), or UNIX, which permit you to search the collection by keyword. The data included with these files will be updated as the collection is expanded. They're a great way to browse through the collection off-line.

The photos don't have captions right on them, but the Smithsonian has taken advantage of features in the GIF89a and JPEG specifications to embed the captions with the images, enabling you to keep the captions and photos together.

To help find your way around, first drop into the /catalogs directory and get yourself a copy of P1TREE.GIF.

This is a map of the directories on the system, which shows the file areas and also the directories where you can get viewing and management software to view the images.

One area where the exhibition shows depth rather than breadth is in the art directory. The Smithsonian uses this area to show off the extensive collection of African-American art at the National Museum of American Art.

You can find old masters in many places on the Internet but you're going to find many of these pieces only in Smithsonian.

The Smithsonian is the last resting place for many of the icons of American aerospace technology, so naturally you'll find images of them here as well, from the Wright Brothers' Kitty Hawk to space craft. You'll find most of these in the air-space directory.

The Science and Nature section has photos from the

The Smithsonian has many images recording early American life, such as this picture of Cheyenne Indian Dull Knife.

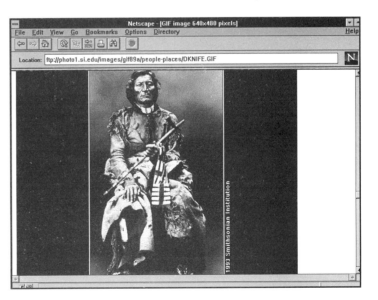

ftp://photo1.si.edu/images/gif89a/people-places/DKNIFE.GIF

National Zoo, with which the Smithsonian is associated. That zoo has had many extraordinary denizens, including Ling-Ling, the famous giant panda. You'll find pictures of her and others in this section.

Although the files have DOS-compatible file names, they do make sense. All the panda pictures, for example, are listed as panda1, panda2, and so on.

This collection is relatively new, and given the size of the Smithsonian's holdings, it's likely to expand significantly, at which time the search tools provided will become not just conveniences, but necessities.

For those hard-to-find graphics or those important moments in American life and development, this is the gallery you'll want to visit. ▲

Charles Lindbergh's Spirit of St. Louis is one of many classic American aircraft seen in the Smithsonian's image archive.

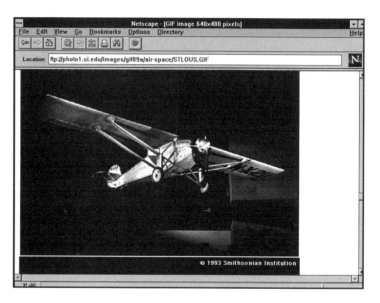

ftp://photo1.si.edu/images/gif89a/air-space/STLOUS.GIF

SimTel Archive

 gopher **file://oak.oakland.edu/SimTel/**

SEE RELATED SITES:

Ch 9 CLIP ART & ICONS

THE SIMTEL Archive is one of the most important sites on the Internet for software and other files related to Intel-based computers such as PC-compatibles. The archive specializes in software and files for MS-DOS, Microsoft Windows, and Microsoft Windows NT.

In addition to lots of programs to help you create, view, manipulate, convert, and catalog graphics files, you'll find a collection of clip art material

A sample of clip art from the SimTel Archive.

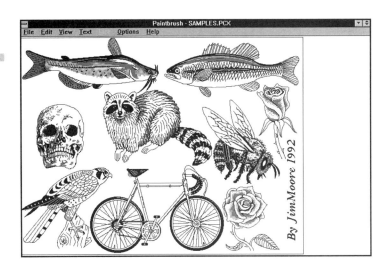

file://oak.oakland.edu/SimTel/msdos/deskpub/clipeze.zip

and icons.

SimTel directories are reasonably well organized, with files grouped into many subdirectories. While the files are only listed by name, at the top of each subdirectory you'll typically find an index that provides a fuller description of file contents and purpose.

You'll find most of the clip art in the msdos/deskpub/ directory. The artmart1.zip file contains transportation images, artmart2.zip has food, artmart3.zip contains images of spices, and artmart4.zip has cartoon-style drawings of families and people. These are PCC images, which is a PCX cut-out image, so any PCX-compatible program such as Windows Paintbrush can read these images and combine them with other images.

The clipeze1.zip file contains some high-quality clip art focusing on animals and

plants with a few other images thrown in. The clipit1.zip file contains more images, most of them poor to mediocre in quality. The ecuatif1.zip file contains TIFF images of Ecuadorian natives.

The msdos/graphics/ directory doesn't contain images, but it does contain hundreds of programs for viewing graphics, creating fractals, ray-tracings, converting graphics files from one format to another, and for cataloging graphics in various ways. If you need a graphics utility for a PC, this may be the place to look.

In the win3 directory tree, you'll find most of the important files in the graphics/ subdirectory. There are a couple of clip art collections here, neither of them notable for quality. Like the msdos directory tree, however, you'll find graphics utilities of various kinds. ▲

20

Smithsonian Photographs Online

http://photo2.si.edu/

SEE RELATED SITES:

Ch 14 SCIENCE & NATURE
Ch 18 TRAVEL & GEOGRAPHY

WE'RE GIVING THE Smithsonian Institution a couple of entries here to distinguish between photographs of its huge and varied collection of objects, and photographs of the rest of the world taken by its photographers.

This World Wide Web site, run by the Smithsonian's Office of Printing and Photographic Services, shows off the work done by the Institution's own photographic staff, who not only provide photos of Smithsonian exhibits, but who assist research staff at the Smithsonian by providing photographs for their work.

Two major themes dominate this site: photographs of scientific work and photographs of places. Sometimes they are part of the same assignment. For example, a photo display on sea turtles in Tortugeuro, Costa Rica, has a strong selection of photos of Tortugeuro, as well as photos of sea turtles and another section on the Costa Rican rain forest.

Another section shows several images of a solar eclipse, and you'll find a fairly extensive collection of underwater photographs from Belize, Panama, and the Florida Keys.

Washington D.C. scenes are a major part of this site. One section has a selection of aerial scenes of Washington, while another covers lesser-known monuments such as memorials related to the Spanish-American War, Seabees, military nurses, and the crew of the Space Shuttle Challenger. There's also a section devoted to the famous cherry trees around the Tidal basin. You'll also find photos of the Clinton inauguration, and a Web version of a book devoted to the Vietnam memorial. ▲

An iguana in the Costa Rican rain forest.

http://photo2.si.edu/turtles/12053.gif

Steve Jackson Games

 http://www.io.com/sjgames/

THE ILLUMINATI ARE online, and so are its art files. You can find them on the home page for Steve Jackson Games, in the links to the graphics files for its card game Illuminati New World Order.

Specializing in role-playing games, Steve Jackson Games is more familiar among Internet circles as the company that fought off the Secret Service when the U.S. government confiscated the company's BBS and files for the then-upcoming GURPS Cyberpunk, a computer hacker role-playing game.

GURPS, short for Generic Universal Role Playing System, is SJG's main RPG product, but skulking around the abundance of links on SJG's home page, we only found image files for INWO, In Nomine, and the company's news organ, Pyramid.

Following the link to INWO and then the link to INWO Artwork near the bottom of the page took us to a short list of sample files from the card game. Each set of files contained four to six preview size images (as it says near the top of the page), with the larger version available when selected. The individual images in the Illuminati I & II files varied in size (18 to 70Kb), and the images in other files were consistently on the small size (20 to 25Kb).

We found a much larger collection of images under In Nomine and following the link to Artwork. Even with our speedy Internet connection, we had time to visit the refrigerator while our computer pulled up the nearly 60 preview images. These are all beautifully crafted images, each available in a much larger version. A few of the files were less than 100Kb, but most of the images ranged in the 200 to 300Kb range.

Browsers can also capture the front-page art of SJG's magazine *Pyramid* by following the link to Cover Images. Each of the magazine's 15 editions is shown as in-line images, with the expanded versions loading up quickly at 50 to 100Kb.

None of the images on the SJG home page are annotated or explained, but visitors can read the text files for explanations of the games. While the site is sprinkled with other art, it's no secret that the art files at SJG will grow as the company produces more games.

The Illuminati, on the other (gloved) hand, are secret. That's all we can say. You aren't cleared for more information. ▲

Whether angels vs. demons or government vs. government, the image files on Steve Jackson Games home page let you choose your own side.

http://www.io.com/sjgames/in-nomine/artwork/splash-fight.jpg

Sandra's Skating Archive

http://haskell.cs.yale.edu/sjl/www/skate-images/images.html

SEE RELATED SITES:

Ch 8 CELEBRITIES & ENTERTAINMENT

Ch 12 NEWS, WEATHER, & SPORTS

HERE WE'VE GOT this nice, sophisticated sport that everyone pays attention to maybe every four years around the time of the Olympics. It's a sport of grace and great athleticism, as Sandra's Skating Archive shows.

This is a comprehensive collection of images about figure skating, assembled from sources all over the world. It's organized into a variety of sections, based on the original source of the images and the type of skating depicted in them.

The images vary in quality, from absolutely professional to marginal. Remember, however that we're talking about shooting pictures of people who are whizzing along in low light at 20 miles an hour and doing all kinds of leaps, jumps, and turns, and most of the images on here are quite acceptable quality. ▲

Nancy Kerrigan at the 1994 Winter Olympics.

http://haskell.cs.yale.edu/sjl/www/skate-images/sunet-mirror/women/
kerrig2a.gif

20

SkyView

http://skview.gsfc.nasa.gov/skyview.html

SEE RELATED SITES:

Ch 16 SPACE

WE ONCE WERE treated to a tour of the stars by an avid amateur astronomer with a backyard telescope mounted in his homemade observatory. It was an impressive display, but at 3 a.m. on a February morning in Alberta, Canada, it tends to be rather chilly.

While SkyView doesn't serve hot chocolate or brandy after a session of star watching, it does provide astronomers, both the backyard amateur and the professional, with an impressive display of the skies.

SkyView is a Virtual Telescope, whose database contains slices of every portion of the sky, taken in the periodic sweeps of the sky that astronomers undertake.

You fill in a form to tell SkyView what portion of the sky you want to see (you can use the astronomical coordinates or the common name of a star or galaxy) and it retrieves an image of that portion of the sky.

Furthermore, the basic interface here gives the user a choice of 16 different wavelengths, from radio waves to gamma rays at the other end of the spectrum.

If you're an amateur at this, you'll want to experiment with the type of survey you use to see what kind of images you get back. Some retrieve more useful data than others for a particular part of the sky.

Those who are more

The image at right was obtained by filling out SkyView's standard form, specifying that we wanted to see an infrared image of the area of the star Sirius.

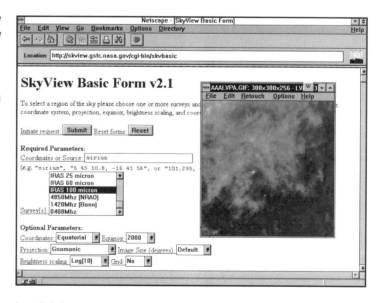

http://skview.gsfc.nasa.gov/cgi-bin/skvbasic

familiar with astronomy can have a field day (or night, which is what astronomers of our acquaintance prefer). The site has an advanced interface that allows overlays of images and other effects.

Folks running X Window (primarily on UNIX machines) can run an X Window session with SkyView, enabling them to manipulate the retrieved images directly. ▲

Comet Shoemaker-Levy Home Page

 http://newproducts.jpl.nasa.gov/sl9/sl9.html

See Related Sites:

Ch 16 Space

THE IMPACT OF the comet Shoemaker-Levy on Jupiter caused at least as many ripples in the terrestrial astronomy community as it did on the giant planet. This was such a major astronomical event that one person who actually keeps track counted nearly 60 sites with serious Shoemaker-Levy 9 coverage in June 1995.

There's no official site, but the home page maintained by the Jet Propulsion Laboratory is a very comprehensive and well organized effort that has hundreds of links to resources elsewhere.

All told, it claims 1,182 images of the collision, taken by 64 observatories around the world.

By the summer of 1995, it also had about five million accesses, which says something about its quality, and the popularity of the subject (and the speed of the server, to boot). To save some time, there's a link to the top 20 images accessed during July 1994, when the impact occurred.

Most popular of all is an image taken in near infrared light by a Spanish observatory. It shows the impact of the first comet fragment rising as a bright flash on the lower-left edge of Jupiter (one of Jupiter's moons confuses things by appearing to the right of the planet in many photos of the event).

You can also look at a collection of animations of the impact. Most, such as the Fragment R Impact Animation, using Keck images, are based on actual telescope images, and show the bright fireball as it flares up from the planet. If you don't mind just a little fiction, you can try the animation done by John Spencer from Lowell Observatory, in which you ride in the comet train itself, and see the flashes of earlier pieces of the comet as, pulled by Jupiter's gravity, they curve into its surface. It's available in small (394Kb) and large (1220Kb) versions and well worth getting.

For another look at the impact, access the link to MIT

20

First ever photos of a collision in our solar system, from the Calar Alto observatory in Spain.

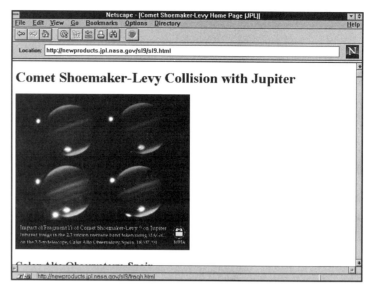

Netscape - [Comet Shoemaker-Levy Home Page (JPL)]
File Edit View Go Bookmarks Options Directory | Help
Location: http://newproducts.jpl.nasa.gov/sl9/sl9.html

Comet Shoemaker-Levy Collision with Jupiter

http://newproducts.jpl.nasa.gov/sl9/image17.html

at the bottom of the page, or go directly to **http://www-erl.mit.edu/flolab/csl9press/csl9hj.html**, for an animation that shows how the shock waves from the impact would have propagated through Jupiter's atmosphere, shaking the gaseous planet nearly from pole to pole. ▲

Supermodel Home Page

 http://www.supermodel.com/

SEE RELATED SITES:

Ch 8 CELEBRITIES & ENTERTAINMENT

THERE ARE MODELS and then there are supermodels. We're not sure who decides when a mere model becomes a supermodel, but the Supermodel Home Page will let you know.

When we looked there was only one model represented, Krissy Taylor, who tragically passed away suddenly in 1995 as her career was taking off.

The site is promising more models will appear, so if you're interested in the most beautiful of the beautiful, this is where you should have a look.

On the home page, click on the face of the model you'd like to look at. You'll get a menu offering you a choice of a biography, magazine covers, or memorabilia related to the supermodel—you can order posters, a press release photo, or the "comp card" that models show to advertising agencies and photographers, which shows them in various poses,

Krissy Taylor on the Supermodel Home Page.

http://www.supermodel.com/krissytaylor/gallery/krissy08.jpg

hair styles, and clothing. There's also a fashion show where the model displays different types of clothing, and a gallery of photos.

If you're interested in just pictures, the photo gallery is the obvious place to go. Typically you'll find several pages of pictures, and you can hit the Next button, or click on a row of numbers at the top (the one in reverse video is the page you're currently on).

These women get photographed a lot, so you're going to find glamorous pictures everywhere you look. Most of the pictures are rendered on the screen directly, but in the photo gallery you can click on an image to see it larger. ▲

Singapore Art and History Museum

 http://www.ncb.gov.sg/nhb/museum.html

SINGAPORE'S GEOGRAPHICAL POSITION, in a crucial Strait between India and China, has made it not only a critical point for commerce in South Asia, but open to a variety of artistic influences.

This site celebrates both history and art with a rich set of offerings demonstrating how Indian, Chinese, Malay, Javan, and Western influences have shaped Singapore's artistic traditions. They are also a fine introduction to many styles of art in South Asia. The online version of this museum has many special exhibitions, most of them illustrated, to show both history and art.

When we visited, this museum had an online display entitled Alamkara, from a Sanskrit word meaning ornamentation or decoration. It was an extensive exhibit of the items of courtly decoration in India, some of them dating back to the 3rd century B.C.

Remember that the great passion of European rulers early during the Age of Discovery was to find a passage to India? America was a mere roadblock to the riches of Asia.

This exhibit shows why India was so desirable a conquest. The courts of the Indian subcontinent were incredibly wealthy and opulent, with hordes of skilled craftsmen who turned the most ordinary household items—a pair of sandals, a drinking goblet— into *objets d'art*. Those arts were eventually to significantly influence western art and decoration, particularly after an 1851 exhibition in London of decorative items brought back from India by the British East India Company.

This well-organized exhibit was easy to navigate, with plenty of images and excellent text descriptions, especially useful for Westerners unfamiliar with the motifs and the religious ideas behind Asian arts.

A table of contents describes basic divisions of the exhibits—Kings and Courtiers, Ornamentation, Self-Adornment, Heroism, Devotion, Food, Pleasure and Love, each of which will have 4 to 21 photos of items in the exhibit. Some particularly small simple items, have only thumbnails, while complex paintings with fine detail can be enlarged by clicking on them.

Clicking on a division brings up a rather long essay on the topic, but these essays are well-written, and put the art in its historic context.

A folio from the Panchatantra, which illustrates essential kingly qualities, such as love, diplomacy, money, and punishment.

http://www.ncb.gov.sg/nhb/alam/alam/kingsjpg/folio(101).jpg

You'll find examples of illustrated manuscripts, jeweled boxes, temple decorations and friezes, paintings, jars and pots, tapestry, combs, and other items from courts and wealthy households.

Another section covers postcards of Singapore produced between 1900 and 1930. They show some interesting scenes of not only the architecture, but the society of the time, including a group of wealthy people enjoying opium, which was a financial mainstay of Singapore for many years (and manufactured by the state until World War II). The on-screen images here were smaller than we would have liked.

A section on the fall of Singapore to the Japanese in 1942 contains several text documents about the war, plus an image archive showing scenes of the Japanese advance and British surrender. The images come from both sides involved in the war.

A section showing 19th century prints of Singapore displays the city in its early colonial days. The prints were compiled from the many travelogues and journals that enjoyed huge popularity in Europe during the 19th century, as colonial powers expanded around the globe and travel became faster and safer.

This museum specializes in both art and history, and you'll find the latter emphasized in most of the exhibits here. Singapore historically occupied a pivotal role in English expansion in Asia, between its developments in India and its later expansion into China.

You'll find a comprehensive hypertext history of Sir Thomas Stamford Raffles, who guided its early growth, and much other British exploration in the region. Raffles, whose name still adorns Singapore's most famous hotel, and the world's largest flower, served most of his career before the era of photography, so illustrations in this area are primarily maps and portraits.

Another section of the museum contains the work of Chinese artists who came to Singapore after World War II. Their work employs Western techniques and themes, but the subtleties of Chinese brush work are also evident. Some important players in Singapore's post-war art scene had strong ties to France and French art academies, and that influence is evident in much of this work, which tends to be more Western than Chinese in style. Unfortunately, these images are displayed in rather small sizes. ▲

20

David Elliott's Land of the Squishy

 http://www.btw.com/dce/

DAVE ELLIOTT IS a hobbyist who likes to fool around with image manipulation tools such as Adobe Photoshop, KPT Bryce, and Ray Dream designer.

The unusual name of this site comes from Elliott's view that the computer tools available today give artists powerful tools to manipulate surfaces and objects plus other options—such as the Undo button—that allow experimentation without making everything permanent.

We're not sure how much he had to undo at this gallery, but it's a particularly good site for looking at what these new tools are capable of. It's organized into a variety of galleries,

but in spite of the different names they didn't look all that different.

In galleries one and two you'll find a collection of landscapes and experiments with ray-tracing of artificial objects. Then there's the Forbidden Gallery, with "nekkid pitchers, guvmint secrets, illegal stock tips." If you believe that, go there. Even if you don't, go there.

While Elliott copyrights his images, he offers them freely for any purposes, so if you're looking for some knockout images for use in a presentation, report, or even advertising, you might want to check this site out. (He does request

An untitled image, done using KPT Bryce.

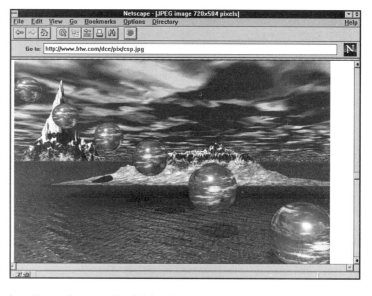

http://www.btw.com/dce/pix/csp.jpg

a free copy of anything the images are used on.)

Elliott obviously loves to play with these tools, and his work shows a breadth of techniques using various backgrounds, textures, and image manipulation techniques.

His tech notes section isn't terribly technical, and offers some simple insight into the tools he uses to create these images. ▲

Star Wars

The Star Wars Home Page

 http://force.stwing.upenn.edu:8001/~jruspini/starwars.html

The Purdue Star Wars Picture Archive

 http://www.mgmt.purdue.edu/~vkoser/starwars/pics.html

 **SEE RELATED SITES:**

Ch 13 PHOTOGRAPHY
Ch 15 SCIENCE FICTION

WHAT ELSE IS there to say about *Star Wars*, the ultimate science fiction movie that ushered in an entire new generation of fandom? Not much, so let's just look at some pictures.

The Star Wars Home Page does not contain a very large collection of images on its own, instead providing links to many other sites. If you're looking strictly for art, click over to the Star Wars Multimedia Files link. Here you'll find a mouthful of .wav sound files, several ray-traced files (very large), missing scene images, and links to (when we visited) seven other archives.

The link to the Star Wars Video Archive at CMU is not to be missed. This Star Wars Multimedia Archive contains about 20 different blooper scenes and a handful of other meaningful moments from all three films, plus the Energizer Bunny Commercial.

We also enjoyed the pictures available on the link to A New Hope: Behind the Scenes Page. You might imagine this as more of a back porch page than a home page, with both B&W and color photographs of the actors, directors, and film crew.

The Purdue Pictures Archive contains many well-scanned *Star Wars* images in three categories: People, Ships, and Miscellaneous. None of the three provide preview images, which is good, because both the People and Ships files are very large. The Miscellaneous file is dedicated to several scans of posters and some other artwork.

The size of the Purdue images varies, and the labeling leaves a bit to the imagination. Although a few of the images are fuzzy, the majority of them are clean and usable. ▲

20

General Tarkin, Princess Leia, and Darth Vader are audience to the power of the Death Star. One of three ray-traced images available on the Star Wars Home Page.

http://force.stwing.upenn.edu:8001/~jruspini/multi/tarkin.jpg

Swedish University Net

 ftp.sunet.se/ftp/pub/pictures/

WHEN YOU RUN across a large graphics archive on the Internet, the odds are good that it either got its pictures from SUNET, or its pictures have been posted to SUNET.

SUNET is the kind of place you go in a pinch. If you need a graphic of something special, and can't find it anywhere, you might check at this rather quirky site, because it is a huge archive of pictures.

It has pictures in some areas, such as history, or famous scientists, where it can be difficult to find anything on the Internet.

The collection policy is basically one of "make a contribution when you can." No attempt is made to make a complete archive. If there's only one picture in a category, so be it. If there are 400, that's great too.

The result, however, is that you'll run across graphics you'd never expect to find—when, for example, would you want a picture of the prize-winning preserves at the '93 L.A. County Fair?

But when you might expect to find something, you could be disappointed. Only two men, Bill Clinton and Mel Gibson, are listed under the people/men directory, and each by one picture.

You just never know who will show up at SUNET.

http://ftp.sunet.se:80/ftp/pub/pictures/people/misc/elvis-n-nixon.gif

The Clinton photo, however, is a rather famous and funny one that didn't receive wide publication, and for good reason: the President's gesture (pointing his right index finger into the curled fingers of his left hand) to explain some concept, taken out of context, could be misconstrued.

Most of the categories in this book have a parallel category on SUNET. We'll run down the list of major categories for you: advertisements (mostly liquor and soft drinks), animals, anime-manga (animation), architecture, art, ASCII art, astronomy, chemistry, collections (such as calendars or illustrated books), comics, computers, fantasy, fractals, history, maps, money, music, people, plants, ray-tracing, sports, television and film, and vehicles.

The art gallery contains the work of more than 80 artists, including Renaissance, Impressionist, and contemporary artists. Some have only a few works in the archive, while others have a strong representation of their major interests.

We did some quick calculations on the animals directory and came up with more than 400 photographs of critters ranging in size from whales to microscopic intestinal parasites.

The sport section has images from several areas, including many where it could be difficult in a pinch to come up with a graphic, such as fencing, skating, volleyball, windsurfing, and rally sports.

Then there's wacky stuff, like a photo of Albert Einstein sticking out his tongue, that

20

you would only run across by accident.

Pictures here come from a variety of sources. Some are posted from newsgroups, others are scanned from magazines or calendars (it would be risky to use any image taken off here for other than personal use, because many contain no copyright information).

Quality varies as well. Some are poorly scanned, while others are high resolution, full color images.

The directory structure (in English) is logically organized, and many of the images have accompanying text files which explain their origins, contents, and sometimes copyright information.

If you're on a slow connection, be sure to check for the text files accompanying pictures, because you can download them in a few seconds, before spending a lot of time downloading a large image file that wasn't what you wanted. ▲

Einstein's tongue.

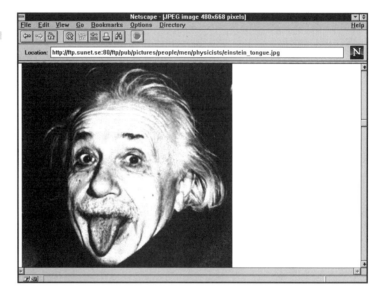

http://ftp.sunet.se:80/ftp/pub/pictures/people/men/physicists/
einstein_tongue.jpg

Synthetic Images, Online Gallery of

 http://www.seas.gwu.edu/faculty/musgrave/art_gallery.html

SEE RELATED SITES:

Ch 11 FRACTALS

KEN MUSGRAVE, WHO as a student assisted Benoit Mandelbrot, the father of fractal geometry, is the premier artist for fractals that resemble natural landscapes, a technique which he calls the "Romantic era" of fractals.

Musgrave's work has turned up on fractal calendars, scientific journals, and on the covers of many documents at George Washington University, where he works. A programmer who is well versed on the technicalities of ray-tracing and fractal math, Musgrave is also a consummate artist.

Some of the text on this site is the programmer speaking, but the images are solidly artistic. You won't find anything here that isn't visually compelling.

After viewing his gallery, full of luscious, haunting images, you might well agree with Musgrave that nature speaks fractal. Simple fractal formulas can so easily duplicate natural features that Musgrave concludes fractal math may be at the root of natural creative processes.

In the Landscapes gallery you'll find a collection of images of mountains, lakes, deserts, and rivers. Musgrave has spent considerable time developing techniques for modeling clouds, erosion,

atmospheric haze, the different colors of light and shadow, and the result is some outstanding images.

Musgrave has mastered the rainbow, so you'll find examples of that in some of his mountain and lake pictures.

By the way, Musgrave's images are all stored in the relatively efficient JPEG format, and most are under 40Kb in size (with many less than 20Kb), which means this is a very modem-friendly site, for those with slower connections.

Musgrave's new worlds to explore are the ones he makes on his computer. As he says in his online autobiography, "In five to ten years I'll have my own damn planet, and you won't see much of me around this one any more."

Musgrave's planets, organized into a solar system that looks remarkably similar to the one we live in, are not yet complete, but considering that it took about 4.5 billion years for nature to get the real world this far, Musgrave isn't doing badly.

You'll find several images of Musgrave's counterpart to Earth, which he calls Gaea, a watery planet with a single moon. There's a ringed Saturn, and a model of Neptune that, created several years before the Voyager space craft

20

A haunting landscape image from Ken Musgrave's art gallery.

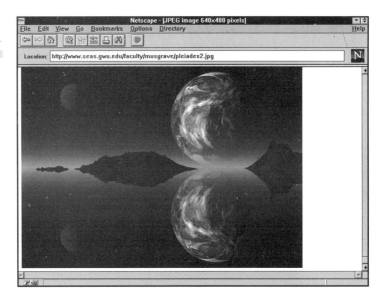

http://www.seas.gwu.edu/faculty/musgrave/pleiades2.jpg

skimmed the planet, turned out to be remarkably like the real thing.

You can download a copy of an MPEG movie for a "deep zoom" on Gaea. And we mean deep: from a few million miles away you head for the planet's horizon, and drop through the atmosphere until you see mountain tops, eventually coming to a stop above a valley of alpine meadows.

The movie isn't as smooth as what you will find in a movie theater, but Musgrave promises that some day you'll zoom around this planet, accompanied by a Yale Symphony Orchestra soundtrack.

The Artistic Renderings section includes some variations on the landscapes, although with offbeat colors. Look under the Psychedelia section for some of those. Another variation is the mini-gallery of Vasarely imitations, regular patterns with a "lens" or "waterdrop" variation.

You can continue to drill down in this gallery by selecting additional mini-galleries. The Mini-Gallery Of Offbeat Images will take you to yet another mini-gallery, and going to Fire Renderings will take you to yet another. Appropriately, deep down in this virtual gallery are a few images of hell, the fractal version. I don't want to go there.

The Scientific Visualization gallery has only a couple of images in it, but Musgrave's image of the Martian landscape raises the possibility that fractals may someday be an important way to "visit" distant planets in virtual reality.

Finally, if you'd like to see what some of Musgrave's students are doing, zip over to http://www.seas.gwu.edu/seas/eecs/Research/Graphics/ ProcTexCourse/index.html, where you can see how our future computer graphics artists are coming along. ▲

This mountainous landscape can be seen in many variations at Ken Musgrave's site.

http://www.seas.gwu.edu/faculty/musgrave/nimbus.jpg

TAEX Clipart Collection

http://leviathan.tamu.edu:70/1s/clipart

T

SEE RELATED SITES:

Ch 9 CLIP ART & ICONS

SOME CLIP ART collections have a few pictures of many things, while others, like the Texas Agricultural Extension Service clip art collection provides many images on a few topics.

As an agricultural institution, its people produce numerous documents and reports related to agriculture and agricultural economics, so you'll find an extensive collection of those images here, with a sprinkling of a few others.

This is one of the few clip art collections with a search engine in it, which makes it particularly handy. Rather than browsing for hours, you can enter keywords and pull up all the images whose one-line descriptions include those keywords.

Collections typically contain images of food products, vegetables, flowers, domestic animals, and a smattering of birds, fish, wild animals, children, and general images of

people, both in regular and cartoon drawing styles.

Clicking on a collection brings up a menu of sub-collections, often organized by disk (they're designed to fit on 1.44-megabyte floppy disks). Clicking on a sub-collection produces a menu where you can either see clickable "contact sheets" or grab the images individually, as GIF, PCX, or TIFF images, based on the one-line descriptions.

Although the clip art comes from various sources, the interface is the same for all of them, making it relatively easy to find your way around.

Quality here is not uniformly high. Many images lack the polish one finds in professionally-done clip art. Our recommendation is to use the search engine to locate images using keywords, rather than to spend a lot of time browsing here. ▲

A vegetable scene from TAEX.

http://leviathan.tamu.edu:70/I/clipart/fsl/0001-0120/fsl0067.gif

Teen Idols Page

 http://www.cris.com/~Dspiral/idol.shtml

SEE RELATED SITES:

Ch 8 CELEBRITIES & ENTERTAINMENT

THE TEEN IDOLS Page is building a solid collection of photos of young teen males from recent films and television shows who are making young (and sometimes old) hearts throb.

If you're not into the young Hollywood scene, you may not recognize some of these names—Andrew Keegan, Brad Renfro, Eddy Furlong, Elijah Wood, Luke Edwards, and so on. One, River Phoenix, is better known because of his untimely death. But many are the stars of the future, young men who already are recognized as having the looks and style that it takes to be officially designated a teen idol.

There actually are newsgroups called alt.fan.teen.idols, and alt.binaries.pictures.teen-idols, and it's there that many of these photos were collected.

This is a clean site, by the way, with no nudity. Well, okay, sometimes not all the buttons are done, and there may be a guy or two who had to take off his shirt, but that's pretty normal behavior for teen-age boys with buff bods.

You'll find links to a few other important sites here as well: one to a page devoted to ending child labor in India, and links to some of the television shows and movie sites where teen idols are featured. ▲

Andrew Keegan, at the Teen Idols Page.

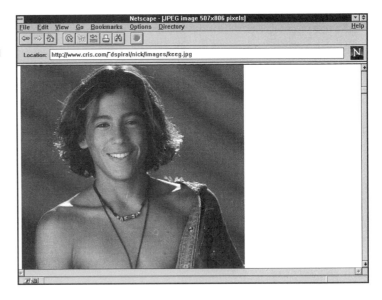

http://www.cris.com/~dspiral/nick/images/keeg.jpg

Time-Life Photo Gallery

 http://www.pathfinder.com/

 **SEE RELATED SITES:**

Ch 2 ANIMALS

Ch 8 CELEBRITIES & ENTERTAINMENT

Ch 13 PHOTOGRAPHY

Ch 14 SCIENCE & NATURE

Ch 16 SPACE

BEFORE THE AGE of television, most of the visual images of the 20th century came from still photographs.

And no publication played a more important role in shaping how Americans, in particular, saw themselves, than *Life Magazine*.

Its photographers were the elite of their time: not only technically sound, but artists in framing their images, psychologists in working with their subjects, and journalists in covering their topics.

Time-Life's Photo Gallery is a small collection of some of the most important images published by Time-Life's photographers, among the thousands that were published in *Time* and *Life* in their heydays.

We wish it were more extensive. This is in many ways an important archive. But what's here is a promising start.

This gallery is not intended to chronicle every moment in the development of American culture or world history since the 1920s, but it does offer a view of many of the classic images of that time.

The gallery is divided into two menus, one covering animals, space, celebrities, the '50s, and World War II. Clicking on the More button brings you to the second gallery, which covers flight, the Civil War, landscapes, sports, and

400 I ▼ TIME-LIFE PHOTO GALLERY

something called Eyewitness.

Clicking on an image map brings up the images from a particular section. The pictures within a section show up as thumbnails, about a dozen at a time. Clicking on the thumbnail opens a moderately sized photo, plus some text. Many of the images are in black and white, although the space, flight, and landscape areas in particular depict mostly modern subjects and are in color.

The latter is a section of photos from Alfred Eisenstadt, one of the original *Life* photographers, and said by *Time* to have had more published photographs than any other photographer in history.

The space area is primarily moon exploration, rocket launches, and a few planet images, most in color.

The flight menu has mostly current American bombers and fighter aircraft. In the sports section you'll find a few classic images from track, baseball, rodeo, and boxing. The Civil War section has a few images of soldiers and battle scenes, and the famous picture of Lincoln at Antietam.

The landscapes, all in color, are classic compositions of nature and man-made features such as the pyramids and St. Peter's Square.

The '50s section is a fun one, recording some of the cultural and entertainment themes of the time: the hula hoop, rock and roll, *I Love Lucy,* and early drive-ins.

The celebrities section is heavy on movie folk from the 1940s and 1950s. You'll find Groucho Marx, Rita Hayworth,

Groucho Marx, in Night in Casablanca, at the Time-Life Photo Gallery.

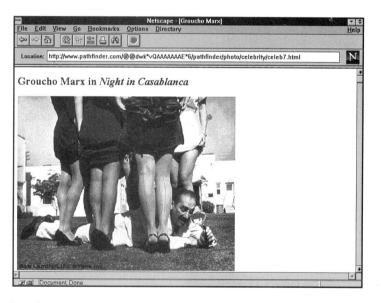

http://www.pathfinder.com/pathfinder/photo/celebrity/celeb7.html

Brigitte Bardot, Judy Garland, and a couple of early Elizabeth Taylor photos here. All of these images are in black and white.

The World War II section has photos of key moments in the war: photos of soldiers in some of the key battles, gaunt prisoners at Buchenwald, and some of the aircraft that partici-pated in the war. Most of these images are in black and white, which is understandable given that color photography was only beginning at the time.

You can purchase many of the images, as posters, cards, or 16" × 20" prints from the order section, as well as a calendar of "Eisie's" most famous pictures. ▲

Treasures of the Louvre

 http://www.paris.org/Musees/Louvre/Treasures/

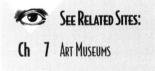

THIS SITE IS kind of a "Best of the Louvre" effort, which means it focuses on the cream of the Louvre's vast collection, rather than providing an in-depth look.

Don't confuse it with the WebMuseum, which is far more comprehensive. Trea-sures of the Louvre is the "offi-cial" presence of the Louvre on the Web.

The exhibit doesn't offer a comprehensive look at the Louvre's massive and priceless collection, but what you will find here are images of many of the world's most famous pieces of art. The emphasis is on popularity and fame, rather than depth.

Because these works are the "official" Louvre presence on the Net, it's worth going there. For one thing the reproduc-tions are top notch. You'll find copies of the "Mona Lisa" all over the Net, but some are scanned from books. This version has more of the lumi-nosity and detail of the origi-nal. While many of the images at this site are rather small, even when displayed in their full version, the "Mona Lisa" is big, glorious, and detailed.

This site is divided into sections covering the type of art: painting, sculpture, antiqui-ties from the Mediterranean, Egypt, and the Orient, sculp-ture, prints and drawings, and other objects of art.

The paintings section has the most content. The pieces on display there include the "Mona Lisa;" "Portrait of a Man, called the Condottiere" by Antonello da Messina; "The Gypsy Girl" by Frans Hals; "Liberty Leading the People" by Eugène Delacroix; "The coronation of Emperor Napoléon and Empress Josephine" by Jacques-Louis David; and a few others.

The Greek and Roman antiquities sections contain only the Winged Victory of Samothrace, a marble statue from 190 B.C., and the Venus de Milo.

The Louvre is even stingier in the sculpture and prints sections, each of which has only a single piece, while the objects of art area has only two decorative objects. ▲

The official "Mona Lisa."

http://www.paris.org/Musees/Louvre/Treasures/gifs/Mona_Lisa.jpg

Dystopian Visions Image Galleries

http://underground.net/~koganuts/Galleries/index.html

SEE RELATED SITES:

Ch 8 CELEBRITIES & ENTERTAINMENT

Ch 13 PHOTOGRAPHY

Ch 15 SCIENCE FICTION

When we did a Yahoo search on "Star Trek," we found 129 entries to the four generations of the TV series, the movies, role playing games, and fan clubs. This came as no surprise, as the original series has split into four successful television shows and movies, and its popularity shows no signs of losing momentum.

Scrolling down through this page, you'll find links to image collections for Star Trek: The Original Series, Star Trek: The Next Generation, Star Trek: Deep Space Nine, and Star Trek: Voyager. You'll also find links here to image galleries for The Terry Farrell (Deep Space Nine's Lt. Jadzia Dax) Fan Club, Star Wars, Indiana Jones, animation and comic sketches, and film directors John Woo and Quentin Tarantino.

You can tell this site was created by a true fan, as almost every image appears in pre-view format with annotated notes. However, this is not the place to look for scenes from any television episodes or films. These galleries are de-voted primarily to signed and unsigned publicity photos of the cast members from the various incarnations of *Star Trek*. ▲

A publicity photograph of
Leonard Nimoy as Captain
Spock in Star Trek VI: The
Undiscovered Country.

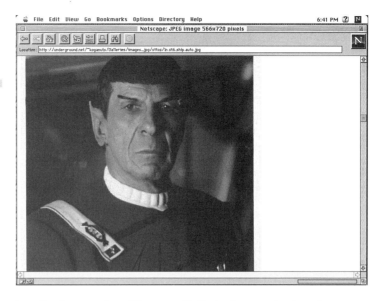

http://underground.net/~koganuts/Galleries/images_jpg/sttos/
ln.st6.ship.auto.jpg

A spacey painting of the
ST:TNG cast. One of the few
non-photograph images
available through the Dystopian
Visions Image Galleries.

http://underground.net/~koganuts/Galleries/images_jpg/sttng/
cast.tng.painting.jpg

Venice

  http://www.tcp.com/pub/anime-manga

SEE RELATED SITES:

Ch 3 ANIMATION & CARTOONS

IF YOU'RE BROWSING the Internet looking for animated movies to download, you already know that the files are huge, ranging from 100Kb for pieces of films into multi-megabyte dimension.

The Venice FTP site specializes in hard storage of anime and manga art, with the former being the more difficult to find. Venice provides .mpg, QuickTime, and .avi formats, as well as few .gz-compressed files.

If you're using a browser such as Netscape to reach Venice, you'll find only directories here. There is no previewing of images, but the file details are displayed and you can check the file size before downloading. If you're not well-versed in anime or manga, you'll find that the file-naming structure leaves a bit to be desired.

From the root directory, selecting the "anime" file will take you to the subdirectory for the different animation formats. While there are only a few .mpgs and .avi files, the QuickTime folder contains more animation than were able to find anywhere else on the Internet. There are also several files of stuffed anime documents.

For manga, Venice is the holding pen for 20+ "manga-creators," a.k.a., people who have scanned in multiple images of manga art without the storage space on their own server. Venice is their anime warehouse.

A few of the files contain only a handful of images, but there are also sound files, software files, fan fiction, mailing list information, and such. Do NOT miss the "sorted" file, where you can find images from most anime on the market. ▲

One of the many anime images to be found on Venice.

http://www.tcp.com/pub/anime-manga/sorted/Nadia/Images/nadia.gif

Virtual Portfolio

 http://www.dircon.co.uk/maushaus/folio.html

SEE RELATED SITES:

Ch 13 PHOTOGRAPHY

THE VIRTUAL PORTFOLIO is clearly a commercial site, intended to showcase the talents of some of London's top photographers, but you don't have to buy anything to get a charge out of these great images.

With 17 photographers in the gallery, each represented by up to a dozen photographs, you're getting the cream of some of the world's top advertising photographers and illustrators. They're reasonably generous with the images that you get when you click on one of the thumbnails here.

When you log in, you can fill in a form to let them know who you are, or skip the formalities and head right into the gallery. It's set up so that you can look at images by photographer, by photographer's agent, or by subject.

The bread and butter of top commercial photographers comes in areas such as industrial and architectural photography, cars, fashion, lifestyle, and still life pictures, which in this case are usually product shots, pictures for annual reports, and the like.

The subject index will get you into these areas the fastest, and will be most useful for those who want to see what some of the world's most successful commercial photographers are turning out these days. Generally, clicking on a subject will bring up the names of two to four photographers who have some pictures in that area in this gallery.

However, these are versatile photographers who didn't get where they did by turning assignments down, so you'll find a real mix of topics in most of their portfolios.

If you're really, really interested in talking to them more, the agency that runs this site can contact the photographers or you can contact most of them by e-mail. ▲

An image by Paul Rees.

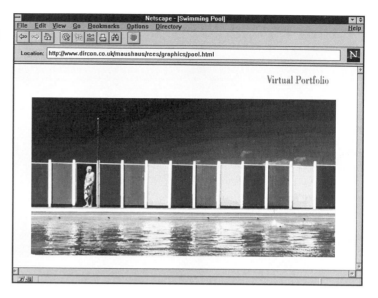

http://www.dircon.co.uk/maushaus/rees/graphics/pool.html

Virtual Gallery (Korea)

 http://203.248.135.66/gallery/

 SEE RELATED SITES:

Ch 6 ART IN CYBERSPACE

Ch 13 PHOTOGRAPHY

ONE OF THE Internet's great achievements in the long run will be to break down many national barriers.

We give you, as an example, the Virtual Gallery, a Net-based gallery that showcases work from some of the top photographers in Korea.

The Webmasters at this site have made a valiant, if not always successful, effort to present menus and information in English, but the pictures tell the story, and they are beautifully done and displayed.

From the opening page, you have several options, and the nomenclature used here—events, exhibitions, galleries, artists, and portfolios—doesn't make it immediately obvious that no matter where you go you're going to find images.

Under Events, we found information about the '95 Kwangju Biennial, a major art show in Korea, with artists from around the world. Images from many of those artists were available.

You'll find the work of individual artists under the exhibitions, galleries, artists, and portfolios sections, and most of these are simply different ways to get to the work of the four photographers represented here.

When we visited, the site was showing a posthumous exhibition by Doo-Kyung Sung, one of Korea's best known photographers, whose photos of the liberation of Seoul during the Korean War were on display. Another posthumous exhibition featured photographs by Seokje Lim, portraying the life and work of Korean miners.

Photographer Bohnchang Koo was showing work from several series of surrealistic images in the exhibitions area.

Under Galleries we found many exceptional images from Keon-hi Park, who explores visually simple themes—landscapes, the face, figure, and actions of a model, open landscapes, with a sense of mystery and powerful compositions. ▲

An image from Bohnchang Koo's "Lost Paradise" virtual show.

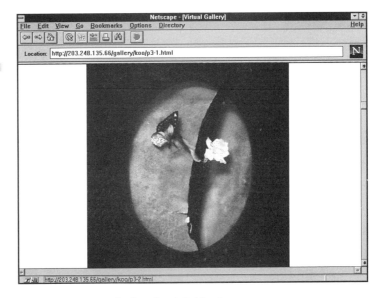

http://203.248.135.66/gallery/koo/p3-1.html

Views of the Solar System

http://www.c3.lanl.gov/~cjhamil/SolarSystem/homepage.html

SEE RELATED SITES:

Ch 16 SPACE

VIEWS OF THE Solar System is billed as a hypertext educational site, and it demonstrates very well the educational potential of the Internet.

You can easily navigate your way through this presentation, with its lineup of Sun and planets waiting to be clicked. Clicking on one brings up a page with statistics about the planet, background documents on its features, and many illustrations and photographs to illustrate it.

Photos are often available in a number of formats, depending on how much resolution you want, and how much time you're prepared to spend downloading the image.

Sections are not cookie-cutter versions of each other. Instead, the special characteristics of each part of the solar system emphasized. The section on the Sun, for example, has images of sunspots, solar prominences, and pictures of the sun itself taken with visible and X-ray portions of the spectrum. You can watch movies and animations that show eclipses, solar prominences, and convection within the Sun itself.

The section on Mars discusses features like Martian volcanoes, seasons, and what future space missions from Mars expect to learn.

Views of the Solar System also contains extensive information about lesser-known system inhabitants, such as asteroids. Some, such as Gaspra, which the spacecraft Galileo passed by only 1000 kilometers, have an extensive gallery of images of their own.

A clever Planetary Data Browser lets you create lists of objects in the solar system, sorted by a variety of factors, including their weight, orbital period, and other factors. ▲

The asteroid Gaspra, about 12 miles long, as seen by the spacecraft Galileo.

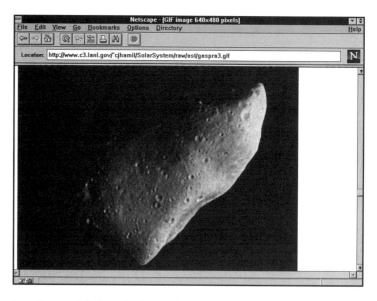

http://www.c3.lanl.gov/~cjhamil/SolarSystem/raw/ast/gaspra3.gif

Bas van Reek Art Building

http://www.xs4all.nl/~basvreek/

SEE RELATED SITES:

Ch 5 ART GALLERIES
Ch 6 ART IN CYBERSPACE
Ch 7 ART MUSEUMS

VOTED A COOL Site of the Day at one point, this gallery has a touch of campy humor to it. As you go through its gallery, you are accompanied by several gape-mouthed aliens who stare at every thumbnail. Clicking on a text link next to that brings up a larger version of the painting they're staring at.

And this gallery is equipped with a necessary utility that far too few galleries in real life, let alone the Net, are equipped with: a toilet.

It's easy to navigate this site because the terminology will be immediately familiar to most people. This cyber gallery has floors, and on each floor you might find rooms, and in each room you'll find views of the art.

The first floor is dedicated to a few versions of van Reek's own work. His style is simple and graphical, and usually employs simple lines with unusual patterns and colors. His favorite theme, apparently, is kissing and there are several versions of this tender activity in the gallery. The second floor features electronic art, primarily digital images that have been manipulated in some way.

The third floor has guest rooms, where guest artists show off their work. These rooms are navigated the standard way, going from view to

A virtual tour guide reacts with surprise to Bas van Reek's display.

http://www.xs4all.nl/~basvreek/galroom3.html

view within each room.

The fourth floor is the multi-media floor, which means downloadable WAV audio files, most of them less than 30Kb.

The fifth floor houses the gift shop. Here you'll find Bas van Reek wrist watches, some with variations of the Kiss theme. ▲

Vermeer, Paintings of

 http://www.ccsf.caltech.edu/~roy/vermeer/

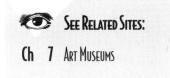

SEE RELATED SITES:

Ch 7 ART MUSEUMS

THIS SITE COVERS in depth, one of the great masters of European painting. Jan Vermeer (1632–1675) used light, space, and texture to reveal the depth of humanity in his subjects, who are generally folk going about ordinary duties in their homes: working around the house, or visiting each other. His work also includes a few traditional subjects, such as a landscape of Delft, Vermeer's life-long home, and some biblical stories and themes.

This site covers the total output of Vermeer that is known to survive, and gives you several ways to look at the artist's work. You can click on a map showing you where all the world's Vermeers are known to hang, you can view a list of cities where they hang, you can view a chronological index of all the paintings (which is the fastest way to get to a specific painting), or you can view a clickable bitmap, which has pictures of all the

"The Milkmaid," perhaps Vermeer's most famous painting.

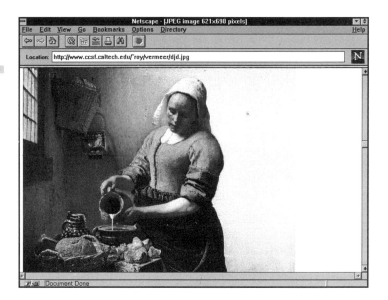

http://www.ccsf.caltech.edu/~roy/vermeer/djd.jpg

paintings. Click on an image to bring it up.

The map is rather fun, and for those who aren't familiar with the world of fine art, it's an interesting lesson in how widespread the art of an old master is likely to be after a few centuries. In Vermeer's case, the paintings can be found in 13 world cities, in Europe, and the Eastern U.S.

Webmaster Roy Williams also helpfully offers images in three forms: a small 25Kb GIF, a 50Kb JPEG that will generally fill your screen, or a screen-overflowing 150Kb JPEG, which is good for looking at details. ▲

Vern's SIRDS Gallery

 http://www.sirds.com/

THERE ARE FEW forms of art that deserve the term "computer-generated" like Single Image (Random Dot) Stereograms.

SIRDS, sometimes called stereographs or hollusions, are those apparently abstract images that, when you unfocus or cross your eyes just the right way, suddenly reveal a three-dimensional image.

First described in 1960, by Bela Julesz, they've only become popular in the last few years as programmers developed the code required to easily generate them.

Several sites on the Internet describe this phenomenon, but this one appears to be one of the better organized sites, with solid libraries and galleries containing the work of SIRDS creators from all over the world.

It's actually not that difficult to see SIRDS directly on your computer screen. In fact, it may be easier than seeing them in print if the printing quality is poor.

Vern Hart has arranged the images by author, and you can also access a single directory, which lists all of the images, with thumbnails, or a text version without thumbnails. The thumbnails are small, so even though there were 75 when we looked, it wouldn't be impossible to look at them this way with a modem connection.

However, you'll be better off looking at the galleries in many cases. For example, when you look at the thumbnails in the gallery of SIRDS created by Peter Chang and Gareth Richards, or Pascal Massimino, you'll see not only the SIRDS images, but also small pictures beneath showing what the original image looked like. That's a handy crutch for those people who just can't seem to see the three-dimensional images.

SEE RELATED SITES:

Ch 10 COMPUTER-GENERATED ART

Some of the images are a bit large to be able to view on your browser. An 800×600-pixel image may have to be downloaded and viewed outside of your browser in a program which can reduce its size somewhat. ▲

There's a prop-driven aircraft headed right toward you.

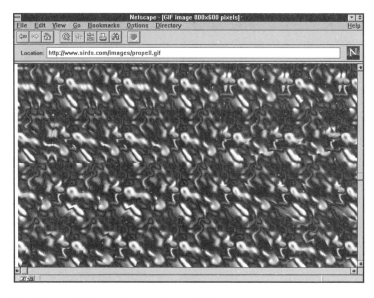

http://www.sirds.com/images/propell.gif

Virtual Tourist

 http://wings.buffalo.edu/world/

See Related Sites:

Ch 18 Travel & Geography

Cyberspace is different from real space, but not so different that wanderlust, of the old get-up-and-go, turn off the computer type doesn't strike once in a while.

But wait. Leave the computer on. You don't have to leave the beloved confines of your desk to travel the world. You can travel through cyberspace courtesy of the Virtual Tourist, or even make contact with real space, courtesy of Virtual Tourist II.

This site lets you go graphically to places around the world, either because you're looking for a Web site (Virtual Tourist) or for pictures, maps, and other information about real places (Virtual Tourist II).

When you fire it up, you get a map of the world. Clicking on any of the regions will give you a color-coded map of the region, depending on the colors of the countries in the region, they will have maps of their own showing the location of their Web sites, or you'll go to a plain text list of all the Web sites in that area.

If you don't need pictures, of course, you can start right away with the text version, which is maintained by CERN at http://www.w3.org/ hypertext/DataSources/WWW/ Servers.html.

Now, let's say that you're not a true cybernaut for whom virtuality is reality, and you're actually interested in seeing some of these places by physically traveling there. You want Virtual Tourist II, which is linked to Virtual Tourist I, or directly at http:// wings.buffalo.edu/world/vt2/. VT2 is tied in with City Net, and its aim is not to help you locate Web sites, but to help you locate information and maps about real places.

City Net is fairly new, so its coverage of the world varies in quality from location to location, but it does what it can to bring you a map of the area as well as related information, some of it from the CIA Fact Book.

As an aside, if you're looking for some simple maps to use on your own Web site or for other purposes, click on the link of "maps used in this service" at the Virtual Tourist. There you'll find some maps you can freely use for your own purposes. ▲

A map showing cities in Switzerland with Web sites.

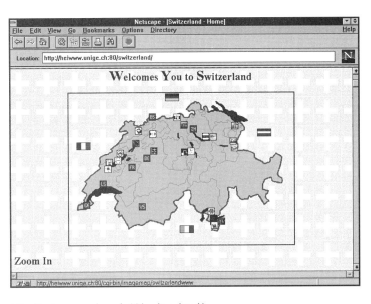

http://heiwww.unige.ch:80/switzerland/

World Art Treasures

http://sgwww.epfl.ch/BERGER/index.html

 **See Related Sites:**

Ch 4 Architecture
Ch 7 Art Museums

World Art Treasures is based on a massive (100,000 slides) archive of images in a Swiss collection.

This site has a unique way of getting at that collection, developing "programs" around themes, so that every image fits into a historical or artistic concept. The museum says it is bypassing the "database" approach to its collection, and prefers to "give birth to a true experience through the new technology" of the World Wide Web.

That approach provides a context in which you move from one image to the next in a sequence that makes sense from a historical point of view. In other words, if you want to learn something about the subjects that are delivered here as "programs," you'll be happy, but if you're simply trying to find a particular image, you'll have to be lucky as well.

When we visited, four programs were in place, with the promise of more to come.

One program covers art from Egypt, China, Japan, India, Myanmar/Burma, Laos, Cambodia, and Thailand. Clicking on this section, you

An ancient Roman portrait from the Egyptian city of Fayyum.

http://sgwww.epfl.ch/BERGER/Le_fayoum/

can choose a country, then select from the dozen or so images that show up from that country on a clickable image map. Though the collections are not large, with 10–20 images from each country, they do convey the flavor of the country's ancient art.

The images here are top notch: sharp, well lit, well composed. Clicking on an image map produces a full screen picture of the image. Then clicking on a Zoom link does exactly that, zooming in by about a factor of two times.

The second program, called Pilgrimage to Abydos, takes a particularly interesting approach. Abydos is an Egyptian temple built by Seti I around 1300 B.C. Clickable maps guide you through the temple, and by clicking on the maps or on links in the text, you see the images and corridors that a devotee of the time would have seen.

The third program covers Roman portraits from the Egyptian center of Fayyum. Consider the time they were made, these images of the deceased are extraordinarily realistic and luminous, similar to the icons of the Eastern Christian churches. Although the portraits are scattered all over the world, this site brings them together in one place. Oddly, this section of the exhibit is lacking almost entirely in explanatory notes, which makes it difficult to know what you're looking at. ▲

Wearable Wireless Webcam

 http://www-white.media.mit.edu/~steve/netcam.html

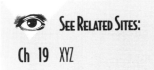

SEE RELATED SITES:

Ch 19 XYZ

ON ONE HAND the Wearable Wireless Webcam is just another one of those crazy things found on the Internet, another person with Web space and nothing constructive to do with it.

On the other hand, it's the wave of the future.

Of course, if it's crazy enough we'll cover it anyway, but we think Webmaster Steve Mann is having fun with an important idea, which is probably the best way to get an idea across to other people.

The important idea here is to use video and graphics effectively over the Internet or other communications media to convey what's going on in one place to people in another place.

This is not radically new: video conferencing software is making its way into more companies than ever, and programs like CU-SeeMe allow video conferencing over the Internet. But Mann adds portability and the Internet to the equation.

Mann's idea is to stick a virtual reality helmet and a video camera on his head, and tie them, through a wireless link, to the Internet. Frames from the video show up at this site, so you can see what Mann is seeing. It's wireless mainly to allow freedom of motion.

An earlier version was simply the video camera, but in a later version, Mann pipes the input from the video camera both to the Internet and to the viewing screen of the virtual-reality helmet, an outfit that Mann calls the VisualFilter. In effect, you are seeing exactly what Mann is seeing.

To see what Mann is seeing, click on the first image on the home page, or the Put Yourself In My Shoes link and you'll go to his latest escapade with the camera. Frankly, virtual reality is generally more interesting than reality, and we weren't exactly blown away by what looked to be pictures of machines at a trade show.

Furthermore, navigation at this site is strange. You really don't know what you're going to get when you click on some links or linked graphics, so you'll probably have to stumble around for a while, and find yourself going in circles, before you get the hang of it.

Still, Mann has some very good ideas about how this technology could be used, and to his knowledge this is the only example of a mobile camera on the Net. It's worth visiting. ▲

Steve Mann and his Wireless Webcam.

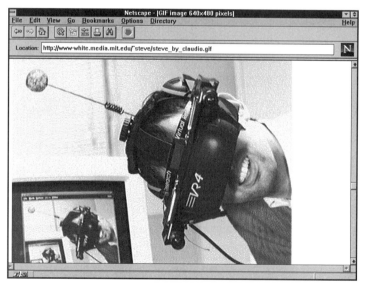

http://www-white.media.mit.edu/~steve/steve_by_claudio.gif

Wooden Toys

http://www.pd.astro.it/forms/mostra/mostra_i.html

SEE RELATED SITES:

Ch 7 ART MUSEUMS

FEW CHILDREN WILL grow up without hearing the story of Pinocchio, the wooden doll who, through the skill and faith of Gepetto the carver, becomes a real boy.

Behind that Italian tale is a centuries-old tradition of wood carving, for practical purposes and for fun.

This Web site explores the latter, with a lovingly restored and preserved collection of wooden toys.

These are not your plywood cutouts from the local fleamarket, but elaborate and painstaking reproductions of real objects, or playful and amusing caricatures.

Most were made between 1900 and 1940, a time before cheap plastic toys made their entrance. Collectors items now, they once were the prized possessions of real children.

The exhibit is largely uncommented, but the titles of each section are in English.

In a section on outdoor games you'll find sleds, wagons, pedal cars, even a boat in which pulling the oars would drive the wheels, plus a doll house and rocking horses.

A section on games shows toys used for racing, or board games. The home-made toy section has some custom made objects, such as dolls, carts and horses, while the toy theaters and targets section shows theaters used for puppet shows.

The most amusing section may be the hand-crafted and industrial toys section, which includes wooden toys turned out for the mass market, most of them in the 1920s and 1930s, when cartoon characters such as Walt Disney images were the big thing. You'll also find wooden trains and boats in this category. And here is where you'll find Pinocchio, and not just one but several variations on the long-nosed theme. ▲

Pinocchios at the Wooden Toys site.

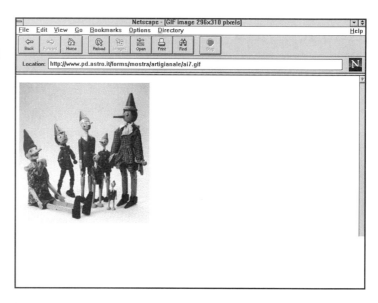

http://www.pd.astro.it/forms/mostra/artigianale/ai7.gif

The World's Women On-Line

 http://www.asu.edu:80/wwol/

SEE RELATED SITES:

Ch 6 ART IN CYBERSPACE

IS WOMEN'S ART different from men's art?

We won't answer that question for you, because you'll probably want to visit this site before making an intelligent assessment.

This site illustrates a very positive trend in the art world, which is to put special exhibitions online as well as in galleries.

In this case, the real galleries are Bejing and Washington, which only a small percentage of us were likely to be in between August 30 and September 15, 1995, when the original exhibition was mounted in connection with the United Nations' Fourth World Conference on Women in Bejing.

This site was under construction when we visited, but already had a very large collection of images.

Navigational tools were very limited when we were there: all the artists were in alphabetical directories, and when you accessed a directory, tiny thumbnails would appear next to each artist's name. Clicking on the name produced a larger image, which can be clicked to full screen view, with more information about the artist.

The guidelines for this exhibition are fairly loose, so the subjects are as varied as the artists. Some are abstract, others representational or

"United Fire" by Samira Badran, Palestine.

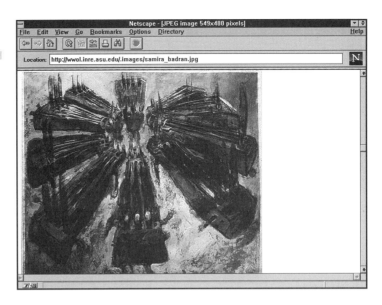

http://wwol.inre.asu.edu/.images/samira_badran.jpg

primitive. Some clearly deal with specifically women's issues, or with issues such as war, while others do not.

We're hoping that other navigational tools are developed for this site, so users could access them by country or by medium, for example, or to have a "next image" button that will take you, slide by slide, through the exhibition.

Nevertheless, this is an im-pressive site that offers expo-sure to artists rarely seen any-where else, and some insight into women and art.

Although artists are limited to just one picture, there are many, many artists here. Under the letter A alone, for example, 40 artists were listed. Most tend to be from the United States or Canada, but many artists from Europe, the Middle East, and Asia are also visible. ▲

Wentworth Gallery

 http://wentworth-art.com/wwg/index.htm

SEE RELATED SITES:

Ch 5 ART GALLERIES

WENTWORTH GALLERIES WILL be familiar to many in the eastern half of the United States be-cause the firm has 37 real gal-leries in addition to its new online gallery.

You'll find a good selection of images here from successful artists from all over the world.

You won't find many revo-lutionary or ground-breaking pieces here: Wentworth's key audiences are consumers and businesses who are less interested in art as a social statement or avant-garde breakthrough, than in something they can be comfortable with and enjoy on their walls.

Aiming to please this market, and its assorted wallpapers, color schemes, psychologies, room settings, and personalities, the Wentworth selection online is selected with an eye to variety. Do you want classical, Renaissance-looking work? Their painter, Armand, can deliver. How about something bright and cheery, with vivid skies and flowers? Try one of Barbara McCann's tropical pieces. You've got Impression-ism with North American scenes, Impressionism with a European flavor, and Impression with (tasteful and stylish) female subjects.

There's even a "whimsical" section for doctors and lawyers who want to add a bit of humor to the lives of the people who turn up in their offices, and who could probably use a bit of humor about that time.

By the way, if you like something here, Wentworth has a program to deliver a dozen or more pieces to your office or home, if you're in a city where it has a gallery. You can then select a specific work of art that matches your requirements. ▲

"Summer Portrait" by Frane Mlinar.

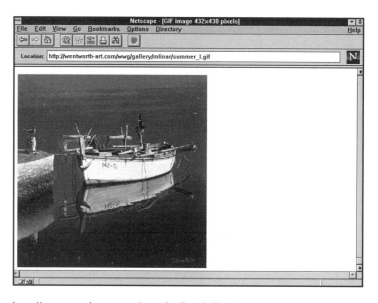

http://wentworth-art.com/wwg/gallery/mlinar/summer_l.gif

Danny's X-Files Home Page

 http://www.stack.urc.tue.nl/~danny/x-files.html

IT IS TRULY difficult to trust any site dedicated to the X-Files. Take this page, for example, created by "Danny." Who is this Danny? Why is he interested in these files? Where did he get these pictures? Is he cleared for this information?

We kept a low profile while digging through the site, discovering graphics, articles, sounds, and even more than a few links to other sites. One might think—considering the way these different home pages are linked—that there might be some sort of conspiracy going on.

For graphics, Danny's imagemap leads you to X-Files Pictures, a long index of .jpgs that gets quickly to the point: photographs of Mulder, Scully, and of Mulder and Scully. The photographs we looked at were clean, but undescribed. If the photographs aren't evidence enough for you, look at them while listening to the downloadable sound files of "Mulder & Scully-isms."

The file names provide little insight to what the images contain, however. If you have a modem slower than 28.8Kb, you might have to dedicate some time to searching through them all before you find what you're looking for.

It would be difficult to sweep Danny's list of X-Files links under the carpet. We found links to videos, more FAQs, more picture archives, pages dedicated to either Mulder or Scully, to X-Files magazines, FTP sites, newsgroups, and mailing lists. ▲

Fox Mulder and Dana Scully
watching out for UFOs.

http://www.stack.urc.tue.nl/~danny/pictures/x-files/both/xfilest3.jpg

Yokhoh Team Home Page

http://pore1.space.lockheed.com/SXT/homepage.html

SEE RELATED SITES:

Ch 16 SPACE

THE YOKHOH ("Sunbeam" in Japanese) satellite, launched by Japan in 1991, was designed to study non-visible radiation such as X-ray and gamma rays from the Sun. These wavelengths are typically absorbed by the Earth's atmosphere and can be seen much better from an orbiting platform.

Contrary to the image of the Sun usually seen by standard optical telescopes, where the solar surface is marred by only the occasional sunspot or flare-up, this satellite reveals the sun as a raging fireball, full of turbulence. The bright spots in these images typically have temperatures around 2 million degrees Celsius.

The satellite automatically generates a collection of images each day, and the site includes a gallery of images taken in the past.

Many of the images show the huge jets of gas that periodically extend from the Sun's surface, while others show the "sun spots" that mark its surface from time to time.

You can click on one link to see where the Yokhoh satellite is in orbit around the Earth at the moment. Another link takes you to the most recent photo of the Sun taken by the satellite.

You'll also find a link to some movies of the Sun, made by putting still images into a movie sequence. Most are large, up to 27 megabytes, but the lab has created a mini-movie of about 1.5 megabytes, within reasonable reach of dedicated modem users.

The movies provide an important alternative perspective to the still images. You can see that what appears to be haziness on still images is in fact bright clouds of radiation extending well away from the Sun's surface. ▲

Insets (above) show details of exploding loops on the Sun's surface.

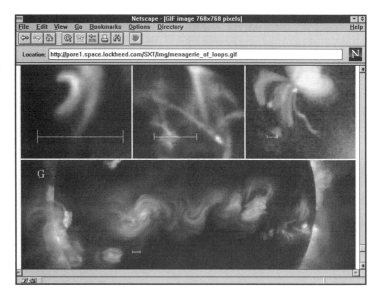

http://pore1.space.lockheed.com/SXT/img/menagerie_of_loops.gif

CHAPTER

21

_____

Search Strategies & Techniques

 ### In This Chapter

> ➤ _Searching the Net without installing lots of extra software_

> ➤ _Finding graphics by file name and file type_

> ➤ _Searching the World Wide Web by subject_

> ➤ _Where to find all the major search tools_

> ➤ _Accessing and searching WAIS image archives_

 ### In Other Chapters

> ➤ _For specific search programs on the CD-ROM, see Chapter 27._

> ➤ _You'll find some directories of graphics on the Net in Chapter 26._

> ◀ _Many specific graphics archives are covered in Chapters 2 through 20._

The Internet sites listed in this book will help you find almost every imaginable kind of graphics image. The authors of this book have purveyed thousands of sites and hand-selected the best so you wouldn't need to do all that searching yourself. Nonetheless, there will be times when you still might like to strike out on your own. When you have a very specific image in mind, quite often it's easier to use an automated search tool than to look through even the most well-organized listing. You may also need an image or information file that lies hidden away in some obscure corner of cyberspace. But no matter how particular or peculiar your needs, they will probably be met by something somewhere out on the Net. With the arsenal of powerful Net search tools at your disposal, you may rest assured: If it's there, you can find it. This chapter (and the next one) will tell you how.

Searching the Easy Way

Ask your average Internet guru how to search the Net, and he is likely to launch immediately into an incomprehensible tutorial on each of the overwhelming number of search programs available. First, he'll try to introduce you to Archie, Veronica, and Jughead. He'll tell you you've got to take several hours to install and configure separate programs for each of them. Just when you start wondering why no 1970s cartoons come up when you run the programs, he'll switch to a less appealing discussion of Crawlers, Gophers, Worms, and something called "Lycos." By the time he starts in about WAIS, CERN, and Yahoo, you've probably decided the old-fashioned library might be quicker and easier.

All those tools have their uses, and this chapter will give you the run-down on each of them. All the programs are on the CD-ROM for you, too. But here's a little secret: 99 percent of the time, you won't need the extra software. In the old days (the '80s, that is), you did. But now all you really need to put every search tool and technique on the Net to work for you is a decent World Wide Web browser (like

Netscape) and a little inside know-how. This chapter provides the know-how.

Most gurus like to show off their skills and the things they can do with all those search programs are certainly impressive. However, you probably do searches because you just want to find something. If there's a way to find the same things the gurus find using one tool you already have, you'd probably be more than happy to use the space on your hard drive for the information you wanted to find instead of a raft of search programs. So here's how.

What Am I Looking For?

First things first. Do you know what you're looking for? If not, browsing through this book or "surfing" through the World Wide Web will suit you just fine, and will turn up plenty of interesting things. But if you know what you want, an automated search is definitely the way to go. Since this is a book about graphics, let's assume you want a specific kind of image, for example, a picture of the Three Stooges, a 3D rendering of a DNA molecule, or even a simple cartoon of a pig. Each of these three examples would suggest a different search technique, and in this chapter, you'll learn exactly how to locate each of them.

How To Find a Specific Image

The first decision you need to make when searching for graphics on the Net is whether to jump right in and look for a specific file or to poke around for some related text information first. Since the file is probably what you really want, doing a search for it right away would seem to make sense—especially since there are comprehensive, freely accessible, and automatically searchable indexes of almost every file on the Net. The only problem is that these indexes, called Archie servers as a pun on the word

21

"archive," only know the names of the files and the names of the disk directories they're stored in. They don't have any text description attached, so a picture of five elephants juggling on bicycles might be called "ejob5.jpg". You could search Archie for the text "elephant," "juggle," and "bicycle" all day and not find the picture.

The good news is that people are generally nice and they often give files descriptive names. Most Internet computers allow long file names, so there very well might be a picture file named "elephants-juggling.gif" stored right next to "ejob5.jpg". And the even better news is that many images have such specific content that you can easily guess what somebody would name the image file. If you were looking for an image of the old *Three Stooges* TV show, an Archie search for the word "stooges" would be a pretty good bet.

"All good and fine in theory," you say. "But how do I actually *do* it?" Crank up your Web browser (see Chapter 26 if you need help on that part) and let's explore how to ask Archie to lead you straight to Larry, Curly, and Moe.

Archie on the Web

Like almost every search tool on the Internet, there are many ways to access Archie. Many people still use special dedicated programs like the WSArchie software found on the CD-ROM in the back of this book. But installing a separate program just to do an occasional Archie search is actually unnecessary; you can now access Archie through gateways on the World Wide Web just as easily. Copies of the global Archie database are installed on many different computers in many different places throughout the world, and several of those also host WWW gateways, usually named either AA or Archieplex. By connecting to any one of those gateways, you can do an Archie search of nearly every publicly accessible file system on the entire Internet.

So which address should you use? Start by pointing your browser to:

http://pubweb.nexor.co.uk/public/archie/servers.html

(To "point to" this site, simply click in the Location area of your browser and type in the address exactly as shown here. After the document comes to you over the Internet, it should look similar to Figure 21.1.)

TIP You are connecting to a computer at Nexor, the British company that makes Archieplex server software and maintains a public list of Archie gateways. This document is very popular, and the computer that delivers it to Netizens like you is often overburdened, so you may have a long delay when you load this page. To avoid having to download it every time you want to do an Archie search, you can load it once and then save it on your own computer. (In Netscape, select File/Save As.) From now on, instead of accessing the file from the U.K., you can just open the file on your computer. You can even add the local file to your Bookmark hotlist in Netscape by selecting File/Open File to open it and then selecting Bookmarks/Add Bookmark.

Figure 21.1

You can conduct Archie searches through these World Wide Web gateways without installing any special Archie software on your computer.

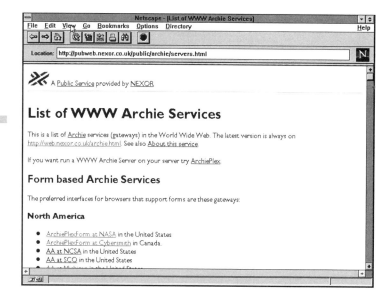

If you are using a browser that supports forms, choose one of the form-based Archie services on the list, such as ArchiePlexForm at Cybersmith in Canada (located at http://www.csi.nb.ca/archgate.html). If your browser doesn't support forms, you can still search Archie using the techniques described further down the Archie Server's document.

The Canadian Archieplex form page is shown in Figure 21.2. To run a search, click in the "What would you like to search for?" box and simply type the letters you want to search for. For the search type, you'll almost always want Case Insensitive Substring Match unless you know the exact name of the file you're looking for. As for impact on other users, which controls how much of the server's attention your query will get, only the most humble users choose anything nicer than Nice but only the most obnoxious jerks choose Not Nice at All.

TIP Which Archie server you use should depend on the time of day, since most servers are overburdened during daylight hours. If you're burning the midnight oil, use the server closest to you. But if it's 10 a.m. and you're in North America, choose a server in New Zealand or Taiwan, where it's the middle of the night and the computers have nothing better to do than chat over the Internet with foreigners. You'll get your answer much faster that way, and the people trying to access the busy local servers will get their answers faster, too.

Figure 21.2

Finding every publicly accessible file in the world containing a particular word in its file name is as simple as typing the word into a form box and pressing a button.

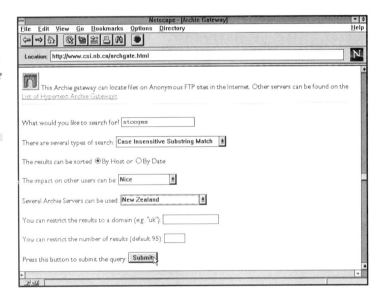

Click on the Submit button, and in a few seconds (sometimes longer at busy times), you will have a list of every publicly archived file in the world containing "stooges" in its name. As you can see in Figure 21.3, the result pops right up in your browser as a nicely formatted Web page that you can then save on your computer if you wish.

NOTE In theory, all Archie servers and gateways are created equal. But Archie and Archieplex, like many programs on the Net, can mess up. For instance, one time I searched several Archie servers from the NASA Archieplex form for many different words and they couldn't seem to find anything about anything. When I searched the same servers for the same words from the identical-looking Canadian Archieplex form, it found lots of matches quite easily. On another day, I got no results when the Canadian Archieplex form queried the Canadian server, but the same form querying the servers in New Zealand and Taiwan found plenty of good stuff. The moral of the story: if you don't get any matches, try a different form/server combination. It will probably work.

Figure 21.3

Archie finds the Three Stooges hiding in Finland, at Boston University, and several other locations around the globe.

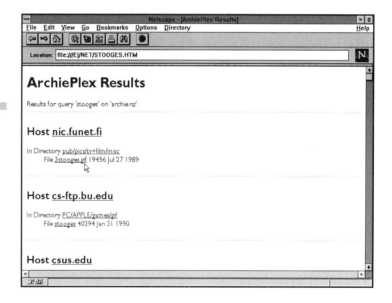

Theoretically, the underlined file names shown on the search result page are hotlinks directly to the files you're after. In reality, though, the search for Larry, *et al.* isn't quite over yet. Since I know that GIF is a graphics file format, I'd expect 3stooges.gif to be an image of the boys.

But when I clicked on it, all I got was a message saying that the file couldn't be found. This isn't too surprising, since it's dated 1989 and of questionable importance to the on-going operation of the Finnish university where it's located. And, alas, the next file in the search list appears to be some sort of hexadecimal machine code for an Apple computer game or something. But just a couple more steps down the search list is another file named 3stooges.gif, apparently located in the personal directory of an AI student named Cox at some college somewhere. This one's dated 1994, and sure enough, a click of the mouse brings back the familiar faces in Figure 21.4. If you really love these guys, you'll find many other images as you browse the links in your search list.

Figure 21.4

Sure enough, Archie helps us discover the joys of modern technology at its finest.

Before we move on to another search technique even more useful than Archie, you should realize that Archie doesn't just look at file names; it indexes directory names, too. For example, the directory pub/pictures/TV.film/ Three stooges at ftp.sunset.se was turned up by the Archie search. This could be exciting: a whole directory full of images! As it turns out, there's only one picture in the directory and it's just a sketch of Moe made by Larry. Other directories in the search list contained several sound files, but the gold mine of Stooge-pics you were hoping for doesn't seem to exist.

Veronica in GopherSpace

The image files that Archie finds are almost hiding in a long list of other types of files with similar names. You can, of course, tell Archie to look for images containing the letters GIF or JPG or PCX if you want to increase the chances of hitting a graphics file. But wouldn't it be nice if you could just say, "Just find me image files. Nothing else." And while we're making out a wish list, it would also be handy if the files had short descriptions attached to them so we could search the descriptions for key words, too.

We're not the first to wish for those features in a file archiving and searching system. In fact, most of the public file servers are part of a worldwide cross-indexed archive called GopherSpace (named after the University of Minnesota's mascot). In the old days, you had to have a special program called a Gopher to browse and search GopherSpace. But Gopher access capability is now built into most decent World Wide Web browsers. When Netscape, for instance, follows a link that leads into GopherSpace, you see the title Gopher Menu followed by a list of files folders or icons representing graphics, text, or binary (program) files. Each item has the file name and sometimes a short description next to it. Figure 21.5 is a typical region of GopherSpace.

Figure 21.5

Some links on the World Wide Web will take you into GopherSpace, a worldwide distributed archive of files and menus.

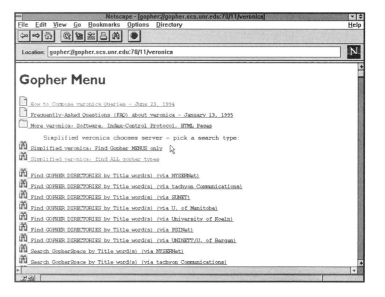

A Gopher menu may at first glance look like a directory listing of some disk drive, but the items on any one menu may actually be located on any Gopher server in the world. A Gopher menu is not a disk directory at all, but rather a group of links that somebody somewhere thought should be listed together. Sometimes they are indeed all on one hard drive; but half of them could be in Australia, while the other half are in England, while the menu itself is stored in Canada. File folder icons represent links to other Gopher menus, not subdirectories on a disk.

Many Gopher menus are searchable. When you click on a searchable link (which has its own icon—usually a pair of binoculars), a simple search form will appear and you can enter a word to look for throughout the menu structure. All of this is pretty snazzy (as file systems go) and cruising GopherSpace sure beats plowing through less able file retrieval systems like FTP (File Transfer Protocol, see Chapter 22). However, Veronica is what makes Gopher-Space really show its stuff. Veronica is a master searchable index of public GopherSpace in its entirety. Like Archie (from whom, as you undoubtedly guessed, Veronica gleaned its name), all Veronica needs from you is a few letters or words to search for, and away she goes to fetch every file in the global GopherSpace that matches your query. Almost all of the files Archie has access to are also in GopherSpace, so Veronica can find them, too.

Often, however, Veronica has access to longer descriptions of the files than Archie does. And more importantly, Veronica knows what type of file she's looking at, and tells you by displaying the appropriate icon on the search result Gopher menu. So you can go straight to the graphics files and ignore the rest.

Let's step through a Veronica search so you can get an idea of how it works.

First, pull up the list of Veronica servers at http://www.scs.unr.edu/veronica.html (see Figure 21.6). Notice the nifty simplified search feature on this page that offers to automatically try servers in random order until it finds one that's not busy. Often, though, you'll actually get a quicker response just by choosing a server from the list. (Yet another one of those Net things that works nicely in theory,

I guess.) Be sure to save this page on your hard disk (so you won't have to download it again every time you want to do a Veronica search) before selecting either a server or the simplified search link.

TIP "Straight to the graphics and ignore the rest," I say. But the rest may still be a heck of a lot of files! Veronica searches often turn up thousands upon thousands of matching files, only 200 or so of which are shown unless you request to see more. Even with handy icons to guide you, weeding through 200 files or more for the graphics images is no fun.

But not to worry. If you know what you're doing, you can tell Veronica to find just graphics files, and ignore everything else. Simply enter **-tlg** as one of the words to search for. This will command Veronica to show you only graphics.

For example, if you want to search for a picture of a pig, tell Veronica to search for:

pig -tlg

You won't get any programs or menus or text files named "pigs in medieval Europe." Just pure pulchritudinous portraits of pork.

Figure 21.6

The list of Veronica search servers includes a simplified search feature that tries multiple servers at random for you. Too bad it's often slower than trying a couple of different servers yourself.

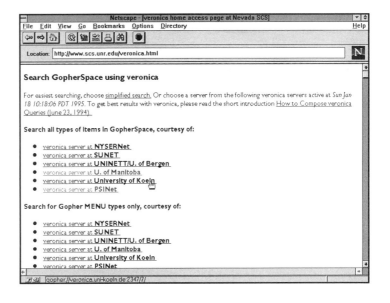

The Veronica search form is pretty basic: you just type the keywords and hit the enter key. Along with the words to search for (which can be entered in any order), you can also give special commands to Veronica. For more information on the command language, choose the How to Compose Veronica Queries link from the Veronica server list page. As mentioned in the previous tip, all you really need to know is that if you enter **-t1g** as if it were one of your search words, Veronica will return only graphics images and ignore all other file types. Sometimes you may also want to include menus and Web pages with the command **-t1gh1** (a dash followed by the letters t1gh and the number 1) instead of just **-t1g**. Figure 21.7 shows a Veronica query for graphics images whose names or descriptions include the letters "pig." Veronica responds by building the Gopher menu, which leads to a sty-full of images.

Figure 21.7

Are there pigs in GopherSpace? There's only one way to find out...

Some image types, however, aren't yet supported by browsers. If you try to load one of those, you'll either see a generic "graphics file" icon or be asked to configure a viewer program. In most browsers, you can still save the file as if it had been loaded and it will be transferred to your hard disk.

Browsers are adding support for more graphics file types all the time, so be sure you've got the latest version!

When Archie and Veronica Won't Work

Consider DNA. The stuff of life. It would be handy to have a picture of it, wouldn't it? One of those ray-traced double-helix renderings would fit the bill—if you could find one. And where better to look for a scientific still-life than where the supercomputers and scientists themselves hang out: the Net.

Could Archie and Veronica help you? Well, yes and no. Yes, either of them could probably find you thousands of files with the letters DNA in their names. But no, you wouldn't be able to weed the "cool**dna**pics" out of the "ma**dna**nnys" and "od**dna**vigators." There are just too many other words that contain the letter combination DNA, and too many different "obvious" file names for molecular portraiture. Knowing those scientific types, they'd probably name the image file you want something like deoxy11ribo42n or raytrace2458 anyway. Archie hates that. And even the extra-long file names that Veronica sees in GopherSpace probably wouldn't help decipher the obscure naming conventions of molecular biologists.

> **NOTE** You may have heard about Jughead, another search tool with a close relationship to Archie and Veronica. Jughead is basically a GopherSpace searcher like Veronica, but with its searches restricted to a particular local server. Jughead has a few features that Veronica doesn't, and can be useful if you know a great Gopher site that you want to search in depth. But since Jughead is very similar and much more limited in scope than Veronica, it isn't mentioned much in this book. We'll jump right to the more powerful stuff instead.

So what you need is something that will search for text files that refer to images. Finding every World Wide Web page in the world containing the words "DNA," "molecule," and "image" would be a good start. Fortunately, there are several excellent Web search engines that let you do just that. There are also "master" search pages that make access to a variety of search engines quick and easy. But before we go to the master pages—which don't have much information on the engines they access—we'll check out the best Web searchers individually and determine how to use them.

Web Indexes and Crawlers

The best Web search engines get their information from software "robots" called Crawlers or Worms. These programs pretend that they're users, and surf the Web day and night in search of new pages. As they crawl around through link after link, they index every page they visit. To make sure the crawler doesn't miss new pages (which may not be referenced by many links from other pages yet), almost all Web search services encourage people to submit the addresses of anything new they think might not have had a crawler visit yet.

Some search services still rely on human-collected references, but explosive growth is threatening to make the "handmade" index a thing of the past, as most of these indexes get more and more hopelessly out of date. However, the very best services do have skilled people behind the scenes, weeding out subtle redundancy that automated crawlers don't always catch.

Lycos

One of the most comprehensive and popular crawler-built search engines is Carnegie Mellon University's Lycos (see Figure 21.8). To get there, point your browser to:

http://lycos.cs.cmu.edu

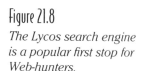

Figure 21.8

The Lycos search engine is a popular first stop for Web-hunters.

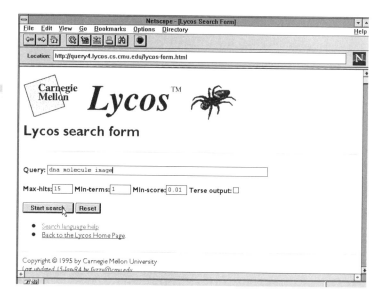

Searching Lycos' multi-million-entry index is as simple as typing in the words you want to find and clicking on the Submit button. There is a fancy language you can use for this-but-not-that-or-maybe-this kind of searches, but for almost all practical purposes just typing in some key words will work just fine. Lycos finds every document with any of the words, and sorts them so the most documents with the most matches appear at the top of the result list. If you have a complex search where you think you need to use a logical language to tell Lycos what you're really after, the Lycos search language link on the Lycos search form page will tell you what you need to know.

The listing of how many documents matched which words is a sometimes-handy, sometimes-useless feature that no search engine other than Lycos gives you. If you scroll down to the actual search list, you will see that the first document, The Image Library of Biological Macromolecules in Denmark does indeed look like a pretty good source for DNA images. The second site on the Lycos search result list (the Silicon Graphics Image Gallery) also has one nice picture of DNA. The other 14 documents that Lycos found, however, didn't seem to have much promise as image sources.

We got lucky this time: The Image Library of Biological Macromolecules sure sounds like a place to find images of DNA, so the best thing to do if you were looking for a DNA image would be rush right down the hotlink to Germany (Deustchland) and see what it has available. Since this is a tutorial on searching, let's just look around a little more. Would the other Web search services have found the same site? Might they find something even better?

There are four other search engines that I'd consider to be on par with Lycos. In order of popularity, they are: the World Wide Web Worm, AOL's WebCrawler, the InfoSeek Demo, and the ALIWEB servers. Reverse the order of that list and you'll get my personal order of preferred usage. Why? Mostly because the most popular servers are often continually clogged so you have to wait forever for an answer. (This is especially true of the WWW Worm.) Though ALIWEB isn't quite as comprehensive as the others, it has many "mirror" servers all over the world; you can almost always get a very quick response from one of them.

InfoSeek probably takes the prize for the most consistently comprehensive, but your result list is limited to 10 items unless you sign up to pay 10 to 20 cents per search for the commercial version of the service. Though WebCrawler is sometimes a bit slow, its responses are nicely formatted and quite extensive. The commercial online service America Online (AOL) recently bought WebCrawler and promises to keep it fast and free so that everyone on the Internet will like them. We'll see.

We'll cover how to access all these (and more) from central locations shortly, but in case you ever need the individual addresses, here they are:

WWW Worm: http://www.cs.colorado.edu/home/mcbryan/wwww.html

WebCrawler: http://webcrawler.com/

InfoSeek free demo: http://www.infoseek.com:80/doc/help/InfoSeekIntro.html#Demo

Master list of ALIWEB servers: http://web.nexor.co.uk/public/aliweb/doc/search.html

In theory (have you noticed that there's a lot of "in theory" on the Net?), all these crawly critters do about the same thing: index every Web page everywhere. In practice, the differences in their responses to a query are often dramatic. For example, Figure 21.9 shows the results of querying AOL's WebCrawler for "dna molecule image."

Almost all the sites that WebCrawler found were missed by Lycos, and vice versa—though both did put the Image Library of Biological Macromolecules near the top of the list. That's why its almost never a waste of time to try the same query on more than one search engine.

InfoSeek

Now you might think that between Lycos and Web-Crawler—both of which attempt to search the entire World Wide Web—you probably found just about all the links to DNA images that are out there. Not so. To prove it, try the free demo of InfoSeek right on the Netscape home page (see Figure 21.10). You can just press Netscape's Net Search button, or use any browser to visit:

http://home.netscape.com/home/interenet-search.html

InfoSeek turns up at least two DNA image sites that both Lycos and WebCrawler missed. This only reinforces the point that it pays to do the same search on several search engines.

Figure 21.9

WebCrawler is another easy-to-use search engine.

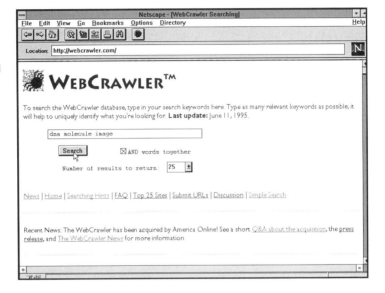

Figure 21.10

InfoSeek offers a free "Search the Web" service as a public service and an advertisement for its commercial search services.

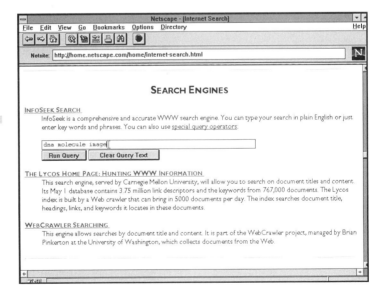

ALIWEB and CUI W3

Searching the Web successfully may take a few tries with different word combinations and different search engines, but the basic idea is still just about as simple as anything could be: type in a word, push a button, and away you go. That is (here comes that ugly phrase again), "in theory." In reality, one of the biggest headaches you'll experience while searching is the wait for overburdened servers to respond to your queries. These services are free—and increasingly essential for finding anything on the Net. Even major universities can't afford enough hardware and bandwidth to keep up with the millions upon millions of searches that flood their servers.

Pouring more tax dollars and educational funds into expensive new servers is one solution. Another approach is to duplicate similar services in many different sites around the world so when one site bogs down, you can simply hop to a less frequently used server. You saw this in action earlier in this chapter when we discussed how to "surf" Archieplex servers depending on the time of day.

Unfortunately, robot search tools like WebCrawler and Lycos complicate the problem of an overburdened network by taking up even more server time cruising around visiting and indexing sites with wanton abandon. ALIWEB is one approach to indexing that tries to lighten the network load while providing a superior Net-wide index service. Like Archieplex, ALIWEB is mirrored on many different servers throughout the world. So when your local ALIWEB is busy, you can simply hop over to one in Europe or the Pacific rim. Furthermore, the ALIWEB index is constructed by a semi-automatic system that consumes less of the Net's resources than most indexing robots. If you want to know more about how ALIWEB works, check out the information page at:

http://web.nexor.co.uk/public/aliweb/doc/introduction.html

Of course, you don't need to know or care about the altruistic concepts behind ALIWEB to make good use of the search service itself. Just pull up the list of ALIWEB servers at http://web.nexor.co.uk/public/aliweb/doc/search.html and select either the ALIWEB site nearest you or, if you get a slow response from your local server, select a server site where it's the middle of the night. Figure 21.11 shows the ALIWEB search form (at the Indiana server).

Figure 21.11

Like other search services, ALIWEB is accessed through a simple fill-in-the-blanks form.

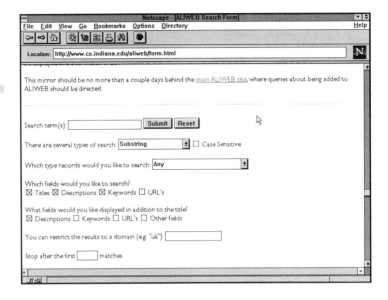

You'll want to use ALIWEB for finding graphics on the Net. However, I'm not going to show you how to use the ALIWEB search form itself for two reasons. First, it's simple enough so that you probably get the idea already. But more importantly, there's a stronger, better, faster way to access ALIWEB—and much, much more.

For starters, you should know that ALIWEB is incorporated into a larger, more comprehensive index called the CUI W3 Catalog. This catalog combines several directories and indexes of the Web with ALIWEB into one big searchable database. The Web page in Figure 21.12 lists the contents of CUI W3. If you want to access this information page or the list of search form servers for CUI W3, just go to:

http://iamwww.unibe.ch/~scg/W3catalog/doc/w3catalog.html

Or then again don't. Read on to find out how to use the Internet's most powerful search interface instead.

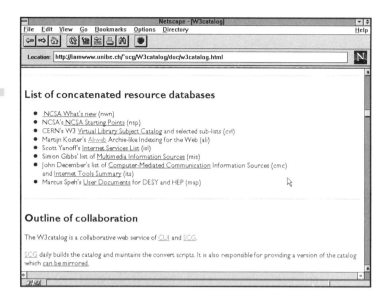

CUSI (and the Return of the Stooges)

Okay, I admit I've been stringing you along. The truth is
that the truly enlightened don't use any of the search
forms we've covered in this chapter so far. Instead, you'll
want to use the super-duper master search interface called
CUSI, or Configurable Unified Search Index. The idea here
is simple: Put access to every major Internet search tool on
one Web page.

Why did I just spend half a chapter introducing you to
all these search forms you'll never use? Don't worry: it
wasn't just to make you feel lucky that you can use CUSI
instead! The fact is that CUSI only becomes useful if you
have some basic understanding of the search engines that
are hiding behind it. Otherwise, it would just look like
a confusing bunch of pull-down lists of gibberish. But
now that you know what Archie, Archieplex, Lycos, Web-
Crawler, InfoSeek, ALIWEB, and CUI W3 all mean, you
can use CUSI to access them all—and many other search
tools too.

As an example, let's see if the World Wide Web has any
images of our stoogely trio that Archie's archives didn't
reveal. We'll use CUSI to search the CUI W3 database for
the keyword "stooges."

Figure 21.13 shows the WWW Indices section of the CUSI form page (see the preceding note for instructions on pulling up CUSI). To search the CUI W3 Catalog for the keyword "stooge," just type in the Search term box and click on the Submit button. A few seconds later, the page in Figure 21.14 reports that it can't find any stooges in CUI W3. Oh well.

Figure 21.13

Searching the index of your choice from CUSI is as simple as tappity-tap-tap-click.

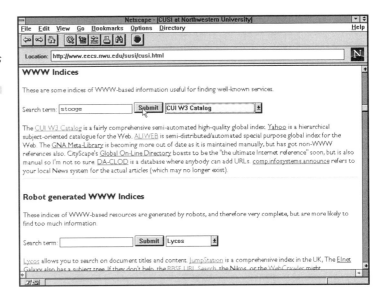

Figure 21.14

"Gee, Larry, the CUI W3 Catalog couldn't find us. We must not be on the Internet yet. Yuk, yuk."

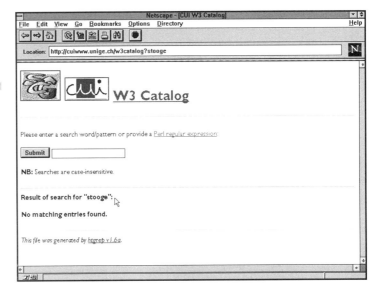

But what the heck—CUSI makes searching so easy we might as well try another index. Maybe one of the index-generating robots will have stumbled upon a stooge or three that all the CUI W3 sources missed.

I chose WebCrawler from CUSI's list of Robot generated WWW Indices, and entered "stooge" as the Search term (see Figure 21.15). Near the top of the result list were three Web pages entitled The Three Stooges. Movie clips, sound files, and yes, a small collection of graphics images proved to be only a link or two away after all.

TIP ▼ The Northwestern University CUSI form doesn't offer access to the World Wide Web Worm—probably because the Worm server is so over-worked that getting a response is almost impossible most times of the day. If you want a CUSI form with the WWW Worm on it, try the one at SunSITE Northern Europe (http://sunsite.doc.ic.ac.uk/cusi/).

Figure 21.15

Now there MUST be some stooges in here somewhere...

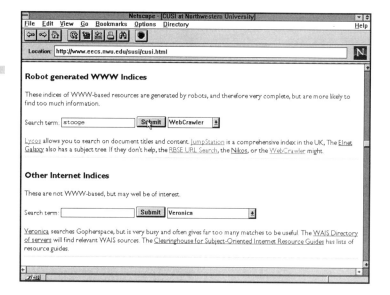

TIP You may have noticed that Archie and Veronica are on the CUSI super-search form, too. Although you can access them through CUSI, you may find that the Archieplex and Veronica search servers that your favorite CUSI page accesses are often too busy to answer your queries. You may also find that Veronica sometimes doesn't understand commands (like the **-tlg** "just graphics, please" command) issued through CUSI. If you encounter these problems, just hop over to the lists of Archieplex or Veronica servers mentioned earlier in this chapter and send your request to a different server.

Likewise, if the Web search engines used by your CUSI form are busy, try the master list of ALIWEB servers mentioned earlier.

Be sure to take a peek at the bottom part of the CUSI form, too. Though the search tools located there aren't much use for finding graphics, having a searchable library of software, dictionaries, Internet standards, and other reference works may come in handy.

Summary

To summarize the search strategies covered in this chapter: If you're looking for something so specific that you can guess part of the file name or title, use Archie or Veronica. When you know (or suspect) that a particular WAIS archive may contain an image you want, head for the WAIS gateway. In most other situations, the Web search engines on a CUSI page should do the trick. But when you really have only a vague idea of what you're after, or you just want to see what's new, you might want to browse one of the major Net directories that has a graphics heading or section. (The next chapter guides you to the best of these directories.)

Almost all of the search services on the Net are developing and changing rapidly. As you are reading this book, new and improved engines are undoubtedly becoming available. So when you visit the search form and directory pages referenced in this chapter and the next, keep your eyes peeled for links to new search engines as well.

CHAPTER

22

Online Directories
of Graphics

In This Chapter

> *The best graphics sections of major Internet directories*

> *Graphics directories and resource lists from academia and government*

> *The greatest graphics home-page hotlinks*

In Other Chapters

◀ *Many of the sites in Chapters 1 through 20 have hotlink lists
to other resources.*

◀ *Searching the Net for specific graphics is covered in
Chapter 21.*

Introduction

To say that the Net is growing and changing would be like saying, "Tut, tut. Looks like rain," during monsoon season in Southern India. For every great graphics site covered in this book, you can bet there will be two even better sites online soon. Many of these new sites will be accessible from your favorite current sites through hotlinks. But there are also some master directories where you can go to find the latest and best in graphics on the Net. This chapter takes you to the most comprehensive and most consistently updated "sources of sources."

Some of the sites covered in this chapter are well-known directories to all sorts of not-necessarily-graphics-related resources, but we'll go straight to the graphics parts of their listings. We'll also go to some "well-kept secret" sites that offer extensive graphics resource links.

The Mother of All Directories

 http://www.yahoo.com/

If you haven't visited the Yahoo directory of World Wide Web sites and Internet resources, you haven't really been on the Net. Even before it earned its own button in Netscape's browser, Yahoo was the most visited (and best) Net directory. And, well, as much as we hate to follow the seething masses, we have to admit that Yahoo should be your first stop for finding the latest graphics on the Net.

Yahoo isn't comprehensive, and it isn't meant to be. (A listing of a million sites isn't much help as a directory, no matter how well organized it may be.) Instead, Yahoo aims to selectively list a generous number of the best and most generally useful sites in each category. And you have to hand it to Yahoo: it actually does it. The sites included are amazingly consistent in quality, considering the vastness of Yahoo's topical domain. Be warned, however, that as the Net gets more vast, Yahoo is of necessity getting less selective. Still, they will continue to be the standard by which all other directories are measured.

So jump on the bandwagon and point your Web browser to http://www.yahoo.com/, or skip straight to one of the graphics-oriented directory pages. The best four pages are listed here. Start on one of these and follow the boldface links to other Yahoo pages and hot graphics Web sites.

Computer Graphics: http://www.yahoo.com/Computers/
                     Graphics/

Multimedia Pictures: http://www.yahoo.com/Computers/
                     Multimedia/Pictures/

Art in General: http://www.yahoo.com/Art/

Photography: http://www.yahoo.com/Art/Photography

Better check out the What's New link from the Yahoo home page while you're there, too. Don't try the Random Link service, though. It's almost certain to be a complete waste of time. (Well, okay, maybe just this once…)

TIP   The CUI W3 Catalog search service includes all the Yahoo pages (and several other directories mentioned later in this chapter) in its index. So you can automatically search Yahoo as you conduct other Net searches from the CUSI form discussed in Chapter 21. You can also search Yahoo with the Search button at the top of each directory page.

Commercially Sponsored Directories

The ultimate relationship between business, government, and academia on the Net is uncertain to say the least. Many old-time Internetters are already grumbling in their rocking chairs about how things aren't the way they used to be, and how these young hooligans in business suits just want a free ride on the network backbone of their government and academic elders.

But it's hard to deny the benefits that business has already brought to the Net, not the least of which are some of the best directories to Net resources of all types. Most commercial Internet providers and services offer some form of publicly accessible directory pages, and some of these have become indispensable reference resources for Netizens everywhere.

You'll also find some fantastic free images and information in smaller businesses' home pages and even some large companies' public offerings, if you know how to look (see Chapter 21). As the major directories and search indexes include more and more business pages and files, corporate-sponsored resources will become an increasingly valuable part of the Internet universe.

Overall, business on the Net has retained much of the "good citizen" flavor enjoyed by the earlier Internet pioneers. Whether that spirit will thrive or die now that secure commercial transactions and big budget advertising have hit the wires remains to be seen. But whether you're waiting for the Net future with checkbook or textbook in hand, you'll find some great directories with .com and .net on the end of their address locators. The following described sites are currently the best for finding graphics.

If you're an old Net hand from the DOD-and-University days, just try to brace yourself for the shock of seeing slick corporate ads at the top of some of the following directory pages. Like Dorothy said when she found out that her Ph.D. wouldn't get her a job (but her knowledge of Internet protocols would), "We're not at Kansas State anymore."

GNN's Whole Internet Catalog

 http://gnn.com/gnn/wic/index.html

The online version of The Whole Internet Catalog runs neck and neck with Yahoo for the title of most popular directory on the Net. Like Yahoo, it deserves the popularity. In the graphics departments, however, The Whole Internet Catalog doesn't have nearly as many good links as Yahoo. Still, there are some good ones here that the Yahoos missed so a quick stop at http://gnn.com/gnn/wic/index.html should be part of your surf schedule if you're looking to ride the latest graphics wave.

The Whole Internet Catalog was originally a book published by O'Reilly and Associates. Bringing it online was their first step into the electronic publishing and service now called Global Network Navigator (GNN), which was recently purchased by America Online. Be sure to check out the Arts & Entertainment/Digital Images and Computers/Publishing & Multimedia category listings as well as the Computers/Graphics page.

As you follow the links to graphics sites, you'll notice one unique and especially nice feature of The Whole Internet Catalog. When you click on a directory listing, you get a paragraph summarizing and describing the site you selected rather than a direct jump to the site itself. Then if you want to go there, you can just click a button marked "GO." If the site doesn't sound as interesting as its one-line title suggested, you can quickly skip back to the directory.

Power Index and InfoBank

 http://www.webcom.com/~webcom/power/

 http://www.clark.net/pub/global/graphics.html

Many Internet service providers like to offer a home page with a directory of the Web to get their users surfing as far and fast as possible. These directories also tend to promote the company's identity, presence, and service products. These vary in quality, but generally have few links to good graphics resources. Fortunately, WebCom's Power Index is an exception —though they lump all forms of graphics rather deceptively under the "Multimedia" page at:

http://www.webcom.com/~webcom/power/multimedia.html

TIP Strangely enough, WebCom misses a great chance to publicize themselves by failing to provide any obvious link to their home page or company information from their directory pages. Even if you want to find out about them, you'll have to know the old Net trick of lopping off the last part of the address to get to:

http://www.webcom.com/~webcom/power/

Whenever you encounter a page that seems to be part of a larger web of documents, but has no links to them, try chopping the last word of the address off. Most servers are smart enough to give you a default document, which is usually a home page.

You'll find another graphics index at:

http://www.clark.net/pub/global/graphics.html

If WebCom makes information about their company tricky to get, InfoBank makes it practically impossible. Though their short list of graphics topics contains some good hard-to-find resources, neither this page nor their home page gives you the slightest clue who they are. They don't seem to be associated with the service provider who owns the clark.net in their address, so their identity remains a mystery to me. Pretty decent directory, though.

EinNET Galaxy

 http://www.einet.net/galaxy/

EinNET is a military-consulting-firm-turned-commercial-enterprise that knows all about the Net's changes of life from a defense and education network to a business haven. They also seem to know how to provide a vital public service while courteously and effectively promoting their business. If you're thinking about publishing on the Web, visit:

> http://www.einet.net/galaxy/Engineering-and-Technology/
> Computer-Technology/Computer-Graphics-and-Art.html

and

> http://www.einet.net/galaxy/Arts-and-Humanities/Visual-
> Arts/Pictorial-Arts.html

The visual organization is simple and clean, but everything the reader wants is easy to find and pleasantly presented. A group of simple, self-explanatory links to the home page, company information, and other key resources at the top of each page; convenient links to higher-level topics and "See also" cross references; carefully selected, relevant news items and articles of interest above the directory listings; and subtle and attractive graphics touches. If more Web pages were like this, the virtual world would be a far friendlier place.

By the way, you can hop up to the Visual Arts topic list for other Galaxy pages of interest as well.

Of course, the talents of Galaxy's Webmasters are less important than the quality of the links to other Web sites. Fortunately, these are as current and well chosen as Galaxy is well designed. We can only hope that EinNET will be emulated as an example for other businesses and services to establish their identities by offering free services on the Net.

The Virtual Library

http://www.w3.org/hypertext/DataSources/bySubject/Virtual_libraries/ Overview.html

The World Wide Web was invented at CERN, the European Laboratory for High Energy Physics. In accord with the Web's globally distributed nature, CERN has organized a distributed directory to the Web called the Virtual Library. Each topic is maintained by a different site with links back and forth to the Virtual Library home page at CERN itself. Though CERN is a scientific research center, the Virtual Library as a whole results from the combined efforts of the international academic, military, and business communities. Most pages do tend to be more academically oriented than other major Internet directories, though.

In your worldwide quest for graphics, you will find two of the Virtual Library sites especially helpful. One is the Computer Graphics and Visualization page at:

http://www.dataspace.com/WWW/vlib/comp-graphics.html

and the other is the Graphic Design page at:

http://www.dh.umu.se/vlib.html

Both of these pages offer paragraphs describing the focus and scope of the sites rather than simply a laundry list of hotlinks.

CHAPTER 23

Getting Graphics from the Net

In This Chapter

➤ *Software and hardware you need to get graphics from the Net*

➤ *How to download quickly and easily*

➤ *File formats and other techie stuff you need to know*

➤ *Decompressing and converting image files*

➤ *Transferring graphics through e-mail and newsgroups*

In Other Chapters

➤ *To install and configure the software you need, see Chapter 26, "What's on the net.graphics CD."*

◀ *For places to find graphics worth getting, see Part I, "Best Graphics Sites on the Net."*

◀ *For help finding a specific file by name or topic, see Chapter 21, "Search Strategies & Techniques."*

➤ *For more on using graphics and video, see Chapter 24, "Viewing & Using Graphics from the Net."*

The first 21 chapters of this book help you find graphics files and graphics-related information on the Internet. But finding the perfect image doesn't do you much good unless you know how to bring it home to your computer and work with it once you've got it. This chapter gives you a quick but complete run-down on everything you need to know to snag and snazz-up graphics from the Net.

Life in cyberspace is just like real life in that there are usually many ways to do things. You could spend years studying all the different approaches to handling Net graphics. But, unless you're hoping to achieve ultimate Internet enlightenment and graphics guruhood, you'd probably prefer just to learn the fastest, easiest, and most efficient way to get everything you need. So that's what this chapter teaches you. Gurus-to-be will either need to pick up some thicker books or hope for a better reincarnation next time.

Software and Hardware You Need

For 90 percent of what you're likely to do with graphics on the Net, you probably won't need any hardware or software beyond the basics mentioned there. When software other than Netscape is necessary to accomplish certain tasks, we'll recommend the programs you need.

If you've been around the Net for a while (or you've read other books written by people who have), you may be used to thinking of a Web browser as a cute-but-nonessential toy. And it is true that you can access most graphics using a combination of older programs such as FTP, Gopher, Telnet, and so on. The CD included with this book even includes the best versions of these programs in case you want to use them instead of a Web browser. But take my advice: Don't.

Finding and getting graphics with a text-only tool is like flying an airplane with no windows. Sure, modern navigation software makes it possible—but you'd darn well better know exactly where you're going before you take off, and have a lot of trust in technology. With a text-based file transfer program like FTP, you pick some files, cross your fingers, and wait until it's over to see what you get. When you access the same files with a browser like Netscape, you can see each one as it comes to you and stop or change your mind at any time while you're still connected. Also, many excellent graphics are in WWW directories that are specifically set up for access by WWW browsers. In theory, you can still get those graphics files with FTP. However, without interactive browsing, chances of finding them and knowing which one you want are about nil.

Okay. End of lecture. In this chapter you'll learn how to access everything through Netscape. If you're still chained to an ancient non-Web-compatible UNIX shell account, you can find out how to set up the old-style file transfer programs in Chapter 26, "What's on the net.graphics CD."

How To Download Quickly and Easily

There's a bunch of technical stuff you ought to know about file formats, translation, compression, and that sort of thing. We'll get to that shortly. But first, let's jump right to the point: Getting the picture. You know where it is because some earlier chapter in this book told you. You know you want it. How do you get it?

That depends mostly on what type of address you have for it. Generally, an Internet file address (called a Uniform Resource Locator, or URL) will begin with one of three words: http, gopher, or ftp. All of these are accessible through Netscape or another comparable Web browser, but the exact technique for retrieving files differs a bit for each address type.

NOTE Before we examine how to access each of these three address types, you should know that transferring files from other computers into your computer is called *downloading*. And, yes, sending files from your computer to another one is called *uploading*. If you're new to this, it can be easy to forget which is which. Just think of the Great Spirit of the Internet hovering high above your lowly personal computer, and the correct meanings of down and up will be hard to confuse.

Hot Off the Web Press

No matter what type of address your file has, the first thing you should do is crank up your browser and enter the URL in its Location or Address box. If the address begins with http (which stands for HyperText Transfer Protocol), you should see a normal Web page nicely formatted with text and graphics. Figure 23.1 is an example. Several of the links on this page lead directly to graphics files. When you click on one of those links (or, on this page, any of the small graphics images), a full-size image will download and display (see Figure 23.2). If you want to keep it, simply select File/Save As from the menu and enter the name you want to save it under (see Figure 23.3). Or, if you're not sure you want it but you might want to go back and get it later, select Bookmarks/Add Bookmark to save the address itself for later use.

Figure 23.1

World Wide Web pages often contain links to graphics images. In this page from The Graphics Alternative Gallery, both the small images and parts of the text are linked to pictures.

Figure 23.2

Clicking on a link is all it takes to pull up this full-sized graphic.

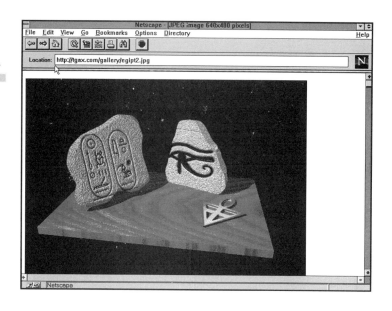

Figure 23.3

If you want a copy of the image to remain on your computer's hard drive, you have to remember to save it.

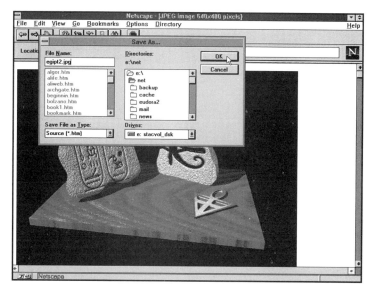

Going for Gopher

Gopher is a system for linking and indexing files located on computers around the world. Though Gopher predates the World Wide Web by a few years, almost all modern Web browsers also allow you to access Gopher menus. When you enter an address that begins with the word gopher, you should see a list of documents and file folders.

The friendliest Gopher menus include a document called "Index" or "00Index" or "Contents" or something like that. This document usually gives you a lot more information about the items listed than the menu names alone could. To view the document, simply click on it and it will pop up in your browser as shown in Figure 23.4.

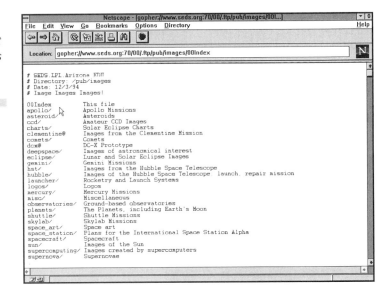

Figure 23.4

This is the "00Index" document at the top of the list. It describes what's in each of the menu folders.

Once you decide which of the menus you'd like to investigate, click on your browser's Back (left arrow) button to return to the Gopher menu, then choose the file folder you want. You will get another bunch of file folders or documents. Figure 23.5 shows the Gopher menu I got when I selected the space_art folder. The icons for text documents look like pages of text, while graphics images look like little geometric shapes on a page.

Again, there appears to be an index to this list of images, called 00Index. (Not all Gopher systems have convenient index documents like this, so when you get one be grateful for the privilege of reading it!) Ah, but all is not as well as it seems. A comparison of the index file (see Figure 23.6) and the actual file list (see Figure 23.5) reveals that the index is very out of date. Many images listed in the index (including the promising-looking thumbnail page) are missing from the file list, and many new images have been added to the file list but not the index. The lesson here is that things usually change too fast on the Net for mere humans to keep up. When you find a hand-made index file, take it with a grain of salt. Figure 23.7 is an example of an excellent image from the file list that wasn't in the outdated index.

Figure 23.5

Selecting the space_art folder from the Gopher menu leads you to this file list of images.

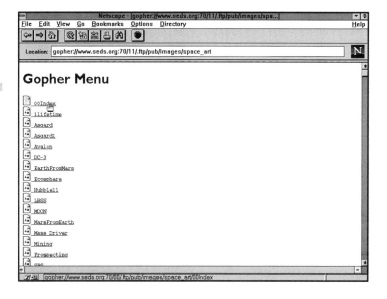

Figure 23.6

Here are the actual contents of the 00Index text file shown at the top of the list in Figure 23.5. Note that the index doesn't include many of the files on the menu, and vice versa.

Figure 23.7

This "Ecosphere" image was probably added to the file archive recently, since it wasn't mentioned in the text index.

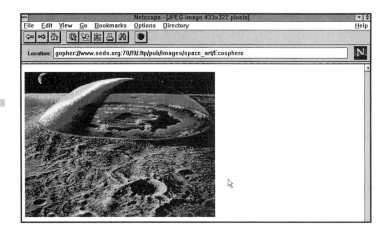

To download the image in Figure 23.7, all I did was click on the Ecosphere document name listed in Figure 23.5. I then had to select File/Save As to store the image on my computer's hard drive. Always remember to save the image (or add its address to your bookmark list) if you want to use it later.

Good Old FTP

Sure, the Web and Gopher space are fun and functional. But let's face reality: the vast majority of files in the world are still accessible only through good old-fashioned File Transfer Protocol (FTP). Fortunately, almost all Web browsers can access FTP sites as easily as they do WWW and Gopher sites.

Figure 23.8 is what you'll get if you point Netscape to an address starting with the letters ftp. (This specific page is from a popular NASA archive of space images.)

Unlike a Gopher menu, everything in an FTP file list is always on one specific computer in one specific directory. And you see even shorter file names than most Gopher sites provide. Fortunately, indexes or contents lists are often available on the major public FTP sites. Scrolling down a bit from Figure 23.8 reveals a text file called CONTENTS. Clicking on its name pops up the information in Figure 23.9.

Individual image files are also often accompanied by short text files describing their contents. Downloading the text description is a quick way to see what an image depicts without waiting for the large graphics file to transfer. The file names listed in Figure 23.8, for example, don't tell you much at all about the images. But clicking on one of the corresponding text files (see Figure 23.10) provides a much better idea what the picture may look like.

Figure 23.8

The /pub/SPACE/GIF directory contains a wealth of images from NASA's archives. (Not too surprising, since it is one of NASA's archives.)

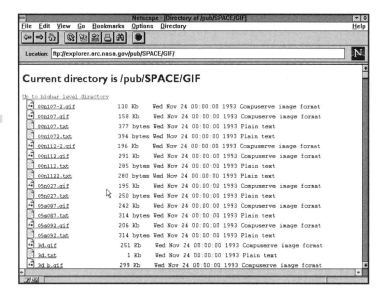

Figure 23.9

Following this introductory message, this text file details a complete list of the contents of the directory shown in Figure 23.8.

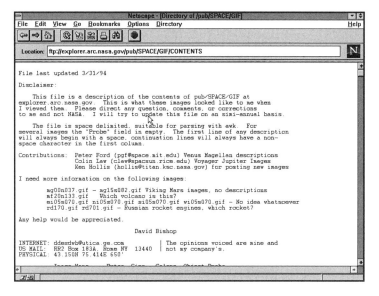

Figure 23.10

This text description file not only helps you decide if you want to download the accompanying image, but also gives you information about the subject that might not be obvious when viewing the image itself.

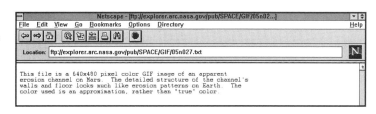

One of the advantages of using a Web browser instead of a text-based FTP program is that you can see images as they download to your computer. You may decide after seeing the top part of an image that it isn't of interest and you don't want to wait for the rest. To cancel the transfer, just press the Stop button in your browser. This can save a lot of time—both for you and the busy server computer you're downloading from.

The Techie Stuff

So far getting graphics from the Net sounds easy. Well, don't get too comfortable yet. The examples in this chapter so far were chosen specifically to avoid some all-too-common headaches that you're almost certain to encounter. With the directions this chapter provides, you will be able to avoid the roughest parts of the I-road and still get where you're going and back. On the way, however, you have to go through some rough spots just so you can see what "fun" you're missing. (So buckle up.)

Chronic Decompression

Image files are big—usually worth several thousand words at least. And many of those words are wasted if you just store images as a huge list of colored dots—500 black dots can be much more efficiently described as "500 black dots" than "black dot black dot black dot black dot black dot... etc." So it isn't unreasonable that most sites save disk space and transfer time by compressing images (and other files) as tightly as possible.

The unreasonable part is the number of different compression schemes that have, over the years, laid claim to the claim "as small as possible." As compression technology has constantly evolved, the hard drives of the world have become littered with files compressed with outdated programs. Each of these files can only be decompressed (and thus made usable) by the particular algorithm that compressed it. What's worse, different computers often use different (and incompatible) compression and decompression programs even though the programs may internally use the same compression technique. So you'll also need special programs to decompress Mac files, UNIX files, and so on. So it's an old Net tradition to keep oodles of decompression programs at the ready for restoring files compressed in multifarious formats.

In a nutshell, just because you can get a file from someone else's computer over the Net doesn't mean you can actually decompress or decode it into a format readable by your software. And the plot thickens. There are programs that can compress any file—text, image, program, whatever—and then there are also programs and algorithms for compressing just graphics files as they're stored. These may be combined, so an image might be compressed and stored in one format, then compressed again by another program and stored in a different format. A very common UNIX procedure uses two different compression programs one after the other, even if the file has already been stored as a compressed image. Unless you're clever, you'll need quite an arsenal of software (and knowledge) to handle different kinds of decompression.

Ah, but of course you are very clever. (You had the good sense to buy this book, right?) So naturally you will use the two (count 'em, two) programs recommended here instead of the 20 or so programs that they replace. So pat yourself on the back and breathe a sigh of relief.

The two programs referred to here depend on your computer type. For Windows users, WinZip will handle all common forms of file decompression, and PaintShop Pro converts between all common (and several not-so-common) compressed image file formats. For Mac users, StuffIt is recommended for file decompression and GraphicConverter is a good choice for converting graphics files. You'll learn how to use these lifesavers later in this chapter.

But first, back to the dismal side of Net life again. Even with WinZip and PaintShop Pro (or their Mac equivalents) at your side, you'll still need to have some knowledge of which formats are which and what to do with them. If you've been working with computer graphics for a while, you've probably faced and tamed the many-headed file format serpent. If not, read on.

File Formats You'll Find on the Net

Of the zillion file formats on the Net, you're actually only likely to encounter a scant few. You can think of these as being divided into two basic categories: files you can use as-is and files you have to do something to first. Usually, you can tell what type of file you're dealing with by the last few letters of the file name, called the *extension* or sometimes *extender*.

Table 23.1 summarizes the most common file extensions for graphics and what software you need to view or use that file type. I've listed video and sound formats in Table 23.1 as well. The graphics conversion and viewing programs mentioned previously won't do anything with these, so you'll need the special viewer programs suggested in the table under each "multimedia" file type (see Chapter 24). Also, be aware that video and sound file formats are still new enough to be outdated quickly, so you'll probably need to juggle many multimedia viewer updates in the next few years.

Fortunately, most graphics files on the Net are in JPEG or GIF format. These formats (and the new PNG format that has replaced GIF) are so space-efficient that running them through an additional compression program wouldn't make them any smaller. So you will seldom have to deal with the messy business of running files through a decompression program before you can use them.

Still, some archive managers simply compress everything automatically whether it actually saves space or not, so even some JPEG files may be hiding in compressed Z or ZIP files. And if you download graphics programs, text tutorials, or C source code, then the files will probably be compressed.

TABLE 23.1 Common graphics and sound file types and what to do with them

If the file name ends in...	It's probably this type of file...
jpg, jpe, jpeg	A ready-to-view image file stored with JPEG (Joint Photographic Experts Group) compression. Most Web browsers will display and save these images without any additional software.
gif, png	GIF is an outdated (but still very common) CompuServe image format now being replaced by PNG. Most Web browsers will display and save these images without any additional software.
tiff, tif, tga, pcx, bmp	Fairly common image file formats (though JPEG and GIF are far more widespread on the Net). The latest generation of Web browsers can display and save these images directly, but if you have an older browser you may need an accessory viewer program such as Lview.
mac, pic, pict, rle, wpg, art, cut, img, lbm, msp, clp, dib, wmf, ras	These are all old or platform-specific image file formats. Use a graphics conversion program such as PaintShop Pro or Graphic Workshop to translate these into one of the more usable formats listed previously—preferably JPEG, PNG, or TIFF.
mpg, mpeg	Video or animation stored in MPEG (Motion Picture Experts Group) format. The latest generation of Web browsers can view these video files directly, or you can use a player such as MPEGPLAY to view them.
wav, avi	Windows audio and video files. Use a player such as Microsoft Media Player.
qt	Apple QuickTime video file format. View with QuickTime for the Mac or Media Player for Windows with QuickTime for Windows software.
au, aiff	UNIX audio file formats. Use a player such as WHAM to listen to the sound.
ps, psd, ai, eps	These are graphics or typeset text pages in the PostScript page description language. You can send them directly to a PostScript-compatible printer or use the software program Ghostscript to view them.
pdf	A document that can only be viewed with Adobe Acrobat software.

Table 23.2 summarizes all the compression formats you're likely to encounter on the Net. All of these except zoo can be handled by WinZip (on the PC) or StuffIt (on the Mac), but the names of the individual decompression programs that handle each file type have been included in the table for your reference.

Note that WinZip will handle zip, tar, gz, z, taz, and tgz files without any additional software. If you need to handle lha, lzh, arj, or arc files, you'll need to tell WinZip where to find the LHA, UnARJ, and UnArc programs (which are also provided on the CD with this book). You probably won't need to handle these types of files, since they aren't nearly as common as the other types. But if you do find a need, see the WinZip online help for help with the (very easy) configuration process.

On the Mac, StuffIt will handle sit, zip, gz, z, and most other common compression formats without additional software. But the SunTar program (also included on the CD) is needed to handle tar, taz, and tgz files.

TABLE 23.2   Compressed File Formats (must be decompressed before use)

File Extension	Decompress with	Description
z	compress or gzip	An aging but ubiquitous UNIX compression format.
tar	tar (UNIX) suntar (Mac) TAR4DOS (PC)	The UNIX "tape archive" utility. Often used in combination with compress.
taz (or tar.z)		A file that must be decompressed first with compress and then with tar.
gz	gzip	"GNU Zip," a modern replacement for the old UNIX compress.
tgz (or tar.gz)		A file that must be decompressed first with gzip and then with tar.
zoo	Zoo	A less successful contender to replace the UNIX compress format.
zip	PKUnzip	The most popular compression type among PC users.
lha, lzh	LHA	A popular and efficient compression program from Japan.
arj	UnARJ	A somewhat passé DOS compression format.
arc	UnArc	The precursor to zip. There aren't many .arc files left out there.
hqx	BinHex	(See the following note on Mac compression formats.)

The Mac has more of its own personal compression formats than anybody could ever want. There's sea and sit, cpt and hqx, and a couple of other variations including AppleLink "packages." If you're a Mac user, the freeware version of StuffIt Expander is a must-have utility for dealing with all this "stuff." PC users probably won't ever have to cope with anything Macish other than hqx files, which are in the BinHex format used for mail transmission and sometimes archival storage on the Net. Most mail programs that handle uuencoded files (discussed later in this chapter) will also handle BinHex. Or you can use the PC BinHex program on the CD that comes with this book.

Being familiar with the file extensions in Tables 23.1 and 23.2 can be helpful even if you never download a graphics file that can't be handled right in your Web browser. In fact, the biggest benefit of knowing how to recognize an obscure graphics or compression format is that you can then avoid it. There are almost always several options for finding the graphics you want on the Net. Suppose, for example, you needed an image of an oversized canine. If you find one file named big.slobbery.dog.tar.z and another file named bigdog.gif, grab the gif and save yourself from wrestling with UNIX decompression schemes and obtuse or unknown graphics file formats. (Assuming, of course, that saliva wasn't the key visual element you were after.) More often than not, a little file name know-how will save you from having to use any conversion programs at all.

Decompressing and Converting a Graphics File

Now that you've got the basic idea, you're ready to step through an actual example of decompressing and converting an image file. Just to illustrate a worst-case scenario, we're going to an archive filled with files of every conceivable combination of obscure file formats. The FTP site is shown in Figure 23.11. (This site was chosen for its admixture of formats, not its contents. But in case you're curious, the actual images here are all logos for the freeware linux operating system. The suggested logos were created by folks around the globe using all different kinds of software—thus the overabundance of incompatible file formats.)

Figure 23.11

This directory probably has more weird file formats than any other single place on the Net.

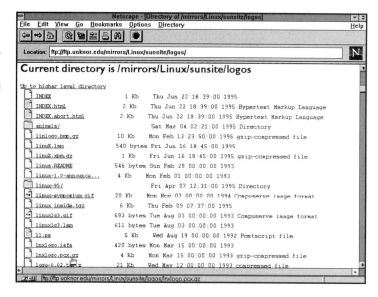

Suppose you wanted to check out the file lnxlogo.pcx.gz. As the name suggests, this is a PCX graphics file compressed with the gzip utility. We'll now step through how to download it, decompress it, and convert it to a more contemporary graphics file format such as JPEG. For this example we'll use the Windows programs WinZip and PaintShop Pro, but Mac users should be able to get the idea and achieve the same results with StuffIt and Graphics Converter.

When you click on the file, Netscape tells you that it doesn't know what to do with this kind of file (see Figure 23.12). Click on Save to Disk, and choose a directory and file name (see Figure 23.13). Notice that the DOS eight-character limit on file names mandates that you drop some letters from the name. In this case, it's okay to drop the .pcx and call the file lnxlogo_.gz as Netscape suggests. Just remember that there's a pcx file in there because when you decompress the file in a moment, you'll tell WinZip to put the .pcx extension back on. If you didn't want to trust your memory, you might tell Netscape to call the file lnx_pcx.gz.

Next, you need to start WinZip (or StuffIt on the Mac) and select Open (see Figure 23.14). Choose the file you just saved in Netscape.

Figure 23.12

Netscape doesn't know how to view a gzip archive, so you should just save the file to your hard disk.

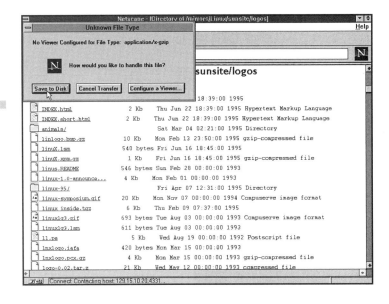

Figure 23.13

Because DOS filenames can only have eight characters plus a three character extension, DOS users need to remember (or—horrors—write down on paper!) any important parts of the original UNIX file name that get chopped off. Mac users don't need to worry about it, since Macs allow long file names.

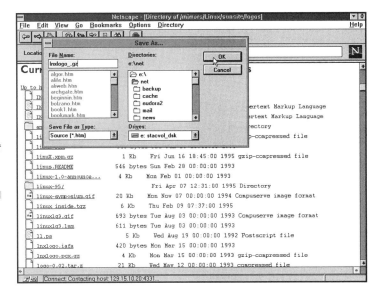

Some compression formats, such as zip and lha, include the full name of original uncompressed files right in the compressed archive file. But the UNIX compress and gzip utilities don't. (Why? Because they only compress a single file into each archive and UNIX allows file names to be long enough so that the .z or .gz extension can simply be added to the end of the original file name.) So WinZip will check with you to see if you want to modify the file name before decompression.

In this case, you should make sure that the file has a .pcx extension, as shown in Figure 23.15.

Figure 23.14

WinZip allows you to open an archive and see what files are inside before extracting them.

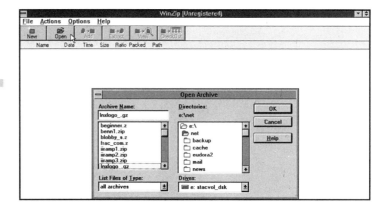

Figure 23.15

If you know what kind of file is hiding in a UNIX archive, be sure to put the right extension on it when you decompress it.

The actual decompression step is a no-brainer: press Extract, pick a directory (see Figure 23.16), and it is done.

Figure 23.16

Decompressing an archived file is a one-step operation.

You now have a genuine, grade-A PCX file. To have a look at it, start PaintShop Pro (you can exit WinZip now). When you Open the file, you see one man's idea of a logo for linux (see Figure 23.17).

PCX is a pretty old standard, and many graphics programs can't read PCX files anymore. So how would you send this graphic to other people? You need to convert it to a more contemporary format such as JPEG.

Figure 23.17

*The decompression worked!
It's an image!*

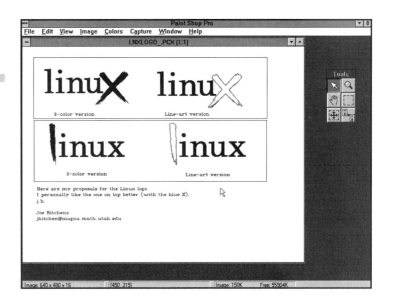

TIP To tell you the truth, JPEG isn't a good choice for storing this particular image. JPEG is what's known as a "lossy" standard, which means that it ever-so-slightly blurs or degrades the image to achieve maximum compression. The degradation is usually unnoticeable for photos or other continuous-tone images, but line art with thin lines and sharp corners can sometimes come out looking a little rough around the edges.

You'd be better off choosing .TIF, .GIF, or .PNG for this image because they preserve every picture-perfect pixel. But for our purposes here we're going to save it as a JPEG anyway, because JPEG is the most popular Internet image standard.

You have two choices for converting between file formats in PaintShop Pro:

▼ You can select File/Open to open the image (as shown in Figure 23.17) and then select File/Save As, choosing any file format you want from the List Files of Type: list (see Figure 23.18). This is the best method when you want to view and convert a single image like this one.

▼ For multiple images, or when you don't care about viewing the image first, you can select File/Batch Conversion and select several files of various formats to be converted automatically (see Figure 23.19). This is a very handy feature.

Figure 23.18

PaintShop Pro can save a graphics file in almost any format you could ever possibly need.

Figure 23.19

The Batch Conversion command makes converting multiple files a piece of cake.

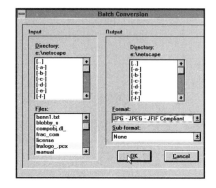

Once the file conversion is complete, you can use it in any graphics application that uses the file type you converted to.

Transferring Graphics via E-mail and Newsgroups

In this chapter, you've seen how to retrieve graphics files from nearly every public archive in the world. As valuable as the millions of files in those global archives may be, sometimes the most valuable file to you personally is the one sitting on your friend's or business associate's hard drive just across town. The only way to get that file is to have him send it to you by putting it on a floppy and sticking it in the mail—but we all know about the hazards of exposing the disk to magnetic fields. Perhaps e-mail is a safer way to go. (Faster, too.)

These days, almost all new e-mail software supports Multi-purpose Internet Mail Extensions, generally referred to simply as MIME. Sending a graphics file in a MIME-compatible mail program is usually as simple as selecting Attach file or Attach document from a menu and specifying the file name. The sender's software will use a standard encoding scheme to prepare the file for transmission over the text-only mail networks, and the recipient's MIME-compatible mail software will automatically decode the file. Whenever possible, you should always use MIME for graphics and other non-text file transfers.

The problem is that "whenever possible" and "always" are not the same thing. Many business people are still using e-mail software that doesn't support non-text files at all, or use older standards than MIME. So you need to know what to do if you get some mail that was encoded with these older standards, such as "raw" uuencoding, xxencoding, and BinHex encoding. You also may need to know what to do if you receive MIME mail but you don't have MIME-compatible e-mail software. (Most commercial online services, including CompuServe and America Online, don't yet support MIME attachments, for instance.)

In the next few pages, you'll learn how to handle all these situations. You'll also learn how to access and decode graphics files from graphics-oriented Internet (UseNet) newsgroups.

TIP Some Macintosh e-mail programs, such as the Mac version of Eudora, call MIME by the name "AppleDouble." (Why is anybody's guess. Free advertising?) Anyway, if you see AppleDouble, AppleSingle, and BinHex on a menu when you try to attach a file, always pick AppleDouble unless the person you're sending the file to specifically requests BinHex encoding.

Decoding MIME Mail

Suppose I happened to be working a bit late (perhaps writing a book or something). It would only be courteous to send my wife an e-mail message to let her know when I'll be home. Better yet, why not send a graphical representation of myself? Then she won't have to wait up and I can keep working into the wee hours of the night. And she'll be happy she married such a thoughtful guy.

So I hop into my e-mail program at work—Eudora, let's say—and send a quick message to her CompuServe mailbox with a GIF file attached. It's easy enough to send attachments in Eudora; just make sure the little MIME mask is showing and select Transfer/Attach Document (see Figure 23.20).

Figure 23.20

Gonna be a late night at the office. Better e-mail myself home so my wife doesn't get too lonely. Sending a GIF of my face as a MIME attachment in Eudora should do the trick.

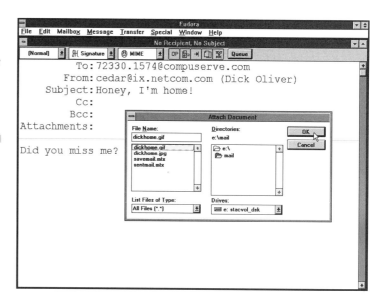

Unfortunately, when Jan receives the message in her CompuServe mail, she won't see the graphic at all. Instead, she just sees a bunch of ASCII gobbledy-gook and a notice saying "This is a multipart MIME message." But being a savvy sort of gal, she naturally knows just what to do. She saves the message to a file (see Figure 23.21) and starts up Information Transfer Professional from her net.graphics CD. (If she were a Mac user, I probably wouldn't have married her. But if your sweetie is a Mac user, she or he could use the MPack software, which is also on the CD.)

TIP Notice that she gives the message the file extension mme when she saves it. This is the standard extension for MIME-encoded files, and it will help her decoding software figure out what type of file it's dealing with.

Using Information Transfer Pro is straightforward. She selects File/Decode, selects the file she just saved the message to (see Figure 23.22), and confirms that the decoded file should be given the same name it had before my mail program encoded it (see Figure 23.23). In a flash, she's got a GIF graphics file instead of a useless string of letters and numbers (see Figure 23.24).

Figure 23.21

Alas, the MIME attachment doesn't do me justice when it arrives as several hundred lines of weird looking text. (I hope she saves it to a file and decodes it back into a graphics image again.)

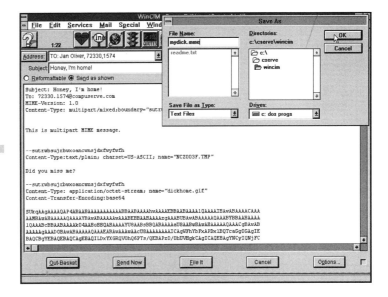

Figure 23.22

Information Transfer Professional can decode MIME attachments and other older encoding standards that your e-mail software might not be prepared to handle.

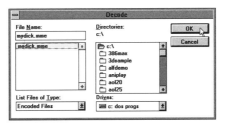

Figure 23.23

The MIME attachment includes the name of the original file, so all Jan has to do is click on OK to restore my beloved visage.

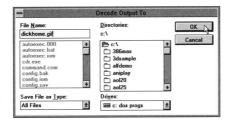

Figure 23.24

In a few seconds, the graphics file is restored to its original glory and saved on her hard drive.

Once the file is decoded, she can view it with any graphics viewer. Of course, I thoughtfully gave her a CompuServe GIF format image, so she can pull it up right in her WinCIM CompuServe Information Manager software just by selecting File/Open. Imagine her delight at seeing the face of her betrothed home in time for supper! (See Figure 23.25.)

Figure 23.35

The next best thing to being there.

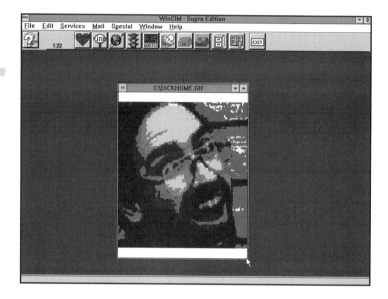

Retrieving Graphics from Newsgroups

This may sound a bit old-fashioned, but we don't have a color scanner at home. Just call me cheap: I take the photos of the kids to the office when I want to scan them for Windows wallpaper. In any case, my heartstruck honey-pie wouldn't have any way to scan a photo of herself (or perhaps of the dinner getting cold) to send me in reply to my little attempt at telepresence. Ah, but being rather resourceful, she might think, "I bet I could find a good graphic to send him on a newsgroup!"

UseNet newsgroups are a great way to find information about almost anything, as long as you don't mind weeding through a lot of messages to get it. The alt.binaries.pictures newsgroups are especially useful because most of the postings are graphics images, not text. That's where Jan would be sure to turn for a way to express her appreciation for my heartwarming graphical missive.

Now if you're a true newsgroup aficionado, you probably use a dedicated newsreader program like the WinVN program on the enclosed CD. But for casual or occasional reading (that is, less than 20 hours a week glued to the newsreader), the built-in newsreading capabilities of Netscape are your best bet. You can select Directory/Go to newsgroups from the menu and browse through the outline of all the available newsgroups, or simply enter **news:** followed by a newsgroup name into the Location box if you already know what group you want to read. For example, Jan might enter:

news:alt.binaries.pictures.animals

which would bring up the list of recent "articles" shown in Figure 23.26.

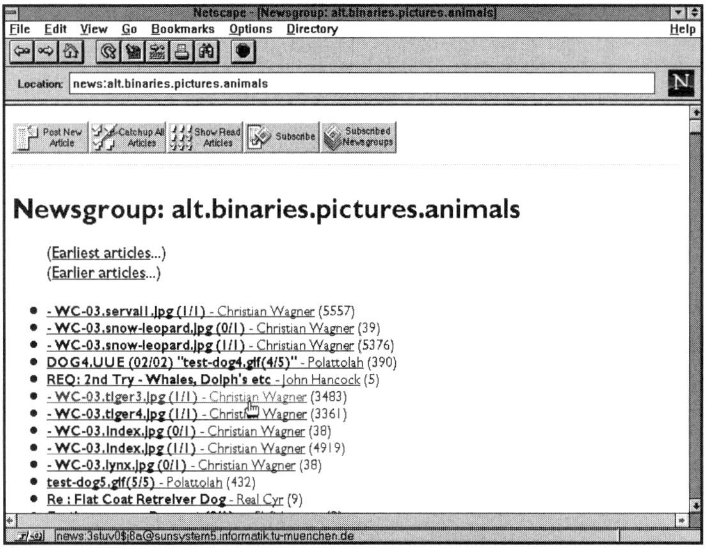

Figure 23.26

You can use Netscape to read newsgroups, including groups like this one, which feature images instead of text discussions.

The articles on "binaries" newsgroups are sometimes text and sometimes encoded non-text files. On "graphics.binaries" newsgroups, text messages are customarily limited to requests for images and brief comments on images. For example, the article entitled "REQ: 2nd Try - Whales, Dolph's etc" is a text message requesting whale and dolphin pictures. Its small size (in parentheses after the title) confirms that it doesn't contain a graphics file. Most of the other messages shown in Figure 23.26 are encoded images.

The subject of an image is usually, though not always, pretty obvious from the title. If Jan was thinking "Tiger," for instance, she might click on "WC-03.tiger3.jpg." The resulting download is shown in Figure 23.27.

Figure 23.27

At first glance, this "image file" doesn't look much like an image file at all.

Did she make a mistake? This looks like C source code, not an encoded image. No, the source code is just a little routine to decode the picture on a UNIX machine if you don't already have a decoding program. Scrolling down a bit (see Figure 23.28) reveals the telltale "random junk" that comprises the actual encoded image data.

Most pictures posted to newsgroups don't contain the C source code—they assume you already have a decoding program, and just include the image itself encoded in uuencode format. Jan knows of course that uuencoding is by far the most common encoding used on newsgroups, so when she saves the message to a file (see Figure 23.29), she gives it the .uue extension that her decoding program will expect.

To turn the promise of an image into a viewable picture, Jan would turn to Information Transfer Pro again. It will handle uuencoded files as easily as MIME files. (Actually, the actual encoding used in MIME files is a variation on uuencoding. But you needn't worry about that sort of picky business.) In fact, the procedure for decoding a uuencoded file is exactly the same as explained earlier for decoding a MIME file. Just select File/Decode (see Figure 23.30), specify a file name to give the decoded image (see Figure 23.31), and away you go.

Figure 23.28

Under the short source code—
which you can safely ignore—is
the actual encoded image.

Figure 23.29

When you save uuencoded
images from newsgroups, give
the file an extension of .uue.

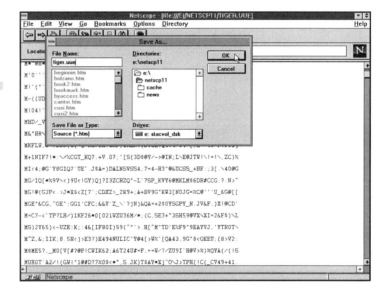

Most dedicated newsreader programs will handle encoding and decoding of images automatically. If you frequent the graphics newsgroups, you should install and try out the WinVN (for Windows) and Nuntius (for the Mac) newsreaders included on the CD-ROM with this book.

Figure 23.30

Information Transfer Professional will decode newsgroup files in a snap.

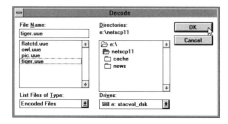

Figure 23.31

Be sure to give the DOS file name the appropriate extension for the image type you downloaded—in this case, it should be .jpg.

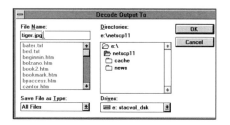

Once the image is decoded, it may be viewed in any graphics program capable of loading JPEG images. You can even load it right in Netscape to have a quick peek at it: just enter **file:///** (that's three slashes, not two) in the Location box, followed by the drive and directory name of the file. Use a | (vertical bar) after the drive letter instead of : because the colon has a different usage in Internet URLs. Figure 23.32 shows the tiger image displayed in Netscape.

With a bit of cropping and color correction in her favorite graphics program (PaintShop Pro would work fine), Jan might just have the perfect image to call me home.

Figure 23.32

Netscape displays the tiger liberated from the text file.

Encoding Graphics for E-mail

Even though this chapter is supposed to be about getting graphics, while we're at it let's explore how to send graphics through e-mail and newsgroups as well. Again Information Transfer Pro (or MPack on the Mac) should be your tool of choice for encoding if your e-mail program doesn't have MIME and uuencoding capabilities built in.

Basically, encoding works just like decoding with one added step: telling the Information Transfer Pro software which encoding method to use. Select Configure/Encode and you'll get the dialog box shown in Figure 23.33. For e-mail transfers, just pick MIME as the Encode Method. For posting to newsgroups, pick UU as the Encode Method. Don't use the XX encoding method—nobody really does anymore. Generally, you will want to pick DOS/Windows under End of Line string unless someone specifically asks you to pick UNIX (most UNIX decoders will work fine with the DOS/Windows end of line string anyway).

For MIME transfers, that's all there is to it, but for uuencoding you have a ton of options for the Encode File Format. For starters, just stick with Single File.

NOTE If you plan to post to a newsgroup, be sure to read its FAQ (Frequently Asked Questions) document to see what format is preferred on that particular newsgroup. You should also download several files and make sure the files you plan to upload are formatted in the same way.

Click on Configure to use the encoding method you've chosen just once, or click on Save to use it as the default encoding method from now on. Then select File/Encode (see Figure 23.34), choose the file, confirm the name for the encoded file, and you're done.

Figure 23.33

Before you encode a graphics file for transmission through e-mail, be sure to pick the MIME encoding method on the Configure/Encode dialog box.

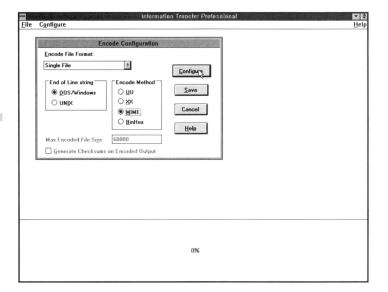

Figure 23.34

Encoding a file is as simple as pointing to it.

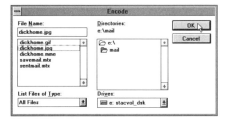

The encoded file can be loaded into any e-mail program and sent as if it was an ordinary text file. Most e-mail software allows you to specify a text file to send simply by giving the name and location of the file on your hard drive. For example, Jan could send her encoded picture to me using CompuServe's WinCIM software as shown in Figure 23.35.

NOTE The Information Transfer Pro software also supports a fairly common form of encoding called BinHex. If you get mail that includes the word "BinHex" in the first few lines of the message, or if you download a file from the Internet with the extension .hqx, just feed it to Information Transfer Pro just as you would a MIME file. (Mac users are especially likely to send you BinHex files, and all Mac decoding software supports BinHex.)

Summary

In this chapter, you've seen how to get graphics files through every major Internet service. You've also seen how to handle all common (and a few not-so-common) graphics file storage and compression formats.

Now that you can get graphics from the Net in every conceivable way, the next chapter will give you some pointers (and software) for viewing, manipulating, altering, printing, and otherwise enjoying the graphics once you've got them. You'll learn to handle sound, movies, and interactive 3D virtual reality, too.

Meanwhile, I'd better get home. Who knows what Jan will e-mail me next, and besides—I can smell dinner through the window of the office (which is attached to our house).

24

Viewing and Using Graphics from the Net

In This Chapter

➤ *Configuring and using graphics viewer software*

➤ *Motion video, sound, and 3D "virtual reality" on the Net*

➤ *Enhancing, correcting, and manipulating images*

➤ *Printing graphics yourself and using service bureaus*

➤ *Using graphics from the Net with other programs*

In Other Chapters

◄ *For information on graphics file formats and conversions, see Chapter 23.*

➤ *You'll find more on using graphics software to create images in Chapter 25.*

Introduction

I've read (and written) quite a few thick books that could have sported the title "Viewing and Using Graphics." Because just about every type of graphics you could want is out there on the Net, this chapter could get big fast. But I'm restraining myself: Here, I stick to the bare essentials of what everyone who gets graphics from the Net ought to know, and cover only a few of the very best graphics utilities. If you want more in-depth coverage of graphics tools and techniques, you may want to check out a more comprehensive book such as my *Tricks of the Graphics Gurus* or *PC Graphics Unleashed*, both from Sams Publishing.

Seeing What You Got: Graphics Viewers

Chapter 23 explains how to get graphics from the Internet. But graphics have to be seen to be of much use. The following sections will help you get your graphics files from your hard drive to your screen where you can enjoy them.

Offline Viewer Programs

There are hundreds of graphics viewer programs. The venerable Windows Paintbrush (or even more venerable MacPaint) is one that you almost certainly already have, and any graphics pro has five or six more programs that can view graphics files. In this chapter, I'm going to use three programs—ACDSee, LView Pro, and PaintShop Pro—as examples of the type of graphics programs that you'll need to deal with the graphics you get from the Net. But if you're an avid user of CorelDRAW!, Photoshop, or any other major graphics package, you can do almost everything described with your favorite software.

Online Viewer Programs

There are two exceptions worthy of note: real-time online viewing and format conversion. Though many packages can serve these functions in a pinch, few have the versatility of PaintShop Pro when it comes to converting between the plethora of graphics file formats you may encounter on the Net. And no graphics program I've ever seen (including PaintShop Pro) works as well as ACDSee or LView Pro when it comes to online viewing.

In this chapter, I explain why the choice between ACDSee and LView Pro depends on your individual setup. But I strongly recommend that you try out all of these programs (which are on the CD with this book), even if you already have some software that duplicates their functions. You may find it well worth the modest shareware registration fees ($15 for ACDSee, $30 for LView Pro, and $69 for PaintShop Pro) just for the extra convenience and power that these utilities offer when handling graphics from the Net. You may also find that the virtues of PaintShop Pro lure you away from far more expensive programs!

NOTE ▶ ACDSee, LView Pro, and PaintShop Pro are all Windows programs. Mac users will enjoy similar functionality in the JPEGView, NIH Image, and GraphicConverter software, which are all on the CD-ROM as well. (Note that JPEGView can view several types of graphics files, not just JPEGs!) I'll use the Windows programs as examples in this chapter, but users of other operating systems and graphics programs should find it quite easy to locate the corresponding menu choices in their software.

Netscape's Internal Viewer

Before I go into the details of configuring an online viewer, let me make one thing clear: You don't absolutely need a separate online viewer program to get graphics from the Net. Netscape and most other Web browsers can view JPEG, GIF, and a couple of other less common types of images without any additional software. Web browsers and file transfer programs can also download any graphics file to your hard drive even if they don't have the ability to view that type of file. So in the discussion that follows, we're talking about convenience and efficiency more than necessity. Of course, there's a lot to be said for convenience and efficiency—especially if you're paying (or being paid) to access graphics on the Net.

Netscape gives you the ability to see JPEG and GIF images immediately as you download them. What an external online viewer gives you is the ability to see other graphics file formats, such as PNG, PCX, and TIF files. You can also set up Netscape (or any Web browser) to use an external viewer program for JPEG and GIF files. You should know the advantages and disadvantages of doing this.

External Viewer Programs

First, however, you should see what it actually looks like to use an online viewer with Netscape. Figure 24.1 shows a Web page with a small graphics image linked to a larger, high-resolution version of the same image. When I configured Netscape to use an external viewer (you'll learn how to do that shortly) and clicked on the image link, a small "Viewing Location" dialog box with a progress bar pops up as the image downloads. When the download is complete, a separate Window appears with the full-sized image in it (see Figure 24.2). This window is actually created by the viewer program, not Netscape itself.

Figure 24.1

When Netscape uses an external viewer program, you will see a progress dialog box as images download.

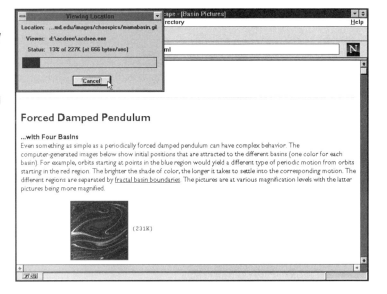

Contrast this with what happens when Netscape's own internal viewing is enabled. As Figure 24.3 shows, you can see the partial image take shape as it is downloading instead of seeing only a progress bar until the download is complete. Seeing the partial image as it comes to you can be a real time-saver, especially if you decide after seeing a little bit that it isn't worth finishing the download. Another advantage of using Netscape's built-in viewer is that the image appears right in the Netscape window and does not hide the location box and navigation buttons.

Figure 24.2

After the download is complete, the viewer program displays the image in a separate window.

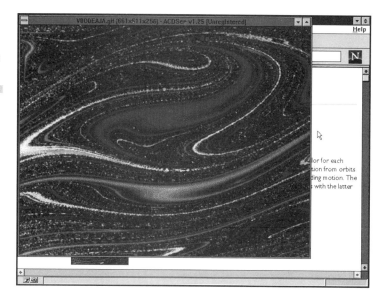

Figure 24.3

When you don't use an external viewer, you can see the image appear gradually as it downloads.

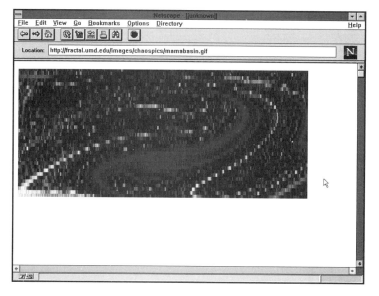

So why would you ever want to use an external viewer for JPEG and GIF images? Because some viewers, such as LView Pro and PaintShop Pro, give you tools for adjusting the color balance, contrast, and other qualities of an image before you save it to your hard disk. They also allow you to convert color images to grayscale, and complete many other handy image processing tasks. (Exactly how to do these tasks is covered later in this chapter.) You may find it quite convenient to be able to correct and enhance images immediately as you download them. If so, using an external viewer may be a good choice for you. I personally prefer to wait and do all my image processing after I disconnect from the Net, so I use Netscape's internal viewer.

Choosing an External Viewer

There are several common file types that Netscape's internal viewer can't handle, though. For these, configuring an external viewer is usually much better than simply saving them, sight unseen, on your hard drive. So now you have another choice: which external viewer program to use. There are dozens available, but two stand out as by far the best for Windows users: ACDSee and LView Pro. Each of these has strong advantages and disadvantages, which you need to understand to make an intelligent choice.

ACDSee

ACDSee is faster, smaller, and less expensive to register than LView Pro. I prefer it as my online viewer for three reasons:

▼ It supports PNG files, which LView Pro version 1.B does not yet support (this may change soon, and PaintShop Pro does also support PNG).

▼ It's much faster than LView Pro—which matters when you pay for Net access by the hour, as I do.

▼ The shareware registration fee is only $15, instead of $30 for LView Pro.

ACDSee also has a great directory browsing and image preview interface for selecting and viewing images on your hard drive when you're not online.

LView Pro

LView Pro has compelling advantages over ACDSee, too. These include:

▼ It allows you to save files by choosing Save As after a download.

▼ LView Pro has many image processing functions built in.

▼ LView Pro supports some UNIX portable bitmap formats (.ppm and .pbm files), which ACDSee doesn't.

TIP Now saving files may seem crucial—isn't that the whole point of downloading them from the Net? Yes, but I know a secret. It just so happens that Netscape automatically transfers files to a "temporary" directory on your hard drive (and leaves them there permanently) every time it sends a graphics file to an external viewer. So ACDSee's lack of a Save command isn't absolutely devastating. The files get saved, even though Netscape doesn't tell you about it. You just have to remember to go to the directory specified under Options/Preferences/Applications and Directories/Temporary Directory (usually "c:\temp") and move or rename the files you want. But it is awfully nice to be able to save the images just where you want them, with the file names you choose, while you're online instead of having to move them later.

Figure 24.4 shows LView Pro in action. Notice that there is a menu bar from which you can save, edit, and retouch images. As Figure 24.2 revealed, ACDSee doesn't have any menu bar at all.

The image processing functions of LView Pro are also very nice. You can adjust the color balance, brightness, contrast, sharpness, "gamma" values, and other image characteristics immediately, even before you save an image. LView Pro also allows you to save all images in JPEG format (or whatever your favorite graphics file format may be), no matter what format they were stored in on the Net, and gives you complete control over the compressed size and quality of JPEG images.

The image processing capabilities of LView Pro largely overlap PaintShop Pro (which is covered later in this chapter), so you may be able to get by with LView Pro as your only image processing program if you don't do a lot of sophisticated enhancement work. If I had to pick just one program handling graphics from the Net, LView Pro would probably be it.

Figure 24.4

LView Pro allows you to save and retouch images in any format you like immediately after downloading them.

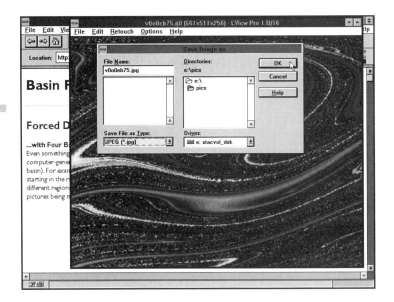

But I don't have to pick just one, and I don't mind sorting graphics files after I get offline if it means maximum speed when I'm online. So I generally don't use LView Pro at all except when I'm producing images for my own Web pages (see note). Instead, I use Netscape to view JPEGs and GIFs online, ACDSee for online viewing of other file formats, and PaintShop Pro (plus an arsenal of other commercial graphics programs) for image processing work.

NOTE LView Pro also has several unique features that you will find essential if you plan to produce images for posting on the World Wide Web. (Chapter 25 covers these features in depth.)

Programs change and new ones arrive constantly, so these are not necessarily long-term choices. If there's a moral to this story, it's that carefully choosing your graphics tools according to your own individual needs is often better than simply adopting a one-size-fits all program.

Enough agonizing over decisions. In the following few paragraphs and figures, you'll learn how to set up Netscape to use ACDSee as an online viewer for all the file formats it supports other than JPEG and GIF. If you decided to go with LView Pro instead, or if you're using a Mac viewer such as JPEGView, simply enter that program's location and name where "ACDSee" is specified.

Configuring Netscape To Use an External Viewer

NOTE The instructions that follow are for Netscape Navigator version 1.2b1. If you are using version 1.1 or 1.0, the configuration screens will look quite different, but the general procedure is the same.

Of course, other browser programs such as Microsoft Internet Explorer have quite different looking configuration screens. If you're using a browser other than Netscape, consult your documentation for help configuring it.

External viewer programs are called "helper applications" in Netscape. To choose which programs Netscape calls on to view various types of files:

1. Select Options/Preferences and click on the Helper Apps tab. You will see a list of file types.

2. Scroll down and click on image/tiff. It will highlight as shown in Figure 24.5.

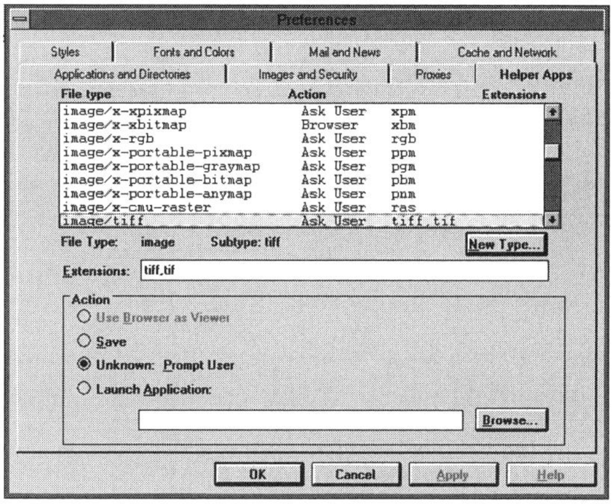

Figure 24.5

Netscape's Options/Preferences/Helper Apps dialog box allows you to configure online viewers.

3. In the Action section below the list, choose Launch Application.

4. You can either enter the path and file name for the acdsee.exe program or click on Browse and navigate to it on your hard drive as shown in Figure 24.6. Click on OK.

Figure 24.6

To choose a viewer, first pick a file type, then select Launch Application and Browse.

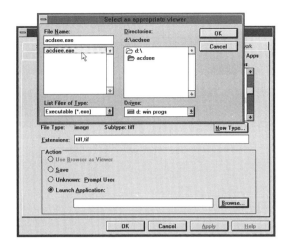

Netscape doesn't have a predefined file type for the other image types that ACDSee can view, so you'll need to create one.

1. Click on New Type. Enter image as the Mime type and other as the Mime SubType, as shown in Figure 24.7. Then click on OK.

Figure 24.7

To specify a viewer for image types not already on the list, you'll need to click on New Type.

2. Enter the following in the Extensions box:
   png,pcx,tga,bmp,pcd

3. Choose Action/Launch Application and specify the path and file name acdsee.exe as you did in step 4 in the preceding list.

4. Your screen should look similar to Figure 24.8. Click on OK.

Figure 24.8

For new Mime types, you need to specify the file Extensions that the viewer can accept.

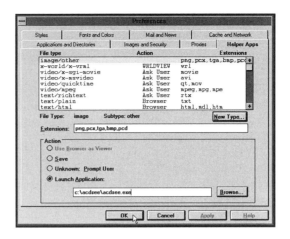

Netscape will now use its own internal viewer for JPEG and GIF files, and automatically send TIF, PNG, PCX, TGA, BMP, and Photo-CD files to ACDSee for online viewing.

Multimedia and 3D Viewers

You can set up online viewers for more than just graphics files. In fact, Netscape and other Web browsers will let you set up an online viewer for any kind of data file whatsoever. Motion video and sound files are becoming increasingly common on the Net, and experimental 3D "virtual reality" is beginning to appear online as well.

Multimedia File Formats

There are four types of motion video files that you're likely to encounter: On the PC, Autodesk flic (FLI and FLC) files and Microsoft Audio/Video Interleave (AVI) files are the most used. On the Mac, QuickTime (QT) files are the norm, and the Motion Picture Expert's Group (MPEG) format is an increasingly popular cross-platform standard. Unfortunately, I don't know of a single inexpensive viewer that can play back all these formats.

On Windows PCs, Microsoft's free Video for Windows utility (included on the CD-ROM with this book) comes close. It can handle FLI, FLC, and AVI files and a QuickTime extension is optional. There are some shareware programs, such as Media

Blast Off! and Multimedia Swiss Army Knife (both also on the CD-ROM) that try to replace and improve on Microsoft's media player. Unfortunately, the current versions of all the AVI utilities I've seen are either buggy or more cumbersome to use than the software they're aiming to replace (in my personal opinion). You might want to try these utilities anyway—some folks I know do prefer them and haven't experienced any problems with them. Or you might decide to be an old fuddy-duddy like me and stick with the plain-vanilla Microsoft Media Player.

NOTE The version of Video for Windows included on the CD-ROM with this book is for Windows version 3.1. A similar media player comes included with Windows 95.

Neither the Microsoft Media Player nor any of its competitors currently support MPEG, which is by far the most popular video format on the Net. Fortunately, there is an excellent MPEG viewer that works great with Netscape. In fact, there are two good Windows MPEG players, called MPEGPLAY and VMPEG. An excellent MPEG player for the Mac is called Sparkle. All of these are included on the CD-ROM with this book.

For PC users, I strongly recommend VMPEG because it is much faster than MPEGPLAY. It also doesn't require the 32-bit extensions to Windows, which MPEGPLAY needs and which can cause problems on some machines. Furthermore, the demonstration version of MPEGPLAY is limited to files smaller than 1Mb (which isn't very big for a video file). The only limitation on the demo version of VMPEG is that it will only play the first 15 seconds of sound, and the rest of the video is silent. Since many MPEGs on the Net don't even have sound tracks, this isn't that big a deal (but it's a good incentive to register for the full version of VMPEG!).

The AVI, QuickTime, and MPEG video formats all support sound tracks synchronized to the video sequence. You may also wish to play sound-only files, which commonly come in one of two formats: Windows waveform (WAV) files, or UNIX audio (AU, SND, or AIFF) files. The standard Windows media player will handle WAV files, and Netscape comes with a built-in player for AU, SND, and AIFF files. If you have trouble with these players (some sound cards are less "100% compatible" than others), you can try using the shareware WHAM and WPLANY sound players included on the CD-ROM instead.

Configuring Netscape for Multimedia

You can configure Netscape to use mulitmedia viewers exactly the same way you configured it to use an external graphics viewer (see Figure 24.9):

1. Select Options/Preferences, and click on the Helper Apps tab.

2. Choose a MIME file type from the list.

3. Select Launch Application, and type in or Browse to the viewer for that file type.

Most viewers will be installed in their own subdirectory, but the Microsoft Media Player will be in your Windows directory (usually c:\windows) under the name mplayer.exe.

Figure 24.9
Multimedia "helper applications" can be set up in Netscape just as easily as graphics viewers.

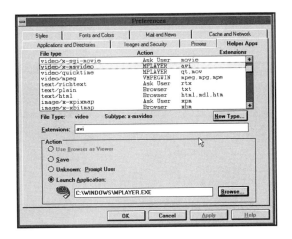

TIP If you have a modem connection (rather than a high-speed network connection) to the Net, you may be better off not configuring Netscape to use multimedia viewers. Why? Because video and sound files are usually very large and take a while to download and view. If you configure Netscape to simply save them for later viewing (after you get offline), you'll save both time and money. Also, many multimedia viewers don't have "save" functions, so the videos you view with them online only get saved to your "temporary" directory.

Figures 24.10 and 24.11 show VMPEG and the Video for Windows media player as they appear when invoked by Netscape. VMPEG plays the video in a small window (optionally magnified to four times its actual size). Depending on your hardware configuration, Microsoft media player will either play in a Window or darken the entire screen and play the video in the center of this black backdrop.

Figure 24.10

VMPEG gives you a control bar in one window, and plays the video in another.

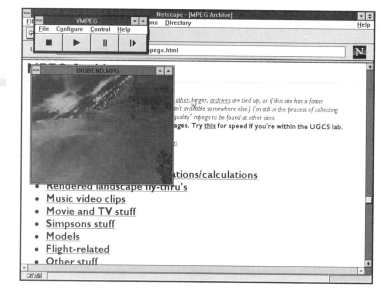

Figure 24.11

Microsoft's media player shows the first frame of the video in a window, but switches to a full-screen view when you hit the play button.

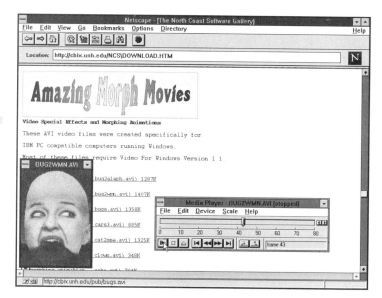

3D Virtual Reality on the Net

Extending the flat universe of the World Wide Web into three dimensions is an exciting prospect. Imagine what "surfing the Net" would be like if instead of clicking on text links you could walk down a realistic rendering of a corridor, click on a doorway, and enter a 3D room located inside a distant computer. This type of interactive network of "virtual realities" isn't here yet, but it's coming fast. A number of browser programs running on powerful Silicon Graphics workstations can now simulate very realistic worlds in real time as they download them from remote computers.

The first official standard has even been published for a Virtual Reality Modeling Language (VRML), which does for 3D worlds what the Web's HTML standard does for text. VRML demands a lot from your computer's processor to render the models. However, the amount of data that actually has to travel over the Net is quite small, since models and worlds are succinctly described by mathematical surfaces. This means that VR on the Net is actually faster and more practical than transferring "plain old" video files.

Unfortunately, Windows and Mac machines aren't quite powerful enough yet to handle the 3D rendering involved in serious Internet-based VR. But they're oooh so close! In fact, a preliminary version of the first Windows-based VRML browser is already publicly available. The alpha-test version is shown in Figure 24.12, but by the time this book gets printed you should be able to download the beta-test version of WorldView from:

http://www.webmaster.com:80/vrml/

Several VRML models and worlds come with WorldView, and additional models (including the mock-up of the Star Trek space ship Reliant shown in Figure 24.12) can be found at:

http://www.vrml.com/models/

If you want to ride the cutting edge of Net technology (and you have a 486/50 or faster computer), get WorldView and install a new Mime type called x-world with a sub-type x-vrml on the Netscape Helper Apps.

Hot links between VRML models and worlds weren't yet implemented when this chapter was written. But the complete and easy-to-use interactive navigation controls let you fly around and through models, and you can even use World View as a stand-alone Winsock-compatible browser without Netscape. Doing so would be a bit futile since there is currently only one place on the Net to go—but if there were more .wrl sites, you could go to them! And there will definitely be many more by the time you read this.

So keep your eyes peeled for the coming explosion of interactive 3D on the Net. Meanwhile, the rest of this chapter returns from the futuristic land of Virtual Reality to the present-day reality of using 2D graphics. After some pointers on how to enhance and process the images you download from the Net, you'll also get some tips on printing and using graphics in other software.

Figure 24.12

Virtual Reality on the Web is here! A preliminary testing version of WorldView for Windows is now available for free.

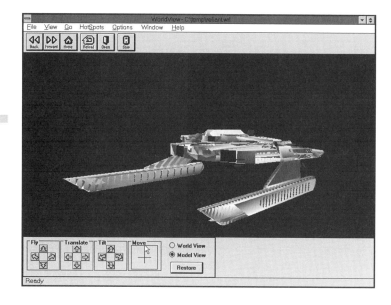

Retouching Images

A comprehensive tutorial on the delicate art of image retouching is obviously beyond the scope of this book. Still, you don't have to be a highly trained professional to learn the basics of correcting and enhancing images. And many of the graphics you may find on the Net will be sorely in need of some repair work if you hope to print them or even use them for on-screen viewing. The quick-and-dirty run down that follows isn't going to qualify you for a degree in graphics arts, but it will show you how to use PaintShop Pro or a comparable graphics program to make almost any image better suit your needs. Of course, you can use the same software and techniques to improve any images that you plan to put on the Net, as well.

Color Correction

Almost all photographs, and many computer-generated pictures, can benefit from color correction. This tends to be especially true of images from the Net because you will often want to look at them on your computer screen and then print them—perhaps on a relatively low resolution black-and-white laser printer or low-end color inkjet. Each of these devices requires vastly different color adjustments. A good looking screen image may be almost solid black when printed on your laser, and an image designed to be printed on paper will almost always look bleak and washed-out when viewed on a monitor.

There are also plenty of poorly scanned snapshots on the Net that need color correction to look good on any display device or printer. As a worst-case scenario, let's say you got hold of one of those and really wanted to use it. For example, Figure 24.13 is a rather flat image of a flat-coated retriever that I retrieved from the alt.binaries.pictures.animals newsgroup. Pictures of flat-coated retrievers are hard to come by (this one was actually posted in response to a request by someone), so if one wanted a masthead for the Flat-Coated Retriever Breeder's Journal one might just have to make do with this rather poor shot.

I don't know this dog's name and "the flat-coated retriever" may get a bit stale after a while, so I'll refer to it by the nickname of a similar looking dog I once knew: "Fry-Brain." (He got the name because he liked to keep his head under the woodstove until he singed all the hair off the top. He moved kinda slow after the first winter of that, but he was still a gentle and friendly sort of fellow.) There wasn't much they could do for the original Fry-Brain, but we can bring this one into PaintShop Pro for some graphical grooming (see Figure 24.14).

Figure 24.13
A bad picture of a good dog.

Brightness and Contrast Enhancement

Fry-Brain's primary problem is that he's too dark. In PaintShop Pro, the Colors menu and the Colors/Adjust sub-menu give several options. You might be tempted to rush right in and select Brightness/Contrast, which could certainly do Fry-Brain some good. But there are a few other choices you should consider as well. To consider them intelligently, you should carefully take note of the range of tones in the image, rather than simply glancing at it and pronouncing it "dark."

TIP For simplicity, I'll treat this as if it were a grayscale picture. However, it is generally a good idea to correct a color image before you turn it into a grayscale image, even if you plan to print it on a black-and-white printer. Converting to gray before you balance the image can result in some degradation of an image due to the combining of similar-valued colors into a single shade of gray. By optimizing the image first, you can often bring out distinctions between subtle shades that will then be retained when you eventually convert to gray.

Figure 24.14

*PaintShop Pro can do all the
tricks you'll need to make this
unusable image acceptable.*

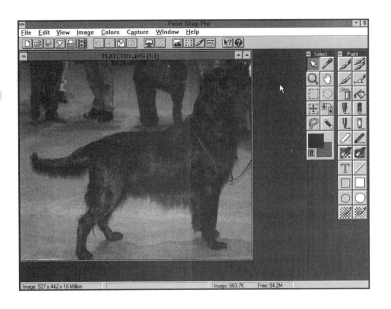

When you look closely, you'll notice that Fry-Brain appears
too dark for specific reasons:

▼ Fry-Brain's coat lacks highlights.

▼ In between his darkest and lightest, Fry-Brain has a very
small range of tones.

These distinctions may seem like hair-splitting, but they are
actually essential in adapting an image for successful printing,
especially on a low-resolution output device like a laser printer.
(Even 600 dots-per-inch is considered low-resolution when
you're printing grayscale images.) To see the range of tonal
values in an image, you can select View/Histogram Window.
The histogram is a graph of the relative amount of each brightness level in the image, as shown in Figure 24.15.

The histogram of a good image almost always covers the
entire range of tones from the far left of the graph to the far
right. You can see from Figure 24.15 that Fry-Brain's histogram
is bunched in two very small areas. In the next few figures,
you'll see how each of the available color adjustment controls
affects the image and its histogram.

Figure 24.15

Opening the Histogram Window gives you a graph of the relative brightness of an image.

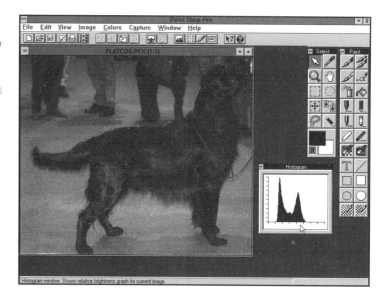

TIP From this point, the figures show the images (and the histogram) after I pressed OK for the corresponding color adjustment. You won't see this change until after you click on OK. (To make these illustrations easier to follow, I just opened the same control a second time and specified the same adjustment.)

Also note that I went back to the original, unmodified image before each adjustment shown. So this series of images represents different alternatives for correcting the image, rather than subsequent corrections applied one after the other.

Adjusting the brightness and contrast are intuitively the easiest corrections to apply, and are quite effective for many images. As you might expect, increasing the brightness simply moves the entire histogram to the right and increasing the contrast spreads the histogram out horizontally. Figure 24.16 shows the Brightness/Contrast control from the Colors/Adjust menu of PaintShop Pro, along with the results on the image and its histogram. (Compare this and the subsequent figures with Figure 24.15 to see how each adjustment changes the original image and histogram.)

Figure 24.16

A small preview image lets you see what you're doing when you make color adjustments in PaintShop Pro.

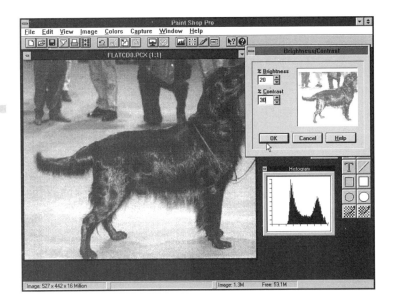

Gamma Correction

Another common tool for adjusting the balance of light and dark in an image is gamma correction. If you choose Gamma Correction from PaintShop Pro's Colors/Adjust menu, you are asked to specify a single number between 0 and 5 as a correction factor. Numbers greater than 1 will brighten the image, while numbers less than 1 will darken it. The difference between this and direct brightness control is that gamma correction achieves its results by changing the "shape" of the histogram rather than simply shifting it to the left or right. For example, notice that the gamma correction of 2.0 shown in Figure 24.17 increases the relative amount of light tones, rather than simply making all the tones lighter. This can be important, since simply shifting a dark image too far to the right can lose information by turning a range of light colors all pure white. Gamma correction keeps all the tones distinct, but changes their values.

If this distinction still seems a bit elusive, don't worry too much about it. As you work with images, try gamma correcting a few and you'll start to get the feel of which images benefit from it. Generally, gamma correction alone will leave an image too "flat," as Figure 24.17 demonstrates. So gamma correction is usually most helpful when used in conjunction with contrast enhancement. The pros will often use the combination of gamma correction/contrast instead of the more obvious combination of brightness/contrast. Gamma correction is also often used as a final step in adjusting for a particular printer, which may print certain tones too dark or too light.

Figure 24.17

Gamma correction is more subtle—but generally more useful in conjunction with other corrective measures—than simple brightness adjustment.

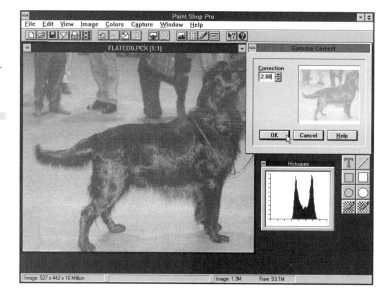

Tonal Corrections

When you start getting used to looking at histograms and correcting images' tonal range, you may start to think in terms of specific regions of the histogram and their role in the overall image. The brighter tones, or highlights, tend to add spark and character, while the darker tones, or shadows, provide the visual anchor and underlying mood. In between are the midtones, which give an image a pleasing range of tonal variety. With the Highlight/MidTone/Shadow control on the Colors/Adjust menu, you can manipulate each of these regions independently or in conjunction with one another. This takes a bit of practice to get used to, but is the most powerful way to really improve most images.

Essentially, these controls let you horizontally stretch the histogram any way you like. When the control box pops up, Highlight will be set at 100%, MidTone at 50% and Shadow at 0%. If you leave them at those values, the image will not change at all. But if you set Highlight to, say 80%, then the rightmost part of the histogram will be "pulled" to the right, making the bright tones brighter and turning any tones in far right 20% of the graph to pure white. Similarly, if you set Shadow to 20%, the bottom part of the histogram will stretch to the left and the dark tones will get darker. Changing the MidTone setting pulls the center of the histogram to the left or right, making the middle range of tones either darker (for settings below 50%) or brighter (for settings above 50%).

If I were going to prepare Fry-Brain for output on my laser printer or a printing press, I would start with Highlight/MidTone/Shadow adjustments and then apply slight contrast enhancement and gamma correction. Figure 24.18 shows Highlight, MidTone, and Shadow values that significantly improve the image by spreading the histogram out nicely.

Figure 24.18

Adjusting the highlights, midtones, and shadows gives you more flexibility than simple brightness and contrast controls can provide.

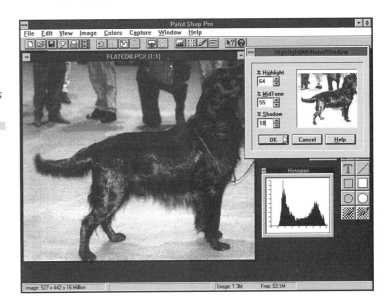

Correcting Color Images

There are two more color correction tools available in PaintShop Pro (and most other photo editing programs), but they are primarily for full-color rather than grayscale images. Even though the figures shown here are not color, we'll discuss these controls anyway. Most images on the Net are in color, so you will probably need to use color correction as often as tonal corrections.

Figure 24.19

The standard Windows color selector uses hue, saturation, and luminance to navigate through color space.

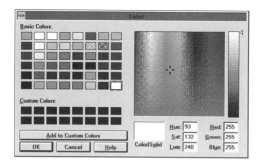

When you select Hue/Saturation/Luminance from the Colors/Adjust menu in PaintShop Pro, you get a control box like the one shown in Figure 24.20. By adjusting the settings for % Hue, Saturation, and Luminance, you can move your whole image through "color space" to a more desirable location. Increasing the luminance is essentially the same as brightening the image. Saturation controls the richness of color, and you will often find that photographic images benefit greatly from increased saturation. Adjusting the hue allows you to eliminate a "color cast" that may have come from the film or lighting conditions where a photo was taken, or to deliberately give the image an artificial or surreal coloring.

Since Fry-Brain is predominantly black, this image didn't need much color correction other than bumping the luminance way up. I also pulled the hue over a little bit to make the ground brown instead of pale green, and enriched the colors slightly by increasing the saturation.

Hue, Saturation, and Luminance aren't the only way to describe color. Any image can be represented on a computer screen or TV by combining the three primary colors: red, green, and blue.

In fact, since RGB is what your computer monitor uses, you may prefer (as I usually do) to adjust the RGB values of a photo rather than the HSL values. Figure 24.21 shows the Red/Green/Blue controls from the Colors/Adjust menu.

Figure 24.20

By adjusting hue, saturation, and luminance you can eliminate color problems in an image.

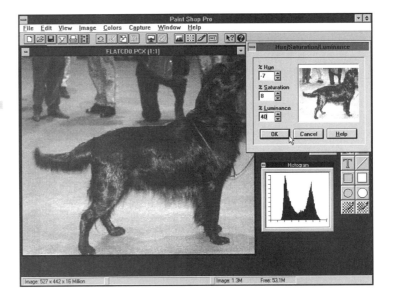

Figure 24.21

Red, green, and blue adjustments are theoretically equivalent to hue, saturation, and luminance adjustments, but require a different intuitive way of seeing images.

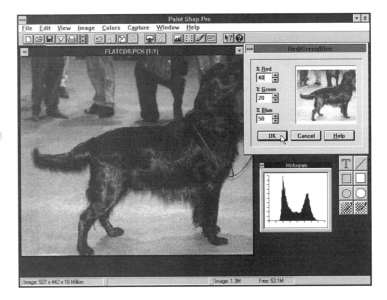

TIP Using red, green, and blue to "make" colors is actually a trick, based on the physiology of the red, green, and blue receptors in our eyes. (An image which appears yellow on TV may actually emit no light in the "yellow" region of the physical spectrum; It just fools your eye by stimulating the same receptors that real yellow light would stimulate. As you can see, there's more to color than meets the eye.)

To represent an image on a reflective surface such as a piece of paper or canvas, you can use a combination of cyan, magenta, and yellow pigments (informally called blue, red, and yellow by some artists). Printers usually also add black ink to make up for the inaccuracies of low-luminance colors when printed with the three secondary-color inks. This way of creating color is called cyan, magenta, yellow, black (CMYK). PaintShop Pro does not directly support CMYK color manipulation and separation, but all high-end commercial graphics programs do.

Equalization

Having just graduated from Dick Oliver's crash correspondence course in color theory, you may be feeling like color correction is either an attractive career choice or a quagmire to be avoided. You might also wonder if some of this could be automated somehow. If the basic idea for most images is merely to spread out the histogram to use the full range of tonal values, why can't the computer just figure it out and do it for you? Well, it can—quite often with spectacular results. Alas, at other times the results are disastrous, and some hand correction is almost always necessary.

To automatically redistribute the tones in your image over the entire histogram, select Colors/Histogram Functions/Equalize. Fry-Brain's response to this (see Figure 24.22) is typical: the range of tones is dramatically improved, but there weren't enough colors in the image to fill all the "gaps" that stretching the histogram opened up. So the transitions between colors becomes too abrupt.

Selecting Colors/Histogram Functions/Stretch also stretches the histogram, but much more gently. Occasionally this is enough to correct an image completely, but usually it's more of a place to begin before further massaging with the other tools we've discussed. Figure 24.23 shows the result of stretching Fry-Brain's histogram twice. Even after two times, the difference between this and the original in Figure 24.15 is not very dramatic.

Figure 24.22

Equalizing the histogram dramatically improves some images and destroys others. For this one, the result was a mixed blessing.

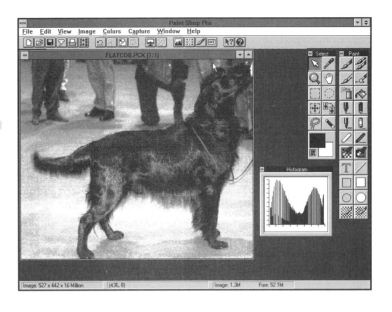

Figure 24.23

Stretching the histogram is gentler than equalizing it.

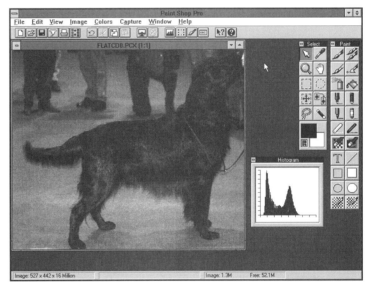

When used with the tone and color correction tools, equalization and histogram stretching are essential tools that can save you a lot of fussing and fiddling.

Image Enhancement and Filtering

A good photographer or publishing professional can do very impressive color correction in a traditional darkroom. Other forms of digital image enhancement, however, are difficult or impossible to do without a computer. Image filters based on a mathematical technique called "convolution" may seem especially magical in their ability to bring out detail, sharpen or soften edges, and automatically produce complex-looking special effects like embossing. But you don't have to understand the math or the magic to use filters. In fact, PaintShop Pro's Image/Filter Browser control (see Figure 24.24) makes it almost brainless to choose and apply a filter.

Figure 24.24

Use the filter browser to preview any of PaintShop Pro's image filters.

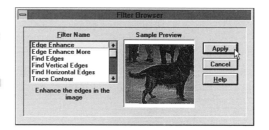

Because filters are so easy to use, I'm not going to ramble on about each one. Table 24.1 gives you an example of each type of filter. You should be able to tell from these examples and the filter browser which filter might do your image some good. When in doubt, try it! You can always select Edit/Undo afterward if you need to. I will mention that the edge filters give better results on images that aren't scanned with a hand scanner, as Fry-Brain appears to have been. The extra "noisy edges" are by-products of the scanning process.

Selecting and Painting

You might wonder how I isolated Fry-Brain from the background to make the example image used in Table 24.1. (Isolating a subject from its background becomes especially important when you want to produce Web pages. More on that in Chapter 25.)

The hard way would be to outline the dog with the "lasso" hand-selection tool. Given the irregular boundaries of a flat-coated retriever, that would be impossible with a mouse and tiresome with a drawing tablet.

An easier way would be to use the "magic wand" tool to automatically select a similarly colored area. In this image, Fry-Brain is fairly well contrasted with the background, so this approach has promise. By double-clicking the magic wand I could even adjust the tolerance to best capture the range of colors that distinguishes Fry-Brain from the ground. Selecting a region this way generally takes some trial-and-error to find the best tolerance, but in high-contrast images it can save a lot of work. Figure 24.25 shows the Magic Wand control box and tool, ready to make a selection.

Figure 24.25

The "Magic Wand" tool automatically selects a region based on color similarity.

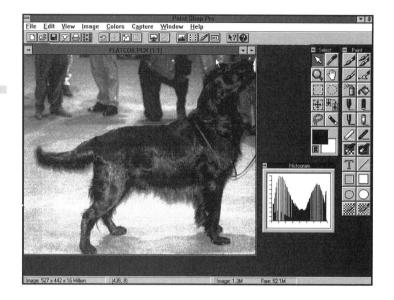

After highlighting Fry-Brain (and some unwanted but similarly colored background details) with the magic wand, I could then select Edit/Copy and Edit/Paste/As New Image to produce a cut-out picture as in Figure 24.26. By carefully tweaking the tolerance and using the other painting tools to smooth the edges, I could get a better outline than this. Figure 24.27 shows a start at this approach, but I didn't bother finishing because it was a lot of picky work and I could see that, for this particular image, there was a better way.

The better way in this case was to use the brightness and contrast controls to fade most of the background out to pure white. Figure 24.28 shows the result, which has much cleaner edges than any magic wand selection could achieve on a low-resolution image.

Table 24.1. Fry-Brain Gets Filtered

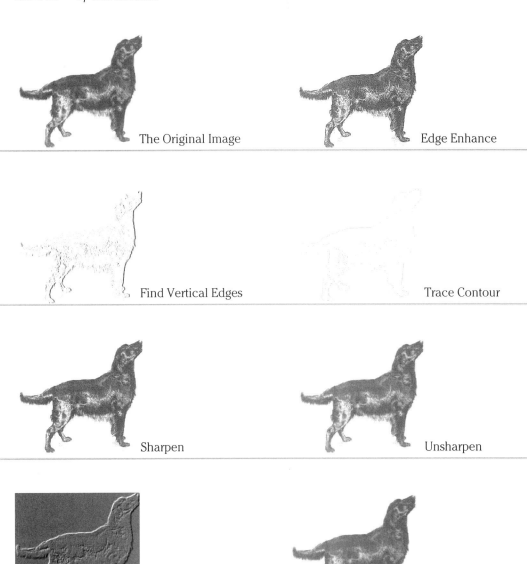

The Original Image

Edge Enhance

Find Vertical Edges

Trace Contour

Sharpen

Unsharpen

Emboss

Erode

Find Edges

Find
Horizontal Edges

Blur

Soften

Add Uniform Noise

Dilate

Median

Mosaic

Figure 24.26

By pasting a magic wand selection into a new image, you can cut a subject away from the background. Sort of.

Figure 24.27

Careful tuning of the magic wand tolerance and meticulous hand editing can liberate even the most complex object from any background.

Figure 24.28

Using brightness and contrast controls to "wash out" a light background sometimes works wonders that no magic wand can match.

NOTE All the tools mentioned in the following paragraph are on the select palette and paint palette on the right side of the PaintShop Pro main window. Similar tools are also found in almost every major image processing or photo editing program. For more details on how they work, consult the online help for PaintShop Pro or your favorite comparable software.

To remove the rest of the background, I first eliminated the people's legs and shadows with the rectangular selection tool, the lasso selection tool, and the Edit/Clear menu command. Then I went in by hand with the paintbrush and "push brush" tools to clear away the stuff around Fry-Brain's head. Finally, I touched up a bit with the softening tool to eliminate any jaggy edges. I chose to leave the small shadows under his feet, but I did use the image clone tool to get rid of that pesky leash. In Figure 24.29, Fry-Brain is finally free. With a bit more work, the edges could be improved, but you get the idea.

Figure 24.29

A bit of touching up with the painting tools and he's a free dog.

Deforming Images

Retouching images can be a lot of work. It can also be a lot of fun, and image deformation tools may be the most fun you can legally have with a computer (what with the new censor-the-Net craze and all). As with filters, PaintShop Pro gives you an interactive preview browser for deformations (see Figure 24.30). Since the results of these effects are almost always completely obvious even in the small preview window, using deformations is pretty much a no-brainer. Rather than waste paper talking about how to use them here, I'll simply give you Table 24.2 as a quick reference guide.

Figure 24.30

The deformation browser is your own computer-controlled funhouse mirror.

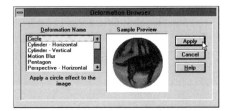

Not all image processing programs have as wide a variety of deformations as PaintShop Pro, but most have a few to play with at least. The Mac program NIH Image isn't quite as spiffy as PaintShop Pro in this regard, but it will help you accomplish most image processing tasks quite well.

Printing Graphics

You might not think of printing an image as something that takes much thought or preparation: you simply turn on your printer, select File/Print in your graphics program, and look at the paper as it comes out. On most Windows and Mac systems equipped with a decent laser printer, this quick-and-dirty approach works fine—if your objective is simply to see an acceptable black-and-white approximation of your image on paper. However, if your goal is to duplicate the printout or achieve the best possible print quality, a little extra thought and work can make a big difference.

Using a Service Bureau

The first choice you should think about is whether or not the printer on your desk can produce the level of quality you need. Though I'll show you some tricks to improve the quality of duplication from an ordinary laser printer and photocopier, few laser printers can do a professional-quality job of generating originals for duplication on an offset press. A 300 dot-per-inch (dpi) laser is barely acceptable for black-and-white "line art" and really not good enough for any but the most amateurish looking photographic or grayscale images. The current norm of 600dpi is fine for photos and artwork to be printed in an informal newsletter, but not suitable when a truly polished look is desired. (If you own a 1200dpi or higher resolution printer, you are a graphics pro who knows the ropes and probably doesn't need to read the rest of this chapter!)

The cost for a service bureau (a company that specializes in printing services) to print a graphic to film at 2400dpi is less than you may think (often as low as $5 or $10 per image if you have several images in a document). So if you're producing your company's annual report with some graphics from the Net, go to the pros. But if you're willing to live with the best you can get from your laser printer, read on for some helpful pointers.

TABLE 24.2. Fry-Brain Gets Deformed

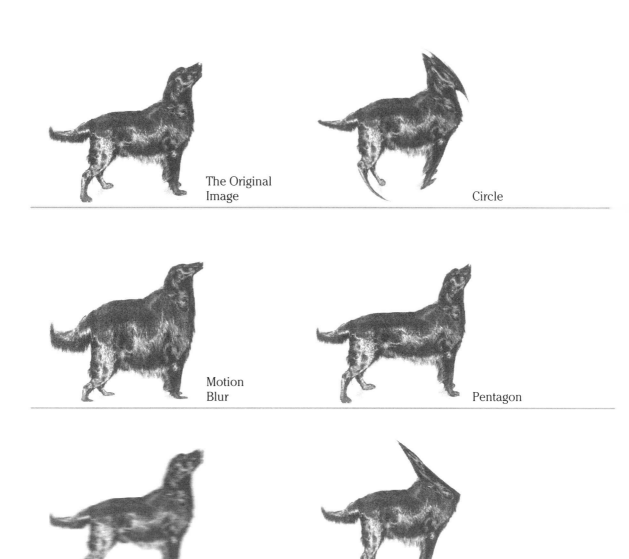

The Original Image

Circle

Motion Blur

Pentagon

Pinch

Punch

Cylinder—
Horizontal

Cylinder-
Vertical

24

Perspective—
Horizontal

Perspective—
Vertical

Skew

Wind Blur

Then there's color. Today's low-cost color inkjet printers can produce amazingly good output, suitable for all but the most demanding color proofing. But of course printing large quantities of a color image requires professional color separation and printing services. In between these two extremes, however, there is a growing range of low-cost options: Slide service bureaus will make an absolutely stunning color slide out of any graphics image straight from a computer disk for $3 to $10 per slide. Many service bureaus also offer fairly high-resolution color prints and large format posters made from your computer files for similarly attractive prices. For the occasional fun project or special presentation, these services can be cheaper than even the most affordable inkjet printer.

Many imaging and printing service companies accept submissions by modem or over the Internet, and some have Web pages as well. Soon, you will be able to compare services on the Web, transmit files over the Net, and receive the results in the mail a day or two later. For the time being, however, the best place to hunt for a service bureau is still your local yellow pages under printers or imaging services, or the classified ads in the back of national computer magazines.

Dithering

No, it isn't something your Great-Aunt Millie or the Three Stooges do habitually. Dithering is a perfectly serious term for reducing the number of colors or tones in an image while pretending not to. By far the most common application of dithering is the preparation of a color or grayscale image for printing on a black-and-white printer.

There are two basic approaches to dithering:

▼ *Halftoning* means representing different levels of gray by varying the size of the black-and-white dots.

▼ *Stochastic screening* (also known as *diffusion dithering* and by other names) uses different densities or patterns of dots, but the individual dots themselves are all the same size.

Technically, true half-tones are impossible on a laser printer or other device with a fixed horizontal and vertical resolution. But they can easily be simulated by arranging the smaller dots to look like larger dots, and this is how most laser printers and software printer drivers automatically convert grayscale images before printing them.

When you're going to send output from a 600dpi laser to an offset press, half-toning is usually the method of choice, and the default settings for your printer and software will usually produce the best results. But if you plan to use a photocopier or a 300-dpi printer to produce the final documents, stochastic screening will copy better and can make images look much smoother and less "grainy."

Regardless of the duplication method you use, some conversion and color correction almost always improves the output as well. In the next few paragraphs, I'll step through the preparation of a good quality image from the Net for printing on a laser printer.

Preparing an Image for Printing

I think Fry-Brain has done his share of tricks in this chapter, don't you? Let's give the poor dog a break and pull up a nice photo/art collage from the NASA space image archives instead. Figure 24.31 shows an artist's rendering of a DC-3 in orbit over Earth, loaded into PaintShop Pro.

NOTE The first step in preparing an image for printing should be to make sure you have the legal right to print it. An image does not need to include a copyright notice to be legally protected as a copyrighted work under U.S., Canadian, and most other nations' laws. Almost all Web pages and image archives include an e-mail address, which means that requesting permission to use an image is usually quite easy and painless. So if you're not sure, ask!

This image looks perfect on the computer screen. However, in print, it will come out much too dark. This is the single most common problem you'll encounter when printing computer images. It's quite difficult to get used to the faded, washed-out look that an image should have on the screen in order for it to print well on a printer. Every time it gets duplicated by a photocopier or press, it will get even darker and higher in contrast as well.

The best way to correct this problem is with gamma correction. Don't use the brightness control, because it's very easy to lose important details of the image that "wash away" to white when an image is brightened. Gamma correction avoids this by lightening the dark regions much more than the light regions. As shown in Figure 24.31, I chose a gamma correction factor of 2.50 for this image. If I were planning on sending this to an offset press or photocopying it, I would pump up the gamma correction as high as I could without producing a choppy, "speckled" look.

Figure 24.31

This image looks good on the screen, but requires gamma correction to print well.

Figure 24.32 shows the image after the gamma correction specified in Figure 24.31 was actually applied. The amount of gamma correction you need depends on the type of dithering you're going to do and the individual printer and driver software you're using. Unfortunately, trial and error is the only way to ensure the best results for your setup and any particular image. A faded-but-still-visible look on the screen is a good place to start, though.

TIP Another sneaky trick for approximating what an image will look like when printed is to turn down the brightness control on your monitor and turn the contrast control all the way up.

If half-toning is appropriate for your needs (see the previous discussion), you can choose File/Print or place the image in a desktop publishing document once you've gamma corrected it. PaintShop Pro also gives you the ability to choose from several dithering methods by selecting Colors/Decrease Color Depth/2 Colors.

You'll almost always want to leave the Grey Values and Weighted items selected on the left part of the dialog box. But each of the various Reduction Methods on the right side will work well with some images, and less well with others. Generally, one of the Error Diffusion methods is best. The differences between them are quite subtle, though I find Stucki dithering best for a majority of laser-printed images. Table 24.3 shows you the results of each of these methods on the gamma-corrected DC-3 image.

The last image in Table 24.3 demonstrates another key to successful dithering: dither the image at the size it will be printed at the full resolution of your printer. For example, a 600 x 480 pixel image like this one would print two inches high on a 300dpi printer. If you want it to be 4 inches high at 300dpi (or 2 inches high at 600dpi), you should select Image/Resample and enter 1200 by 960 as the dimensions before you dither it. This will "blow up" this image to twice its previous height and width (four times the total resolution), and the dithering pattern will be that much smaller and less noticeable.

TIP If you plan to photocopy an image after you print it, dither at a resolution of about 200dpi for the best results. For example, the 600 x 480 image in Table 24.3 would copy well if it were printed about three inches high. If you plan to photocopy an image after you print it, dither at a resolution of about 200dpi for the best results. For example, the 600 x 480 image in Table 24.3 would copy well if it were printed about three inches high.

TABLE 24.3.   Dithering in Orbit

Nearest Color

Ordered Dither

Floyd-Steinberg Error Diffusion

Burkes Error Diffusion

Stucki Error Diffusion

Stucki (at 4x resolution)

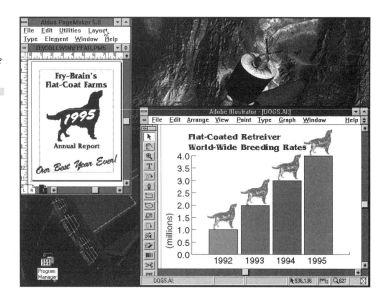

This chapter could go on with more and more uses for graphics, but these hints and tips should be enough to get your creativity flowing (see Figure 24.33). And speaking of creativity, what about creating and publishing your own graphics on the Net? Once you start surfing, you'll soon want to be a part of the Net waves yourself. Read on, and Chapter 25 will put you on the path to electronic posting and publishing.

25

Putting Graphics on the Net

In This Chapter

➤ *Creating images for the Net*

➤ *Uploading to FTP sites and other services*

➤ *Publishing on the Web*

In Other Chapters

◀ *Sending graphics through e-mail and to newsgroups is covered in Chapter 23.*

◀ *For help enhancing and correcting images, see Chapter 24.*

Most of this book focuses on graphics that you can get from the Net and view on your computer. But a PC ain't a TV. The most exciting difference is that you can put images onto the Net for others to access almost as easily as you can see what others have "posted." In this chapter, you learn how to become a creative, active netizen.

(Oh, and I suppose Al Gore would never forgive me if I didn't say, "The information superhighway is a two-way street" somewhere near the beginning of this chapter. Now that that's over with, I promise to drop the government-issue car analogies for the rest of the book.)

Some Preliminary Considerations

There are four ways to acquire images for posting on the Net: the first three are to beg, borrow, or steal. Posting someone else's graphics files with permission (begging) is a perfectly respectable thing to do, and scanning (borrowing) images with permission amounts to the same thing. Passing on a neat image you found without bothering to check with its creator (stealing) is probably the most common origin of images on the Net, and many netizens don't mind at all. The only drawback is that stealing happens to be illegal in almost every country in the world, so you may encounter the inconvenience of being sued, heavily fined, or put in jail. If that sort of thing doesn't bother you much, go for it—you can come up with some really nice images.

Fortunately, there is a way to avoid both the hassle of getting permissions and the hassle of watching the judge fall asleep during yet another copyright infringement suit: Create some images yourself. In the old days, they called people who did that sort of thing "artists," but don't let the label intimidate you. Nowadays, creating images can be as easy as running an inexpensive hand scanner over your family album, or clicking your mouse on an interesting part of a computer-generated "fractal." Creating images that somebody on the Net would actually like to see may be a bit more challenging of course, but you don't have to be Vincent van Gogh to add some spice to your home page on the Web or shoot an illustration for the prize-winning cake recipe you've decided to share with the world. Heck, there's probably somebody somewhere on the Net who would even get a kick out of those snapshots of you standing on your head juggling four tractor tires with your feet while playing the kazoo.

Of course, if you are Vincent van Gogh (reincarnated), or the modern equivalent, millions of eyeballs eagerly await the Internet premiere of your next masterpiece. As the many chapters in this book have shown, thousands of graphic artists and photographers have found the Net to be an effective place to publicize their work—or simply "get it out there" for the world to see.

Before you stock up on cybernetic champagne and virtual fromages for your first opening on the Net, you should pause to consider some technical issues. If you aren't aware of the unique limitations that various venues on the Net impose on your images, your enthusiastic patrons could end up staring at blank screens (or worse) when they try to puruse your work.

Of Depth and Resolution

Two forces are always at odds when you post graphics on the Net: your eyes want graphics to be as detailed and accurate as possible, but your clock and wallet want images to be as small as possible. Intricate, colorful graphics mean big (and we're talking BIG) file sizes, which can take a long time to transfer even over a fast connection. These large-footprint graphics files can also fill up space on your hard drive like retirement community developers in Arizona. You probably don't want to buy too many big new hard drives just to hold graphics—or big new monitors capable of displaying ultra-high resolution images, for that matter.

For most professional graphics applications, quality is king and you've just got to sacrifice the disk space and buy the big monitor. But on the Net, visual quality usually has to take a back seat to file size—especially now that most people on the Net are using 25.8K modems and not high-speed university trunk lines.

So how do you find the right balance? And how do you maximize the quality of your images while minimizing file size? To make these choices, you need to understand what your options are, and how color depth and resolution work together to create a subjective sense of quality. So read the next few paragraphs carefully—they contain a concise summary of what you need to know about color and resolution.

The vertical and horizontal resolution are the height and width of the image, measured in pixels (the individual dots that make up a digital image).

Color depth is the number of bits of information used to describe each pixel. Each bit can have two values, so two bits can have four unique values (2×2), four bits can have sixteen unique values (2×2×2×2), and so on. For most images you'll put on the Net, a color look-up table or "palette" is included in the image file to specify which actual color corresponds to each value.

If you use enough bits per pixel, however, you can describe the color itself in terms of its red, green, and blue color components and you don't need a color look-up table. Most often, these "true color" images use 24 bits per pixel, which provides more colors than the human eye can distinguish. Some graphics cards use only 15, 16, or 18 bits to display true color images, but the graphics files themselves usually include all 24 bits of color information even if you can't see them all on your graphics card.

All these factors together determine the overall size of the image file. Table 25.1 shows all the common color depths and resolutions and the resulting theoretical size of the image, including the color look-up table.

TABLE 25.1 How color depth and resolution affect the theoretical (uncompressed) file size (1K=1,024 bytes=8,192 bits).

Bits per pixel (Number of colors):	1(2)	4(16)	8(256)	15(32,768)	24(16,777,216)
160×120 pixels	3K	10K	20K	35K	58K
320×200 pixels	8K	31K	64K	117K	188K
640×480 pixels	37K	150K	300K	563K	900K
800×600 pixels	59K	234K	469K	879K	1,406K
1024×768 pixels	96K	384K	769K	1,440K	2,304K

Achieving Maximum Compression

Most images will actually take much less space on your hard drive than Table 25.1 indicates, because they are stored in a compressed format. How much an image can be compressed depends on the image itself: a truly random "sea of static" image wouldn't compress at all, and a solid color image would compress to well under 1K no matter what its resolution. Generally the GIF and JPEG images most often found on the Net achieve somewhere around 4:1 compression (meaning that a file would typically take up a quarter as much space as is listed in Table 25.1). The new PNG standard achieves slightly higher compression ratios than the GIF standard it replaces, and represents about the best compression you can currently get without losing any image data.

"Lossy" JPEG compression, however, can squeeze images even smaller. They'll usually start showing noticeable degradation at compression ratios greater than 4:1, but true color photographic images will sometimes tolerate JPEG compression as tight as 10:1 without too much uglification.

You can control the JPEG compression ratio in many graphics programs, including LView Pro (included on the CD with this book). Figure 25.1 shows the JPEG I/O... dialog box from LView Pro's Options menu. You can control the compression ratio for saving JPEG files by sliding the JPEG Compression/ Compression Quality setting between 20% (low quality, small file size) and 95% (high quality, large file size).

Table 25.2 indicates how these settings affect the file size. If you were surfing the Net, would you rather wait nearly half a minute to see this image in its full glory, or watch it pop onto your screen at 75% quality in less than six seconds? That's the kind of difference that makes JPEG a hard format to beat for storing true color graphics on the Net. Unfortunately, larger images than this 320×200 example will usually not compress quite as efficiently.

Figure 25.1

LView Pro allows you to trade reduced file size for image quality when saving JPEG images.

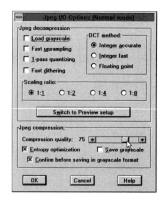

TABLE 25.2 Relative file sizes of the image in Figure 25.4, and approximate transfer time over a 25.8Kbps modem connection.

Color depth	Actual file format	Approximate file size	Approximate compression ratio	Transfer time
24 bit	Uncompressed TGA	190.5K	1:1	95 seconds
8 bit	Compressed GIF	51.4K	4:1	26 seconds
24 bit	"Near perfect" JPEG	54.3K	4:1	27 seconds
24 bit	95% JPEG (Figure 25.4a)	32.5K	6:1	16 seconds
24 bit	75% JPEG (Figure 25.4b)	11.3K	17:1	6 seconds
24 bit	50% JPEG (Figure 25.4c)	7.3K	26:1	4 seconds
24 bit	25% JPEG (Figure 25.4d)	4.6K	40:1	2 seconds

NOTE Be aware that some viewers are better than others at displaying JPEG images, and so you can't be quite sure what people will see when they look at JPEGs that you post on the Net.

How Big is Too Big?

Pumping up the JPEG compression is great for snapshots where ideal image quality probably isn't the primary concern. But what about that artistic masterpiece you spend years of your life creating? How good an image can you realistically put on the Net and expect someone to really download it?

First, consider the limitations of what most computer users are able to view. On a 15" or 17" monitor, 1024×768 true color images are noticeably superior to those with lower resolution or fewer colors. Higher resolutions than that, however, have no visual benefits unless you plan to make a big poster out of them or something.

TIP To estimate how long it will typically take for your images to download, you can assume that a standard 28.8 kilobit-per-second modem with a good connection to a Net site can pull about 2 kilobytes per second.

Therefore, a lossless 1024×768 true color image would take around 5 to 10 minutes to transfer, depending on its compression ratio. You probably aren't going to upload or download too many of those at a time, but a dedicated fan of your creations would probably tolerate the wait. Users with a high-speed (64Kbps or more) network connection would be even more likely to sit through the download, but they might still suffer through a significant wait, especially considering the delays induced by overburdened servers at many sites.

Remember, though that many people are still accessing the Net through 14.4Kbps or slower modems.

Usually, even the most finicky artists will refrain from clogging archives with 1024×768 images. I suggest you do the same and consider 800×600 the "high end" for 256-color images, and 640×480 the top of the line for true color images. Most Net users can download an image of that size in well under 5 minutes.

Even five minutes is a long time to tie up your computer and Internet connection for a single image, though. Many people will simply "pull the plug" on a transfer after 60 seconds no matter how nice an image they'll miss. So for practical purposes, even fine art images should really be limited to 640×480 with 256 colors (under 100K in size) unless there's a truly compelling reason to post a higher resolution version.

All this applies to stand-alone, high quality images which are intended to be viewed or printed offline. On the World Wide Web, where multiple graphics may be included on a page (sometimes for no other purpose than to add some "flair"), you should be much more conservative with graphics file sizes. As a general rule, any Web page that includes more than 50K worth of graphics should only be accessed from another, less graphics-intensive page. Links to the graphics-intensive page should warn the readers so they can turn off their Web browsers' automatic graphics downloading if they are using a dial-up modem connection. Most individual images incorporated into Web pages are around 160×120 resolution.

Later in this chapter, I say much more about preparing graphics for the Web. But first, I discuss some important things to keep in mind when you produce images and then I step you through the production and preparation of an image for posting to a Net archive or newsgroup.

Uploading Graphics

Compared to creating an image, uploading it is a relatively trivial task. More challenging, in fact, is the endeavor of finding a good place on the Net to upload to. Chapters 2 through 19 of this book should help with that, but do remember that most public sites have special directories for uploads—you can't simply transfer an image to the directory you'd like people to be able to download it from. Many sites also require special permission, some form of registration, or membership to upload. Check out any "readme" or other text files you can find at each site before you try to foist unwanted graphics files on them.

You are always expected to be very familiar with the guidelines and FAQ documents for any newsgroup you upload to as well. Each of the binaries.pictures newsgroups has its own preferred format for uuencoding and splitting long files, so pay careful attention to these details. Chapter 23 of this book gives you instructions on encoding and decoding graphics files for transmission to newsgroups and through e-mail.

Once you've properly encoded an image, you can post to a newsgroup right from your everyday e-mail program or even from a Web browser such as Netscape Navigator. To upload a file to most other archives, however, you'll need to install an FTP program. WS_FTP for Windows and Fetch for the Mac are excellent shareware FTP programs and are included on the CD-ROM with this book. You'll find directions for installing them in

Chapter 26 and on the CD itself. Most "all-in-one" Internet access software and all major commercial online services also include FTP software.

Using FTP

"The user interface for this FTP client is designed with the novice FTP user in mind. Usage should be obvious. For more information on FTP please refer to the many different NETNEWS groups or one of the recent books on the Internet."
—John Junod, in the WS_FTP documentation

Well, this is "one of the recent books on the Internet" so I guess I should explain the obvious here. But, hey, don't waste your time reading it until you go ahead and try WS_FTP (or whatever FTP program you prefer) first. I bet you'll get the idea pretty quickly. If so, skip this section in the book. If not, don't feel dumb—it's not quite as obvious as he makes it out to be. Here, I'll step you through an example by uploading the image named UROS.JPG to a site dedicated to POV-Ray (one of the software programs used to create the image).

1. The first thing you'll see when you start up WS_FTP is the Session Profile dialog box. (The Profile name list at the top contains a number of popular FTP sites that you might want to check out later.) To tell WS_FTP where to go, click on the New button and enter the information shown in Figure 25.2 and in steps 2 through 4.

Figure 25.2

The Session Profile dialog box lets you specify the FTP site you'd like to upload to (or download from).

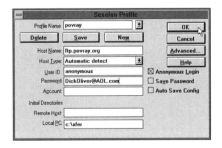

2. The Host Name is simply the address of the FTP site. (Note that you don't need to put ftp:// in front of the address like you would if you were accessing the site with a Web browser.)

3. Unless you have private access to a site, the User ID will be anonymous and the Password should always be your full e-mail address. (Some sites do allow you to log on with the password "guest" but that's considered rude—sort of like going to a party with a paper bag over your head.)

4. I entered **c:\xfer** as the Local PC initial directory because that's where I had put the file I wanted to upload. If you're familiar with the directory structure at the site you're going to, or somebody told you which directory you should upload to, you can also specify an initial directory for the Remote Host. Otherwise, just leave it blank.

5. Before clicking on OK, click on Save to save the site information for future use.

6. When you do click OK, you will automatically log onto the FTP site you specified. (If it doesn't work, make sure your Winsock is set up and connected.)

7. The first thing you should always do is press the LogWnd button at the bottom of the screen (third button from the left), so you can see any message that the FTP server tried to give you as you logged on. Figure 25.3 shows the logon message I got from the povray.org server.

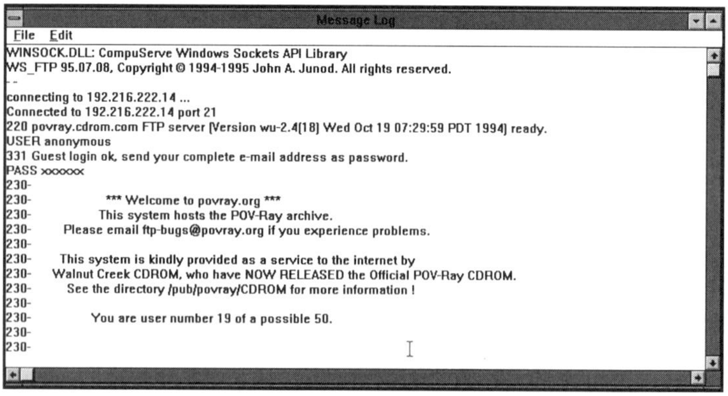

Figure 25.3

To see these messages from the remote host, I clicked on the LogWnd button.

```
                                        Message Log
 File   Edit
WINSOCK.DLL: CompuServe Windows Sockets API Library
WS_FTP 95.07.08, Copyright © 1994-1995 John A. Junod. All rights reserved.
- -
connecting to 192.216.222.14 ...
Connected to 192.216.222.14 port 21
220 povray.cdrom.com FTP server [Version wu-2.4[18] Wed Oct 19 07:29:59 PDT 1994] ready.
USER anonymous
331 Guest login ok, send your complete e-mail address as password.
PASS xxxxxx
230-
230-              *** Welcome to povray.org ***
230-          This system hosts the POV-Ray archive.
230-      Please email ftp-bugs@povray.org if you experience problems.
230-
230-      This system is kindly provided as a service to the internet by
230-      Walnut Creek CDROM, who have NOW RELEASED the Official POV-Ray CDROM.
230-      See the directory /pub/povray/CDROM for more information !
230-
230-          You are user number 19 of a possible 50.
230-
230-                                       I
```

You may often encounter a message telling you that too many people are trying to access the FTP server, and you can't get on right now. If that happens, the only things you can do are to try again later (maybe late at night, their time) or try any "mirror" sites that the message may tell you about. This time, I got onto the server as user number 19, meaning that 18 other people are accessing it at the same time.

8. After you've read the messages, close the Message Log window. You'll see something like Figure 25.4, with your local directories and files on the left and the remote system's directories and files on the right. Since I didn't specify a remote directory, I start out at the "root" directory, which contains three subdirectories (bin, etc, and pub) and no files. If there were any files, they would be listed in the large blank space below the directory list.

Figure 25.4

Faced with a list of directories like this, you should almost always head for the pub.

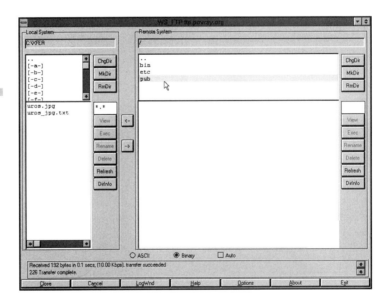

9. Almost all FTP servers have a pub directory, which sometimes stands for "public" and sometimes stands for "publications." In either case, it's usually the directory you want to go into, which you can do by clicking on it and hitting the ChgDir button, or just by double-clicking on the directory name.

10. Sites that allow uploads will almost always have one or more directories named "upload," or "incoming" or something similar. At this site, the "pub" directory contained many other directories for various topics, each of which has its own "incoming" subdirectory. It didn't take too much thought to figure out that the directory I was looking for was /pub/povray/incoming. When I got there (Figure 25.5), I saw four files. As it turns out, three of them (.message, Instructions, and README) all contain exactly the same text. Obviously, they want to make sure everybody gets that message!

Figure 25.5

Always view any files named README or .message before trying to upload to a site.

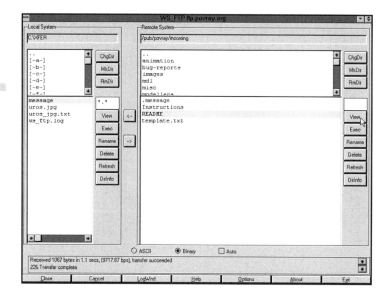

11. By clicking on any one of those files and then clicking the View button, you would get the message shown in Figure 25.6. This message is pretty typical for FTP sites, though the exact file naming conventions and text description formats vary from site to site. Always, always, always find, read, and obey the upload instructions for every site you upload to! You'd be amazed how many people don't, and how many hours are wasted uploading files that are then immediately deleted because the people who uploaded them didn't follow the instructions for that site.

Figure 25.6

The requirements outlined in this README file are typical of most upload sites.

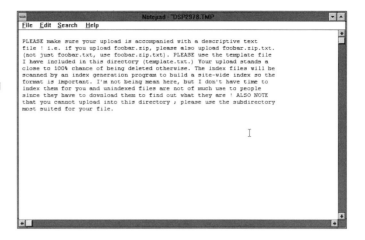

12. In this case, I happened to have already downloaded the template.txt file and filled it out properly, as shown in Figure 25.7. If you hadn't done this, you would need to download the template.txt file (by highlighting it and clicking on the <-- button), close your FTP connection (by clicking on the Close button), and prepare the text file before logging back on and uploading.

Figure 25.7

Prescience granted me the ability to prepare this file ahead of time so I could show you how to upload it.

TIP Notice that since I'm using a DOS/Windows system, I can't give the text file the name it's supposed to have according to the instructions in Figure 25.6. Instead of uros.jpg.txt I'll have to name it uros_jpg.txt on my machine and change the name after I upload it to their UNIX system, which supports multiple dots (.) in filenames.

13. Now it's time to actually do the upload. As Figure 25.8 depicts, all you have to do is hop into the appropriate subdirectory (in this case /pub/povray/incoming/ images), highlight the image file in the Local System

window, and hit the —> button. The Transfer Status
dialog shown in Figure 25.9 appears, and a minute or so
later the transfer is complete.

Figure 25.8

*To upload files, go to the
appropriate directory on the
remote host, highlight the files
on your local computer, and hit
the right-arrow button.*

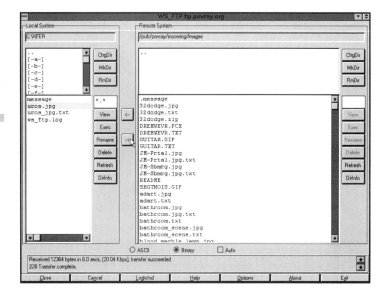

Figure 25.9

*A status box helps you predict
how long the transfer will take.*

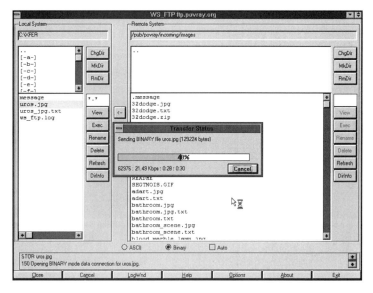

14. Don't forget the accompanying text file. You can upload
multiple files by highlighting them all before clicking on
the - -> button. Image files must always be transferred
with the Binary radio button (near the bottom of the

screen) selected (Figure 25.8). Text files, however, should always be transferred as plain text by selecting the ASCII radio button instead (Figure 25.10). Otherwise, file format differences may make the text unreadable on other computer systems. If you're uploading a mixture of binary and text files, select the Auto radio button and WS_FTP will automatically switch between binary and ASCII uploading as appropriate.

Figure 25.10
Always transfer text files as ASCII instead of Binary.

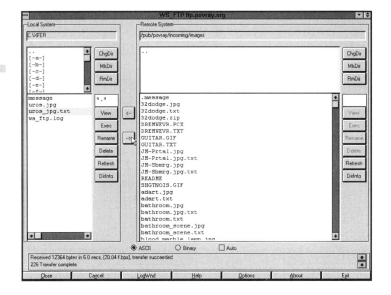

15. Once both the image and text files have been transferred, scroll down the remote file list to make sure their file names are really there.

16. As a final step, you may need to rename the text file to match the conventions for the site. Here, I selected uros_jpg.txt and hit the Rename button (Figure 25.11) and entered uros.jpg.txt as the new file name.

17. You could transfer more files in the same session, or just hit the Close button in the lower lefthand corner to log off. (Don't just exit WS_FTP without hitting Close, or the remote host might continue to "hold your place," which could prevent other users from accessing the site.)

Figure 25.11

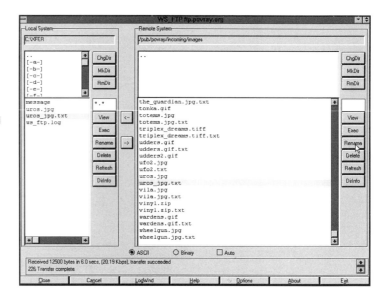

Graphics on the World Wide Web

Shuffling graphics files back and forth with FTP is all good and fine, but the World Wide Web is where you want to be if you're putting graphics on the Net. After all, why leave your images languishing in some archive directory when they could be up on a Web page for all the world to see?

Right now, setting up your own Web site if you're not a student or teacher is a moderately large undertaking. First you have to shop around for some server space to rent. This can be nerve-racking because Internet services are popping up in droves and neither prices nor specifics of service contracts have settled into any sort of stable state yet. In a quick search of the Net under the topic "web service provider," I came up with prices for posting a single Web page from $10 a month to $100 a month, and prices for a few megs of commercial server space from $50 a month to $1,000 a month for the same advertised services. Would the $50 a month provider be able to handle a flurry of visitors to a commercial site if they did a special promotion to bring in people? Would the $1,000 a month provider? Who knows.

Of course, you need to know this sort of thing if you're going to set up some kind of shop on the Net, and many other things besides. Even if you're only interested in posting a few personal pages, you don't want to end up like the customers of several Web service providers lately who found out that maintaining a server is harder than they thought and suddenly closed their virtual doors, leaving their customers with no place for their lovely Web pages.

I'm not going to recommend names or warn against any particular service providers for the Web, both because I don't have personal experience with enough of them to pass judgment and because the industry is so new that the criteria for judging changes monthly. Perhaps the best advice I can give is to surf around the Web and find some pages similar to what you'd like to do, then ask their owners who they use for a provider and if they're happy with the service. You'll also find more good advice and information on setting up and maintaining a presence on the Web in other Que books, including *Running a Perfect Web Site* by D. Chandler and *Launching a Business on the Web* by David Cook and Deborah Sellers.

If you do happen to be enrolled in, or on the faculty of, even a moderately sized educational institution, you should be able to park a few noncommercial pages on its servers for free. Also, all the major online services and Internet access companies are planning on offering free or very cheap personal Web space to their customers within the next year or two. I'd venture to predict, in fact, that well over 90% of the readers of this book will have their own Web pages in that time span.

To make my prediction a reality, you'll need to learn some of the codes used to "mark up" text so that Web browsers know where to insert graphics, links to other pages, and other formatting. These codes are called hypertext mark-up language (HTML), and they're actually very easy to work with once you get the basic ideas. I teach you most of the HTML you will probably need later in this chapter. But before you start marking up text for the Web, you should step back and consider the overall design of your Web page(s) and the graphics that will be displayed on them.

To make these considerations more concrete, I've designed the interface to the CD-ROM that comes with this book as a web of HTML pages, with many hotlinks out into the World Wide Web. In the following discussion of graphics for the Web, I refer to the CD pages as a working example. You can use Netscape (or another browser) to explore the pages and peek at the HTML "source code" behind them.

Designing Graphics for the Web

Web pages are not paper pages, and shouldn't be designed as if they were. As you have explored the Web, you've probably noticed that one of the most common uses of graphics is to help readers orient themselves in a vast homogeneous worldwide sea of pages. The role of graphics as a navigational aid is far more important on the Web than in a book or magazine, where there are physical cues to location. Printed publications can also rely on font, layout, and paper type to establish a visual identity and help readers distinguish one part of a publication from another. On the Web, none of that can be reliably controlled, so the graphics are all you've got to visually distinguish one page from another and your pages from all the rest.

Most Web page designers establish that identity by creating a set of icons, accents, and graphical titles for their pages, in addition to any graphical content that may go along with the text itself. Sometimes these icons are very generic—like a house that links you to a site's home page, or left and right arrows to leaf back and forth through a sequential series of pages. Generally, it's better to give your navigation icons a unique thematic look that reminds readers that the pages are all part of a single site.

When I designed the graphics for the CD-ROM Web pages, I first identified the major subject areas:

Home page/table of contents

Hotlinks to the Net

Images and Videos

PC Software

Mac Software

About the Authors

I knew that some of these areas would contain multiple pages, but should be visually grouped together. For each area, I created a graphical page header to go under the titles of the pages in that area, as well as a small icon to use as a navigation link to the area from other areas. I used a bright color scheme and "traveling spark" icon to tie the elements together visually, and generic icons like a house, a globe, and the letters "PC" and "Mac" to identify each area. I also made a simple horizontal rule with the same color scheme for use as a replacement of the generic horizontal rule. Figure 25.12 shows the home page and hotlinks graphics. You can view the CD Web pages or the /cdweb/webart.htm page to see the others.

Figure 25.12

These simple icons help create a visual identity for the Web pages on the CD.

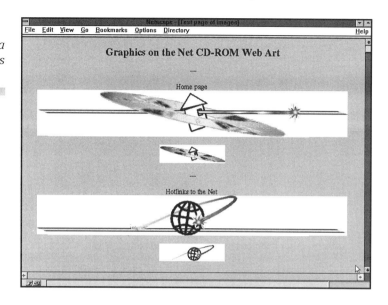

Displaying Graphics with HTML

Once you have the graphical elements of your Web pages, you're ready to create the pages themselves. A complete tutorial in HTML is beyond the scope of this book, but the basic idea is so simple I can show you enough to make a good Web page pretty quickly.

Web pages look fancy when viewed with a browser, but they're just plain old text underneath. To tell the browser where to put graphics, headings, and other visual emphasis, you "mark it up" with special codes called tags.

Suppose I had the following text, and wanted to make a Web page out of it:

NET.GRAPHICS CD-ROM
The Online Companion to the Internet Graphics Gallery Book
Introduction.
Think of this CD-ROM as your own personal Internet, packed with hundreds of megabytes of images, software, and other graphical goodies from the real Internet. Starting on the

"home page" you're reading now, you can browse through the CD-ROM just as you would "surf" the World Wide Web. This Web page is linked to many others that will help you see what's on the CD and select the programs and graphics you'd like to view or "download" to your hard drive.

One difference between this CD-ROM and the Net is that getting files from this CD is much faster and cheaper. It would take you many thousands of hours to download everything on the CD if you had to get it from the Net, and that doesn't count any time spent searching. Of course, we couldn't fit everything from all the world's graphics archives on one CD-ROM. But when you want something that isn't here, you can use our link pages to jump straight to hundreds of hot graphics sites on the Net—without even leaving your browser!

To tell the Web browser which part of the text is a heading, I insert tags at the beginning and end of each heading. A tag is nothing more than a special code word (or several code words) enclosed in angle brackets. The <H1> and </H1> tags begin and end the largest size heading, like this:

<H1>NET.GRAPHICS CD-ROM</H1>

I can also use H2, H3, H4, H5, and H6 to make smaller sub-headings. (Though six levels of headings are available, you should try to stick to three levels only.) So I might do this:

<H1>NET.GRAPHICS CD-ROM</H1>
<H2>The Online Companion to the Internet Graphics Gallery Book</H2>
<H3>Introduction</H3>

A normal paragraph of text can begin with a <P> tag and end with </P>, but the HTML conventions allow you to take a shortcut and simply put a single <P> tag at the beginning or end of each paragraph. This bends the rules a bit, but won't cause any problems in any browser and saves typing.

You must also enclose the entire body of an HTML document between a <BODY> tag and a </BODY> tag. In front of the <BODY> tag, you must place a title for the document (which will show up on hotlists and in a special title window in some browsers). In front of the title you put a <HEAD> and a <TITLE> tag, and after the title you put </TITLE> and </HEAD> tags. (You can put other things in the document head, but the title is all you usually need.) Then at the very beginning and end of the entire document, you put an <HTML> tag and an </HTML> tag. So the whole thing would look like this:

```
<HTML>
<HEAD><TITLE>Net.Graphics CD-ROM Home Page</
TITLE></HEAD>
<BODY>
<H1>NET.GRAPHICS CD-ROM</H1>
<H2>The Online Companion to the Internet Graphics Gallery
Book</H2>
<H3>Introduction</H3>
Think of this CD-ROM as your own personal Internet, packed
with hundreds of megabytes of images, software, and other
graphical goodies from the real Internet. Starting on the
"home page" you're reading now, you can browse through
the CD-ROM just as you would "surf" the World Wide Web.
This Web page is linked to many others that will help you see
what's on the CD and select the programs and graphics you'd
like to view or "download" to your hard drive.
One difference between this CD-ROM and the Net is that
getting files from this CD is much faster and cheaper. It would
take you many thousands of hours to download everything on
the CD if you had to get it from the Net, and that doesn't
count any time spent searching. Of course, we couldn't fit
everything from all the world's graphics archives on one
CD-ROM. But when you want something that isn't here, you
can use our link pages to jump straight to hundreds of hot
graphics sites on the Net—without even leaving your
browser!<P>
</BODY>
</HTML>
```

All these tags may seem complex at first, but the basic sequence is the same for all HTML documents, so you only have to learn it once—and you don't even need to remember it after that, because you can always cut and past the tags from your first page.

There are other tags of course, like <I> and </I> that start and end a section of italicized text. Similarly, <B> and </B> start and end boldface text. The <HR> tag inserts a horizontal rule (line) across the page, and <BR> inserts a single line break (the <P> tag usually is interpreted to insert two line breaks, skipping a line between paragraphs).

You can also indicate numbered or bulleted lists. Numbered lists are called ordered lists; they begin with the <OL> tag, and end with </OL>. Bulleted lists are called unordered lists; they begin with <UL> and end with </UL>. Each new item on the list starts with an <LI> tag, and you can put an optional </LI> tag at the end of each line if you want to.

Table 25.3 summarizes the most commonly used tags. As you can see, they are not at all hard to learn and use.

TABLE 25.3   The most common HTML tags.

Usage	Opening tag	Closing tag
Entire document	<HTML>	</HTML>
Document header	<HEAD>	</HEAD>
Title (within header)	<TITLE>	</TITLE>
Document body	<BODY>	</BODY>
Top level heading	<H1>	</H1>
2nd level heading	<H2>	</H2>
3rd level heading	<H3>	</H3>
Italic text	<I>	</I>
Bold text	<B>	</B>
Monospaced text	<TT>	</TT>
Centered text	<CENTER>	</CENTER> (This "unofficial" tag doesn't work with all browsers)
New paragraph	<P>	(</P> is optional)
Line break (within a paragraph)	 	
Horizontal rule	<HR>	
Ordered list	<OL>	</OL>
Unordered list	<UL>	</UL>
New line in list	<LI>	(</LI> is optional)
Image	<IMG>	
Anchor/link	<A>	</A>

Images, Links, and Anchors

There are two tags in Table 25.3 that I haven't mentioned yet: <IMG> and <A>.

These are, in fact, the most important ones, and require some explanation.

The <IMG> tag tells the browser to insert an image. You must specify where to find the image file, and how to place the next line of text in relation to the image. The image location, called the source, can be a file name on the same computer as the HTML text file, or an Internet URL address pointing to a file on some other computer somewhere. Usually, you will put the images in the same directory as the HTML pages, so you can simply specify a file name with the SRC= attribute, like this:

```
<IMG SRC="cdhome.gif">
```

All major browsers now support inclusion of GIF and JPG images, and are promising support for several other image formats (including PNG) in their next versions.

The next line of text after an image is assumed to be a caption, and will be placed immediately to the right of it. You can specify whether the caption should be aligned with the TOP, MIDDLE, or BOTTOM of the image with the ALIGN= attribute. For example:

```
<IMG SRC="cdhome.gif" ALIGN="BOTTOM">
```

Basically, you should enclose the word TOP, MIDDLE, or BOTTOM in quotes, although most browsers allow you to cheat and leave the quotes off.) If you don't want the next line of text to be placed next to the image, just put a paragraph <P> tag after the <IMG> tag, and leave the ALIGN= attribute out.

The <A> and </A> tags are what make the Web a web: they provide "hypertext" hotlinks to other documents, and also allow you to jump around within a single document. To insert a link, called a hypertext reference, an HREF= attribute in the <A> tag specifying the file name of a local file or the address of any document or file on the Net. Any text that falls between the <A> and </A> tags will be highlighted (in most browsers, colored and underlined). When readers click on that text, they will hop to the file you specified in the HREF= attribute. Here's how a link looks:

...you can use our <A HREF="cdnet.htm">link pages</A> to jump straight to...

You can include an image within a link, and a colored border will appear around the image. When the reader clicks on any part of the image, he will jump to the address in the link's HREF. For example, if you wanted to allow readers to jump to a document named cdpics.htm by clicking on an icon named gopics.gif or an accompanying caption that reads "Click here for images and videos," you would write:

```
<A HREF="cdpics.htm"><IMG SRC="gopics.gif"> Click here
for images and videos.</A>
```

Putting all this together, a simple but complete hypertext document made by marking up the text given above might look like this:

```
<HTML>
<HEAD><TITLE>Net.Graphics CD-ROM Home Page</
TITLE></HEAD>
<BODY>
<CENTER>
<H1>NET.GRAPHICS CD-ROM</H1>
<H2>The Online Companion to the <I>Internet Graphics
Gallery</I> Book</H2>
  <IMG SRC="cdhome.gif">
</CENTER>
<H3>Introduction</H3>
Think of this CD-ROM as your own personal Internet, packed
with hundreds of megabytes of images, software, and other
graphical goodies from the real Internet. Starting on the
"home page" you're reading now, you can browse through
the CD-ROM just as you would "surf" the World Wide Web.
This Web page is linked to many others that will help you see
what's on the CD and select the programs and graphics you'd
like to view or "download" to your hard drive.<P>
One difference between this CD-ROM and the Net is that
getting files from this CD is much faster and cheaper. It would
take you many thousands of hours to download everything on
the CD if you had to get it from the Net, and that doesn't
count any time spent searching. Of course, we couldn't fit
everything from all the world's graphics archives on one
```

CD-ROM. But when you want something that isn't here, you can use our <A HREF="cdnet.htm">link pages</A> to jump straight to hundreds of hot graphics sites on the Net—without even leaving your browser!<P>
<HR>
<A HREF="cdpics.htm"><IMG SRC="gopics.gif"> Click here for images and videos.</A>
</BODY>
</HTML>

As a matter of fact, the above HTML listing looks an awful lot like the cdhome.htm document on the net.graphics CD-ROM.

By looking at the HTML source for this and other pages on the CD-ROM, you will probably be able to pick up enough HTML to start you well along your way to publishing on the Web.

I haven't touched on many parts of HTML, such as forms and tables, in this brief account. Later in this chapter, I will discuss some fancier HTML graphics tricks, but for a complete guide to HTML authoring you might like to pick up a good book on the subject, such as Laura Lemay's *Teach Yourself Web Publishing with HTML in a Week* from Sams publishing.

I will share one more non-graphics related HTML technique here, because it's the only part of basic HTML that I haven't already mentioned. The <A> tag, called an "anchor" tag, can be used as a named reference point. You can jump to it from other parts of an HTML document. To create a named anchor, use the NAME= attribute:

<A NAME="introduction"></A>Once upon a time...

You can then jump to the "introduction" anchor by creating a link from some other part of the document. Put a # character before the anchor name in the HREF= attribute, like this:

<A HREF="#introduction">Click here</A> to go to the introduction.

You'll see extensive use of anchors and links in the cdnet.htm, cdpc.htm, cdmac.htm and cdalpha.htm documents on the CD-ROM.

Plan To Be Mangled

The graphics-savvy among us can pull off some jazzy stunts to make their Web pages display in style. But before I tell you how to toot your graphical horn, let me remind you that not all browsers play in the same key.

Figure 25.13 shows the beginning of an HTML document from the CD-ROM, as it looks in Netscape Navigator version 1.2 for Windows.

Figure 25.13

Part of a fairly simple Web page (cdpc.htm) displayed in the Netscape browser.

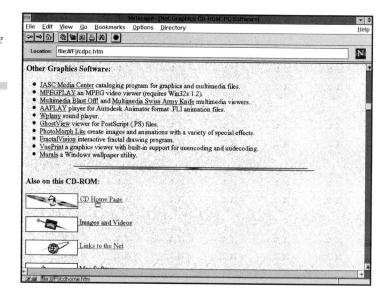

This page is all pretty straightforward HTML, so you'd think it might look pretty much the same in any browser. Not so. Figures 25.14 through 25.16 reveal that it may appear quite different to readers using different software to access the Web. That's quite in line with the spirit of HTML, which is intended to be a content-oriented (rather than appearance-oriented) standard. But it does imply two things for those of us who carefully design and lay out colorful graphics on our Web pages: First, always check to see how your pages look in various common browsers before you post them on the Net. Second, don't get too hung up on fine-tuning the exact appearance of your page in a particular browser. Instead, focus on general organization and strong content that will be compelling no matter how the reader looks at it.

Figure 25.14

The same page as Figure 25.15, as seen by Spry's Enhanced Mosaic browser.

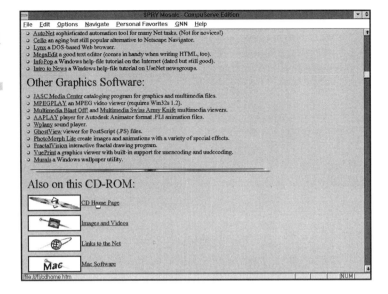

Figure 25.15

Cello, another common browser, depicts graphics, hotlinks, and lists quite differently than Netscape or Mosaic.

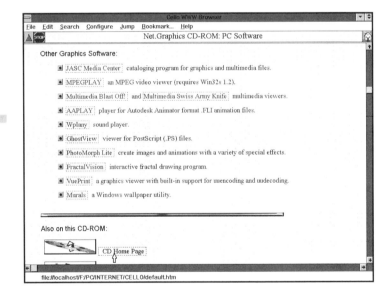

Figure 25.16

The DOS-based Lynx browser only displays graphics as a separate document when the reader clicks on the word "IMAGE."

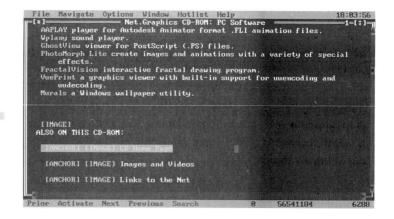

TIP
     Figure 25.16 is a good reminder that many people will not see any of the graphics you put on your Web pages. Even those using graphics-capable browsers often surf with graphics downloading turned off to reduce download times over a slow modem connection.

HTML gives you a way to send a special message to readers who don't see your graphics: Each image can be given an ALT= attribute that will display the text you specify whenever the image itself can't be shown. Here's an example:

             `<IMG SRC="triangle.gif" ALT="WARNING:">` This page is radioactive on some monitors.

If the image file triangle.gif can't be displayed, most browsers would display the word WARNING: instead.

Using a Dedicated HTML Editor

As I hope you've gathered, using HTML to create Web pages is not a particularly mysterious or arduous task. You can learn to do it quickly within any text editor or word processor. If you do a lot of work in HTML, however, you will probably want to use a dedicated HTML editing program.

     My personal favorite HTML editor is HTML Assistant for Windows. But I'm definitely going against the mainstream in that choice, and I openly confess that many of you will find HoTMetaL, which is by far the most popular HTML editor, more to your liking. I've included both of these (and the similar Mac programs HTML Editor and HTML Pro) on the CD-ROM with this book, so you can try them for yourself. But before you decide on looks alone, let me tell you why I strongly recommend against HoTMetaL.

To save a few bytes of space in the file, HoTMetaL crunches all the lines together, but then wastes space by including irrelevant and unnecessary attributes in many tags. The result is a completely unreadable mess which makes the C programming language seem like easy reading. Two years from now, when the current version of HoTMetaL is ancient history but your Web pages still need updating—or next week, when you want to borrow some pieces from an HTML page to make another one—you may eventually have to untangle this unsightly gob by hand. Good luck.

HTML Assistant, on the other hand, lets you put line breaks wherever you think they should be (Web browsers don't pay any attention to line breaks until they see a <P> or a <BR>) so your HTML documents will be readable by human beings (including yourself).

Figure 25.17 shows the HTML Assistant interface, and Figure 25.18 shows HoTMetaL. I didn't include an illustration here comparing the messy code you'll get out of HoTMetaL to a cleanly crafted page produced in HTML Assistant, but you can easily see the difference by creating and saving a page in HoTMetaL and comparing it to the example HTML documents on the CD-ROM.

Figure 25.17

HTML Assistant shows the actual HTML source text, and offers an extensive toolbar.

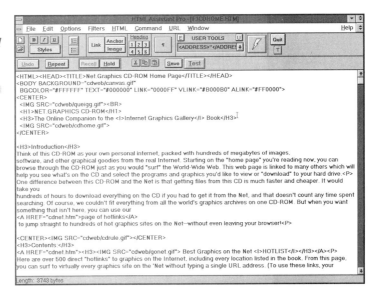

Figure 25.18

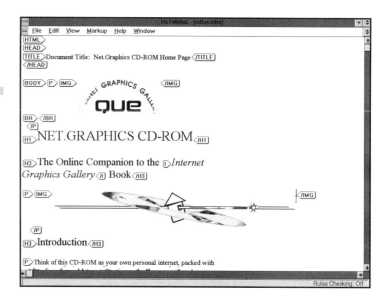

NOTE You should know that HTML Assistant is a bit looser with official HTML syntax than HoTMetaL. You may find, in fact, that HoTMetaL refuses to open many documents that use perfectly valid but non-standard extensions to HTML.

I've never found a browser that had trouble with HTML Assistant's loose coding, but if you want absolutely airtight HTML, you should make sure all attributes have quotes around them (like this: ALIGN="BOTTOM" not this: ALIGN=BOTTOM) and put the following line at the very beginning of every document:

<!DOCTYPE HTML PUBLIC "-//IETF//DTD HTML//EN//2.0">

Nobody pays any attention to this line yet, but future browsers might use it to identify the version of HTML you were using.

Both HoTMetaL and HTML Assistant (as well as their Mac counterparts, HTML Editor and HTML Pro) are shareware, and the registered versions offer many enhancements over the versions included on the CD-ROM. So once you pick a favorite, be sure to register it with the author. See the online documentation for details.

Interlaced and Transparent Images

Because browsers display images differently, you can't always assure that the graphics on your Web pages look the way you intended them to look. Nor can you be sure how long a reader will have to wait for an image to download and appear. Fortunately, the GIF file standard (and its new successor, PNG) gives you a couple ways to increase the likelihood that readers will see something like what you meant for them to see, and that they will see it as quickly as possible.

The "as quickly as possible" part is easy: simply save any large images as interlaced GIFs. In a non-interlaced image file, the top line of pixels is stored first, then the next line down, then the next line after that, and so on. In an interlaced file, only every other line is saved and then the missing lines are filled in at the end of the file. Many Web browsers will display interlaced GIFs as they are being read, so a "rough draft" of the image appears very quickly, and then the details are filled in as the download finishes. This can have a dramatic psychological effect, making the images seem to "come up" much faster even though they take the same total amount of time to download.

Most graphics programs that can handle GIF files allow you to choose whether to save them interlaced or noninterlaced. In PaintShop Pro, for example, you can choose the File sub-format on the Save As... dialog box just before you save a GIF file. In LView Pro, just check Save GIFs Interlaced on the Options menu before you save a file.

LView Pro also supports an even more useful GIF feature: transparency. Because different browsers use different background colors (and most allow individual users to select their favorite background color), it can be difficult to make non-rectangular graphics look good on a Web page. By choosing a color in your GIF image to be transparent, however, you can ensure that it will look its best on any color background. Figure 25.19 shows two versions of the same image—one with transparency, and one without.

To turn the bottom image in Figure 25.19 into the top one, I loaded it into LView Pro and selected Options/Background Color. This brought up the palette selection dialog box shown in Figure 25.20. I then selected color number 215 as the background color, hit OK, and saved the file as a GIF.

Figure 25.19

With transparency, you can incorporate non-rectangular shapes into a page.

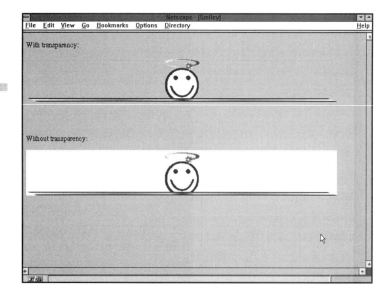

Figure 25.20

LView Pro lets you preview which portion of an image will be transparent when you select a background color.

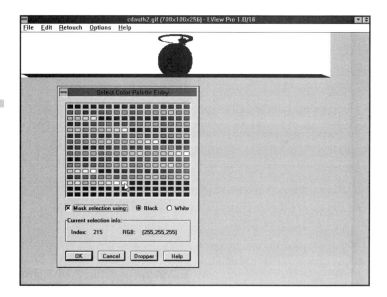

Notice that LView Pro even gives you a "masked" preview of which part of the image will be transparent. You may also note that the white face didn't become transparent, even though it was exactly the same color as the white background. That's because when I created the image, I purposefully filled the face with a different palette color (number 214 instead of 215). This works because transparency uses the palette index number and not the actual physical color to decide what's transparent.

(In case you're wondering what software I used to paint the face a different color, it was PaintShop Pro. I selected Colors/ Edit Palette..., double-clicked on palette color 214, turned it white, and then used the bucket fill tool to fill the face with it.)

Netscape Extensions and HTML 3.0

Transparent and interlaced GIF images work in most browsers, and even browsers that don't display them as transparent or interlaced will still display the image itself. There are also a number of even fancier tricks that only work in Netscape Navigator and a few other new browsers such as MS Internet Explorer. You should use them with caution until they become more widely supported, but as many as 75% of the people browsing the Web already do use Netscape or another browser which supports most of the Netscape extensions. Given the huge number of pages on the Web that use the Netscape extensions, you can bet that the other 25% will "get a real browser" before too long. Some of the extensions are also part of the new HTML 3.0 standard, though even some of those that don't make the final standard are certain to gain widespread browser support.

Centering

One Netscape extension is so ubiquitous that I included it on my list of the most common "standard" HTML tags: you can center lines of text (and images) by enclosing them between <CENTER> and </CENTER>. The powers that be have resisted adding this tag to the official standard because it goes against the concept that HTML isn't supposed to tell a browser how to display text, but simply what kind of text it is. That's a nice theory. Meanwhile, I'd say over half the pages on the Web use centering and all major browsers are planning to support it. (There's a lesson about standards committees in there somewhere.)

Backgrounds

Background tiling is another unofficial extension that looks like it probably will make it into the HTML 3.0 standard, and is quickly gaining universal support. This powerful feature allows you to specify an image file to be used as a "wallpaper" tile behind all text and images in a document. It is implemented as an attribute in the <BODY> tag like this:

<BODY BACKGROUND="blues.gif"> (document text goes here) </BODY>

As Figure 25.21 shows, background tiling can be combined with transparent images to add a great deal of flair to your pages. Be warned, however, that as of version 1.2, even Netscape Navigator itself doesn't always handle backgrounds and transparent images correctly. Background tiling can also significantly increase the time it takes for a page to download and display.

Figure 25.21

Netscape and other browsers, including Microsoft Explorer, have added some magical graphics tricks to the HTML language.

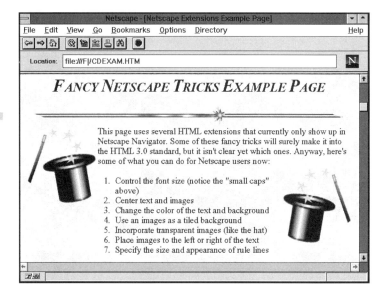

A faster and more reliable way to wield some control over the background in Netscape is to use the body color extensions. These simply allow you to specify a color for the background, text, and hotlinks. No extra images need to be loaded or processed, so images still download and display quickly. The format for specifying colors is currently **"#*rrggbb*"** where *rr*, *gg* and *bb* are two-digit hexadecimal values for the red, green, and blue components of the color. If you're not familiar with hexadecimal numbers, don't sweat it: just remember that **FF** is the maximum, **00** is the minimum, and **88** is in the middle. To make the background white, the text black, and the links blue, you would say:

```
<BODY BGCOLOR="#FFFFFF" TEXT="#000000"
LINK="#0000FF">
```

The Web pages on the CD-ROM with this book all use this color specification. They also specify a color for links that have already been visited with ALINK= and a color for links to "blink" when they're activated with VLINK=.

Note that if your request for a background color cannot be honored (either because the user has selected Always use mine on Netscape's Preferences/Style and colors page, because the computer can't make that color, or any other reason that might come up), your text color specifications will also be ignored. The idea is to avoid accidentally putting white text on a white background and that sort of thing.

TIP Because many computers display "dithered" colors that can create distracting patterns behind text, you should always stick to the basic colors that almost every computer will show without any dithering. These are:

Black:	#000000
White:	#FFFFFF
Red:	#FF0000
Green:	#00FF00
Blue:	#0000FF
Yellow:	#FFFF00
Magenta:	#FF00FF
Cyan:	#00FFFF

Medium grey (#808080) and light grey (#A0A0A0) are usually pretty safe, too—but not as reliable as the "pure" colors above.

Text Wrapping and Other Extensions

The cdexam.htm page from the CD-ROM depicted in Figure 25.21 uses several other Netscape extensions. If you take a peek at the file, they should be pretty self-explanatory. I will only point out here how easy it is to wrap text around an image. By typing

<IMG SRC="magic.gif" ALIGN="LEFT">

you can insert an image on the left margin and all subsequent text will automatically wrap around the right side of it. The ALIGN="RIGHT" attribute works similarly.

For more information about HTML 3.0 and Netscape extensions, including some really hot stuff I haven't discussed here such as clickable image maps and dynamic documents, hop to the Creating Web Documents item on the Netscape Help menu, and follow the links to the latest updates and tutorial pages on these topics.

NOTE You may have seen (or even created) some pages on the Web that seem to animate background colors, use multiple text colors in a single document, and employ "moving" images. These effects were achievable in Netscape Navigator versions 1.0 and 1.1 due to a bug in the HTML interpreter that allowed multiple <BODY> tags in a single document. Much to the disappointment of many web.artists, this bug has been removed in version 1.2 and later.

Some of the neat animation effects are still possible with the new dynamic document extensions. Check out the latest pages over at netscape.com for details.

CHAPTER

26

What's on the net.graphics CD-ROM

In This Chapter

> *About the Web pages on the enclosed CD-ROM*

> *Overview of the PC and Mac software on the CD-ROM*

> *Overview of the images and videos on the CD-ROM*

In Other Chapters

‹ *For help setting up a Web browser to view the pages on the CD-ROM, see Chapter 26 or the README.TXT file on the CD-ROM.*

‹ *If you aren't yet connected to the Net, see Chapter 26.*

‹ *For instructions on configuring viewers programs to work with your Web browser, see Chapter 23.*

‹ *Chapters 23, 24, and 25 offer instructions and helpful tips on using many of the programs on the CD-ROM.*

Almost every word in this chapter is also in the Web pages on the CD-ROM itself. Those Web pages also include many images and details about the contents of the CD-ROM that aren't in these printed pages. So if you have a Web browser program (preferably Netscape Navigator), start it up and open the _START_.HTM file on the CD-ROM without further ado! This printed chapter is intended primarily as an additional reference that you can read while away from your computer, or when your computer is busy doing something else.

If you don't have a Web browser, read the README.TXT file on the CD-ROM for advice on getting one.

Think of the net.graphics CD-ROM as your own personal Internet, packed with hundreds of megabytes of images, software, and other graphical goodies from the real Internet. With the Web page interface, you can browse through the CD-ROM just as you would "surf" the World Wide Web.

One difference between the CD-ROM and the Net is that getting files from the CD is much faster and cheaper. It would take you hundreds of hours to download everything on the CD if you had to get it from the Net, and that doesn't count any time spent searching. Of course, we couldn't fit everything from all the world's graphics archives on one CD-ROM. But when you want something that isn't there, you can use our page of hotlinks to jump straight to hundreds of hot graphics sites on the Net—without even leaving your browser!

Best Graphics on the Net Hotlist

Here are over 500 direct "hotlinks" to graphics on the Internet, including every location listed in the book. From the CDNET.HTM Web page, you can surf to virtually every graphics site on the Net without typing a single URL address. (To use these links, your browser must be connected to the Internet. For help installing and configuring a browser, see the README.TXT file on the CD-ROM.)

Images and Videos

We've selected hundreds of images and videos from a wide variety of the best sources on the Internet, and put them on the net.graphics CD-ROM for you to explore.

Featured Artists and Galleries

Tour our gallery of 25 outstanding artists and check out select images from some of the Internet's greatest graphics galleries on the CDARTS.HTM page and in the /artists/ subdirectories. And don't miss our exclusive sampler collection of WebGraphics to use in your own Internet publications; they are on the CDCAMEO.HTM page and the /webgrafx/ subdirectories. These royalty-free background textures, 3D borders and rules, and abstract button symbols are from Gini Schimtz of Cameo Graphics, who also created the popular WildTiles! CD-ROM collection of tileable art textures. See the /webgrafx/readme.txt file for more details and contact information.

Digital Videos

There are also over 50 computer-generated animations and digital video sequences provided on this CD-ROM for you to explore and enjoy. If you have multimedia viewers configured to work with your Web browser, you can click on the following links to view these videos. Or you may prefer to simply start the appropriate media player programs and open the video files in the /video/flic, /video/avi, and /video/mpeg directories from within the player programs themselves.

If you wish to view the images and videos from within your Web browser, you will need to configure it to use "Helper Apps" capable of viewing the following formats:

▼ GIF and JPG images. Most browsers already support these internally.

▼ TIF and PCX images. Use any of the image viewers recommended on the PC and Mac software pages.

▼ MPEG (.MPG) videos. Use VMPEG on the PC or Sparkle on the Mac.

▼ Audio-Video Interleave (.AVI) videos. Use Video for Windows on the PC, or AVI-QuickTime on the Mac.

▼ Autodesk Animator FLIC (.FLI) videos. Use AAPLAY or Video for Windows on the PC or MacAnim Viewer on the Mac.

For instructions on configuring Netscape Navigator (and similar Web browsers) to use these viewer applications, see Chapter 23 in this book, or your browser's documentation. If you don't configure a viewer for TIF files and videos, you can still tour the gallery pages, but you will get an error notice when you click on links to the artwork and animations.

Andover Advanced Technology, publishers of PhotoMorph software, have also provided the interactive "Digital Video Kickstart" tutorial on creating digital video and using PhotoMorph. To start the "Digital Video Kickstart" tutorial, run VIPRPRES.EXE in the /video/avi subdirectory, and open the _TUTOR.HPW file. (This tutorial is only for Windows users, and is not available to Mac users.) You may want to check out the _ONLINE.HPW presentation as well.

Graphics Archive Sampler

We're also pleased to feature an extensive sampling of graphics from Walnut Creek's CD-ROM collections and Internet archives. A description of each collection is accompanied by a single sample image on the CDWC.HTM Web page, and several sample images from each collection are in the /wc/ subdirectories. Use a Web browser or a viewer program such as ACDSee or JPEGView to view the images in these directories, and read the text files named 00_INDEX.TXT in each subdirectory for a brief description of each image file included.

Walnut Creek's CD-ROM is the host of one of the world's largest and most popular public archives on the Internet. They also publish many high-quality CD-ROM collections of files from the Internet and other sources. Purchasing a CD-ROM is often considerably easier and less expensive than finding and downloading even a few of the same files from the Internet directly, especially for large graphics and animation files. The collections featured on the net.graphics CD-ROM are:

▼ **Clip Art Cornucopia (/wc/clipart)**   Dinosaurs from a massive clip-art collection.

▼ **Fractal Frenzy (/wc/fractal)**   Wild computer-generated art by Lee Skinner.

▼ **GIFs Galore (/wc/gifs)**   Art and photography of all sorts in GIF format.

▼ **RayTrace! (/wc/raytrace)**   Realistic computer-rendered images created with the POV-Ray freeware ray tracer.

▼ **Space and Astronomy (/wc/space)**   Images from NASA missions and telescopes.

▼ **Travel Adventure (/wc/travel)**   Photos from Europe, the U.S., and the Caribbean.

▼ **Visions (/wc/visions)**   Royalty-free stock photos.

▼ **Amazing Animations (/wc/amazing and /video/flic)**   3D animations in Autodesk .FLI format.

Walnut Creek's other offerings range from MSDOS/Windows shareware to Linux/FreeBSD boot floppies to royalty-free images. The /wc/catalog.txt file lists all current Walnut Creek titles as of April 1995. To find out what's new since then, contact the address given at the end of the catalog file and on the CDWC.HTM Web page.

Software for Internet Graphics

There are two types of programs on this CD-ROM: Those you need to get started with graphics on the Net, and those you might like to check out later when you get more serious (or more playful). In order to save you hours of wading through software you don't need yet, we've carefully selected 10 programs that we think are the best and most essential for exploring and using graphics on the Net. We recommend that you check these out first and install any you don't already have on your hard drive. You can browse through the rest of the software on the CD-ROM when you need something more exotic or feel like trying out some useful and fun tools.

NOTE Most of these programs are shareware, which means that you can try them for free (usually for up to 30 days) to see if they meet your needs. If they do, you must send a registration fee directly to the author. See the online help and documentation for each program for more details and contact addresses.

Open CDPC.HTM or CDMAC.HTM with your browser for detailed description and installation information for each Windows and Mac program on the CD-ROM. These pages also include links to some excellent Internet sources for the latest versions of Windows and Mac shareware and freeware.

Index

travel sites, 153
China News Digest, 157
Covered Bridges of
Southeastern
Pennsylvania, 43,
230-231
CIA World Factbook, 157
Durham Cathedral, 43,
246-247
Glensheen, 43, 281-282
Global Network Navigator
Travel Features, 158
Grand Canyon, 158,
221-222
Grand Canyon River
Running, 158
Loma Prieta Earthquake
Photos, 158
Lonely Planet, 158
Multiworld, 158, 327
Russia By Pictures, 159
Salem, 369-370
Smithsonian Photographs
Online, 380
Space Shuttle Earth
Observations, 159
Travel Adventure
(net.graphics CD-ROM),
575
UK Guide, 159
Vietnam Pictures
Archive, 159
Virtual Hawaii, 159
Virtual Tourist, 414-415
Web Travel Review,
154-157
Xerox PARC Map Viewer,
159
see also graphics on the Web
**GraphicConverter
software, 493**
**Graphics and Visualization
Laboratory Web site,
286-287**
graphics on the Web, 11-12
downloading
accessing graphics, 462
decompressing files,
468-479
FTP sites, 466-468
Gopher sites, 463-466
via newsgroups, 482-486
file formats, 470-473
lists of sites, *see* graphical
sites

posting graphics on the Web
acquiring images, 536-537
compression options,
539-540
downloading time,
estimating, 540-543
size/resolution
considerations, 537-538
uploading graphics to the
Web, 542-551
printing, 525
dithering options, 528-532
gamma corrections,
529-530
securing copyrights, 529
service bureaus, 525-528
retouching
brightness/contrast
enhancement, 508-510
color corrections, 507
deforming, 524-525
equalizing colors, 516-517
filtering, 517-518
full color corrections,
513-516
gamma corrections,
511-512
selecting/painting,
518-523
tonal corrections, 512-513
searching for, 429-430
Archie, 430-434
CUSI (Configurable
Unified Search Index),
446-449
Jughead, 439
Veronica, 435-438
Web crawlers, 440-445
see also browsers
transferring, 478-479
encoding graphics for
transfer, 487-489
MIME-compatible
software, 479-482
UseNet newsgroups,
482-486
graphics viewers
3D graphics (VRML), 505-506
offline, 492
online, 492-493
configuring external
viewers for Netscape,
499-501
configuring Netscape for
multimedia, 503-504
external viewers, 494-498

multimedia formats,
501-503
Netscape internal viewer,
493-494
**Graphics Visualization
Laboratory Web site, 125**
greeting cards, 20
Grotesk Web site, 282-283
**Grotesque in Art Web site,
62, 284**

H

**headings for Web pages
(HTML tags), 554**
**Herpetocultural Home
Page, 27**
history sites
Age of Enlightenment, 69,
256-257
American Memory, 112-116
ArtServe, 168, 191
Astarte Gallery, 52, 205
British Library, 69, 214-215
Royal British Columbia
Museum, 363-364
Salem, 369-370
Singapore Art and History
Museum, 70, 387-389
Smithsonian, 170, 376-378
Smithsonian Photographs
Online, 126, 380
**Hollywood Online Web site,
72-73**
home pages, *see* **Web sites,
building**
**Hot Pictures: Russian
Photography Web site, 117,
288-289**
**hotlists (favorite bookmarks),
13**
**HoTMetaL (HTML editor),
562-564**
**HTML (hypertext mark-up
language), 551, 553-554**
anchor (hypertext) tags,
557-559
body tags, 554-555
browser display variations,
560
dedicated HTML editors,
562-564
formatting tags, 555
heading tags, 554
image tags, 557